Learn Encryption Techniques with BASIC and C++

Gilbert Held

Wordware Publishing, Inc.

Library of Congress Cataloging-in-Publication Data

Held, Gilbert, 1943-
    Learn encryption techniques with BASIC and C++ / by Gilbert Held.
      p. cm.
    Includes index.
    ISBN 1-55622-598-9 (pbk.)
    1. Computers--Access control.   2. Data encryption (Computer science).
    3. BASIC (Computer program language).   4. C++ (Computer program language).
    I. Title.
    QA76.9.A25H42   1998
    005.8'2--dc21   98-34653
                                                          CIP

ISBN 1-55622-598-9

10 9 8 7 6 5 4 3 2 1

9809

Product names mentioned are used for identification purposes only and may be trademarks of their respective
companies.

All inquiries for volume purchases of this book should be addressed to Wordware
Publishing, Inc., at the above address. Telephone inquiries may be made by calling:

(972) 423-0090

Contents Summary

Contents

Contents

Preface

"Bid $3.62 million on the 46th Street project," "potential corporate acquisition requires suspension of training activities through the end of month," and "meet me at 7 P.M. in the Radisson lobby to discuss…" are but a few examples of personal communications that for one reason or another should be confidential.

Today, we live in a world whose "communications dimensions" have rapidly shrunk due to the explosive growth in the use of computer-based networks. Messages that took hours or days to reach a recipient a decade ago are now delivered near instantaneously to most areas on the globe. Although advances in communications technology have considerably enhanced our quality of life, it has also provided the con artist, computer hacker, and persons many would classify as being in the lower elements of society with the ability to electronically take advantage of others. An unscrupulous person may commit electronic fraud by ordering items and billing the cost to others, or read personal messages and take actions that are harmful to other persons. In other situations, the inadvertent viewing of a personal message concerning a potential corporate reorganization, pending personnel action, or similar activity can result in an exponential increase in the rumor mill, while employee productivity decreases in an inverse proportion to these rumors.

While it is doubtful if fraud or rumors will ever cease as long as humans populate the earth, there are steps you can consider to keep personal communications personal. Some steps, such as routing messages correctly, avoid the embarrassment of an unintentional recipient. Other steps, such as converting your message into a sequence of characters that is not meaningful to an unintended recipient or casual observer, provide a mechanism to protect the content of your message. It is this area that is the focus of this book, providing practical methods readers can use to obtain a degree of privacy and security for messages that are transmitted over internal corporate communications networks or via public electronic messaging systems.

The focus of this book is upon the use of cryptology to encipher and decipher messages. As we examine different encipherment methods, we will also focus our attention upon the development of programs written in the C++ and BASIC programming languages that can be used to automate the encipherment and decipherment process.

Many readers by now will realize that the techniques covered in this book are available to any person who obtains a copy of this book. While this fact means the techniques to obtain message privacy are in the public domain, it does not mean that the use of those techniques results in public messages.

Most techniques covered in this book are based upon the use of keywords, phrases, or the selection of a random sequence of characters. Although almost any enciphering technique can be broken given a long enough message and time, the objective of this book is to provide readers with a mechanism to prevent the inadvertent reading of messages as well as delay the translation of messages intercepted by hackers, rascals, and scoundrels. Thus, a message concerning a bid due on Tuesday may be worthless to a person who reads the contents of your message on Thursday. By carefully considering the use of different enciphering techniques and keywords, phrases, or random character sequences to govern the encipherment process, you can keep personal communications personal as well as obtain a degree of message security that will enable you to conduct your business in a more efficient and effective manner.

As a professional author, I consider reader feedback extremely important and encourage you to send me your comments. Let me know if the information and techniques presented in this book satisfied your requirements or if there are other areas you would like me to tackle in a future edition. You can write to me via e-mail at **235-8068@mcimail.com** or through my publisher whose address is on this book.

Gilbert Held
Macon, GA

Acknowledgments

From proposal to publication a book requires the efforts of many individuals besides the author. Since I spend a majority of my writing time at home, the cooperation and assistance of my family was essential and once again is greatly appreciated. Concerning that assistance, a special acknowledgment and loud "thanks" goes to my son, Jonathan Held. Jonathan took up his father's challenge after taking a graduate course covering C++. Over a series of many evenings Jonathan both converted and improved upon the original BASIC language programs and program modules as he developed the C++ programs and program modules included in this book.

As an old-fashioned author, I like to write my manuscript and depend upon the professional skills of Mrs. Linda Hayes to turn my longhand notes and diagrams into a suitable manuscript. Thus, once again I am indebted to Linda Hayes for her fine work.

Editing a complex manuscript takes a very special skill, especially when the manuscript consists of numerous files, line art, text, and sidebars that have to be carefully put together. This author sincerely thanks Beth Kohler for her fine editing effort during the publication process.

While many persons can write manuscripts, only a select few have the ability and position to judge the viability of a book proposal, arrange for the editing of a manuscript, and coordinate the thousand and one items ranging from the book cover design to its production schedule that enable the finished product to reach the market. It is with sincere appreciation that I thank Mr. Jim Hill for his cooperation and assistance as well as his vision and foresight in noting the role of this book in fulfilling the requirements of readers.

About the Author

Gilbert Held is an internationally recognized author and lecturer who specializes in the application of computer and communications technology. The author of more than 30 books about personal computers, data communications, and business topics, Gil is the only person to twice receive the coveted Interface Karp Award. He has also received an award from the American Publisher's Institute.

Gil managed a nationwide communications network for the federal government for over 20 years. This network supports one of the largest numbers of dial-in encryption devices in use throughout the free world. Gil is a frequent lecturer and often conducts seminars on such topics as LAN and WAN internetworking, data compression, and personal computer hardware and software. In recognition of his work, Gil was selected by *Federal Computer Week* as one of the top 100 persons in government, industry, and academia whose efforts made a difference in the acquisition and utilization of computer equipment. Gil teaches graduate school courses at Georgia College and State University in such areas as LAN performance and data communications.

Chapter 1

Technology and Terminology

The primary purpose of this chapter is to acquaint you with a core set of terms associated with the field of cryptology. You should note that your primary objective is to obtain a level of knowledge which provides the ability to develop and use practical encipherment techniques to hide the meaning of messages transmitted over different types of electronic mail systems. Many of the techniques we will cover are not unbreakable to a trained analyst; however, they will provide varying levels of message protection that can make it difficult and, in many cases, very time consuming to understand the meaning of a message. In fact, some practical techniques we will cover in this book may require more than 60 billion trials to correctly understand the meaning of a message. Because each trial could require the printing of an intercepted message, a 10-line message could conceivably require a person to scan 600 billion printed lines!

Although the United States National Security Agency (NSA), the United Kingdom's MI5, and Russia's modern version of the KGB have probably programmed supercomputers to use artificial intelligence in an attempt to understand the meaning of intercepted messages, few, if any, commercial organizations have the financial resources to obtain the required hardware to develop programs to perform similar operations. Thus, the more sophisticated techniques presented in this book should provide you with a mechanism to protect the meaning of your communications from the casual observer, the inadvertent observer, and most, if not all, intentional illicit intercepters.

To acquaint readers with the terminology associated with the field of cryptology, we will both discuss different terms as well as their meaning through the use of several examples. In doing so we will review the main types of ciphers that are covered in detail in succeeding chapters. When appropriate, we will discuss the use of different ciphers from a historical perspective; however, our intention is not to provide readers with information on the historical evolution of ciphers but to show some of their practical uses from a historical basis.

A secondary objective of this chapter is to discuss the subroutines and programs we will develop and include via program listings throughout this book. This discussion will acquaint readers with the rationale for selecting the C++ and BASIC programming languages that are used to develop subroutines and programs and file naming conventions which can facilitate the use of the subroutines and programs included in this book.

Ciphers Versus Codes

One of the major areas of confusion for many readers is the difference between a cipher system and a code system. Although both systems are designed to conceal information while it is transmitted, they do so using different substitution techniques.

If you're a video buff and remember such war films as *The Longest Day*, *Tora, Tora, Tora*, and similar films, you noted the transmission of messages whose contents appear to be meaningless. Such messages as "Paul has a long arm," "The soup is in the kitchen," and "Ralph needs shoes," for example, represent coded messages in which words and phrases are substituted for other words or phrases to disguise the meaning of the message. In other films, you may remember a soldier or sailor using equipment to intercept a message and preparing a punched paper tape containing the contents of the message. The paper tape was then placed into a special tape reader that read the tape and produced a new tape. The soldier or sailor would then read the message on the new tape and yell across the room, "Let's get this message to the Captain" or a similar line.

Those movies illustrated the use of specially constructed decipherment machines which were designed to read enciphered messages and reproduce the original text of the message known as plaintext or cleartext. The intercepted message punched on paper tape consisted of a series of what appeared to be randomly picked characters, such as the sequence "QAFRT..." That character sequence represented an enciphered message in which each plaintext character in the message was replaced by a ciphertext character according to a predefined algorithm.

In a cipher system, the plaintext, which represents a set of data prior to encipherment, is operated upon without regard to their meaning. In a code system, words or phrases are replaced by other words or phrases to hide the meaning of a message. Thus, the message FIRE THE CORPORATE LAWYER might be transmitted as GJSF UIF OPSQPSBUF MBXZFS using a simple cipher discussed later in this chapter. When transmitted in a code, the message could become SELL THE CORPORATE DONKEY, assuming SELL was the code for FIRE and DONKEY was the code for LAWYER.

Because many code systems normally do not change the meaning of more than a few terms in a message, such systems immediately provide a hint as to the contents of a message. In addition, the observation of a series of messages can provide a reasonable set of clues that will enable someone to determine the meaning of coded messages. Another obstacle to the use of codes, especially when they are only used infrequently, is the requirement to have prior knowledge of all of the substitutions. Some code systems used by military and diplomatic personnel are based upon the creation of code books that may have tens of thousands of terms and their equivalent codes. Not only are such code books difficult and time consuming to prepare but, in addition, their distribution and replacement by a new code book if an existing book should become lost or compromised can create a logistical nightmare. Although still popular for military and diplomatic use in certain situations, the efficient use of a code system requires the development of the previously mentioned code book which provides the basis for encoding and decoding messages. In comparison, many cipher systems only require knowledge of one or a few items of information known as keys to encipher and decipher a message. Thus, from a practical point of view, encipherment and decipherment operations can be easier to perform than encoding and decoding operations associated with conventional code book-based systems, especially as the length of a message increases. In addition, many cipher systems can be expected to provide a higher level of message protection than obtained from the use of a code system. Due to the preceding, the focus of this book is upon different encipherment techniques.

Cipher Terminology

As previously described, a cipher system is a system in which a substitution process occurs on individual characters or groups of characters without regard to their meaning. The actual enciphering process can be performed by hardware, software, or manually by the brainpower of one or more persons.

Plaintext and Enciphered Text

The use of a cipher system requires a message or text to operate upon. The original, unaltered contents of the message or text is known as plaintext or cleartext. Through the use of a cipher system, the meaning of the plaintext message is hidden. The process of hiding the meaning of the plaintext is known as enciphering, while the resultant text is referred to as enciphered text.

Encipherment

Figure 1.1 illustrates the encipherment process in a block diagram format. In examining Figure 1.1, note that plaintext (x) is converted to ciphertext (y) by an enciphering process (E), such that $y=E_k(x)$, where k is a key. The enciphering process can be considered as an algorithm which operates upon the plaintext based upon the value of a key (k). Thus, the key defines the operation of the encipherment algorithm and different keys result in different ciphertext being created from a fixed plaintext.

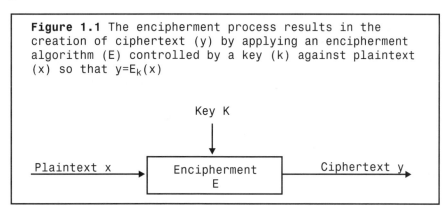

Figure 1.1 The encipherment process results in the creation of ciphertext (y) by applying an encipherment algorithm (E) controlled by a key (k) against plaintext (x) so that y=E$_k$(x)

An example of the use of a modern key can be obtained by constructing a modulo 2 encipherment process. As a bit of review for readers who may not remember modulo arithmetic, when adding numbers using that arithmetic for base n you divide n into the added numbers and retain the remainder as the result of the modulo arithmetic process. That is, for our familiar base 10 the addition of 6 and 8 under modulo 10 results in a value of 4. Table 1.1 illustrates the results of modulo 2 for the four possibilities that can occur per bit position.

Table 1.1 Modulo 2 Addition

0	0	1	1
0	1	0	1
0	1	1	0

To illustrate the encipherment process using modulo 2 addition, let's encipher the word HELP, assuming it was first stored using the 7-bit American Standard Code for Information Interchange. Let's then assume the key was the word BURP. Table 1.2 illustrates the encipherment process using modulo 2 addition.

Table 1.2 Enciphering the word HELP with the key BURP using modulo 2 addition.

Plaintext	H	E	L	P
	1001000	1000101	1001100	1010000
⊕ Key	B	U	R	P
	1000010	1010101	1010010	1010000
Enciphered text	0001010	0010000	0011110	0000000
	LF	DLE	RS	NUL

In examining the entries in Table 1.2, note that as a result of the modulo 2 encipherment process the plaintext HELP is converted into a sequence of 28 bits which represent four control characters—Line Feed (LF), Data Link Escape (DLE), Record Separator (RS), and Null (NUL). Thus, if a person intercepted the enciphered text they would observe the sequence LF, DLE, RS, NUL instead of the word HELP.

Decipherment

The process of converting or restoring ciphertext back into its original plaintext contents is known as decipherment. Figure 1.2 illustrates the decipherment process in a block diagram format. Decipherment (D) can be considered the inverse of the encipherment process, requiring the use of an algorithm which converts ciphertext back into its original plaintext. Decipherment is also controlled by a key (k), which is applied to ciphertext (y) to produce plaintext (x), such that $x = D_k(y)$.

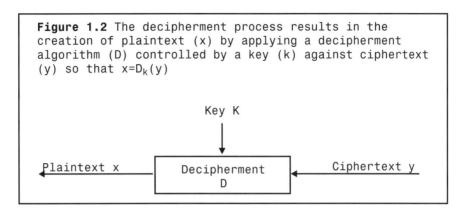

Figure 1.2 The decipherment process results in the creation of plaintext (x) by applying a decipherment algorithm (D) controlled by a key (k) against ciphertext (y) so that x=D_k(y)

You can obtain an appreciation for the decipherment process by deciphering the previously enciphered message. Assuming you have the key BURP and received the message LF DLE RS NUL, you would use modulo 2 subtraction to reconstruct the original plaintext message. Thus, an understanding of the decipherment process requires a brief overview of modulo subtraction.

Under modulo subtraction, if the minuend is greater than the subtrahend the result is obtained by subtracting the subtrahend from the minuend. If the minuend is less than the subtrahend, you would first add the value of the next base position to the minuend prior to subtracting the subtrahend. For example, under base 10 9-5 is 4, while 5-9 is 6 since a value of 10 is added to the minuend (5) prior to subtracting the subtrahend (9).

Since our previous encipherment was performed using modulo 2 addition, we will use modulo 2 subtraction to perform a decipherment operation. Table 1.3 illustrates the modulo 2 subtraction process for all four possible combinations per bit position.

Table 1.3 Modulo 2 Subtraction

0	0	1	1
0	1	0	1
0	1	1	0

Now that you have an appreciation for modulo 2 subtraction, let's turn our attention to deciphering the previously enciphered message. If you are the recipient of the message, you would receive the enciphered text

LF DLE RS NUL. Assuming you have the key BURP, you would then perform a modulo 2 subtract process to decipher the enciphered text into its original plaintext. This decipherment process is illustrated in Table 1.4.

Table 1.4 Deciphering the message LF DLE RS NUL with the key BURP using modulo 2 subtraction.

Enciphered text	LF	DLE	RS	NUL
	0001010	0010000	0011110	0000000
⊖ Key	B	U	R	P
	1000010	1010101	1010010	1010000
Deciphered text	1001000	1000101	1001100	1010000

Keys and Key Space

In examining Figure 1.1 and 1.2, the key—no pun intended—to enciphering and deciphering is the key that controls the operation of the enciphering and deciphering algorithms. Although a person may obtain a copy of an enciphered message and have knowledge of the algorithm used to encipher the message, you must use the correct key to successfully decipher the message. Thus, the number of possible values of a key, referred to as an algorithm's key space, is an important consideration in selecting an enciphering algorithm. This is because an algorithm with a limited key space is very susceptible to a trial-and-error process in which different keys are applied in an attempt to decipher an intercepted message. For example, if a sequence of nine decimal digits is used to form a key, its key space is 10^{10}, or 10 billion, key values.

Although it is relatively easy to program a computer to generate a series of 10-digit sequences to use at different times, it is probably not realistic to expect a mortal to remember those sequences. Thus, a tradeoff will occur between key space and practicality if we wish to develop ciphers that can be easily used in a manual process. In addition, from a practical point of view, it is many times easier to remember words or phrases instead of a sequence of digits. Thus, many of the cipher systems discussed in this book are based upon the use of an alphabetic key in the form of a word or phrase. This usually provides an increased retention capability over the use of a sequence of digits. Even if you automate the enciphering process through the use of a program executed on a personal computer, under certain situations you may prefer to use a word or phrase in place of a digit sequence to facilitate the use of the program.

Another reason for using alphabetic or alphanumeric keys instead of a key restricted to digits is the significant increase in the key space afforded by the use of alphabetic or alphanumeric keys. For example, a two-digit key provides 10*10, or 100, unique keys. In comparison, the use of two uppercase or two lowercase alphabetic characters in a key provides 26*26, or 676, unique keys, while the use of two alphanumeric characters in which alphabetic characters are limited to a single case results in 36*36, or 1,296, unique keys.

Table 1.5 contains the key space obtained by the use of digits, letters, and alphanumeric characters for keys varying in length from 1 to 20 positions. The field width column indicates the number of characters in a key. You should note that the discussion of key space will be limited to the use of all uppercase or all lowercase letters when alphabetic or alphanumeric keys are used unless otherwise noted. Although the use of both uppercase and lowercase letters significantly increases the key space, it also increases the potential for confusion. That is, it becomes quite easy to remember a word or phrase but to forget which letters are uppercase and which letters are lowercase. For that reason we will normally restrict the use of keys in this book to letters of a single case. That is, if our key is limited to eight positions and we wish to use the word "computer," we would enter the key as "COMPUTER" or "computer," but not as "Computer," unless we develop a program which is case insensitive and converts all characters to one case.

Table 1.5 Key space based on characters used and field width.

Field Width	Digit Combinations	Letter Combinations	Alphanumeric Combinations
1	1.00000E+01	2.60000E+01	3.60000E+01
2	1.00000E+02	6.76000E+02	1.29600E+03
3	1.00000E+03	1.75760E+04	4.66560E+04
4	1.00000E+04	4.56976E+05	1.67962E+06
5	1.00000E+05	1.18814E+07	6.04662E+02
6	1.00000E+06	3.08916E+08	2.17678E+09
7	1.00000E+07	8.03181E+09	7.83642E+10
8	1.00000E+08	2.08827E+11	2.82111E+12

Field Width	Digit Combinations	Letter Combinations	Alphanumeric Combinations
9	1.00000E+09	5.42950E+12	1.01560E+14
10	1.00000E+10	1.41167E+14	3.65616E+15
11	1.00000E+11	3.67034E+15	1.31622E+17
12	1.00000E+12	6.54290E+16	4.73838E+18
13	1.00000E+13	2.48115E+18	1.70582E+20
14	1.00000E+14	6.45100E+19	6.14094E+21
15	1.00000E+15	1.67726E+21	2.21074E+23
16	1.00000E+16	4.36087E+22	7.95866E+24
17	1.00000E+17	1.13383E+24	2.86512E+26
18	1.00000E+18	2.94795E+25	1.03144E+28
19	1.00000E+19	7.66467E+26	3.71319E+29
20	1.00000E+20	1.99281E+28	1.33675E+31

In examining the entries in Table 1.5, you should note that E+6 represents one million, while E+9 represents one billion. Thus, a six-character alphanumeric field produces 2.17 billion combinations even when we restrict our alphabet to all uppercase or all lowercase letters! Readers should also note that a nine-character field would be required to obtain just one billion key combinations if the key was restricted to digits. Thus, we can maintain a large key space with a lesser number of key characters or increase our key space by using alphanumeric characters instead of restricting our key to digits or letters.

Types of Encryption Systems

There are two types of encryption systems—private and public key based. The previously described method of encipherment and decipherment based upon the use of the same key for encryption and decryption is referred to as a private key based encryption system. That is, the key must remain private and cannot be disclosed to the person or persons who are intended recipients of an encrypted message. Otherwise the key is said to be compromised, meaning that any message encrypted using the key is potentially compromised. Another term commonly used to reference a private key based encryption system is a "symmetric" key system. Here, the term symmetric is used to reference the fact that the same key is used at both ends of the process.

One of the major problems associated with the use of a private key based encryption system is key generation and key distribution. For example, if you only need to send an encrypted message between two persons using a private key system, a single key used by each person becomes sufficient. If three people need to send encrypted messages to each other you could use one common key; however, if that key is compromised, then any messages transmitted between any of the three persons could become compromised. Thus, many organizations using a public key based encryption system commonly elect to use different keys for encryption between different persons. This means that the use of a public key based encryption system linking three persons or corporate offices would require three keys, while a system linking four persons or offices would require four keys.

This also means that for n users or organizational locations the number of unique keys required becomes 2^n-2. While this may not be a problem for a small number of users or organizational locations, as those numbers increase they can reach a point where the administration process to include key generation and distribution becomes unmanageable. This is particularly true when you consider the use of modern electronic mail systems where employees may have to communicate with hundreds or thousands of persons. In this type of situation a private key based encryption system obviously becomes unsuitable. Similarly, it would be virtually impossible to use a private key based encryption system to secure electronic commerce from browsers to World Wide Web servers. Fortunately, the efforts of mathematicians resulted in the development of another type of encryption which significantly alleviates the previously described key generation and distribution problems associated with private key based encryption systems. This type of encryption is referred to as a public key based encryption system.

Public key based encryption dates to the late 1970s when mathematicians discovered certain mathematical relationships that resulted in a key used to encrypt a message being unable to perform decryption while another key in a matched pair of keys could be used for decryption. The mathematical relationship requires the use of two keys, one which remains private while the second can be provided to anybody, and can even be posted on a person's home page on the Web. That key is referred to as a public key.

Under public key encryption, a person wishing to send an encrypted message to another person or organization acquires the recipient's public key and uses that key to encrypt the message. The recipient uses their private key to decrypt the message. Since each user or organization in a public key system only has to maintain two keys, one public and one private, regardless of the number of persons or locations in the system the total number of keys required for n users becomes $2*n$. Thus, for a large n the number of keys required is significantly reduced from the 2^n-2 keys required for a private key based encryption system.

The use of a public key based encryption system results in keys providing one-way encryption and decryption based upon the type of key used, public for encryption, private for decryption. Thus, another term commonly used to reference a public key encryption system is an asymmetric encryption system.

From a mathematical perspective the ciphertext, $E_k(x)$, is computed using a public key (k_p) which has a mathematical relationship to the private key (k_r). Unlike a private key system where $D_k(E_k(x))$ results in the reconstruction of the original plaintext, $D_k(x)$ cannot be easily computed from k_p without knowledge of k_r. Instead, $D_k(x)$ is easily computed when the private key (k_r) is known. The key to the use of a public key system is the ability for individuals to generate their own public and private keys so that they can freely distribute their public key to persons they may wish to communicate with in a secure manner. Through the use of exponentiation and large prime numbers it becomes possible to generate relatively long public and private keys. While it is possible for other persons to use similar algorithms to generate public and private keys in an attempt to decrypt data encrypted by another person, the time required to factor relatively long primes would require the use of supercomputers for decades. Thus, you can be reasonably assured that properly developed public and private key pairs provide a high degree of protection for messages well into the future.

Key Generation, Management, and Distribution

An enciphering system that produces billions of possible key combinations may be extremely vulnerable if keys are selected in a manner in which their possible composition can be easily guessed. For example, a birth date or home address would not be advisable for use as a key as they represent one of the first trials in a trial-and-error process an unauthorized person will more than likely attempt to use as a key. Ideally, keys should be generated based upon some random process. However, if you're traveling and wish to use your laptop or notebook computer to transmit or receive private messages enciphered according to a predefined key, you would probably prefer to remember PCATV instead of Q4R51. Because PCATV is obviously an easier guess than Q4R51, you can consider using a random process to generate keys and store those keys for use over a predefined period of time on a computer file enciphered using a different key. Then, employees would only be tasked with remembering one key for a period of time to access a list of keys and the period of time each key is valid for use. This technique is one of many methods associated with key management.

Key management can be considered the process of generating, maintaining, and distributing keys. In addition, this activity is responsible for defining what action or actions to take in the event a cipher system or key to a cipher system is lost or compromised.

The key management process, as well as functions associated with this process, will vary from organization to organization based upon a variety of factors. Those factors may include the number of employees that require knowledge of an enciphering key, their geographical distribution, and the integrity of the firm's internal mail service. Additionally, the type of key system, public or private, will significantly affect the key distribution method. Some organizations post public keys on their Web servers or deliver those keys via internal interoffice mail in a manner similar to which computer passwords are distributed. Other organizations distribute keys via registered mail, through the use of the corporate electronic mail system enciphered using the current key, or in plaintext. Obviously, the repeated distribution of new private keys in plaintext or enciphered using the currently-in-use key opens the organization to a potentially compromising situation. However, you should remember that many organizations simply want a mechanism to keep personal communications personal and are not looking for nor do they seek an elaborate method to guarantee that their communications will never be broken. Although some sophisticated methods to distribute keys are discussed in succeeding chapters, our primary focus of attention will be placed on practical and efficient methods to distribute keys.

Regardless of the manner in which new keys are distributed, they should be distributed because employees will leave the organization, lose their keys, misplace a message containing a listing of keys, and do other things which in hindsight can compromise a system.

 Perhaps one of the more interesting public compromises of security occurred when a president of the United States was photographed with a document folded in his suit pocket. The document was folded in such a manner that a keyword was prominently displayed in the photograph that appeared in newspapers. Fortunately for national security, the keyword denoted a classification associated with a special type of communications and did not reflect the key used to encipher communications. Unfortunately for many persons involved in national security, the display of the keyword resulted in a large amount of unpaid overtime required to rapidly change the keyword used to classify the type of communications exposed to the public.

At some federal agencies, private keys are changed on a quarterly basis, while other agencies change keys on a monthly, weekly, and even a daily basis. The driving force behind the frequency of key changes should be the worth of the data whose contents are being hidden by encipherment and the potential threat to that data. The latter may be extremely hard to judge, since most persons will not know their electronic conversations have been targeted for interception until it is too late. In addition to the potential threat, you must balance key changes against the effort required to develop and distribute new keys on a periodic basis. If the system you devise is difficult to implement or requires too much effort to effectively use, many potential users may bypass the system you develop. Thus, the old military adage—Keep it simple—is worth remembering when you consider various methods for the generation and distribution of keys.

Types of Ciphers

A visit to a large university or public library will reward you with the ability to locate a large number of books which discuss the use of cipher systems. Some books, such as *The Codebreakers* (Macmillian, 1969) by David Kahn and *Cryptanalysis* (Dover Publications, 1956) by Helen F. Gaines, provide an excellent overview of a variety of cipher systems, primarily focusing upon the historical use of such systems. More recently published works, such as *Security for Computer Networks* by D.W. Davies and W.L. Price, can bring you up to date on recent developments in the construction of cipher systems from a mathematical basis. Reading these and other books will acquaint you with hundreds of types of cipher systems, ranging in scope from an elementary process that can be performed mentally to very complex systems that require the use of a computer. What each of those cipher systems has in common is the ability to be classified into one of two general categories—substitution and transposition.

The remainder of this section focuses on an initial overview of each cipher category and discusses several of the variants used to develop specific types of cipher systems. This is followed by a discussion of the constraints that must be employed in considering the algorithms and key space used to convert plaintext to ciphertext which will enable ciphertext to be carried by many electronic mail systems. Our examination of substitution and transposition cipher systems will be based upon the use of private keys. Although it is quite possible to develop public key based substitution and transposition cipher systems since the former dates from the 1970s while the latter can be traced to the time of Caesar, from a historical perspective the cipher systems we will examine were all developed based upon the use of private keys. Thus, we will respect the historical evolution of encryption and primarily examine the characteristics of substitution and transposition cipher systems via the use of private keys in this chapter.

Substitution Cipher Systems

In a substitution cipher system, each plaintext character is replaced by a ciphertext character using an algorithm which operates upon the plaintext in the sequence in which the plaintext characters appear. In a simple substitution cipher system, the replacement process is unaltered. That is, each plaintext character is replaced by the same ciphertext character. For example, the well-known Caesar cipher, in which the ciphertext represents a fixed displacement in the alphabet, would encipher the message KILL ALL THE LAWYERS as LJMM BMM UIF MBXZFST using a displacement of one character position as the encipherment algorithm.

You can denote the relationship between a plaintext alphabet and a ciphertext alphabet by listing one alphabet above the other. For example, restrict your plaintext and ciphertext alphabets to the 26 uppercase letters. Then, for the simple one-character Caesar cipher displacement, the relationship between the plaintext alphabet (P) and the ciphertext alphabet (C) is as appears below. In this example, the letters in the ciphertext alphabet are displaced by one character position from the letters in the plaintext alphabet. We can denote this relationship between the mapping of plaintext and ciphertext characters as $P_A=C_B$, which indicates that the letter A in the plaintext alphabet is aligned with the letter B in the ciphertext alphabet.

Plaintext alphabet (P):   ABCDEFGHIJKLMNOPQRSTUVWXYZ

Ciphertext alphabet (C):   BCDEFGHIJKLMNOPQRSTUVWXYZA

In a varying substitution cipher, the replacement of plaintext by ciphertext results in a very high probability that repeating plaintext characters are replaced by different ciphertext characters. To accomplish this requires the use of more than one "mapping" alphabet to convert plaintext to ciphertext, a term referred to as polyalphabetic substitution. As an alternative, a random or pseudo-random sequence can be used to generate a variable ciphertext replacement. Varying substitutions through the use of a pseudo-random sequence generated by a key is the basis for many commercially developed enciphering systems as well as the well-known data encryption standard (DES). In separate chapters in this book we will examine the construction of monoalphabetic, polyalphabetic, and pseudo-random number based cipher systems.

Prior to the start of World War II, the U.S. Army Signal Corps successfully constructed a cipher machine called PURPLE that duplicated the cryptographic operations of a Japanese machine. Intercepted Japanese transmissions were fed into PURPLE, producing plaintext information that was then translated into English and distributed under the code name MAGIC to President Roosevelt and top-level civilian and military officials within his administration. Although a series of urgent messages from Tokyo to the Japanese ambassador in Washington was intercepted and deciphered, this then-secret effort did not prevent the Pearl Harbor attack simply because Japan never transmitted a message stating they would attack Pearl Harbor! Whether intentional or not, the lack of an explicit attack message resulted in a degree of complacency within the U.S. government.

The ability to read enciphered messages, while important, does not necessarily mean you will always be able to understand the intentions of others. While effective in many situations, the ability to read enciphered messages is no substitute for the analysis of the contents of those messages. For example, in June of 1942, U.S. naval intelligence decoding of intercepted Japanese transmissions noted that one Japanese unit gave Midway as its post office address. By concentrating U.S. naval forces to meet the Japanese threat, the battle of Midway represented the turning point of the war in the Pacific.

Transposition Cipher Systems

As its name implies, a transposition cipher system rearranges the characters in a message. An elementary transposition system could simply swap plaintext character positions so that position n is mapped to $n+1$ and position $n+1$ is mapped to position n. Then, the message KILL ALL THE LAWYERS would become IKLL LAT LEH ALYWRES. In the preceding example, note that a visual observation immediately provides a good clue as to the meaning of the plaintext.

As an alternative to the transposition of plaintext characters, some cipher systems are based upon the use of an algorithm which transposes the characters of a mapping alphabet or series of mapping alphabets. A variety of transposition systems are covered in a later chapter of this book.

Electronic Mail Transmission Considerations

Until now, I have simply glossed over the contents of the plaintext alphabet and the resulting ciphertext alphabet. The plaintext alphabet represents all possible characters in the character set used to develop a plaintext message. The ciphertext alphabet represents all possible enciphered characters resulting from the enciphering process. It is the plaintext character set and the enciphering process that generates the ciphertext character set you must consider to successfully transmit an enciphered message through many electronic mail systems. The reason for this is the fact that most computer alphabets use eight bits to represent a character. This results in 2^8, or 256, unique characters that can be used to represent both plaintext and ciphertext alphabet sets. Unfortunately, several electronic mail systems are restricted to transmitting seven-bit characters, with the eighth bit in a transmitted byte used for parity. Such electronic mail systems are restricted to transmitting 2^7, or 128, characters. This means that many cipher systems, such as the DES algorithm, that are not restricted with respect to the ciphertext alphabet set it generates cannot be used to directly transfer data across certain electronic mail systems.

Transmitting randomly generated ciphertext that can represent any of the 256 unique characters in an 8-bit character set over a 7-bit electronic mail system requires a conversion of each 8-bit character. One of the earliest programs developed to perform this conversion is UUENCODE, which converts three 8-bit characters into four 7-bit characters. Another program known as UUDECODE is used to reconvert each group of four 7-bit characters transmitted via a 7-bit electronic mail system back into their original three 8-bit characters. Although you can use the UUENCODE/UUDECODE program pair or similar software products to transmit a message created using an 8-bit character set via a 7-bit electronic mail system, all recipients must have the decoding program associated with the encoding program.

To obtain the capability to transmit ciphertext via certain electronic mail systems without requiring recipients to have a 7-bit to 8-bit conversion program, you need to place limits on both the plaintext alphabet set as well as the algorithm used to create ciphertext. Several methods you can use to limit the plaintext alphabet set and the algorithm used to generate a ciphertext alphabet are discussed at appropriate points in succeeding chapters.

Subroutines and Programs

To extend the practical use of encipherment, numerous routines will be developed in this book to perform different enciphering and deciphering related operations. To provide code that can be utilized by a maximum number of readers, program modules are developed using both C++ and QuickBASIC. Concerning the development of C++ modules, this author and his son used the Microsoft Visual C++ compiler to create and execute C++ routines used in this book. Microsoft Corporation's QuickBASIC compiler was used to develop the QuickBASIC subroutines and programs contained in this book.

The selection of C++ as one of two programming languages to use in the development of programming modules was based upon several factors. First, C++ is a very powerful programming language which provides programmers with the ability to perform data manipulations frequently required when using different encryption algorithms. Secondly, C++ is standardized and compilers are readily available, which means that the modules created by this author using Microsoft's Visual C++ can be used by persons with C++ compilers developed by other software vendors. However, since it is possible that some persons may not have a C++ compiler, each program module was also coded using QuickBASIC. In addition, program modules created in both C++ and QuickBASIC are stored on the CD-ROM accompanying this book in both source and binary executable form. This will provide you with a significant degree of flexibility as you can elect to incorporate source modules into Visual C++ or Visual Basic to create Windows-compliant programs, execute the binary modules under DOS to experiment with the creation of ciphertext through the use of different encryption techniques, or modify source code to tailor one or more modules to your specific requirements.

QuickBASIC was also selected for several reasons. First and foremost, every version of PC-DOS and MS-DOS contains a BASIC language interpreter on the DOS distribution diskette. This means that most readers can easily adapt the subroutines and programs presented in this book to execute through the use of a BASIC language interpreter at no additional cost. Readers can use the programs as is, modify one or more programs, or select a number of subroutines that can be viewed similar to a construction set for the design of a program tailored to a specific reader requirement.

A second reason for the selection of QuickBASIC is the availability of QBASIC on all DOS distribution diskettes commencing with release 5.0 of that operating system. QBASIC can execute all subroutines and programs presented in this book without modification, facilitating the use of those subroutines and programs.

The large number of persons with BASIC programming knowledge enables more persons to be able to put theory to practice. The capability of the QBASIC compiler to produce object code permits the inclusion of ready-to-run, executable program files on the CD-ROM. This allows you to directly execute a program without having to modify the source code, as would be required if a BASIC interpreter is used. Of course, you cannot modify the executable program, which may take some of the fun out of the use of the program if you would like to attempt to modify one or more functions.

File Naming Conventions

To facilitate the use of the CD-ROM, a set of file naming conventions was developed and used to reference program listings in this book as well as files on the CD-ROM. Files with the extension .CPP represent C++ language source code files. In this book, those files appear as subroutine and program listings. Files with the extension .BAS are BASIC language source code files. In this book, those files also appear as subroutine and program listings. Files with the extension .DAT reference data files. These files contain plaintext and ciphertext messages which facilitate demonstrating the operation and utilization of the programs developed in this book and are also contained on the CD-ROM. The fourth type of file has the extension .EXE. Files with that extension represent executable programs that readers can directly run on any Windows and DOS-based personal computer.

To enable the largest number of potential readers to use this book, files are stored under two directories on the CD-ROM. The C directory contains C++ language source and executable language programs, while the BASIC directory contains BASIC language source and executable programs. Although it is easy to distinguish BASIC and C++ source programs from one another by their extensions, both programs use the extension .EXE for executable programs. Thus, it is important to remember to note the directory under which an executable program is stored as it serves as a mechanism to distinguish BASIC from C++ executable programs. Refer to Appendix A for a list of files contained on the CD, including their names and description. Table 1.6 summarizes the file naming conventions used in this book for the mythical file XXXX.

Table 1.6 File naming conventions

File Name	Description
XXXX.BAS	The BASIC source code for the program XXXX.
XXXX.CPP	The C++ source code for the program XXXX.
XXXX.EXE	The BASIC version is in the BASIC directory, and the C++ version is in the C directory.
XXXX.DAT	A sample data file.

Chapter 2

Monoalphabetic Substitution Concepts

At first glance, the title of this chapter may evoke a vision of coverage of a medical disease. Thus, let's clarify the scope and content of this chapter by discussing what we intend to cover.

The focus of this chapter is on the use of single letters or characters contained in one alphabet to replace plaintext letters and characters in a message. Because replacement letters and characters are restricted to those included in one alphabet, we use the term "monoalphabet." In recognition of the fact that characters in the alphabet are substituted for plaintext characters, we refer to the encipherment process as a monoalphabetic substitution process.

In some books you may note the term "uniliteral substitution" or "monoalphabetic uniliteral substitution." Here, the word "uniliteral" denotes the fact that the replacement process occurs on a character-by-character basis with one character from the replacement alphabet substituted for each character in the plaintext message.

Evolution

Monoalphabetic uniliteral substitution represents one of the earliest methods of cryptology, with the technique employed by Julius Caesar approximately 20 centuries ago to hide the contents of messages he sent by courier. Although Caesar's method of encipherment was relatively elementary, his name has been associated with a class of displacement enciphering techniques and the term "Caesar cipher" is used to denote encipherment by displacement.

According to historical records, Julius Caesar wrote to Cicero and other friends using a cipher system in which the plaintext letters in his message were replaced by letters three positions further down the alphabet. Thus, in the English language, INVADE would be enciphered as LQYDGH and ENGLAND would be enciphered as HQJODQG.

Augustus Caesar, the nephew of Julius and first emperor of Rome, modified his uncle's technique. Augustus substituted for each plaintext character, reducing the displacement from three positions to one. Whether Augustus had difficulty in counting, arthritis which precluded counting by the use of his fingers, or just wanted to make deciphering easier is unknown. What is known is that any enciphering system in which plaintext characters are replaced by characters in an alphabet displaced from the plaintext alphabet is referred to as a Caesar cipher, while the displaced alphabet is called a Caesar alphabet.

Although a Caesar cipher is a rather elementary enciphering technique, it provided a foundation for the development of more advanced monoalphabetic substitution techniques. Thus, an understanding of that class of ciphers provides you with the ability to recognize the advantages and disadvantages of other techniques whose foundation can be traced to the Caesar cipher.

Prior to examining the use of uniliteral substitution systems, let us define a few terms that will be used throughout this chapter. In doing so, let us restrict our alphabet to the uppercase letters A through Z and ignore lowercase letters, punctuation characters, and numerics for simplicity of illustration (numerics and punctuation characters can be spelled out—ZERO, COMMA, and so on). In fact, in many military systems the English alphabet is restricted to the 26 uppercase characters, so we can be considered as "borrowing" military techniques by initially restricting the alphabet we will use to uppercase letters. However, you can easily expand the examples presented in this chapter to incorporate the use of larger character sets if you so desire.

Alphabets

There are two basic types of alphabets you must consider in developing a monoalphabetic uniliteral substitution system—a plaintext alphabet and a ciphertext alphabet. The plaintext alphabet represents the alphabet from which the characters of a message are constructed, while the ciphertext alphabet represents the sequence of characters used to replace the plaintext characters during the uniliteral substitution process. Because the characters in the ciphertext alphabet are used to replace the characters in the plaintext alphabet, the ciphertext alphabet is also commonly known as a substitution alphabet.

Alphabetic Relationships

The top portion of Figure 2.1 illustrates the elementary relationship between a direct-sequence plaintext alphabet and a direct-sequence ciphertext alphabet. In this example, the ciphertext alphabet was shifted or wrapped five character positions to the right with respect to the plaintext alphabet if the wraparound of each character is considered to represent one positional shift. As you will shortly note, the relationship between the numeric positions representing a ciphertext character (C) and a plaintext character (P) can be expressed as $C=(P+5)$ modulo 26.

Figure 2.1 Plaintext-ciphertext relationship. In this example, the ciphertext alphabet is shifted, or wrapped, five positions to the right. Here, the relationship between the numeric positions representing a ciphertext character (C) and a plaintext character (P) can be expressed as C=(P+5) modulo 26.

Alphabetic Relationship
Plaintext   ABCDEFGHIJKLMNOPQRSTUVWXYZ
Ciphertext   FGHIJKLMNOPQRSTUVWXYZABCDE

Numeric Relationship
Plaintext   00 01 02 03 04 05 06 07 08 09 10 11 12 13 14 15 16
               ⮩17 18 19 20 21 22 23 24 25
Ciphertext   05 06 07 08 09 10 11 12 13 14 15 16 17 18 19 20 21
               ⮩22 23 24 25 00 01 02 03 04

To illustrate the relationship between ciphertext and plaintext characters, assume each of the letters of the plaintext alphabet is sequentially assigned the numbers 0 through 25. Then, the process of encipherment illustrated in the top portion of Figure 2.1 can be expressed as $C=(P+5)$ modulo 26, where C represents the ciphertext character's numeric value, P represents the plaintext character's numeric value, and the modulo 26 process requires 26 to be subtracted when the result of the addition exceeds 25.

For example, 25 mod 26 has a value of 25, while 26 mod 26 and 27 mod 26 have values of 0 and 1, respectively. To verify this relationship, the lower portion of Figure 2.1 indicates the numerical relationships between the characters in the plaintext and ciphertext alphabets. The numeric relationship is based upon the assignment of the values 0 through 25 to the letters in the plaintext alphabet and the shifting of the ciphertext alphabet by five positions with respect to the plaintext alphabet.

From an examination of Figure 2.1, it becomes obvious that the ciphertext alphabet can be shifted up to 25 positions to the right or it can be reversed and shifted to the left. When directly shifted to the right, a series of 25 cipher alphabets can be developed, since the 26th shift results in the ciphertext matching the plaintext. Perhaps the most famous example of the use of a shifted cipher alphabet is the one credited to Julius Caesar in which the original displacement between plaintext and ciphertext was three places to the right. This well-known cipher, as well as other displacement ciphers, is very weak because the reconstruction of plaintext may be reduced to a simple trial-and-error process. However, because you need to start somewhere, this simple displacement process represents a good starting point for our discussion of monoalphabetic uniliteral substitution systems.

The recipient of a message encoded as a monoalphabetic uniliteral substitution system requires a mechanism to convert ciphertext to plaintext. That mechanism is obtained by knowing the displacement used to encode the ciphertext and using that displacement to reverse the process. Mathematically the process can be expressed as $P=(C-n)$ mod 26, where P represents the plaintext character's numeric value, C represents the ciphertext character's numeric value, n represents the displacement used to encode the ciphertext, and the modulo 26 process requires 26 to be subtracted when the result of the addition exceeds 25.

You can use Figure 2.1 to illustrate encipherment and decipherment. For example, assume the message HELP was encoded using a displacement of 5. The resulting ciphertext you would receive would be MJQU. You could convert the characters to their numeric equivalents, resulting in the sequence 12, 09, 21, 25. As previously noted, $P=(C-n)$ mod 26. Since the displacement is 5 positions $(P=(C-5)$ mod 26), this results in the received sequence of 12, 09, 21, 25 being converted to 07, 04, 16, 20. In the plaintext line in Figure 2.1 the numeric sequence 07, 04, 16, 20 represents the characters HELP which represents the deciphered message.

Displacement Alphabets

As previously illustrated in Figure 2.1, you can develop a series of 25 direct ciphertext alphabets with respect to a plaintext alphabet when both are restricted to uppercase English letters. The top portion of Listing 2.1 contains a simple program named SHIFT.BAS which displays all possible displaced alphabets from the standard uppercase English alphabet. In this program, the string array PLAINTXT$ is used to store each letter of the alphabet through the use of a READ statement contained in the first FOR-NEXT loop. The following pair of FOR-NEXT loops causes 25 shifted alphabets to be displayed with respect to the original alphabet which is displayed without any shift occurring. The bottom portion of Listing 2.1 illustrates the result obtained from the execution of SHIFT.BAS.

Listing 2.1 The SHIFT.BAS program listing.

```
Rem PROGRAM SHIFT.BAS
Rem This program produces a sequence of shifted alphabets
Cls
Dim PLAINTXT$(26)
For I = 0 To 25
READ PLAINTXT$(I)
Next I
Data "A", "B", "C", "D", "E", "F", "G", "H", "I", "J", "K"
Data "L", "M", "N", "O", "P", "Q", "R", "S", "T", "U", "V", "W", "X", "Y",
"Z"
For J = 0 To 25
For I = 0 To 25
Print PLAINTXT$((I + J) Mod 26);
Next I
Print
Next J
```

```
ABCDEFGHIJKLMNOPQRSTUVWXYZ
BCDEFGHIJKLMNOPQRSTUVWXYZA
CDEFGHIJKLMNOPQRSTUVWXYZAB
DEFGHIJKLMNOPQRSTUVWXYZABC
EFGHIJKLMNOPQRSTUVWXYZABCD
FGHIJKLMNOPQRSTUVWXYZABCDE
GHIJKLMNOPQRSTUVWXYZABCDEF
HIJKLMNOPQRSTUVWXYZABCDEFG
IJKLMNOPQRSTUVWXYZABCDEFGH
JKLMNOPQRSTUVWXYZABCDEFGHI
KLMNOPQRSTUVWXYZABCDEFGHIJ
LMNOPQRSTUVWXYZABCDEFGHIJK
MNOPQRSTUVWXYZABCDEFGHIJKL
NOPQRSTUVWXYZABCDEFGHIJKLM
OPQRSTUVWXYZABCDEFGHIJKLMN
PQRSTUVWXYZABCDEFGHIJKLMNO
QRSTUVWXYZABCDEFGHIJKLMNOP
RSTUVWXYZABCDEFGHIJKLMNOPQ
STUVWXYZABCDEFGHIJKLMNOPQR
TUVWXYZABCDEFGHIJKLMNOPQRS
UVWXYZABCDEFGHIJKLMNOPQRST
VWXYZABCDEFGHIJKLMNOPQRSTU
WXYZABCDEFGHIJKLMNOPQRSTUV
XYZABCDEFGHIJKLMNOPQRSTUVW
YZABCDEFGHIJKLMNOPQRSTUVWX
ZABCDEFGHIJKLMNOPQRSTUVWXY
```

Since a goal of this book is to provide you with both BASIC and C++ modules you can incorporate into a program of your choice, the BASIC program SHIFT.BAS is also presented as a C++ program. Listing 2.2 provides the C++ program, which when executed produces the same results as those shown in the lower portion of Listing 2.1. As previously mentioned, C++ programs presented in this book were developed using Microsoft's Visual C++ program development package. Although Visual C++ can be considered to represent a "standardized" version of C++, it is probably worthwhile to review some items in the program listing. First, the array PLAINTEXT is used as a character array to contain the uppercase letters A through Z. Those characters are stored in elements 0 through 25 in the array. The increment operators (++) are positioned after each integer used for looping (i and j), which results in each integer being incremented after it is used in the loop. The first printf statement displays a sequence of 25 characters controlled by the i loop with the percent (%) sign used to represent modulo arithmetic. Once 25 characters are printed, the i loop terminates and the second printf statement simply generates a line feed. Both the program SHIFT.CPP and an executable version of the program stored under the filename SHIFT.EXE are contained on the CD-ROM accompanying this book. Source BASIC language programs and executable files are located in the BASIC directory, while source C++ language programs and executable files are located in the C directory.

Listing 2.2 The SHIFT.CPP program listing.

```
/*   PROGRAM SHIFT.C */
/*      This program produces a sequence of shifted alphabets */

#include <stdio.h>

int main()
{
    int i,j;

    char PLAINTEXT[26] = {'A','B','C','D','E',
                'F','G','H','I','J',
                'K','L','M','N','O',
                'P','Q','R','S','T',
                'U','V','W','X','Y','Z'};
    for ( j=0; j<=25; j++)
```

```
{for (i=0; i<=25; i++)
{ printf("%c",PLAINTEXT[(i+j)%26]);
} printf("\n");
}

return (0);

}
```

In addition to a direct relationship between plaintext and ciphertext alphabets, you can reverse the relationship. That is, you can reverse and displace the ciphertext alphabet with respect to the plaintext alphabet. In doing so, the ciphertext can be applied to the plaintext alphabet at any of 26 points of coincidence between the two alphabets. Thus, you can develop a series of 25 reverse ciphertext alphabets with respect to a plaintext alphabet when both are restricted to uppercase English letters. Figure 2.2 illustrates an example of a reverse ciphertext alphabet in which the first letter of both the plaintext and ciphertext alphabets coincide. Note that the reverse ciphertext alphabet can also be shifted or displaced a total of 25 times prior to the relationship between plaintext and ciphertext characters repeats.

Figure 2.2 Reverse ciphertext alphabet. A reverse ciphertext alphabet must be shifted, or wrapped, one position to the left for the letter A in the plaintext alphabet to coincide with the letter A in the ciphertext alphabet.

```
Plaintext         ABCDEFGHIJKLMNOPQRSTUVWXYZ
Ciphertext        AZYXWVUTSRQPONMLKJIHGFEDCB
```

The relationship between a plaintext and ciphertext alphabet can be direct or reversed. For either situation, the characters in one alphabet can be shifted n positions, or $0<n<25$, with respect to the other alphabet prior to the alphabet repeating.

You can denote the relationship between plaintext and ciphertext alphabets through the location where the ciphertext alphabet coincides with the first letter (A) of the plaintext alphabet. This location is commonly referred to as the alphabetic shift key. For the ciphertext alphabet illustrated in Figure 2.1, the shift key can be expressed as $P_A=C_B$, where the P and C denote plaintext and ciphertext alphabets, and the subscript letters indicate the relationship between the two alphabets with respect to the beginning of the plaintext and ciphertext alphabets. For the reverse ciphertext alphabet illustrated in Figure 2.2, the alphabetic shift key can be expressed as $P_A=R(C_A)$, where R indicates a reversal of the ciphertext alphabet beginning with the letter A.

Encipherment

To illustrate encipherment and decipherment operations, I'll use the simple displacement relationship between ciphertext and plaintext alphabets previously illustrated in Figure 2.1. In that example, the alphabetic shift key, $P_A=C_F$, defined the relationship between the two alphabets.

Suppose you wish to encipher the message MEET ME IN ST LOUIS. You would first locate M in the plaintext and note that it is replaced by R in the ciphertext alphabet. Next, each plaintext E would be replaced by a ciphertext J, and so on. The plaintext message's completed encipherment would yield RJJY RJ NS XY QTZNX.

In military systems, the resulting enciphered message would more than likely be rewritten into groups of five characters for transmission to minimize the effect of a transmission error and facilitate the transmission and reconstruction of the original message. Thus, if you were transmitting the message you might consider sending it as:

RJJYR JNSXY QTZNX

Note that in placing the enciphered message into groups of five characters you remove spaces between words. This is usually done to eliminate obvious word groupings that would facilitate the decipherment of the message if it fell into the hands of the wrong party. Because this message has exactly 15 characters, it fills up three groups of five characters. This is not always the case, however, and unfilled groups are normally filled with one or more predefined letters known as message nulls. The most common message null is the letter X and should not be confused with the ASCII null character which represents a blank.

Care should be taken in selecting characters to fill ending message groups and terminating messages. In many military units, messages were terminated with the abbreviation FTA or one or more of those characters was used to terminate an ending message group. Not only was the abbreviation an obscene message concerning the Army, but more significantly, its inclusion in an enciphered message provided an enemy intercepting the message with the ability to rapidly gain knowledge concerning a portion of the substitution process used to encipher the message. Given that insight, with some additional effort, the entire contents of the message becomes vulnerable to decipherment.

Decipherment

Upon receipt of the enciphered message, you must know the relationship between the plaintext and ciphertext to perform our decipherment operation. Although you can use the alphabet relationship previously illustrated in Figure 2.1, that relationship is easier to use for encipherment than decipherment. For decipherment operations, you may wish to reverse the alphabet relationship shown in Figure 2.1, placing the ciphertext alphabet at the top. Then you would look up each letter from the enciphered message in the ciphertext alphabet and replace it with its plaintext alphabet equivalent. This produces the message MEETM EINST LOUIS, which you can rewrite to reflect the correct spacing between words, restoring the original form of the message.

Similar to the coding in the programs SHIFT.BAS and SHIFT.CPP, we can easily test any enciphered message to determine if a simple monoalphabetic substitution process was used. Because only 26 plaintext-ciphertext relationships exist, you can simply displace each character in the enciphered message by a uniform amount and vary that amount 25 times to discover the contents of the plaintext. Thus, a simple monoalphabetic substitution process does not offer a significant level of protection. However, the simple monoalphabetic substitution process represents an excellent starting point for a discussion of more sophisticated substitution processes as well as the development of a series of subroutines and programs that can be used to automate encipherment and decipherment operations. In the remainder of this chapter, I'll create a series of subroutines and programs that will form the basis for coding examples constructed in the rest of this book.

Automating Operations

The process of converting plaintext to ciphertext and the reverse process can be automated to facilitate monoalphabetic operations. As previously explained in Chapter 1, I'll use QuickBASIC and C++ to develop the subroutines and programs presented in this chapter and the remainder of this book.

Using an Alphabetic Shift Key

Listing 2.3 contains the program CIPHER1.BAS which can be used to create a ciphertext alphabet based upon the use of a defined alphabetic shift key. In this program, the string array PLAINTEXT$ is used to store the standard sequence of uppercase letters contained in the English alphabet, while the string array CIPHERTEXT$ is used to store the resulting cipher alphabet shifted according to an alphabetic shift key. Note that the subroutine INITIALIZE is used to initialize the plaintext values into the array PLAINTEXT$. In fact, in this and subsequent programs presented in this book, I'll use common subroutines, when possible, to facilitate the construction of specific programs or program segments developed to perform predefined operations. This will provide you with a "construction set" of routines that can be used to tailor the development of programs to your specific requirements.

Listing 2.3 The CIPHER1.BAS program listing.

```
REM PROGRAM CIPHER1.BAS
DIM PLAINTEXT$(25), CIPHERTEXT$(25)
GOSUB INITIALIZE
1       INPUT "Enter UPPERCASE Alphabetic Shift Key: ", K$
        FOR I = 0 TO 25
        IF K$ = PLAINTEXT$(I) GOTO 2
        NEXT I
        PRINT "You must enter a letter from A to Z"
        GOTO 1
2       REM Position I represents shift key letter
GOSUB FORMCIPHER
```

```
GOSUB PRTOUT
STOP
INITIALIZE:
        REM Initialize plaintext values
        FOR I = 0 TO 25
        READ PLAINTEXT$(I)
        NEXT I
        DATA "A","B","C","D","E","F","G","H","I","J","K","L","M","N"
        DATA "O","P","Q","R","S","T","U","V","W","X","Y","Z"
RETURN
FORMCIPHER:
        REM Routine to form CIPHERTEXT alphabet based upon defined shift
key
        J = I + 1
        FOR K = 0 TO 25
        CIPHERTEXT$(K) = PLAINTEXT$((K + J) MOD 26)
        NEXT K
RETURN
PRTOUT:
        REM Print results
        FOR I = 0 TO 25
        PRINT CIPHERTEXT$(I);
        NEXT I
        PRINT
RETURN
END
```

Returning to Listing 2.3, after the PLAINTEXT$ array is initialized, the INPUT statement displays the message "Enter UPPERCASE Alphabetic Shift Key" which is read into the string labeled K$. The value of K$ is compared against the alphabet to ensure that an uppercase letter was entered. If this is not the case, an error message is displayed and the program branches back to the statement labeled 1, causing the message "Enter UPPERCASE Alphabetic Shift Key" to be redisplayed. Assuming an uppercase letter is entered, the subroutine FORMCIPHER is invoked. In this subroutine, the position in the plaintext alphabet in which the shift key character equaled a plaintext character plus one is saved by assigning I+1 to the variable J. The reason I+1 is assigned to J is because the alphabet needs to be rotated through the position of the alphabetic shift key. For example, assume C was entered as the alphabetic shift key. Its position in the array PLAINTEXT$ is 2 since the index starts at 0. To shift the alphabet so it starts at the letter D you must add 1 to the position of the shift character.

The FOR-NEXT statement in the subroutine FORMCIPHER assigns 26 characters to the array CIPHERTEXT$ by adding the index K in the loop (which varies in value from 0 to 25) to the value of J, using the mod 26 operator. Thus, when K is 0 and the shift key is C, (K+J) mod 26 is 3, which results in D being assigned to CIPHERTEXT$(0). Similarly, when the shift key is C and K has a value of 25, (K+J) mod 26 has a value of 2, which results in the assignment of C to CIPHERTEXT$(25).

Once the FORMCIPHER subroutine is completed, the main part of the program invokes the subroutine PRTOUT. This subroutine prints the new alphabet based upon the entered alphabetic shift key.

Figure 2.3 illustrates several examples of the execution of CIPHER1.BAS. Note that the use of Z as the alphabetic shift key results in a full rotation of the alphabet.

```
Figure 2.3 CIPHER1.BAS execution examples.

Enter UPPERCASE Alphabetic Shift Key: B
CDEFGHIJKLMNOPQRSTUVWXYZAB
Enter UPPERCASE Alphabetic Shift Key: D
EFGHIJKLMNOPQRSTUVWXYZABCD
Enter UPPERCASE Alphabetic Shift Key: Q
RSTUVWXYZABCDEFGHIJKLMNOPQ
Enter UPPERCASE Alphabetic Shift Key: Z
ABCDEFGHIJKLMNOPQRSTUVWXYZ
```

The C++ version of the CIPHER1.BAS program can be located on the CD-ROM under the C directory. That program has the filename CIPHER1.CPP and is contained in Listing 2.4.

Listing 2.4 The CIPHER1.CPP program listing.

```
/* PROGRAM :CIPHER1.CPP
   All C++ code written by Jonathan Held, January 20, 1998,
   using Microsoft's Visual C++ version 5.1.
*/
```

```
//standard include files
#include <iostream.h>

//function prototypes
void check(char &);
void findKey(char, const char [], int &);
void formCipher(const char[], char[], int);
void printResults(const char[], const char[]);

//main program
int main(){

    char PLAINTEXT[26] = {'A', 'B', 'C', 'D', 'E', 'F', 'G', 'H', 'I',
            'J', 'K', 'L', 'M', 'N', 'O', 'P', 'Q', 'R', 'S', 'T', 'U',
            'V', 'W', 'X', 'Y', 'Z'};

    char CIPHERTEXT[26], key;

    int key_location;

    cout << "Enter UPPERCASE Alphabetic Shift Key: ";
    cin >> key;
    check(key);

    findKey(key, PLAINTEXT, key_location);
    formCipher(PLAINTEXT, CIPHERTEXT, key_location);
    printResults(PLAINTEXT, CIPHERTEXT);

    return (0);
}//end main()


//-----------------------------------------------------------------
//Function: check()
//Parameters: key - alphabetic key entered by user
//Return type: none
//Purpose: Ensure key is a valid alphabetic character.  If it is
//a lowercase letter, this procedure will automatically convert it
//to an uppercase one.  This procedure also handles all error
//checking!
//-----------------------------------------------------------------
void check(char &key){
    int key_value;
```

```
   bool error = false;

   do {

       //only change came in this line, where I removed the call
       //to the function toupper()

       key_value = static_cast<int>(key);

       if ((key_value < 65) || (key_value >90)){
           cerr << "\n\aPlease enter an UPPERCASE Alphabetic Shift Key
             (A-Z): ";
           cin >> key;
       }
       else {
       error = true;
       }
   } while (!(error));

   key = static_cast<char>(key_value);
   cout << "\nKey entered was: " << key << endl;

   return;
}//end check()



//-------------------------------------------------------------------
//Function: findkey()
//Parameters: key - alphabetic key entered by user
//            PLAINTEXT - the plaintext alphabet
//            key_location - the location of the key in the
//            PLAINTEXT alphabet
//Return type: none
//Purpose: Find the key in the PLAINTEXT alphabet.  This position
//will be used when we form the cipher.
//-------------------------------------------------------------------
void findKey(char key, const char PLAINTEXT[], int &key_location){

    for (int ix=0; ix<26; ix++){
        if (key == PLAINTEXT[ix]){
            key_location = ix + 1;
            break;
        }
```

```
        }

    return;
}//end findKey()


//------------------------------------------------------------------
//Function: formcipher()
//Parameters: PLAINTEXT - the plaintext alphabet
//            CIPHERTEXT - the cipher alphabet we will create
//            loc - the key location in the plaintext
//Return type: none
//Purpose: Create the ciphertext using modulo arithmetic.
//------------------------------------------------------------------
void formCipher(const char PLAINTEXT[], char CIPHERTEXT[], int loc){

    for (int ix=0; ix<26; ix++){
        CIPHERTEXT[ix] = PLAINTEXT[(ix + loc) % 26];
    }

    return;
}//end formCipher()


//------------------------------------------------------------------
//Function: printresults()
//Parameters: PLAINTEXT - the plaintext alphabet
//            CIPHERTEXT - the ciphertext
//Return type: none
//Purpose: Print the plaintext and corresponding ciphertext based
//on the key the user selected.
//------------------------------------------------------------------
void printResults(const char PLAINTEXT[], const char CIPHERTEXT[]){

    cout << "PLAINTEXT:  ";

    for (int ix=0; ix<26; ix++){
        cout << PLAINTEXT[ix] << " ";
    }

    cout << "\nCIPHERTEXT: ";

    for (int jx=0; jx<26; jx++){
        cout << CIPHERTEXT[jx] << " ";
```

```
    }

    cout << endl;

    return;
}//end printResults()
```

In examining the C++ program listing for CIPHER1.CPP, note that four functions were used—check, findKey, formCipher, and printResults. Each function is documented within the program listing to include a description of their parameter(s), return type, and purpose. The execution of CIPHER1.CPP will produce the same results as the execution of CIPHER1.BAS, which was previously illustrated in Listing 2.3. The executable version of CIPHER1.CPP is named CIPHER1.EXE and is located under the C directory on the CD-ROM included with this book.

Converting to Ciphertext

We can build upon the programs CIPHER1.BAS and CIPHER1.CPP to expand their capability so that they can convert plaintext to ciphertext. Listing 2.5 contains the program listing for this new program which we named CIPHER2.BAS. This elementary program enciphers a one-line message based upon an alphabetic shift key.

Listing 2.5 The CIPHER2.BAS program listing.

```
REM PROGRAM CIPHER2.BAS
        PRINT "This program enciphers a one-line message based upon an
alphabetic shift key"
DIM PLAINTEXT$(26), CIPHERTEXT$(26)
GOSUB INITIALIZE
1       INPUT "Enter UPPERCASE Alphabetic Shift Key: ", K$
        FOR I = 0 TO 25
        IF K$ = PLAINTEXT$(I) GOTO 2
        NEXT I
        PRINT "You must enter a letter from A to Z"
        GOTO 1
2       REM Position I represents shift key letter
GOSUB FORMCIPHER
        PRINT "Enter your message in UPPERCASE:"
        INPUT TEXT$
        MSGLEN = LEN(TEXT$)
GOSUB MSGENCIPHER
GOSUB PRTOUT
```

```
      STOP
INITIALIZE:
      REM Initialize plaintext values
      FOR I = 0 TO 25
      READ PLAINTEXT$(I)
      NEXT I
      DATA "A","B","C","D","E","F","G","H","I","J","K","L","M","N"
      DATA "O","P","Q","R","S","T","U","V","W","X","Y","Z"
RETURN
FORMCIPHER:
      REM Routine to form CIPHERTEXT alphabet based upon defined shift
key
      J = I + 1
      FOR K = 0 TO 25
      CIPHERTEXT$(K) = PLAINTEXT$((K + J) MOD 26)
      NEXT K
RETURN
MSGENCIPHER:
      REM Convert plaintext to ciphertext
      FOR I = 1 TO MSGLEN
      FOR J = 0 TO 25
      IF MID$(TEXT$, I, 1) = PLAINTEXT$(J) THEN GOTO 5
      NEXT J
5     MID$(TEXT$, I, 1) = CIPHERTEXT$(J)
      NEXT I
RETURN
PRTOUT:
      REM Print results
      PRINT "Resulting enciphered message is:"
      PRINT TEXT$
RETURN
END
```

In examining Listing 2.5, let us focus our attention upon the new additions, specifically the lines from PRINT "Enter your message in UPPERCASE" to STOP, and the subroutine MSGENCIPHER.

The statements following the referenced PRINT statement simply accept a one-line message and store it in the string variable TEXT$, obtain the length of the message through the use of the LEN statement and store the length of the message in the variable MSGLEN, invoke the subroutine MSGENCIPHER, and output or print the results obtained from an encipherment of the message by invoking the subroutine PRTOUT. Thus, the key to encipherment once the ciphertext is developed through the use of an alphabetic shift key is the subroutine MSGENCIPHER, which we will now discuss.

The MSGENCIPHER Subroutine

The subroutine MSGENCIPHER contains a nested pair of FOR-NEXT loops in which I is varied in the outer loop from 1 to the last character of the message denoted by MSGLEN. In the inner loop, J is varied from 0 to 25 and is used to match each plaintext character in the message to its equivalent PLAINTEXT array character position through the use of the MID function. For example, when I has a value of 1, MID$(TEXT$, I, 1) extracts the first character from the string TEXT$ which, when used in the IF statement, is compared to the value of the string variable PLAINTEXT$(J). As J is varied from 0 to 25, a value is reached in which the extracted character from TEXT$ equals a character in the PLAINTEXT$ string array and a branch to the statement label 5 occurs. At that location, the character in the string TEXT$ is replaced by the character in the CIPHERTEXT$ array located at position J. Thus, each character in the plaintext message will be replaced by a character from the shifted alphabet whose position coincides with the unshifted alphabet plaintext character.

Figure 2.4 illustrates the execution of the program CIPHER2.BAS using B as the alphabetic shift key to form the cipher alphabet. Note that at this point in time you have to eliminate spaces between words as there is no space character in our plaintext or ciphertext alphabet. Later in this book, I'll develop a routine which will remove spaces between words, enabling a user to enter a plaintext message in a more natural manner.

```
Figure 2.4 A CIPHER2.BAS execution example.

This program enciphers a one-line message based on an
alphabetic shift key
Enter UPPERCASE Alphabetic Shift Key: B
Enter your message in UPPERCASE
? BIDFIVEPOINTTWOMILLION
Resulting enciphered message is:
DKFHKXGRQKPVVYQOKNNKQP
```

The CIPHER2.CPP Program

In developing a C++ version of CIPHER2.BAS, a considerable visual improvement occurred by allowing spaces between words. Listing 2.6 contains a listing of the program CIPHER2.CPP. Since this program is well defined through the use of a significant number of comments concerning its coding, our comments on its coding will be minimized. As noted from the function prototypes section, the program uses five key functions. The getShiftKey function checks for and accepts an uppercase letter as the shift key to be used by the program. The createCipher function creates the ciphertext alphabet based upon the shift key previously entered. The third function, getMessage, retrieves the user's message which can be up to 256 uppercase characters in length. The fourth function, formCipheredMessage, enciphers the previously entered message while the fifth function, printResults, displays the corresponding enciphered message.

Listing 2.6 The CIPHER2.CPP program listing.

```
/*
Program Cipher2.cpp
C++ Code written by Jonathan Held, January 21, 1998, using
Microsoft Visual C++, version 5.0

211 total lines of code.
*/

//standard include files
#include <iostream.h>
#include <string.h>

//function prototypes
void getShiftKey(char &);
void createCipher(const char [], char[], const char);
void getMessage(char []);
void formCipheredMessage(const char[], const char [], char []);
void printResults(const char[], const char[], const char[], const char []);

//main program
int main(){

    //initialize plaintext
    char plaintext[26] = {'A','B','C','D','E','F','G','H','I',
                          'J','K','L','M','N','O','P','Q','R',
```

```
                        'S','T','U', 'V','W','X','Y','Z'};

    //other variables we will use
    char ciphertext[26], message_to_cipher[256], enciphered_message[256], key;

    //function calls

    do {

        //get the uppercase key
        getShiftKey(key);

        //create the cipher key
        createCipher(plaintext, ciphertext, key);

        //get the users message
        getMessage(message_to_cipher);

        //form the ciphered message
        formCipheredMessage(ciphertext, message_to_cipher, enciphered_message);

        //print off the results
        printResults(plaintext, ciphertext, message_to_cipher,
                enciphered_message);

    } while (true);

    return (0);

}//end main()


//------------------------------------------------------------------
//Function: getShiftKey()
//Parameters:  key_desired - uppercase key entered by the user
//Return Type: None
//Purpose: Get the key the user enters; error checking performed
//until user enters a valid value.
//------------------------------------------------------------------
void getShiftKey(char &key_desired){

    bool error = true;

    do {
```

```
            //prompt user to enter an uppercase shift key
            cout << "Enter UPPERCASE Alphabetic Shift Key (CTRL-C to quit): ";
            cin >> key_desired;

            int key_value = static_cast<int>(key_desired);

            //do some error checking
            if ((key_value < 65) || (key_value > 90)){
               cerr << "\nYou must enter a letter from A to Z!" << endl << endl;
            }
            else {
               cout << endl;
               error = false;
            }
      } while (error);

      return;
}//end getShiftKey()


      //-------------------------------------------------------------------
      //Function: createCipher()
      //Parameters:  PTEXT - the plaintext alphabet
      //             ctext - the cipher alphabet we are going to create
      //             user_key - the key the user entered
      //Return Type: None
      //Purpose: Create the cipher stream we will use later to encode the
      //user's message.
      //-------------------------------------------------------------------
      void createCipher(const char PTEXT[], char ctext[], const char user_key){

          int location;

          //find the location of the key in the plaintext
          for (int ix=0; ix<26; ix++){
             if (user_key == PTEXT[ix]){
                //location is one more than ix
                location = ix + 1;
                break;
             }
          }

          //create the cipher text
          for (int jx=0; jx<26; jx++){
```

```
        ctext[jx] = PTEXT[(jx + location) % 26];
    }
    return;
}//end createCipher();


//------------------------------------------------------------------

//Function: getMessage()
//Parameters:  msg_to_cipher[] - the message entered by the user
//Return Type: None
//Purpose: Get the user's message and find out how long it is using
//the standard string function strlen including in the string.h
//library file.
//------------------------------------------------------------------
void getMessage(char msg_to_cipher[]){

    //get the newline character off of the input stream
    cin.get();

    cout << "Enter the message in UPPERCASE characters: " << endl;

    //get the entire line, up to 256 characters
    cin.getline(msg_to_cipher, 256, '\n');

    return;
}//end getMessage()


//------------------------------------------------------------------
//Function: formCipheredMessage()
//Parameters: CTEXT - the cipher alphabet we will use for substitution
//            MESSAGETOCIPHER - the user's message
//            enc_message - the enciphered message to be determined
//Return Type: None
//Purpose: Encipher the user's one-line message.
//------------------------------------------------------------------
void formCipheredMessage(const char CTEXT[], const char MESSAGETOCIPHER[],
                         char enc_message[]){


    int length = strlen(MESSAGETOCIPHER)+1;

    for (int ix=0; ix<length; ix++){
```

```
                //get character from MESSAGETOCIPHER
                char encode = MESSAGETOCIPHER[ix];
                int encode_value = static_cast<int>(encode);

                //handle the case where an input character is not a letter
                //A - Z
                if ((encode_value < 65) || (encode_value > 90)){
                        enc_message[ix] = MESSAGETOCIPHER[ix];
                }
                else {
                   //valid character - the easy way to calculate the ciphered
                   //character is based on the plain text's ascii character value;
                   //since it has to be a capital letter, it must be in the range
                   //from 65 to 90, with A represented by 65, Z by 90. By simply
                   //subtracting 65 from the encode_value (the integer representation
                   //of the plaintext character), we now know what cipher character
                   //to use.
                   enc_message[ix] = CTEXT[encode_value-65];
                }
        }

        return;
}//end formCipheredMessage()



//-----------------------------------------------------------------
//Function: printResults()
//Parameters: PTEXT - the plaintext alphabet
//            CTEXT - the cipher alphabet we used for subsitution
//            MESSAGETOCIPHER - the user's message
//            ENCIPHEREDMESSAGE - the corresponding enciphered message
//Return Type: None
//Purpose: Display the values of all passed-in parameters.
//-----------------------------------------------------------------
void printResults(const char PTEXT[], const char CTEXT[],
                     const char MESSAGETOCIPHER[], const char
ENCIPHEREDMESSAGE[]){

   cout << "\nPLAINTEXT:   ";
   for (int ix=0; ix<26; ix++){
     cout << PTEXT[ix] << " ";
   }

   cout << endl;
```

```
    cout << "CIPHERTEXT: ";
    for (int jx=0; jx<26; jx++){
       cout << CTEXT[jx] << " ";
    }

    cout << "\n\nORIGINAL MESSAGE: " << MESSAGETOCIPHER << endl;
    cout << "\nCIPHERED MESSAGE: " << ENCIPHEREDMESSAGE << endl << endl;

    return;
}//end printResults()
//end file cipher5.cpp
```

Key differences between the BASIC and C++ versions of the CIPHER2 program are in the validation of uppercase letters and termination of the program. The C++ version uses ASCII values from 65 through 90 as a check for uppercase A through Z and recognizes the CTRL-C key combination as a mechanism to quit the program.

Limiting the Effect of Errors

The meaning of an enciphered message can be adversely affected by a human typing error or a transmission or transcription error. In such situations, a mistake which adds or omits a character would jumble the decipherment of the meaning of a message. Thus, we need a mechanism to limit the effect of errors caused by humans or technology. One common mechanism has its roots dating to the development of military systems and is known as character grouping—the most common method being the placement of enciphered text into groups of five characters for transmission.

To place ciphertext into groups of five characters, we will modify the CIPHER2.BAS and CIPHER2.CPP programs by the inclusion of a new subroutine. That subroutine, appropriately named GROUPBY5, replaces the subroutine PRTOUT contained in the CIPHER2.BAS program.

The GROUPBY5 Subroutine

Listing 2.7 lists the contents of the subroutine GROUPBY5. That subroutine uses the variable L as a group counter. When invoked, the subroutine sets the value of L to 1. The FOR-NEXT loop in the subroutine prints one character at a time through the use of the MID$ function, which extracts a character from the string variable TEXT$. After a character is printed, the value of the FOR-NEXT loop index (I) divided by 5 is compared to the value of L. If the value of I/5 equals the value of L, five characters have been printed and a branch to the label 6 occurs. At that label, the PRINT statement generates a space. If the value of I/5 does not equal the value of L, a branch to the label 7 occurs and the FOR-NEXT loop terminates the current index value of the loop.

Listing 2.7 The GROUPBY5 subroutine.

```
GROUPBY5:
    L = 1
    FOR I = 1 TO MSGLEN
    PRINT MID$(TEXT$, I, 1)
    IF I / 5 = L THEN GOTO 6
    GOTO 7
6   PRINT ' ';
    L = L + 1
7   NEXT I
RETURN
```

One of the more famous messages transmitted using groupings of five characters was sent by Takeo Yoshikawa, a Japanese naval ensign assigned as a consulate secretary to the Japanese consulate in Honolulu. At 6 P.M. on December 6, 1941, he sent his final message using what was known as Oite to the Japanese and PA-K2 to American codebreakers. This message contained 44 groups of five characters and was transmitted to Tokyo via RCA communications at a cost of $6.82.

The message transmitted by ensign Yoshikawa reported the arrival of an American battleship and mine sweeper into port and provided a summary of the number of ships at anchor and ships in dock in Honolulu by category—battleships, light cruisers, destroyers, and mine sweepers. The message also noted that it appeared that no air reconnaissance was being conducted by the U.S. fleet's air arm.

Although American cryptanalysts were able to crack messages transmitted in a PA-K2 code, doing so required an average of three days. Unfortunately, the contents of this message were deciphered well after the attack on Pearl Harbor had begun.

The CIPHER3.BAS Program

Listing 2.8 contains the listing of the main body of the program
CIPHER3.BAS. That program includes the subroutine GROUPBY5 which
groups a line of enciphered text into groups of five characters. Figure 2.5
illustrates an example of the execution of the CIPHER3.BAS program
using the alphabetic shift key B, and shows the five-character grouping of
the enciphered message. If you are familiar with military systems, you
may wonder why the GROUPBY5 subroutine leaves the last group with
less than five characters instead of filling the group by adding X's or some
similar group terminator character. The reason for not doing so at this
time is because this program only operates on one message line at a time.
Thus, before you terminate an unfilled group, you should first modify our
program to read and process multiple lines of plaintext.

Listing 2.8 The CIPHER3.BAS program listing.

```
REM PROGRAM CIPHER3.BAS
DIM PLAINTEXT$(25), CIPHERTEXT$(25)
CLS
        GOSUB INITIALIZE
1       INPUT "Enter UPPERCASE Alphabetic Shift Key: ", K$
        FOR I = 0 TO 25
        IF K$ = PLAINTEXT$(I) GOTO 2
        NEXT I
        PRINT "You must enter a letter from A to Z"
        GOTO 1
2       REM Position I represents shift key letter
GOSUB FORMCIPHER
        PRINT "Enter your message in UPPERCASE:"
        INPUT TEXT$
        MSGLEN = LEN(TEXT$)
GOSUB MSGENCIPHER
        REM Print results
        PRINT "Resulting enciphered message is:"
GOSUB GROUPBY5
STOP
INITIALIZE:
        REM Initialize plaintext values
        FOR I = 0 TO 25
        READ PLAINTEXT$(I)
        NEXT I
        DATA "A","B","C","D","E","F","G","H","I","J","K","L","M","N"
```

```
                    DATA "O","P","Q","R","S","T","U","V","W","X","Y","Z"
RETURN
FORMCIPHER:
          REM Routine to form CIPHERTEXT alphabet based upon defined shift key
          J = I + 1
          FOR K = 0 TO 25
          CIPHERTEXT$(K) = PLAINTEXT$((K + J) MOD 26)
          NEXT K
RETURN
MSGENCIPHER:
          REM Convert plaintext to ciphertext
          FOR I = 1 TO MSGLEN
          FOR J = 0 TO 25
          IF MID$(TEXT$, I, 1) = PLAINTEXT$(J) THEN GOTO 5
          NEXT J
5         MID$(TEXT$, I, 1) = CIPHERTEXT$(J)
          NEXT I
RETURN
GROUPBY5:
          L = 1
          FOR I = 1 TO MSGLEN
          PRINT MID$(TEXT$, I, 1);
          IF I / 5 = L THEN GOTO 6
          GOTO 7
6         PRINT " ";
          L = L + 1
7         NEXT I
RETURN
END
```

```
Figure 2.5 A sample execution of the program CIPHER3.BAS.

Enter UPPERCASE Alphabetic Shift Key: B
Enter your message in UPPERCASE:
? BUYFIVETHOUSANDSHARESOFGAMMAINDUSTRIES
Resulting enciphered message is:
DWAHK XGVJQ WUCPF UJCTG UQHIC OOCKP FWUVT KGU
```

The CIPHER3.CPP Program

The C++ version of CIPHER3.BAS follows our naming convention and is stored in the C directory under the filename CIPHER3.CPP. This program is similar to the BASIC language version in that it first asks for the entry of an uppercase alphabetic shift key character. Next, it displays the plain-text and ciphertext alphabet resulting from the shift and prompts you to enter your "original message." Using the shift key the program generates an enciphered message in which the resulting enciphered text is displayed in military fashion in groups of five characters.

Listing 2.9 contains the CIPHER3.CPP program listing. Note that the function printResults places the enciphered text into groups of five characters and adds a space when the variable "counter" does not equal 0 and the value of counter mod 5 equals 0.

Listing 2.9 The CIPHER3.CPP program listing.

```
/*
Program Cipher3.cpp
C++ Code written by Jonathan Held, January 21, 1998, using
Microsoft Visual C++, version 5.0.

248 total lines of code.
*/

//standard include files
#include <iostream.h>
#include <string.h>

//function prototypes
void getShiftKey(char &);
void createCipher(const char [], char[], const char);
void getMessage(char []);
void formCipheredMessage(const char[], const char [], char []);
void printResults(const char[], const char[], const char[], const char []);
void printCipher(const char[]);

//main program
int main(){

    //initialize plaintext
    char plaintext[26] = {'A','B','C','D','E','F','G','H','I',
                          'J','K','L','M','N','O','P','Q','R',
                          'S','T','U', 'V','W','X','Y','Z'};

    //other variables we will use
    char ciphertext[26], message_to_cipher[256], enciphered_message[256], key;
```

```
        //function calls

        do {

            //get the uppercase key
            getShiftKey(key);

            //create the cipher key
            createCipher(plaintext, ciphertext, key);

            //get the users message
            getMessage(message_to_cipher);

            //form the ciphered message
            formCipheredMessage(ciphertext, message_to_cipher, enciphered_message);

            //print off the results
            printResults(plaintext, ciphertext, message_to_cipher,
                        enciphered_message);

        } while (true);

        return (0);

}//end main()


//-------------------------------------------------------------------
//Function: getShiftKey()
//Parameters:  key_desired - uppercase key entered by the user
//Return Type: None
//Purpose: Get the key the user enters; error checking performed
//until user enters a valid value.
//-------------------------------------------------------------------
void getShiftKey(char &key_desired){

    bool error = true;

    do {
        //prompt user to enter an uppercase shift key
        cout << "Enter UPPERCASE Alphabetic Shift Key (CTRL-C to quit): ";
        cin >> key_desired;

        int key_value = static_cast<int>(key_desired);
```

```
      //do some error checking
      if ((key_value < 65) || (key_value > 90)){
         cerr << "\nYou must enter a letter from A to Z!" << endl << endl;
      }
      else {
         cout << endl;
         error = false;
      }
   } while (error);
   return;
}//end getShiftKey()



//-----------------------------------------------------------------
//Function: createCipher()
//Parameters: PTEXT - the plaintext alphabet
//            ctext - the cipher alphabet we are going to create
//            user_key - the key the user entered
//Return Type: none
//Purpose: Create the cipher stream we will use later to encode the
//user's message.
//-----------------------------------------------------------------
void createCipher(const char PTEXT[], char ctext[], const char user_key){

   int location;

   //find the location of the key in the plaintext
   for (int ix=0; ix<26; ix++){
      if (user_key == PTEXT[ix]){
         //location is one more than ix
         location = ix + 1;
         break;
      }
   }

   //create the cipher text
   for (int jx=0; jx<26; jx++){
      ctext[jx] = PTEXT[(jx + location) % 26];
   }

   return;
}//end createCipher();
```

```
//-----------------------------------------------------------------
//Function: getMessage()
//Parameters:  msg_to_cipher[] - the message entered by the user
//Return Type: None
//Purpose: Get the user's message and find out how long it is using
//the standard string function strlen including in the string.h
//library file.
//-----------------------------------------------------------------
void getMessage(char msg_to_cipher[]){

    //get the newline character off of the input stream
    cin.get();

    cout << "Enter the message in UPPERCASE characters: " << endl;

    //get the entire line, up to 256 characters
    cin.getline(msg_to_cipher, 256, '\n');

    return;
}//end getMessage()



//-----------------------------------------------------------------
//Function: formCipheredMessage()
//Parameters:  CTEXT - the cipher alphabet we will use for substitution
//             MESSAGETOCIPHER - the user's message
//             enc_message - the enciphered message to be determined
//Return Type: None
//Purpose: Encipher the user's one-line message.
//-----------------------------------------------------------------
void formCipheredMessage(const char CTEXT[], const char MESSAGETOCIPHER[],
                    char enc_message[]){

    int length = strlen(MESSAGETOCIPHER)+1;

    for (int ix=0; ix<length; ix++){

        //get character from MESSAGETOCIPHER
        char encode = MESSAGETOCIPHER[ix];
        int encode_value = static_cast<int>(encode);

        //handle the case where an input character is not a letter
        //A - Z
        if ((encode_value < 65) || (encode_value > 90)){
```

```
              enc_message[ix] = MESSAGETOCIPHER[ix];
          }
          else {
            //valid character - the easy way to calculate the ciphered
            //character is based on the plain text's ascii character value;
            //since it has to be a capital letter, it must be in the range
            //from 65 to 90, with A represented by 65, Z by 90.  By simply
            //subtracting 65 from the encode_value (the integer representation
            //of the plaintext character), we now know what cipher character
            //to use.
            enc_message[ix] = CTEXT[encode_value-65];
          }
      }


      return;
}//end formCipheredMessage()



//----------------------------------------------------------------
//Function: printResults()
//Parameters:  PTEXT - the plaintext alphabet
//             CTEXT - the cipher alphabet we used for subsitution
//             MESSAGETOCIPHER - the user's message
//             ENCIPHEREDMESSAGE - the corresponding enciphered message
//Return Type: None
//Purpose: Display the values of all passed-in parameters.
//----------------------------------------------------------------
void printResults(const char PTEXT[], const char CTEXT[], const char
MESSAGETOCIPHER[],
                  const char ENCIPHEREDMESSAGE[]){

   cout << "\nPLAINTEXT:  ";
   for (int ix=0; ix<26; ix++){
      cout << PTEXT[ix] << " ";
   }

   cout << endl;

   cout << "CIPHERTEXT: ";
   for (int jx=0; jx<26; jx++){
      cout << CTEXT[jx] << " ";
   }

   cout << "\n\nOriginal Message: " << endl << MESSAGETOCIPHER << endl;
```

```
        cout << "\nEnciphered Message: " << endl;
        printCipher(ENCIPHEREDMESSAGE);

        return;
}//end printResults()


//-------------------------------------------------------------
//Function: printCipher()
//Parameters:  MSG - the cipher text we are displaying
//Return Type: None
//Purpose: Group the cipher in 5-block characters
//-------------------------------------------------------------
void printCipher(const char MSG[]){

    int counter = 0;

    int length = strlen(MSG)+1;

    for (int kx=0;kx<length;kx++){

        if (*(MSG+kx) != ' '){

            if ((counter != 0) && (counter%5 == 0)) {
                cout << " ";
            }

            cout << *(MSG+kx);
            counter++;
        }
    }

    cout << endl << endl;

    return;
}//end printCipher()
//end file cipher3.cpp
```

Processing Multiple-Line Messages

Since you want the ability to read a message containing multiple lines of text, let's modify our previously constructed program by the addition of several subroutines. One subroutine will permit a message to be input from the keyboard or a previously created file. To provide you with the ability to enter text more naturally, this subroutine will also permit you to enter words with spaces between words, since the program will become responsible for their removal. Other subroutines will convert the plaintext message into ciphertext and position the enciphered text into groups of five characters for printing, terminating the last group of characters with an appropriate number of X's to fill any terminating group that has less than five characters.

The MSGFILE Subroutine

Listing 2.10 shows the contents of the subroutine labeled MSGFILE. This subroutine performs three major functions. First, it permits the user to assign filenames for the file used to store a plaintext and resulting ciphertext message or to select the default filenames MESSAGE.DAT for storing the plaintext message and CIPHERTX.DAT for storing the enciphered message. The second function performed by MSGFILE is to remove spaces between words. The third function performed by this subroutine is to store in a file the resulting plaintext message in which any spaces between words were removed.

Listing 2.10 The MSGFILE subroutine.

```
MSGFILE:
        REM Routine to assign I/O files and accept keyboard or file input
        REM and remove spaces between words
                INPUT "Enter filename to store plaintext message,
                    default=MESSAGE.DAT", INFILE$
                IF INFILE$ = "" THEN INFILE$ = "MESSAGE.DAT"
                INPUT "Enter filename to store enciphered message,
                    default=CIPHERTX.DAT", OUTFILE$
                IF OUTFILE$ = "" THEN OUTFILE$ = "CIPHERTX.DAT"
                INPUT "Select keyboard (k) or file (f) message input: ", IN$
                IF IN$ = "F" OR IN$ = "f" THEN RETURN
                OPEN INFILE$ FOR OUTPUT AS #1
        REM Routine to place message on a file removing spaces between words
                PRINT "Enter your message - place a / at the beginning of
                    each line"
                PRINT "that should remain in plaintext and a \ on a
                    separate line"
                PRINT "to indicate the end of the enciphered message"
                PRINT
AGN:            LINE INPUT TEXT$
```

```
                        IF MID$(TEXT$, 1, 1) = "/" THEN GOTO XT
                        NTEXT$ = ""
                        FOR I = 1 TO LEN(TEXT$)
                        NTEXT$ = NTEXT$ + LTRIM$(MID$(TEXT$, I, 1))
                        NEXT I
                        WRITE #1, NTEXT$
                        IF MID$(TEXT$, 1, 1) = "\" GOTO DONE
                        GOTO AGN
         XT:            WRITE #1, TEXT$
                        GOTO AGN
         DONE:          CLOSE #1
         RETURN
```

The first portion of the subroutine MSGFILE prompts the user to enter filenames for storing a plaintext message and its resulting enciphered message. If the user simply presses the Return key, the default filenames MESSAGE.DAT and CIPHERTX.DAT are used. Otherwise, the subroutine prompts the user to enter the appropriate plaintext and ciphertext filenames.

The second major routine in MSGFILE performs the actual placement of keyboard-entered plaintext on a file and removes spaces between words. To facilitate the transmission of enciphered messages, this portion of the subroutine permits users to prefix each heading message line with a forward slash (/) character if they do not want that message line to be enciphered. This allows a header portion of a message to be ignored during the encipherment process. The transmission of the enciphered text with a cleartext header facilitates its distribution to the appropriate recipient. To indicate the end of the message, a backslash (\) character must be entered by itself on a separate line.

The FOR-NEXT loop in the second half of the subroutine MSGFILE uses the LTRIM$ statement to remove spaces between words. This FOR-NEXT loop is invoked only when the beginning of a line does not contain a forward slash character. Since LTRIM$ removes leading spaces in a string, its use in the FOR-NEXT loop places a line of plaintext in which all spaces have been removed into the string variable NTEXT$.

The CONVERTSTORE Subroutine

The following subroutine reads the contents of the previously stored messages a line at a time, converts each message into its enciphered text, and stores the enciphered text on a line-by-line basis in the file whose name is assigned to the string variable OUTFILE$. Listing 2.11 shows the statements in the subroutine CONVERTSTORE which perform the previously mentioned functions.

Listing 2.11 The CONVERTSTORE subroutine.

```
CONVERTSTORE:
        REM Routine to convert and store ciphertext on a file
        OPEN INFILE$ FOR INPUT AS #1
        OPEN OUTFILE$ FOR OUTPUT AS #2
        DO UNTIL EOF(1)
                INPUT #1, TEXT$
                MSGLEN = LEN(TEXT$)
                IF MID$(TEXT$, 1, 1) = "/" THEN GOTO CLEARTXT
                IF MID$(TEXT$, 1, 1) = "\" THEN GOTO DONE1
                REM Convert plaintext to ciphertext
                        FOR I = 1 TO MSGLEN
                        FOR J = 0 TO 25
                        IF MID$(TEXT$, I, 1) = PLAINTEXT$(J) THEN GOTO GOTIT
                        NEXT J
GOTIT:                  MID$(TEXT$, I, 1) = CIPHERTEXT$(J)
                        NEXT I
CLEARTXT:               WRITE #2, TEXT$
        LOOP
DONE1:          CLOSE #2
RETURN
```

After opening the file whose name was assigned to the string variable INFILE$ for input and the file whose name was assigned to OUTFILE$ for output, the subroutine uses a DO UNTIL loop to read each message line from the file containing the plaintext message. Within the DO UNTIL loop, each line is processed based upon the first character in the line.

If the first character in a line is a forward slash, a branch to the label CLEARTXT occurs and the conversion of plaintext to enciphered text is bypassed. If the first character in a line is a backslash, the end of the previously stored message has been reached and a branch to the label DONE1 occurs. This terminates the loop, closes the previously opened file #2, and causes an exit from the subroutine to occur.

If the first character in each line is neither a forward slash nor a backslash character, the subroutine converts each plaintext character in the line into its equivalent ciphertext character. This is accomplished through the use of a pair of nested FOR-NEXT loops. The outer loop cycles through each of the characters in a line retrieved from the file containing the plaintext. The inner loop compares on a character-by-character basis the plaintext character to each character in the string array PLAINTEXT$. When a match occurs, a branch to the label GOTIT occurs. At that label, the plaintext character is replaced by the ciphertext character whose position in the array CIPHERTEXT$ is the same as the position of the plaintext character in the array PLAINTEXT$.

The PRTOUT Subroutine

Now that subroutines were developed to place a message on a file and process and convert the message to enciphered text which is stored on another file, I am ready to print the results. To do this I will develop a subroutine named PRTOUT which will process the file containing the enciphered text so that no more than 25 characters or five groups of five characters are displayed on a line. We have limited the printout of enciphered text to 25 characters per line to facilitate manual operations for readers who wish to use the resulting display of the enciphered message in place of the file containing the enciphered text for sending a message.

Listing 2.12 shows the contents of the subroutine PRTOUT. After using an INPUT statement to display the message informing a user to press the Return key, the subroutine clears the display and sets the string variable TEMP$ to a null value. Next, the message "Resulting enciphered message is:" is displayed and the file assigned to the variable OUTFILE$ is opened for input. Note that the enciphered text was previously stored on the file assigned to the variable OUTFILE$; thus, this subroutine will process the enciphered message.

Listing 2.12 The PRTOUT subroutine.

```
PRTOUT: REM Subroutine to print results
        INPUT "Press Return key to display resulting enciphered message", p$
        CLS : TEMP$ = ""
        PRINT "Resulting enciphered message is:"
        OPEN OUTFILE$ FOR INPUT AS #2
        DO UNTIL EOF(2)
                INPUT #2, TEXT$
                IF MID$(TEXT$, 1, 1) = "/" THEN PRINT RIGHT$(TEXT$,
                        LEN(TEXT$) - 1)
                IF MID$(TEXT$, 1, 1) = "/" THEN GOTO NOGROUP
                IF TEMP$ = "" GOTO BLANK          'blank string
```

```
                    TEMP$ = TEMP$ + TEXT$            'concatenate
                    TEXT$ = TEMP$
                    TEMP$ = ""
BLANK:              MSGLEN = LEN(TEXT$)
                    IF MSGLEN >= 25 THEN GOTO BIG
                    TEMP$ = TEXT$
                    GOTO NOGROUP                     'less than 25 characters
BIG:                FOR I = 26 TO MSGLEN             'place remainder of string
                                                     'into temp
                    TEMP$ = TEMP$ + MID$(TEXT$, I, 1)
                    NEXT I
                    MSGLEN = 25
                    GOSUB GROUPBY5:                  'print 25 characters
NOGROUP: LOOP
                    TEXT$ = TEMP$                    'print remainder
                    MSGLEN = LEN(TEXT$)
                    IF MSGLEN <= 25 THEN GOSUB GROUPBY5
                    IF MSGLEN <= 25 THEN RETURN      'done printing
         WHILE MSGLEN > 25
                    TEMP$ = LEFT$(TEXT$, 25)         'get first 25 characters
                                                     'in string
                    TEMPR$ = RIGHT$(TEXT$, MSGLEN - 25)
                    TEXT$ = TEMP$
                    MSGLEN = LEN(TEXT$)
                    GOSUB GROUPBY5
                    TEXT$ = TEMPR$
                    MSGLEN = LEN(TEXT$)
         WEND
                    TEXT$ = TEMPR$
                    MSGLEN = LEN(TEXT$)
                    GOSUB GROUPBY5
RETURN
```

The DO UNTIL loop processes the lines on the enciphered file. First, each line is read into the string variable TEXT$. The first two IF statements check for the presence of a forward slash. If a forward slash occurs in the first character position in a line, the first IF statement causes the line to be printed without the slash. Since a forward slash indicates the line should be treated as cleartext, the second IF statement simply skips the remaining statements in the loop by branching to the label NOGROUP.

The first time PRTOUT is invoked, the string TEMP$ is set to the null string. Thus, the first time through the DO UNTIL loop, the third IF statement causes a branch to the label BLANK to occur. At that label the length of the retrieved line of ciphertext is determined through the use of the LEN function. If the length of the line equals or exceeds 25 characters, a branch to the label BIG occurs. If the length of the line did not exceed 25 characters, there were not enough characters for printing 25 characters on one line. At this point, the characters assigned to the variable TEXT$ are assigned to the variable TEMP$ and a branch to the label NOGROUP occurs to terminate one cycle through the loop.

When the value of TEMP$ is not a null string, the contents of the next line of ciphertext are concatenated, or joined, to the contents of TEMP$. Then, the contents of TEMP$ are assigned to TEXT$ and TEMP$ is reset to a null string. In this manner, you can continue to cycle through the contents of the enciphered file until you either reach the end of the file or the length of the variable TEXT$ equals or exceeds 25 characters.

When the length of TEXT$ equals or exceeds 25 characters, a branch to the label BIG occurs. At that location, the FOR-NEXT loop places the remainder of the contents of TEXT$ that exceed 25 characters into the variable TEMP$. Next, the message length variable MSGLEN is set to 25 and the subroutine GROUPBY5 is called. That subroutine, which was previously discussed and which will be discussed in more detail in the next section in this chapter, actually prints the characters in groups of fives and assigns X's to fill the last group, if that group contains less than five characters.

When all lines in the file assigned to OUTFILE$ are read, the DO UNTIL loop is exited. At this point, you need to print the remaining enciphered text stored in the variable TEMP$. To do this, assign the contents of TEMP$ to TEXT$ and obtain its length. If the length of TEXT$ is less than or equal to 25 characters, invoke the subroutine GROUPBY5 to print the last 25 or less characters in the enciphered message and then exit the subroutine. If there are more than 25 characters in TEXT$, use a WHILE-WEND loop to print the contents of TEXT$. Assign the first 25 characters in TEXT$ to TEMP$ through the use of the LEFT$ function. Next, the remaining characters in the string TEXT$ are assigned to the variable TEMPR$. After the contents of TEMP$ are assigned to TEXT$, the message length is determined and the subroutine GROUPBY5 is invoked. The contents of TEMPR$ are assigned to TEXT$, the length of TEXT$ is determined, and the subroutine GROUPBY5 is again invoked, this time printing the remaining portion of characters that exceeded 25 in length. When less than 25 characters remain in TEMPR$, the WHILE-WEND loop terminates. At that point the contents of TEMPR$ are assigned to TEXT$, its length is determined, and the subroutine GROUPBY5 is invoked for the last time.

Modifying the GROUPBY5 Subroutine

As previously constructed, this subroutine performs the actual printing of characters in groups of five. Now we will modify this subroutine so that it fills the last group with X's if there are less than five characters in the group. Listing 2.13 shows the statement in this modified subroutine.

Listing 2.13 The modified GROUPBY5 subroutine.

```
GROUPBY5:
        L = 1
        FOR I = 1 TO MSGLEN
                PRINT MID$(TEXT$, I, 1);
                IF I / 5 = L THEN GOTO AGROUP
                GOTO NGROUP
AGROUP:         PRINT " ";
                L = L + 1
NGROUP: NEXT I
        NUMX = 5 - MSGLEN MOD 5
        IF NUMX = 5 OR NUMX = 0 THEN GOTO PRTBLK
        FOR I = 1 TO NUMX
        PRINT "X";
        NEXT I
PRTBLK: PRINT
RETURN
```

When the subroutine is invoked, the variable L is set to 1 and the FOR-NEXT loop cycles through the contents of the string variable TEXT$, printing one character at a time. If the index I of the FOR-NEXT loop divided by 5 equals L, five characters have been printed and a branch to the label AGROUP occurs. At that location, the PRINT statement prints a space, providing a space between groups of five characters. Next, the variable L is incremented and the loop ends. If a group of five characters was not printed, a branch to the label NGROUP occurs, bypassing the printing of the space.

Once the FOR-NEXT loop is completed, you must determine if a group did not have five characters, a condition that can only occur when the last line in the enciphered message is processed. Here, the value of the variable NUMX determines the number of X's that must be added to fill the last group. Only if NUMX is greater than 0 or less than 5 do we invoke the next FOR-NEXT loop to print the terminating X's. Otherwise, a branch to the label PRTBLK occurs, which terminates a previous PRINT statement ending with a semicolon so that the next cycle through the subroutine GROUPBY5 will have succeeding groups placed on a new line.

The CIPHER4.BAS Program

The entire program previously developed as modules will be listed to facilitate recognizing how the previously mentioned subroutines and calling program relate to each other. This program is contained in the directory BASIC in the file CIPHER4.BAS on the CD-ROM and is given in Listing 2.14.

Listing 2.14 The CIPHER4.BAS program listing.

```
REM PROGRAM CIPHER4.BAS
DIM PLAINTEXT$(26), CIPHERTEXT$(26)
CLS
        GOSUB INITIALIZE
        PRINT "CIPHER4.BAS PROGRAM accepts spaces between words in a
                plaintext "
        PRINT "message and selectively enciphers the message using a
    simple"
        PRINT "monoalphabetic substitution process."
1       INPUT "Enter UPPERCASE Alphabetic Shift Key: ", K$
        FOR I = 0 TO 25
        IF K$ = PLAINTEXT$(I) GOTO 2
        NEXT I
        PRINT "You must enter a letter from A to Z"
        GOTO 1
2       REM Position I represents shift key letter
GOSUB FORMCIPHER                'create cipher alphabet
GOSUB MSGFILE        .          'assign I/O files, place message on a file
GOSUB CONVERTSTORE              'convert and store ciphertext on a file
GOSUB PRTOUT                    'print results
STOP
INITIALIZE:
        REM Initialize plaintext values
        FOR I = 0 TO 25
        READ PLAINTEXT$(I)
        NEXT I
```

```
            DATA "A","B","C","D","E","F","G","H","I","J","K","L","M","N"
            DATA "O","P","Q","R","S","T","U","V","W","X","Y","Z"
RETURN
FORMCIPHER:
            REM Routine to form CIPHERTEXT alphabet based upon defined shift key
            J = I + 1
            FOR K = 0 TO 25
            CIPHERTEXT$(K) = PLAINTEXT$((K + J) MOD 26)
            NEXT K
RETURN
MSGFILE:
            REM Routine to assign I/O files and accept keyboard or file input
            REM and remove spaces between words
                    INPUT "Enter filename to store plaintext message,
                        default=MESSAGE.DAT", INFILE$
                    IF INFILE$ = "" THEN INFILE$ = "MESSAGE.DAT"
                    INPUT "Enter filename to store enciphered message,
                        default=CIPHERTX.DAT", OUTFILE$
                    IF OUTFILE$ = "" THEN OUTFILE$ = "CIPHERTX.DAT"
                    INPUT "Select keyboard (k) or file (f) message input: ", IN$
                    IF IN$ = "F" OR IN$ = "f" THEN RETURN
                    OPEN INFILE$ FOR OUTPUT AS #1
            REM Routine to place message on a file removing spaces between words
                    PRINT "Enter your message - place a / at the beginning of
                        each line"
                    PRINT "that should remain in plaintext and a \ on a
                        separate line"
                    PRINT "to indicate the end of the enciphered message"
                    PRINT
AGN:        LINE INPUT TEXT$
            IF MID$(TEXT$, 1, 1) = "/" THEN GOTO XT
            NTEXT$ = ""
            FOR I = 1 TO LEN(TEXT$)
            NTEXT$ = NTEXT$ + LTRIM$(MID$(TEXT$, I, 1))
            NEXT I
            WRITE #1, NTEXT$
            IF MID$(TEXT$, 1, 1) = "\" GOTO DONE
            GOTO AGN
XT:         WRITE #1, TEXT$
            GOTO AGN
DONE:       CLOSE #1
RETURN
CONVERTSTORE:
            REM Routine to convert and store ciphertext on a file
```

```
            OPEN INFILE$ FOR INPUT AS #1
            OPEN OUTFILE$ FOR OUTPUT AS #2
            DO UNTIL EOF(1)
                    INPUT #1, TEXT$
                    MSGLEN = LEN(TEXT$)
                    IF MID$(TEXT$, 1, 1) = "/" THEN GOTO CLEARTXT
                    IF MID$(TEXT$, 1, 1) = "\" THEN GOTO DONE1
                    REM Convert plaintext to ciphertext
                        FOR I = 1 TO MSGLEN
                        FOR J = 0 TO 25
                        IF MID$(TEXT$, I, 1) = PLAINTEXT$(J) THEN GOTO GOTIT
                        NEXT J
GOTIT:                  MID$(TEXT$, I, 1) = CIPHERTEXT$(J)
                        NEXT I
CLEARTXT:               WRITE #2, TEXT$
        LOOP
DONE1:          CLOSE #2
RETURN
PRTOUT: REM Subroutine to print results
        INPUT "Press Return key to display resulting enciphered message", p$
        CLS : TEMP$ = ""
        PRINT "Resulting enciphered message is:"
        OPEN OUTFILE$ FOR INPUT AS #2
        DO UNTIL EOF(2)
                INPUT #2, TEXT$
                IF MID$(TEXT$, 1, 1) = "/" THEN PRINT RIGHT$(TEXT$,
                    LEN(TEXT$) - 1)
                IF MID$(TEXT$, 1, 1) = "/" THEN GOTO NOGROUP
                IF TEMP$ = "" GOTO BLANK          'blank string
                TEMP$ = TEMP$ + TEXT$             'concatenate
                TEXT$ = TEMP$
                TEMP$ = ""
BLANK:          MSGLEN = LEN(TEXT$)
                IF MSGLEN >= 25 THEN GOTO BIG
                TEMP$ = TEXT$
                GOTO NOGROUP                      'less than 25 characters
BIG:            FOR I = 26 TO MSGLEN             'place remainder of string
                                                 'into temp
                TEMP$ = TEMP$ + MID$(TEXT$, I, 1)
                NEXT I
                MSGLEN = 25
                GOSUB GROUPBY5:                   'print 25 characters
NOGROUP: LOOP
                TEXT$ = TEMP$                     'print remainder
```

```
                    MSGLEN = LEN(TEXT$)
                    IF MSGLEN <= 25 THEN GOSUB GROUPBY5
                    IF MSGLEN <= 25 THEN RETURN     'done printing
          WHILE MSGLEN > 25
                    TEMP$ = LEFT$(TEXT$, 25)        'get first 25 characters
                                                   'in string
                    TEMPR$ = RIGHT$(TEXT$, MSGLEN - 25)
                    TEXT$ = TEMP$
                    MSGLEN = LEN(TEXT$)
                    GOSUB GROUPBY5
                    TEXT$ = TEMPR$
                    MSGLEN = LEN(TEXT$)
          WEND
                    TEXT$ = TEMPR$
                    MSGLEN = LEN(TEXT$)
                    GOSUB GROUPBY5
RETURN
GROUPBY5:
        L = 1
        FOR I = 1 TO MSGLEN
                    PRINT MID$(TEXT$, I, 1);
                    IF I / 5 = L THEN GOTO AGROUP
                    GOTO NGROUP
AGROUP:         PRINT " ";
                    L = L + 1
NGROUP: NEXT I
        NUMX = 5 - MSGLEN MOD 5
        IF NUMX = 5 OR NUMX = 0 THEN GOTO PRTBLK
        FOR I = 1 TO NUMX
        PRINT "X";
        NEXT I
PRTBLK: PRINT
RETURN
END
```

Note that the main portion of CIPHER4.BAS very closely resembles CIPHER3.BAS. However, calls using the GOSUB statement were added to access the subroutines MSGFILE, CONVERTSTORE, and PRTOUT—the latter subroutine accesses the subroutine GROUPBY5 as previously discussed. You should also note the inclusion of several PRINT statements at the beginning of the program to better describe its operation.

Program Execution

To illustrate the use of CIPHER4.BAS, execute the program just developed. The top portion of Figure 2.6 illustrates the execution of the program which displays program information and enables the user to enter his or her message. In this example, the first two lines of the message were entered with the forward slash as a prefix character to ensure those lines remained in cleartext. After the two-line heading, the next four lines required encipherment and were entered without a forward slash character used as a prefix. Finally, the backslash character was entered by itself on a separate line to indicate the termination of the message.

```
Figure 2.6 The execution of CIPHER4.BAS

CIPHER4.BAS PROGRAM accepts spaces between words in a plaintext
message and selectively enciphers the message using a simple
monoalphabetic substitution process.
Enter UPPERCASE Alphabetic Shift Key: B
Enter filename to store plaintext message, default=MESSAGE.DAT
Enter filename to store enciphered message, default=CIPHERTX.DAT
Select keyboard (k) or file (f) message input: K
Enter your message - place a / at the beginning of each line
that should remain in plaintext and a \ on a separate line
to indicate the end of the enciphered message

/TO ALL BRANCH CHIEFS
/FROM PRESIDENT V.F. SMALL
DUE TO THE STATE OF THE ECONOMY WE MUST TERMINATE
TWENTY PERCENT OF OUR EMPLOYEES BY NEXT FRIDAY STOP
YOU MUST PREPARE YOUR HIT LIST THIS WEEKEND AND TRANSMIT
THAT LIST IN ENCIPHERED FORM TO ME BY NINE AM MONDAY STOP
\
Press Return key to display resulting enciphered message

Resulting enciphered message is:
TO ALL BRANCH CHIEFS
FROM PRESIDENT V.F. SMALL
FWGVQ VJGRT GUGPV UVCVG QHVJG
GEQPQ OAYGO WUVVG TOKPC VGVYG
PVARG TEGPV QHQWT GORNQ AGGUD
APGZV HTKFC AUVQR AQWOW UVRTG
RCTGA QWTJK VNKUV VJKUY GGMGP
FCPFV TCPUO KVVJC VNKUV KPGPE
KRJGT GFHQT OVQOG DAPKP GCOOQ
PFCAU VQRXX
```

The lower portion of Figure 2.6 illustrates the resulting enciphered message printed in groups of five characters. Note that the first two lines of heading information are simply printed without alteration, while the body of the message is both enciphered and printed in groups of five characters. Also note that the last group contained three characters and required the addition of two X's to complete the group of five. You can easily confirm this visually by noting that the message ended with the word STOP. Because a simple alphabetic shift was used for enciphering using the character B as the shift key, each character of plaintext is shifted up two positions in the alphabet. Thus, STOP becomes UVQR. Because VQR are the last three characters in the message, two X's were added to complete the group.

Program Default Files

To understand the contents of the default files created by CIPHER4.BAS, let us examine their contents after the program is executed. Figure 2.7 lists the contents of MESSAGE.DAT and CIPHERTX.DAT based upon the message illustrated in Figure 2.6 being entered when CIPHER4.BAS was executed. As indicated in Figure 2.7, the heading is placed on a file as is, while the body of the message is placed on each file with spaces between words being removed.

```
Figure 2.7 The CIPHER4.BAS file contents.

C>TYPE MESSAGE.DAT
"/TO ALL BRANCH CHIEFS"
"/FROM PRESIDENT V.F. SMALL"
"DUETOTHEPRESENTSTATEOFTHEECONOMYWEMUSTTERMINATE"
"TWENTYPERCENTOFOUREMPLOYEESBYNEXTFRIDAYSTOP"
"YOUMUSTPREPAREYOURHITLISTTHISWEEKENDANDTRANSMIT"
"THATLISTINENCIPHEREDFORMTOMEBYNINEAMMONDAYSTOP"
"\"

C>TYPE CIPHERTX.DAT
"/TO ALL BRANCH CHIEFS"
"/FROM PRESIDENT V.F. SMALL"
"FWGVQVJGRTGUGPVUVCVGQHVJGGEQPQOAYGOWUVVGTOKPCVG"
"VYGPVARGTEGPVQHQWTGORNQAGGUDAPGZVHTKFCAUVQR"
"AQWOWUVRTGRCTGAQWTJKVNKUVVJKUYGGMGPFCPFVTCPUOKV"
"VJCVNKUVKPGPEKRJGTGFHQTOVQOGDAPKPGCOOQPFCAUVQR"

C>
```

The CIPHER4.CPP Program

The C++ version of CIPHER4.BAS contains a number of programming improvements which facilitate the use of the program. The program listing of CIPHER4.CPP is contained in Listing 2.15.

Listing 2.15 The CIPHER4.CPP program listing.

```
/*
Cipher4.cpp
C++ Code written by Jonathan Held, January 23, 1998, using
Microsoft Visual C++, version 5.0.

486 total lines of code.
*/

//standard include files
#include <iostream.h>      //standard i/o operations
#include <string.h>        //used to find the length of a string
#include <ctype.h>         //for character handling
#include <fstream.h>       //file stream processing
#include <stdlib.h>        //standard library functions

//function prototypes - see function headers for more information
void getFileNames(char* &, char* &);
int getInputType(void);
void getShiftKey(char &);
void createCipher(const char [], char[], const char);
bool getMessage(char*, char*, char [], const char[], const char[]);
char* formCipheredMessage(const char[], const char [], char []);
void printResults(const char[], const char[], const char[], const char [],
                  const int);
void printCipherToFile(ofstream, const char[]);
bool encryptText(char *, char *, const char [], const char[], char []);


//-----------------------------------------------------------------
//Function: main()
//Parameters:  argc - the number of command line arguments passed to
//                main
//Return Type: int - 0 execution is normal, 1 abnormal termination
//Purpose: Runs the main part of the program.
//-----------------------------------------------------------------
int main(int argc, char *argv[]){
```

```
//initialize plaintext
char plaintext[26] = {'A','B','C','D','E','F','G','H','I',
                      'J','K','L','M','N','O','P','Q','R',
                      'S','T','U', 'V','W','X','Y','Z'};

//other variables we will use
char ciphertext[26], message_to_cipher[256], enciphered_message[256], key;
char *infile, *outfile;
int input_type;
bool success = false;

//function calls

//this code allows the user to run the program from the
//dos prompt with command line arguments, i.e. the user
//can run the program at the dos prompt by typing
//cipher <input filename> <output filename> <key>
if (argc >= 4){

   infile = new char[strlen(argv[1])+1];
   strcpy(infile,argv[1]);

   outfile = new char[strlen(argv[2])+1];
   strcpy(outfile,argv[2]);

   key = toupper(*argv[3]);
   int key_value = static_cast<int>(key);

   if ((key_value < 65) || (key_value > 90)){
      //print error message
      cerr << "Error: Invalid key used. Goodbye." << endl;
      //force the program to terminate due to error
      exit(EXIT_FAILURE);
    }

   input_type = 1;
}
//user tried to run from the dos prompt but made a mistake
else if (argc >=2 && argc <4){
   cout << "Usage: cipher10 <inputfile> <outputfile> <key>";

   //force the program to terminate due to error
   exit(EXIT_FAILURE);
}
```

```
      else {
         //user wants to manually enter information

         //get file information
             getFileNames(infile, outfile);
         input_type = getInputType();

         //get the uppercase key
             getShiftKey(key);
          }

      //create the cipher key
      createCipher(plaintext, ciphertext, key);

      //process file input
      if (input_type){
         success = encryptText(infile, outfile, plaintext, ciphertext,
                    enciphered_message);
      }
      else {
         cout << "Use a \'/\' to leave a line in plaintext." << endl
              << "Use a \'\\\' to indicate end of message input. " << endl;
         success = getMessage(infile, outfile, message_to_cipher, plaintext,
                             ciphertext);
      }

      //report success of operation
      if (!success){
         cerr << "Error: Invalid filename specified. Goodbye." << endl;
      }

      //delete dynamically allocated memory
      delete [] infile;
      delete [] outfile;

      return (EXIT_SUCCESS);

}//end main()



//----------------------------------------------------------------
//Function: getFileNames()
//Parameters:  infile_name - the input file
//             outfile_name - the output file we will write the
```

```
//              enciphered text to
//Return Type: None
//Purpose: Get file information from the user.
//----------------------------------------------------------------
void getFileNames(char * &infile_name, char * &outfile_name)
{
   char buffer[256];
   int length;

   cout << "Enter filename to store/retrieve plaintext message: ";

   cin >> buffer;
   length = strlen(buffer);

   infile_name = new char[length + 1];
   strcpy(infile_name, buffer);

   cout << "\nEnter filename to store enciphered message: ";

   cin >> buffer;
   length = strlen(buffer);
   outfile_name = new char[length + 1];
   strcpy(outfile_name, buffer);

   cout << endl;

   return;
}//end getFileNames()


//----------------------------------------------------------------
//Function: getInputType()
//Parameters: None
//Return Type: int - 0 indicated keyboard input, 1 indicates file
//              input
//Purpose: Determines if the user will be manually entering text to
//be enciphered or if the user wants a file to be enciphered.
//----------------------------------------------------------------
int getInputType(void)
{
   char type;
   bool error = false;
   int value;
```

```
      do {
          //prompt user for input from file or keyboard
          cout << "Is file input from keyboard (K, k) or file (F, f): ";
          cin >> type;

          //make type an uppercase letter
          type = static_cast<char>(toupper(static_cast<int>(type)));

          //check for an invalid character
          if ((type != 'K') && (type != 'F')){
             cerr << "You have entered an invalid character!" << endl << endl;
             error = true;
          }
          else {
             if (type == 'K')
                value = 0;        //value of 0 represents keyboard input
                else value = 1;   //value of 1 represents file input
             error = false;
          }

      } while (error);

      cout << endl;

      return value;

}//end getInputType()


//------------------------------------------------------------------
//Function: encryptText()
//Parameters:  inp_file - the name of the input plaintext file
//          outp_file - the name of the output ciphertext file
//          PTEXT[] - the plaintext alphabet
//          CTEXT[] - the ciphertext alphabet
//          encoded_msg[] - the message to be encoded
//Return Type: bool, indicating success of operation
//Purpose: Used to encrypt file input.  Takes each line of the input
//file, encrypts it, and saves the result to the specified output
//file.
//------------------------------------------------------------------
bool encryptText(char * inp_file, char * outp_file, const char PTEXT[],
                const char CTEXT[], char encoded_msg[])
{
```

```cpp
bool success = false;
char buffer[256];
char nextChar;

//declare file stream objects
ifstream input(inp_file, ios::in);
ofstream output(outp_file, ios::app);

if ((!input) || (!output)){
   //do nothing - I/O error; user will be notified upon
   //procedure's return to main()
}
else {

   success = true;

   //print plaintext and ciphertext alphabets to the
   //output file
   output << "PLAINTEXT:  " << PTEXT << endl;
   output << "CIPHERTEXT: " << CTEXT << endl << endl;

   while (input.getline(buffer, 256, '\n')){

      //look at the next character
      nextChar = input.peek();

      //if we've grabbed 256 characters, and the very next character
      //is the newline delimeter, we want to ignore it
      if (nextChar == '\n')
         input.ignore();

      //check to see if the user wants the line to appear in plain text
      if (buffer[0] == '/'){
         output << buffer << endl;
      }
      else {
         //encipher the line
         char *msg = formCipheredMessage(CTEXT, buffer, encoded_msg);
         //print the cipher in groups of five to the ouput file
         printCipherToFile(output, msg);
      }
   }

   //notify user where plaintext and ciphertext files are
```

```
            cout << "Plaintext file is: " << inp_file << endl;
            cout << "Encrypted file is: " << outp_file << endl << endl;

        }

    //don't forget to close the files
    input.close();
    output.close();

    //return success of the operation
    return success;
}//end encryptText()


//----------------------------------------------------------------
//Function: getShiftKey()
//Parameters:  key_desired - uppercase key entered by the user
//Return Type: None
//Purpose: Get the key the user enters; error checking performed
//until user enters a valid value.
//----------------------------------------------------------------
void getShiftKey(char &key_desired){

    bool error = true;

    do {
        //prompt user to enter an uppercase shift key
        cout << "Enter UPPERCASE Alphabetic Shift Key (CTRL-C to quit): ";
        cin >> key_desired;

        int key_value = static_cast<int>(key_desired);

        //do some error checking
        if ((key_value < 65) || (key_value > 90)){
            cerr << "\nYou must enter a letter from A to Z!" << endl << endl;
        }
        else {
            error = false;
        }
    } while (error);

    cout << endl;

    return;
```

```
}//end getShiftKey()


//------------------------------------------------------------------
//Function: createCipher()
//Parameters: PTEXT - the plaintext alphabet
//            ctext - the cipher alphabet we are going to create
//            user_key - the key the user entered
//Return Type: None
//Purpose: Create the cipher stream we will use later to encode the
//user's message.
//------------------------------------------------------------------
void createCipher(const char PTEXT[], char ctext[], const char user_key){

    int location;

    //find the location of the key in the plaintext
    for (int ix=0; ix<26; ix++){
       if (user_key == PTEXT[ix]){
          //location is one more than ix
          location = ix + 1;
          break;
        }
    }

    //create the cipher text
    for (int jx=0; jx<26; jx++){
       ctext[jx] = PTEXT[(jx + location) % 26];
    }

    return;
}//end createCipher();


//------------------------------------------------------------------
//Function: getMessage()
//Parameters:  input - the name of the input plaintext file
//             output the name of the output ciphertext file
//             msg_to_cipher - the essage to be encoded
//             PTEXT[] - the plaintext alphabet
//             CTEXT[] - the ciphertext alphabet
//Return Type: bool, indicating success of operation
//Purpose: Allow the user to manually input text from the keyboard.
//Save the text in plaintext to the input file; encrypt the text
```

```
//and save it to the specified output file for later retrieval.
//------------------------------------------------------------------
bool getMessage(char* input, char* output, char msg_to_cipher[], const char
              PTEXT[], const
char CTEXT[]){

    bool go_on = true, success = false;

    ofstream textFile(input, ios::app);
    ofstream cipherFile(output, ios::app);

    if ((!textFile) || (!cipherFile)){
        //do nothing - error will be noted to user later
    }
    else {

        success = true;

        textFile << "PLAINTEXT:  " << PTEXT << endl;
        textFile << "CIPHERTEXT: " << CTEXT << endl << endl;

        //get the newline character off of the input stream
        cin.get();

        cout << "Enter the message in UPPERCASE characters: " << endl;

        while (go_on) {

            //get the entire line, up to 256 characters
            cin.getline(msg_to_cipher, 256, '\n');

            //case user doesn't want the text to be encrypted
            if (msg_to_cipher[0] == '/'){
                textFile << msg_to_cipher << endl;
                cipherFile << msg_to_cipher << endl;
            }

            //case user is done entering text (ASCII value is 92
            //for the newline delimeter
            else if (static_cast<int>(msg_to_cipher[0]) == 92){
                go_on = false;
            }

            //encrypt the text
```

```
      else {
         textFile << msg_to_cipher << endl;

         char enciphered_msg[256];
         formCipheredMessage(CTEXT,msg_to_cipher,enciphered_msg);
         printCipherToFile(cipherFile,enciphered_msg);
      }
   }
}

//close the files
textFile.close();
cipherFile.close();

//notify user where plaintext and ciphertext files are
cout << "\nPlaintext file is: " << input << endl;
cout << "Encrypted file is: " << output << endl << endl;

return success;
}//end getMessage()



//------------------------------------------------------------------
//Function: formCipheredMessage()
//Parameters:  CTEXT - the cipher alphabet we will use for substitution
//             MESSAGETOCIPHER - the user's message
//             enc_message - the enciphered message to be determined
//Return Type: char* - a pointer to the encoded information.
//Purpose: Encipher the user's message.
//------------------------------------------------------------------
char* formCipheredMessage(const char CTEXT[], const char MESSAGETOCIPHER[],
                     char enc_message[]){

   int length = strlen(MESSAGETOCIPHER)+1;

   int encode_value;

   for (int ix=0; ix<length; ix++){

      //test to see if we have an alphabetic character; if not,
      //simply copy it to our encrypted message - this preserves
      //characters such as ' , ! etc...
      if (!isalpha(static_cast<int>(MESSAGETOCIPHER[ix]))){
         enc_message[ix] = MESSAGETOCIPHER[ix];
```

```
        }
        else {
            //valid character - the easy way to calculate the ciphered
            //character is based on the plain text's ascii character value;
            //since it has to be a capital letter, it must be in the range
            //from 65 to 90, with A represented by 65, Z by 90.  By simply
            //subtracting 65 from the encode_value (the integer representation
            //of the plaintext character), we now know what cipher character
            //to use.

            encode_value = toupper(static_cast<int>(MESSAGETOCIPHER[ix]));
            enc_message[ix] = CTEXT[encode_value-65];
        }
    }

    //return a reference to the encoded message
    return enc_message;
}//end formCipheredMessage()


//-----------------------------------------------------------------
//Function: printCipherToFile()
//Parameters: op - the output file we are writing to
//            MSG - the cipher text we are displaying
//Return Type: None
//Purpose: Group the cipher in 5-character blocks in the
//specified output file.
//-----------------------------------------------------------------
void printCipherToFile(ofstream op, const char MSG[]){

    int len = strlen(MSG) + 1;

    //keep track of number of characters
    int counter = 0;

    for (int kx=0;kx<len;kx++){

        if (*(MSG+kx) != ' '){

            //test to see if we need to print a space
            if ((counter != 0) && (counter%5 == 0)) {
                op << " ";
            }
            //if not, we have a character to print
```

```
        op << *(MSG+kx);

        //increment the count of characters
        counter++;
    }
}

//force a carriage return in the output file
op << endl;

return;
}//end printCipherToFile()
//end file cipher4.cpp
```

You can execute the program from the DOS prompt by typing:

CIPHER4 <input file><output file><K>

Here the input and output files can use any extension; however, for consistency it is suggested that the extension .DAT be used. K represents the shift key you want to use, similar to our previous examples. To practice using CIPHER4.CPP, create a text file using a word processor or line editor. For example:

THIS IS A TEST RUN OF THE PROGRAM
/THIS LINE WILL BE IN CLEARTEXT
THIS LINE WILL NOT

The C++ version of the program does not require the ending of file input with a backslash (\) character. Once you save your file as ASCII text, at the DOS prompt enter the previously referenced command line. Then, you can list the contents of the file OUTPUT.DAT by typing TYPE OUTPUT.DAT or by the use of a word processor. Due to the extensive documentation contained in the program we will not duplicate its contents by examining its modules.

Although simple monoalphabetic substitution produces ciphertext that offers little protection to a message, it provides you with a foundation for creating a program with many subroutines. Prior to moving on to more sophisticated methods of encipherment, I'll conclude this chapter by automating the decipherment process. Although you could create several new subroutines and incorporate them into our encipherment program

2

Chapter

through appropriate logic to form one program that both enciphers and deciphers messages, it may be more useful to illustrate the decipherment process by creating a separate program. That program will be named DCIPHER4.BAS to correspond to CIPHER4.BAS, because they both use the same simple monoalphabetic substitution process to encipher and decipher messages.

The DCIPHER4.BAS Program

The process of deciphering a message is the inverse of the encipherment process. For a simple monoalphabetic substitution process, you would first initialize the plaintext and ciphertext alphabets using the previously developed INITIALIZE and FORMCIPHER subroutines. Once the two alphabets are constructed, you would use a new subroutine to decipher the ciphertext characters by comparing each ciphertext character in the message to the ciphertext alphabet. When a match occurs, use the position of the character in the ciphertext alphabet as a pointer to extract a corresponding character from the plaintext alphabet. In addition to creating this new subroutine which is named DECIPHER, you must modify the previously created MSGFILE and PRTOUT subroutines. As you will recall, MSGFILE is used to assign I/O files and accept keyboard or file input, while PRTOUT is used to print the enciphered message. To reflect the new functions performed by those subroutines their names will be changed to DMSGFILE and DPRTOUT, respectively.

The DMSGFILE Subroutine

Listing 2.16 contains the statements in the subroutine DMSGFILE which assigns I/O files and accepts the entry of an enciphered message from either the keyboard or from a file. Because enciphered text was grouped into five-character groups with spaces between groups, the DMSGFILE subroutine is similar to the MSGFILE subroutine in that it removes spaces between groups, while MSGFILE removed spaces between words. Also note that the variable INFILE$ is used to store the name of the file containing the enciphered message, while the variable OUTFILE$ is used to store the resulting plaintext deciphered message. Thus, DMSGFILE assigns files opposite to the manner in which I/O files are assigned by the subroutine MSGFILE.

Listing 2.16 The DMSGFILE subroutine.

```
DMSGFILE:
        REM Routine to assign I/O files and accept keyboard or file input
        REM and remove spaces between words
                INPUT "Enter filename to store enciphered message,
                      default=CIPHERTX.DAT",
INFILE$
                IF INFILE$ = "" THEN INFILE$ = "CIPHERTX.DAT"
                INPUT "Enter filename to store deciphered message,
                      default=MESSAGE.DAT",
OUTFILE$
                IF OUTFILE$ = "" THEN OUTFILE$ = "MESSAGE.DAT"
                INPUT "Select keyboard (k) or file (f) ciphertext message
                      input: ", IN$
                IF IN$ = "F" OR IN$ = "f" THEN RETURN
                OPEN INFILE$ FOR OUTPUT AS #1
        REM Routine to place enciphered message on a file removing spaces
                      between groups
                PRINT "Enter your message - place a / at the beginning of
                      each line"
                PRINT "that should remain in plaintext and a \ on a
                      separate line"
                PRINT "to indicate the end of the enciphered message"
                PRINT
AGN:            LINE INPUT TEXT$
                IF MID$(TEXT$, 1, 1) = "/" THEN GOTO XT
                NTEXT$ = ""
                FOR I = 1 TO LEN(TEXT$)
                NTEXT$ = NTEXT$ + LTRIM$(MID$(TEXT$, I, 1))
                NEXT I
                WRITE #1, NTEXT$
                IF MID$(TEXT$, 1, 1) = "\" GOTO DONE
                GOTO AGN
XT:             WRITE #1, TEXT$
                GOTO AGN
DONE:           CLOSE #1
RETURN
```

Similar to the manner in which MSGFILE was created, DMSGFILE uses the forward slash and backslash characters to indicate to the program that it should bypass conversion (/) or the end of the message is reached (\). Thus, the second part of DMSGFILE, with the exception of wording in PRINT statements, functions in the same manner as the subroutine MSGFILE used in the CIPHER4.BAS program.

The DECIPHER Subroutine

The actual deciphering process is performed by the subroutine DECIPHER whose contents are listed in Listing 2.17. In examining the statements in the subroutine DECIPHER, readers should recognize its close resemblance to the subroutine CONVERTSTORE in the CIPHER4.BAS program. The only difference between the two subroutines is the search mechanisms bounded by the nested FOR-NEXT loops. In the DECIPHER subroutine, each character in the enciphered message is compared against the ciphertext alphabet. When a match occurs, the position of the character in the ciphertext alphabet is used as a pointer to extract a character from the plaintext alphabet. Also note that the first character of each line of data retrieved from the ciphertext file is examined to determine if a forward slash or backslash character is in the first position of the line. Similar to the encipherment process, the decipherment process uses those characters to bypass the decipherment process (/) or to terminate the decipherment process (\).

Listing 2.17 The DECIPHER subroutine.

```
DECIPHER:
        REM Routine to decipher and store plaintext on a file
        OPEN INFILE$ FOR INPUT AS #1
        OPEN OUTFILE$ FOR OUTPUT AS #2
        DO UNTIL EOF(1)
                INPUT #1, TEXT$
                MSGLEN = LEN(TEXT$)
                IF MID$(TEXT$, 1, 1) = "/" THEN GOTO CLEARTXT
                IF MID$(TEXT$, 1, 1) = "\" THEN GOTO DONE1
                REM Convert ciphertext to plaintext
                        FOR I = 1 TO MSGLEN
                        FOR J = 0 TO 25
                        IF MID$(TEXT$, I, 1) = CIPHERTEXT$(J) THEN GOTO GOTIT
                        NEXT J
GOTIT:                  MID$(TEXT$, I, 1) = PLAINTEXT$(J)
                        NEXT I
CLEARTXT:               WRITE #2, TEXT$
        LOOP
DONE1:          CLOSE #2
        RETURN
```

The DPRTOUT Subroutine

The last subroutine required for decipherment is appropriately labeled DPRTOUT to reflect the fact that it prints the results of the decipherment process. Unlike the subroutine PRTOUT which limited the number of characters to 25 per line and required extensive logic to operate on strings and invoke the GROUPBY5 subroutine, DPRTOUT is very simple. DPRTOUT simply reads each line in the file containing the deciphered message, eliminates any forward slash character used as a line prefix, and prints each line as is. Listing 2.18 lists the contents of that subroutine.

Listing 2.18 The DPRTOUT subroutine.

```
DPRTOUT: REM Subroutine to print results
         INPUT "Press Return key to display resulting enciphered message", p$
         CLS
         PRINT "Resulting deciphered message is:"
         OPEN OUTFILE$ FOR INPUT AS #2
         DO UNTIL EOF(2)
                 INPUT #2, TEXT$
                 IF MID$(TEXT$, 1, 1) = "/" THEN PRINT RIGHT$(TEXT$,
                     LEN(TEXT$) - 1)
                 IF MID$(TEXT$, 1, 1) <> "/" THEN PRINT TEXT$
         LOOP
RETURN
```

To illustrate the composition of the resulting decipherment program, Listing 2.19 lists the main portion of the program DCIPHER4.BAS. You should note that two of the five subroutines, INITIALIZE and FORMCIPHER, are exactly the same as those subroutines used in CIPHER4.BAS. The three remaining subroutines, DMSGFILE, DECIPHER, and DPRTOUT, are modified versions of the subroutines MSGFILE, CONVERTSTORE, and PRTOUT. The entire decipherment program which deciphers a message enciphered using a simple monoalphabetic substitution process is stored on the file DCIPHER4.BAS on the CD-ROM under the BASIC directory. The executable program in that directory is named DCIPHER4.EXE.

Listing 2.19 The main portion of the DCIPHER4.BAS program.

```
REM PROGRAM DCIPHER4.BAS
DIM PLAINTEXT$(26), CIPHERTEXT$(26)
CLS
GOSUB INITIALIZE
        PRINT "DCIPHER4.BAS PROGRAM deciphers a message using a simple"
        PRINT "monoalphabetic substitution process."
1       INPUT "Enter UPPERCASE Alphabetic Shift Key: ", K$
        FOR I = 0 TO 25
        IF K$ = PLAINTEXT$(I) GOTO 2
        NEXT I
        PRINT "You must enter a letter from A to Z"
        GOTO 1
2       REM Position I represents shift key letter
GOSUB FORMCIPHER             'create cipher alphabet
GOSUB DMSGFILE               'assign I/O files, place message on a file
GOSUB DECIPHER               'convert enciphered message to plaintext
GOSUB DPRTOUT                'print results
STOP
```

Program Execution

To illustrate the operation of the DCIPHER4.BAS program, you can execute the program with input from the keyboard and from a file. To facilitate a comparison of the deciphered message to the original plaintext message, you can use the enciphered message contained at the bottom of Figure 2.6 as input to DCIPHER4.BAS.

Figure 2.8 illustrates the operation of DCIPHER4.BAS in which keyboard input was selected. In this example, you must use the keyboard to enter the ciphertext message in the same manner as it was displayed as a result of the execution of CIPHER4.BAS. That is, you must prefix each cleartext line with a forward slash, enter each line using the five-character groups contained on the line, and terminate the enciphered message with a backslash character on a separate line.

Figure 2.8 The execution of DCIPHER4.BAS using keyboard input.

```
DCIPHER4.BAS PROGRAM deciphers a message using a simple
monoalphabetic substitution process.
Enter UPPERCASE Alphabetic Shift Key: B
Enter filename to store enciphered message, default=CIPHERTX.DAT
Enter filename to store deciphered message, default=MESSAGE.DAT
Select keyboard (k) or file (f) ciphertext message input: K
Enter your message - place a / at the beginning of each line
that should remain in plaintext and a \ on a separate line
to indicate the end of the enciphered message

/TO ALL BRANCH CHIEFS
/FROM PRESIDENT V.F. SMALL
FWGVQ VJGRT GUGPV UVCVG QHVJG
GEQPQ OAYGO WUVVG TOKPC VGVYG
PVARG TEGPV QHQWT GORNQ AGGUD
APGZV HTKFC AUVQR AQWOW UVRTG
RCTGA QWTJK VNKUV VJKUY GGMGP
FCPFV TCPUO KVVJC VNKUV KPGPE
KRJGT GFHQT OVQOG DAPKP GCOOQ
PFCAU VQRXX
\
Press Return key to display resulting enciphered message

Resulting deciphered message is:
TO ALL BRANCH CHIEFS
FROM PRESIDENT V.F. SMALL
DUETOTHEPRESENTSTATEOFTHE
ECONOMYWEMUSTTERMINATETWE
NTYPERCENTOFOUREMPLOYEESB
YNEXTFRIDAYSTOPYOUMUSTPRE
PAREYOURHITLISTTHISWEEKEN
DANDTRANSMITTHATLISTINENC
IPHEREDFORMTOMEBYNINEAMMO
NDAYSTOPVV
```

The execution of DCIPHER4.BAS using keyboard input will display up to 25 characters per line because input was limited to five groups of five characters per line. In comparison, the use of file input when DCIPHER4.BAS is executed deciphers each full line contained on the file whose name was assigned to the variable OUTFILE$ (Figure 2.9). The use of file input may provide a more natural conversion to plaintext since words do not have to be split among two lines if they do not fit into a five-character group terminating a line.

Figure 2.9 The execution of DCIPHER4.BAS using file input.

```
DCIPHER4.BAS PROGRAM deciphers a message using a simple
monoalphabetic substitution process.
Enter UPPERCASE Alphabetic Shift Key: B
Enter filename to store enciphered message, default=CIPHERTX.DAT
Enter filename to store deciphered message, default=MESSAGE.DAT
Select keyboard (k) or file (f) ciphertext message input: F
Press Return key to display resulting enciphered message


Resulting deciphered message is:
TO ALL BRANCH CHIEFS
FROM PRESIDENT V.F. SMALL
DUETOTHEPRESENTSTATEOFTHEECONOMYWEMUSTTERMINATE
TWENTYPERCENTOFOUREMPLOYEESBYNEXTFRIDAYSTOP
YOUMUSTPREPAREYOURHITLISTTHISWEEKENDANDTRANSMIT
THATLISTINENCIPHEREDFORMTOMEBYNINEAMMONDAYSTOP
```

The DCIPHER4.CPP Program

In concluding this chapter we will turn our attention to the C++ version of DCIPHER4.BAS. This program, which is appropriately named DCIPHER4.CPP, is included on the accompanying CD-ROM under the C directory. In addition, the executable version of the program, named DCIPHER4.EXE, is also included in that directory.

Listing 2.20 contains the contents of the DCIPHER4.CPP program. This program is very similar to previously developed C++ programs, using functions to perform specific tasks. In this program you will note that constants were defined using mnemonics that are associated with constant values. This coding technique was used to facilitate any changes in coding readers may wish to effect.

Listing 2.20 The DCIPHER4.CPP program listing.

```
/*
dcipher.cpp   C++ code written by Jonathan Held
using Microsoft Visual C++, version5.0, on February 22, 1998.
*/

//standard include files
#include<iostream.h>
#include<fstream.h>
#include<stdlib.h>
```

```
#include<string.h>
//function prototypes
void getShiftKey(char &);
void createCipher(const char[], char[], const char);
void formatData(char []);
void getFileToDecipher(const char[], char[]);
void decipher(ifstream, ofstream, const char[], char[]);

//constants we will use
#define FIVE            5
#define TWENTYFIVE     25
#define TWENTYSIX      26
#define TWENTYSEVEN    27
#define SIXTYFIVE      65
#define NINETY         90
#define SIZE          256


//-----------------------------------------------------------------
//Function: main()
//Parameters: None
//Return Type: int - 0 execution is normal, 1 abnormal termination
//Purpose: Runs the main part of the program.
//-----------------------------------------------------------------
int main()
{
   char plaintext[TWENTYSEVEN] = {'A','B','C','D','E','F','G','H',
                                  'I','J','K','L','M','N','O','P',
                                  'Q','R','S','T','U','V','W','X',
                                  'Y','Z'};

   char ciphertext[TWENTYSEVEN], key;


   //get the shift key that was used
   getShiftKey(key);
   //create the cipher text based on the shift key
   createCipher(plaintext, ciphertext, key);

   //decipher the file
   getFileToDecipher(plaintext, ciphertext);

   return (0);

}
```

```
//-----------------------------------------------------------------
//Function: getShiftKey()
//Parameters:  key_desired - uppercase key entered by the user
//Return Type: None
//Purpose: Get the key the user enters; error checking performed
//until user enters a valid value.
//-----------------------------------------------------------------
void getShiftKey(char &key_desired){

    bool error = true;

    do {
       //prompt user to enter an uppercase shift key
       cout << "Enter UPPERCASE Alphabetic Shift Key (CTRL-C to quit): ";
       cin >> key_desired;

       int key_value = static_cast<int>(key_desired);

       //do some error checking
       if ((key_value < SIXTYFIVE) || (key_value > NINETY)){
          cerr << "\nYou must enter a letter from A to Z!" << endl << endl;
       }
       else {
          cout << endl;
          error = false;
       }
    } while (error);

    return;
}//end getShiftKey()


//-----------------------------------------------------------------
//Function: createCipher()
//Parameters: PTEXT - the plaintext alphabet
//            ctext - the cipher alphabet we are going to create
//            user_key - the key the user entered
//Return Type: none
//Purpose: Create the cipher stream we will use later to encode the
//user's message.
//-----------------------------------------------------------------
void createCipher(const char PTEXT[], char ctext[], const char USER_KEY){
```

```
    int location;

    //find the location of the key in the plaintext
    for (int ix=0; ix<TWENTYSIX; ix++){
        if (USER_KEY == PTEXT[ix]){
            //location is one more than ix
            location = ix + 1;
            break;
        }
    }

    //create the cipher text
    for (int jx=0; jx<TWENTYSIX; jx++){
        ctext[jx] = PTEXT[(jx + location) % TWENTYSIX];
    }

    return;
}//end createCipher();


//-----------------------------------------------------------------
//Function: formatData()
//Parameters: data - the array we want to format
//Return Type: None
//Purpose: Get rid of all spaces in the array.
//-----------------------------------------------------------------
void formatData(char data[]){

    for (int mx=0, nx=0; (*(data+nx) != '\0'); nx++){
        if (*(data+nx) == ' '){
            //do nothing - skip over the space in the data
        }
        else {
            *(data+mx++) = *(data+nx);
        }
    }

    //don't forget to add the null terminator
    *(data+mx) = '\0';

    return;
}//end formatData()
```

```
//------------------------------------------------------------------
//Function: getFileToDecipher()
//Parameters: PTEXT - the plaintext alphabet
//            ctext - the corresponding cipher text
//Return Type: None
//Purpose: Prompt the user for the name of the encrypted file
//and the file the user wants to store the decrypted text to.
//------------------------------------------------------------------
void getFileToDecipher(const char PTEXT[], char ctext[])
{
   char fileinput[SIZE], fileoutput[SIZE];

   cout << "Enter name of file to decipher: ";
   cin >> fileinput;

   ifstream input(fileinput, ios::in);

   if (!(input)){
      cerr << "Input file not available. Exiting program." << endl;
      exit(EXIT_FAILURE);
   }

   cout << "Enter name of file for output: ";
   cin >> fileoutput;

   ofstream output(fileoutput, ios::out);

   if (!(output)){
      cerr << "Output file not created.  Exiting program." << endl;
      exit(EXIT_FAILURE);
   }

   decipher(input, output, PTEXT, ctext);

   //don't forget to close the files
   input.close();
   output.close();

   cout << "\nDeciphered text is in " << fileoutput << endl;

   return;
}//end getFileToDecipher()
```

```
//---------------------------------------------------------------
//Function: decipher()
//Parameters: in - the input file we are deciphering
//            out - the output file we are writing the deciphered
//                  text to
//            PTEXT - the plaintext alphabet (used to decipher)
//            ctext - the ciphertext
//Return Type: None
//Purpose: Decipher the input file and write the contents to the
//output file specified by the user.
//---------------------------------------------------------------
void decipher(ifstream in, ofstream out, const char PTEXT[], char ctext[])
{

    char enc_file_data[SIZE];

    //continue this process until we get to the end of the file
    while (in.getline(enc_file_data, SIZE, '\n')){
       if (enc_file_data[0] == '/'){
          out << enc_file_data << endl;
       }
       else {
          //format the data - i.e. get rid of all spaces
       formatData(enc_file_data);

       //dump data to file
       for (int ix=0; ix<strlen(enc_file_data); ix++){

            //used to keep track of what plaintext character
          //we are going to use
          int jx;

          for (jx=0; jx<TWENTYSIX; jx++){
          //find where the encrypted data is in the
          //ciphertext - this location corresponds to
          //the plaintext character location
             if (enc_file_data[ix] == ctext[jx])
             break;
               }

            //conditionals for grouping by five and inserting
          //new lines
          if (!(ix%TWENTYFIVE))
```

```
                    out << endl;

            if ((ix!=0) && (!(ix%FIVE))){
                out << " " << PTEXT[jx];
            }
            else {
                out << PTEXT[jx];
            }
        }
      }
    }

    return;
}//end decipher()
//end file dcipher.cpp
```

The DCIPHER4.CPP program includes five functions as indicated in the function prototype section in the listing. getShiftKey obtains the desired uppercase key entered by the user and createCipher creates the cipher stream that would normally be used to encode a message. The function getFileToDecipher, as its name implies, prompts you for the name of the encrypted file and the file to be used to store the results of the decryption operation. The function decipher deciphers the contents of the input file and writes the results to the specified output file. This function invokes the function formatData for data formatting. In addition, the decipher function uses a for jx statement to locate the encrypted data in the ciphertext since the location corresponds to the plaintext character location. This operation requires the use of a pointer into the ciphertext array and explains why the function createCipher is used to create a cipher alphabet. DCIPHER4.CPP is similar to the execution of DCIPHER4.BAS where, with the exception of an option for typing input from the keyboard, the execution of the C++ program is left for you to perform.

Chapter 3

Keyword-Based Monoalphabetic Substitution

Using the information presented in Chapter 2, Monoalphabetic Substitution Concepts, as a base, this chapter continues the examination of monoalphabetic substitution techniques. This discussion opens with the development and use of a keyword-based mixed alphabet to add a degree of randomness to the development of plaintext and ciphertext alphabets. This will be followed by a discussion of several additional techniques that can be used to develop a ciphertext alphabet. Similar to the material presented in Chapter 2, you will examine different techniques and develop a series of subroutines and programs in Microsoft Corporation's QuickBASIC and C++ programing languages to automate the operation of each technique.

Keyword-Based Mixed Alphabets

The relationship between plaintext and ciphertext alphabets in which one alphabet is shifted from the other by n positions is easy to construct. Unfortunately, it also represents an encipherment method that offers a very limited degree of protection to a message that falls into the hands of the wrong party. To add an additional level of protection to messages, keyword mixed alphabets were developed.

Construction

In a keyword mixed alphabet, a word or phrase is selected as the keyword and is used for the formation of the letters of the alphabet, with repeated letters omitted after their first occurrence. At the end of the word or phrase, the remaining letters of the alphabet are used in their normal sequence, omitting letters previously used in the keyword or phrase. For example, suppose you use the phrase GOD SAVE THE QUEEN as a keyword phrase. The first step in this process is to group the phrase to form a continuous word and eliminate duplicate letters in this newly formed word. This would result in the keyword GODSAVETHQUN, since there were duplicate E's in the keyword. Next, you would add the letters of the alphabet to the keyword you just reduced to contain only one occurrence of each letter. This would result in the keyword-based mixed alphabet GODSAVETHQUNBCFIJKLMPRWXYZ.

Automating Keyword Construction

Listing 3.1 illustrates the statements in the program WORD.BAS which, when executed, produces a keyword-based mixed sequence alphabet. This program contains two subroutines—INITIALIZE and KEYWORD. The first subroutine is the same subroutine previously used in the CIPHER series of programs developed in Chapter 2 to initialize the PLAINTEXT array. The second subroutine was developed to produce a keyword-based mixed sequence alphabet. In this section, the focus is upon the subroutine labeled KEYWORD which actually forms the keyword-based mixed sequence alphabet. After a review of the operation of this subroutine, I'll show you how to incorporate it into a new series of programs which will enable you to create both keyword-based mixed alphabets as plaintext and ciphertext alphabets, and to incorporate a shift key character to encipher a message.

Listing 3.1 The WORD.BAS program listing.

```
REM PROGRAM WORD.BAS TO DEVELOP ALPHABET BASED ON A KEYWORD
DIM PLAINTEXT$(26), CIPHERTEXT$(26), KEY$(26)
    GOSUB INITIALIZE
    INPUT "Enter keyword in CAPS", TEXT$
    GOSUB KEYWORD
    PRINT "Keyword-based alphabet is:"; X$
    STOP
INITIALIZE:
    REM Initialize plaintext values
    FOR I = 0 TO 25
    READ PLAINTEXT$(I)
    NEXT I
```

```
        DATA "A","B","C","D","E","F","G","H","I","J","K","L","M","N"
        DATA "O","P","Q","R","S","T","U","V","W","X","Y","Z"
RETURN
KEYWORD:
    REM Place entered keyword into KEY$ array 1 character per position
        MSGLEN = LEN(TEXT$)
        FOR I = 1 TO MSGLEN
        KEY$(I) = MID$(TEXT$, I, 1)
        NEXT I
    REM ELIMINATE DUPLICATE LETTERS, REPLACE WITH NULLS
        K = 2
        FOR I = 1 TO MSGLEN
        FOR J = K TO MSGLEN
        IF KEY$(I)  KEY$(J) GOTO NOTDUP
        KEY$(J) = " "
NOTDUP:    NEXT J
        K = K + 1
        NEXT I
    REM REMOVE NULLS IN STRING
        X$ = ""
        FOR I = 1 TO MSGLEN
        X$ = X$ + LTRIM$(KEY$(I))
        NEXT I
    REM PLACE REVISED KEYWORD WITH NO DUPLICATE LETTERS BACK IN KEY$
        FOR I = 1 TO LEN(X$)
        KEY$(I) = MID$(X$, I, 1)
        NEXT I
    REM COMPARE KEY$ & PLAINTEXT$ ARRAYS, BLANK PLAINTEXT$ WHEN MATCHED
        FOR J = 1 TO LEN(X$)
        FOR K = 0 TO 25
        IF KEY$(J) = PLAINTEXT$(K) THEN PLAINTEXT$(K) = " "
        NEXT K
        NEXT J
    REM CREATE ONE STRING
        FOR I = 0 TO 25
        X$ = X$ + LTRIM$(PLAINTEXT$(I))
        NEXT I
    REM PLACE SEQUENCE BACK INTO PLAINTEXT$ ARRAY
        FOR I = 0 TO 25
        PLAINTEXT$(I) = MID$(X$, I + 1, 1)
        NEXT I
RETURN
END
```

The use of a mnemonic key to mix a cipher alphabet can be traced to a family of cryptologists that lived in Rome during the sixteenth century. One member of this family, Matteo Argenti, served as the papal secretary of ciphers under Pope Gregory XIV and five succeeding popes. Argenti taught cryptology to his younger brother, Marcello, who served as a cipher secretary to a cardinal and wrote a cryptology manual which contained the first written reference to the use of a mnemonic key to mix a cipher alphabet.

The first keyword mixed alphabet developed by the Argenti family used numerics in place of ciphertext characters. To increase the difficulty of unauthorized decipherment operations, the letters "q" and "u" were merged into a single unit for encipherment and rules prohibiting word separations and punctuation were developed.

The KEYWORD Subroutine

It may be useful to review the operation of the subroutine KEYWORD based upon each group of statements bounded by a REM statement. The first program module simply stores each character in the keyword into an element of the KEY$ string array. The second program module uses a nested pair of FOR-NEXT loops to eliminate duplicate letters in the keyword, replacing each duplicate letter with a null character. To illustrate the operation of this program module, assume that the keyword ALPHA, which has a string length of five, was used. In the program module, the inner loop (J) operates from 2 to 5, while the outer loop operates from 1 to 5. Thus, when I is 1, J varies from 2 to 5. This results in A being compared to L, P, H, and A. If KEY$(I) does not equal KEY$(J), a branch to the label NOTDUP occurs and J is incremented. If KEY$(I) equals KEY$(J) the statement KEY$(J)=" " sets KEY$(J) equal to a null character. After the value of J increments, K is incremented, which results in the second character in the keyword (L) being compared to the third (P) through the fifth (A) characters of the keyword.

The third program module removes the nulls previously inserted in place of duplicate characters. The statement X$=X$+LTRIM$(KEY$(I)) concatenates each element of KEY$ that is a non-null with the previous value of X$ because the string function LTRIM$ removes leading nulls from a string.

The fourth program module takes the recently formed string variable X$ which contains the keyword without duplicate characters and places those characters back into the array KEY$. The fifth program module then compares each character in the KEY$ array to each character in the PLAINTEXT$ array. If they match, the plaintext character is then set to a null. The sixth program module simply adds each non-blank element position of the PLAINTEXT array to the string X$, which now contains the keyword-based mixed alphabet. The seventh and last program module places the keyword-based alphabet into the array PLAINTEXT$.

The use of the previously described WORD.BAS program is illustrated in Figure 3.1, which indicates the QuickBASIC execution screen after the program WORD.BAS was executed three times in succession. The first time WORD.BAS was executed the keyword phrase SEVENBRIDES was used to develop the keyword-based mixed alphabet. The second time the program was executed the keyword phrase BROOKLYNBRIDGE was used, while the third keyword phrase was MICROSOFTWINDOWSISGREAT.

```
Figure 3.1 Results obtained from executing WORD.BAS several times.

C:>WORD
Enter keyword in CAPS SEVENBRIDES
Keyword-based alphabet is: SEVNBRIDACFGHJKLMNOPQTUWXYZ

C:>WORD
Enter keyword in CAPS BROOKLYNBRIDGE
Keyword-based alphabet is: BROKLYNIDGEACFHJMPQSTUVWXZ

C:>WORD
Enter keyword in CAPS MICROSOFTWINDOWSISGREAT
Keyword-based alphabet is: MICROSFTWDNGEABHJKLPQUVXYZ
```

The C++ version of WORD.BAS, which is appropriately named WORD.CPP, is contained in the C directory on the CD-ROM. Following our file naming conventions, the file WORD.EXE in the C directory is the executable version of the C++ program, while the file WORD.EXE located in the BASIC directory represents the executable version of the BASIC program.

Listing 3.2 provides the C++ version of WORD.BAS which was assigned the filename WORD.CPP. When you execute this program you will note several improvements. Those improvements include the ability to repetitively execute the program and to use the CTRL+C multi-key combination to terminate the program execution. Similar to all C++ programs developed for this book, WORD.CPP was written by subdividing activities into functions. Three key functions were developed—getKeyword, checkInput, and createAlphabet. The getKeyword function, as its name implies, prompts you for a keyword and continues prompting until a valid keyword without spaces or non-alphabetic characters is entered. The checkInput function is called by the getKeyword function and performs the actual verification of user input. The third function, createAlphabet, uses the verified keyword to construct the keyword alphabet. Since the program is documented through the use of a liberal amount of comment statements, you are referred to the program listing for a detailed explanation of the manner by which the code functions.

Listing 3.2 The WORD.CPP program listing.

```
/*
word.cpp
C++ Code written by Jonathan Held, February 27, 1998, using
Microsoft Visual C++, version 5.0.  Please read file for
detailed description of how the program works.
*/

#include<iostream.h>
#include<iomanip.h>
#include<string.h>

//function prototypes
void getKeyword(char * &);
bool checkInput(char * &);
void createAlphabet(char *, char []);

//constants
#define TWENTYSIX    26
#define TWENTYSEVEN  27
#define SIXTYFIVE    65
#define NINETY       90
#define SIZE         256

//----------------------------------------------------------------
```

```
//Function: main()
//Parameters: None
//Return Type: int - 0 if program terminated normally
//Purpose: Runs the main part of the program.
//-----------------------------------------------------------------
int main(){

   char *keyword;
   char ciphertext[TWENTYSEVEN]= {'\0'};

   cout << "*** AUTOMATING KEYWORD CONSTRUCTION ***" << endl
        << "***     Hit CTRL-C to quit program    ***" << endl << endl;

   do {

      getKeyword(keyword);
      cout << "\nYou entered\t\t" << keyword << endl;
      createAlphabet(keyword, ciphertext);
      cout << "Keyword alphabet is: " << setw(29) << ciphertext
              << endl << endl;
      delete [] keyword;
   } while(true);

   return (0);
}//end main()



//-----------------------------------------------------------------
//Function: getKeyword()
//Parameters: text - the keyword that the user enters
//Return Type: None
//Purpose: Prompts the user for a keyword and continues until
//a valid keyword has been entered.
//-----------------------------------------------------------------
void getKeyword(char * &text)
{
   bool error = false;

   do {
      char buffer[SIZE];
      cout << "Enter keyword in CAPS (do not use" << endl
        << "spaces or non-alphabetic characters): ";

      cin.getline(buffer, SIZE, '\n');
```

3

Chapter

```
            text = new char[strlen(buffer) + 1];
            strcpy(text, buffer);

            error = checkInput(text);

    } while (error);

    return;
}//end getKeyword()



//------------------------------------------------------------------
//Function: checkInput()
//Parameters: input - the keyword the user entered
//Return Type: bool - true if the input string contains an error,
//                    false otherwise
//Purpose: Checks the user's keyword for invalid characters.
//------------------------------------------------------------------
bool checkInput(char * &input)
{
    bool error = false;
    int count = strlen(input);

    for (int ix=0; ix<count; ix++){

        int char_value = static_cast<int>(*(input+ix));

        //determine if the user did not enter an uppercase character
        if ((char_value < SIXTYFIVE) || (char_value > NINETY)){
            error = true;
            cerr << "You entered an invalid keyword!" << endl << endl;
            break;
        }
    }

    return error;
}//end checkInput()



//------------------------------------------------------------------
//Function: createAlphabet()
//Parameters: input - the keyword the user entered
//            cipher - the keyword alphabet that will be constructed
//Return Type: None
```

```
//Purpose: Creates the keyword alphabet.
//----------------------------------------------------------------
void createAlphabet(char *input, char cipher[])
{
   bool used[TWENTYSIX];
   int index = 0,
       count = strlen(input);

   //no characters are initially used
   for (int ix=0; ix<TWENTYSIX; ix++){
      used[ix] = false;
   }

   //keep track of each character used, start forming the keyword
   //alphabet
   for (int jx=0; jx<count; jx++){

      //get each character of the input string (integer value)
      int char_value = static_cast<int>(*(input+jx));

      if (used[char_value-SIXTYFIVE]){
         //do nothing - the character was already used
      }
      else {
         //mark as used and add to the keyword alphabet
         used[char_value-SIXTYFIVE] = true;
         *(cipher+index++) = static_cast<char>(char_value);
      }
   }

   //go through the list of characters used - those which weren't
   //used should be added to the keyword alphabet
   for (int kx=0; kx<TWENTYSIX; kx++){

      if (!(used[kx])){
         *(cipher+index++) = static_cast<char>(SIXTYFIVE+kx);
      }
   }

   return;
}//end createAlphabet()
//end file word.cpp
```

3

Chapter

In examining the automated creation of three keyword-based alphabets illustrated in Figure 3.1, you will note that the trailing portion of the resulting alphabets is very similar. In fact, the characters U and Z are positioned at the same locations in all three alphabets. If you simply positioned a keyword-based alphabet directly under a plaintext alphabet, there is a high degree of probability that one or more plaintext and ciphertext characters would equate to one another. This situation would obviously provide a valuable clue to the decipherment of an intercepted message. To eliminate or reduce the number of coincidental characters between a plaintext alphabet and a keyword-based ciphertext alphabet, you need to apply an alphabetic shift key to one or both alphabets.

Incorporating an Alphabetic Shift Key

In Chapter 2 you developed a program labeled CIPHER4.BAS that creates enciphered text based upon the use of an alphabetic shift key. In this chapter the discussion of monoalphabetic substitution is continued by examining the development of a keyword-based mixed alphabet as well as the statements in a subroutine contained in the program WORD.BAS to automate the keyword-based mixed alphabet creation process. Combining the use of a keyword-based mixed alphabet with an alphabetic shift key should result in a higher level of enciphered data protection than the separate use of either method. Thus, this section focuses on combining both techniques for enciphering and deciphering messages.

By placing the KEYWORD subroutine contained in WORD.BAS or the createAlphabet function from WORD.CPP into the CIPHER4.BAS or CIPHER4.CPP program, you gain the ability to encipher a message based upon a keyword or keyword phrase and an alphabetic shift. I'll call these new programs CIPHER5.BAS and CIPHER5.CPP.

The CIPHER5.BAS Program

Listing 3.3 illustrates the statements contained in the main portion of CIPHER5.BAS as well as the subroutine INITIALIZE, which required a slight modification from its prior form. You should note that lines terminating with five asterisks (*) as a comment indicate lines that were added to the main program to facilitate an explanation of its operation. Those lines can be removed if you do not wish to burden a user who has no desire to understand the enciphering process with this extraneous information.

Listing 3.3 The main portion of the program CIPHER5.BAS and the modified subroutine INITIALIZE.

```
REM PROGRAM CIPHER5.BAS
DIM PLAINTEXT$(26), CIPHERTEXT$(26), KEY$(26)
CLS
GOSUB INITIALIZE
        PRINT "CIPHER5.BAS PROGRAM enciphers text based upon the use of
                a keyword or keyword"
        PRINT "phrase and an alphabetic shift key using a monoalphabetic
                substitution process."
        PRINT
        INPUT "Enter keyword or keyword phrase in UPPERCASE: ", TEXT$
        PRINT "Plaintext based alphabet is      : ";        '*****
        FOR I = 0 TO 25: PRINT PLAINTEXT$(I); : NEXT I       '*****
        GOSUB KEYWORD                  'form keyword-based mixed alphabet
        PRINT "Keyword-based alphabet is        : "; X$      '*****
1       INPUT "Enter UPPERCASE Alphabetic Shift Key: ", K$
        FOR I = 0 TO 25
        IF K$ = PLAINTEXT$(I) GOTO 2
        NEXT I
        PRINT "You must enter a letter from A to Z"
        GOTO 1
2       REM Position I represents shift key letter

GOSUB FORMCIPHER               'create cipher alphabet
        PRINT "Shifted keyword mixed alphabet is   : ";      '*****
        FOR I = 0 TO 25: PRINT CIPHERTEXT$(I); : NEXT I: PRINT   '*****
GOSUB INITIALIZE               'reinitialize plaintext array
GOSUB MSGFILE                  'assign I/O files, place message on a file
GOSUB CONVERTSTORE             'convert and store ciphertext on a file
GOSUB PRTOUT                   'print results
STOP
INITIALIZE:
        RESTORE
        REM Initialize plaintext values
        FOR I = 0 TO 25
        READ PLAINTEXT$(I)
        NEXT I
        DATA "A","B","C","D","E","F","G","H","I","J","K","L","M","N"
        DATA "O","P","Q","R","S","T","U","V","W","X","Y","Z"
RETURN
```

As indicated in Listing 3.3, first initialize the string array PLAINTEXT$ and then display information about the program. After the keyword or keyword phrase is entered and assigned to the string variable TEXT$, the plaintext alphabet is displayed. Next, the subroutine KEYWORD is invoked to form a keyword-based mixed alphabet. That subroutine is the same as the subroutine previously developed in the program WORD.BAS.

After the subroutine KEYWORD is invoked, the keyword-based alphabet is displayed via the use of another optional statement. The user is then prompted to enter an alphabetic shift character, and the subroutine FORMCIPHER is invoked to create a cipher alphabet. That alphabet is displayed through the use of a pair of optional statements.

Because the subroutine FORMCIPHER creates the cipher alphabet by shifting the previously created keyword-based mixed alphabet, you must restore the plaintext alphabet to its original sequence to correctly convert plaintext characters to their equivalent ciphertext characters. This is accomplished by again invoking the subroutine INITIALIZE. However, because that subroutine previously read the normal letter sequence into the array PLAINTEXT, you must place a RESTORE statement at the beginning of the subroutine. Otherwise, you would receive an "out-of-data" error message.

The Encipherment Process

Figure 3.2 illustrates the execution of CIPHER5.BAS to encipher a short but important message. To understand the encipherment process, examine the composition of the different alphabets displayed by the program.

```
Figure 3.2 A sample execution of CIPHER5.BAS.

CIPHER5.BAS PROGRAM enciphers text based upon the use of a
↳keyword or keyword phrase and an alphabetic shift key using a
↳monoalphabetic substitution process.

Enter keyword or keyword phrase in UPPERCASE: MICROSOFTWINDOWS
Plaintext-based alphabet is: ABCDEFGHIJKLMNOPQRSTUVWXYZ
Keyword-based alphabet is: MICROSFTWNDABEGHJKLPQUVXYZ
Enter UPPERCASE Alphabetic Shift Key: B
Shifted keyword mixed alphabet is: EGHJKLPQUVXYZMICROSFTWNDAB
Enter filename to store plaintext message, default=MESSAGE.DAT
Enter filename to store enciphered message, default=CIPHERTX.DAT
Select keyboard (k) or file (f) message input: K
Enter your message - place a / at the beginning of each line
↳that should remain in plaintext and a \ on a separate line
↳to indicate the end of the enciphered message

/TO: JOHN P. BIDDER
/FROM: PRESIDENT V.F. SMALL
BID NO MORE THAN TWO HUNDRED THOUSAND FOR THE PROPERTY
\
Press Return key to display resulting enciphered message

Resulting enciphered message is:
TO: JOHN P. BIDDER
FROM: PRESIDENT V.F. SMALL
GUJMI ZIOKF QEMFN IQTMJ OKJFQ
ITSEM JLIOF QKCOI CKOFA
```

3

Chapter

The plaintext based alphabet is simply the character sequence A through Z. After a keyword or keyword phrase is entered, the plaintext sequence is modified based upon the keyword or keyword phrase. For example, entering the keyword MICROSOFTWINDOWS results in the keyword-based alphabet MICROSFTWNDABEGHJKLPQUVXYZ because all duplicate characters in the keyword or keyword phrase are eliminated prior to the addition of the characters in the plaintext alphabet that are not in the modified keyword or keyword phrase. The entry of an alphabetic shift key causes the cycling of the keyword-based alphabet so that all characters to and including the alphabetic shift key character are rotated. Thus, the shifted keyword mixed alphabet becomes EGHJKLPQUVXYZMICROSFTWNDAB.

The encipherment process requires each character in the message to be located in the array PLAINTEXT$, which contains the normal alphabetic sequence. When a match is found, the ciphertext character located in the same position in the shifted keyword mixed alphabet in the CIPHERTEXT$ array is extracted and substituted for the plaintext character. Note the positional relationship of characters between the plaintext based alphabet and the shifted keyword mixed alphabet in Figure 3.2. The first character in the message is B, located in the second position in the plaintext alphabet. The second character in the shifted keyword mixed alphabet is G. Hence, B was replaced by G. The second letter in the message is I, located in the ninth position in the plaintext alphabet. In the ninth position in the shifted keyword mixed alphabet, extract a U. Similarly, D is replaced by the character J and the first word in the plaintext message, BID, is enciphered as GUJ.

The CIPHER5.CPP Program

The C++ version of the previously described CIPHER5.BAS program is appropriately named CIPHER5.CPP and is contained on the CD-ROM under the C directory. The executable version of this C++ program follows our naming convention and is named CIPHER5.EXE. To distinguish the BASIC executable version of CIPHER5 from the C++ version of that program, it is important to remember that those versions are located in the BASIC and C directories on the CD-ROM.

Listing 3.4 lists the contents of the program CIPHER5.CPP. As you examine the program listing you will note that the C++ software author, Jonathan Held, replaced the #define statements with the use of integer constants to demonstrate another method you can use to create constants for a C++ program. Similar to other C++ program listings, the listing of CIPHER5.CPP includes a detailed description via embedded comments that indicates how the program operates. The only function that is completely new in Listing 3.4 is the welcome function whose statements are listed at the end of the program. Although the other functions in CIPHER5.CPP were developed for previously covered C++ programs, the entire program is given in Listing 3.4 to provide you with the manner by which functions interact with one another as well as to provide an example of the use of integer constants instead of magic numbers.

Listing 3.4 The CIPHER5.CPP program listing.

```
/*
cipher5.cpp
C++ Code written by Jonathan Held, February 28, 1998, using
Microsoft Visual C++, version 5.0.  Please read file for
detailed description of how the program works.
*/

//standard include files
#include <iostream.h>      //standard i/o operations
#include <string.h>        //used to find the length of a string
#include <ctype.h>         //for character handling
#include <fstream.h>       //file stream processing
#include <stdlib.h>        //standard library functions
#include <string.h>        //string handling functions

//Constants - we don't want to use any magic numbers!
//Notice how now we aren't using #defines as we did before -
//Just another way to create constants for our program.
const int TWO=2, THREE = 3, FOUR = 4, FIVE = 5, TWENTYFIVE = 25,
          TWENTYSIX = 26, TWENTYSEVEN = 27, SIXTYFIVE = 65,
          NINETY = 90, NINETYTWO = 92, SIZE = 256, BIGSIZE = 1000;


//function prototypes - see function headers for more information
void welcome(void);                    //only function that is
                                       //new to this file

void getFileNames(char* &, char* &);   //all other functions have
int getInputType(void);                //been used in previous programs

//keyword or keyword phrase functions:
void getKeyword(char * &);
bool checkInput(char * &);
void createAlphabet(char *, char []);
bool getMessage(char*, char*, char [], const char[], const char[]);

//monoalphabetic substitution functions:
void getShiftKey(char &);
void shiftKeyword(char [], char);      //shiftKeyword modified for this
                                       //program - see function for details
```

3

Chapter

```
//other functions:
char* formCipheredMessage(const char[], const char [], char []);
void printResults(const char[], const char[], const char[], const char [],
                  const int);
void printCipherToFile(ofstream, char[]);
void formatData(char []);
void groupBUFFER(ofstream, int);
bool encryptText(char *, char *, const char [], const char[], char []);
void display(char *);

char BUFFER[BIGSIZE] = {'\0'};


//------------------------------------------------------------------
//Function: main()
//Parameters: None
//Return Type: int - 0 execution is normal, 1 abnormal termination
//Purpose: Runs the main part of the program.
//------------------------------------------------------------------
int main(){

    //initialize plaintext
    char plaintext[TWENTYSEVEN] = {'A','B','C','D','E','F','G','H','I',
                                   'J','K','L','M','N','O','P','Q','R',
                                   'S','T','U', 'V','W','X','Y','Z', '\0'};

    //other variables we will use
    char ciphertext[TWENTYSEVEN]= {'\0'};
    char message_to_cipher[SIZE], key;
    char *infile, *outfile, *keyword;
    int input_type;
    bool success = false;

    welcome();
    getKeyword(keyword);
    createAlphabet(keyword, ciphertext);
    cout << "\nPlaintext-based alphabet is: " << plaintext << endl
         << "Keyword-based alphabet is:   " << ciphertext << endl << endl;
    getShiftKey(key);
    shiftKeyword(ciphertext, key);
    cout << "Shifted keyword mixed alphabet is: " << endl << ciphertext
              << endl << endl;
    getFileNames(infile, outfile);
    input_type = getInputType();
```

```
   //check for manual entry of data
   if (!(input_type)){
      success = getMessage(infile, outfile, message_to_cipher, plaintext,
               ciphertext);
   }
   //user wants to encipher a file
   else {
      success = encryptText(infile, outfile, plaintext, ciphertext,
               message_to_cipher);
   }

   //display the output file only if we were successful
   if (success){
      cout << "Press return to display resulting enciphered message."
               << endl;
      //get the newlines off the current input stream
      cin.get();
      cin.get();
      display(outfile);
   }
   else {
      cerr << "Error executing program!" << endl;
   }

   //delete all dynamically allocated memory
   delete [] keyword;
   delete [] infile;
   delete [] outfile;

   return (static_cast<int>(!(success)));

}//end main()



//------------------------------------------------------------------
//Function: checkInput()
//Parameters: input - the keyword the user entered
//Return Type: bool - true if the input string contains an error,
//                    false otherwise
//Purpose: Checks the user's keyword for invalid characters.
//------------------------------------------------------------------
bool checkInput(char * &input)
{
   bool error = false;
```

```
        int count = strlen(input);

        for (int ix=0; ix<count; ix++){

           int char_value = static_cast<int>(*(input+ix));

           //determine if the user did not enter an uppercase character
           if ((char_value < SIXTYFIVE) || (char_value > NINETY)){
              error = true;
              cerr << "You entered an invalid keyword!" << endl << endl;
              break;
           }
        }

        return error;
}//end checkInput()



//----------------------------------------------------------------
//Function: createAlphabet()
//Parameters: input - the keyword the user entered
//            cipher - the keyword alphabet that will be constructed
//Return Type: None
//Purpose: Creates the keyword alphabet.
//----------------------------------------------------------------
void createAlphabet(char *input, char cipher[])
{
   bool used[TWENTYSIX];
   int index = 0,
       count = strlen(input);

   //no characters are initially used
   for (int ix=0; ix<TWENTYSIX; ix++){
      used[ix] = false;
   }

   //keep track of each character used, start forming the keyword
   //alphabet
   for (int jx=0; jx<count; jx++){

      //get each character of the input string (integer value)
      int char_value = static_cast<int>(*(input+jx));
```

```
      if (used[char_value-SIXTYFIVE]){
         //do nothing - the character was already used
      }
      else {
         //mark as used and add to the keyword alphabet
         used[char_value-SIXTYFIVE] = true;
         *(cipher+index++) = static_cast<char>(char_value);
      }
   }

   //go through the list of characters used - those which weren't
   //used should be added to the keyword alphabet
   for (int kx=0; kx<TWENTYSIX; kx++){

      if (!(used[kx])){
         *(cipher+index++) = static_cast<char>(SIXTYFIVE+kx);
      }
   }

   return;
}//end createAlphabet()


//-----------------------------------------------------------------
//Function: display()
//Parameters: name - the name of the file the user wants displayed
//Return Type: None
//Purpose: Echos the resulting output file to the screen.
//-----------------------------------------------------------------
void display(char *name)
{
   ifstream infile(name, ios::in);
   char input[SIZE];

   if (!(infile)){
      cerr << "Unable to open input file for display." << endl;
   }
   else {
      while (infile.getline(input, SIZE, '\n')){
         cout << input << endl;
      }
   }
```

3

Chapter

```
        return;
    }//end display()


    //------------------------------------------------------------------
    //Function: encryptText()
    //Parameters: inp_file - the name of the input plaintext file
    //           outp_file - the name of the output ciphertext file
    //           PTEXT[] - the plaintext alphabet
    //           CTEXT[] - the ciphertext alphabet
    //           encoded_msg[] - the message to be encoded
    //Return Type: bool, indicating success of operation
    //Purpose: Used to encrypt file input.  Takes each line of the input
    //file, encrypts it, and saves the result to the specified output
    //file.
    //------------------------------------------------------------------
    bool encryptText(char * inp_file, char * outp_file, const char PTEXT[],
                     const char CTEXT[], char encoded_msg[])
    {
        bool success = false;
        char ip[SIZE];

        //declare file stream objects
        ifstream input(inp_file, ios::in);
        ofstream output(outp_file, ios::app);

        if ((!input) || (!output)){
            //do nothing - I/O error; user will be notified upon
            //procedure's return to main()
        }
        else {

            success = true;

            //print plaintext and ciphertext alphabets to the
            //output file
            output << "PLAINTEXT:  " << PTEXT << endl;
            output << "CIPHERTEXT: " << CTEXT << endl << endl;

            while (input.getline(ip, BIGSIZE, '\n')){

                //check to see if the user wants the line to appear in plain text
                if (ip[0] == '/'){
```

```
            if (strlen(BUFFER)>0){

                //empty whatever is in the buffer
                groupBUFFER(output, strlen(BUFFER));
                //adjust the buffer
                strcpy(BUFFER, (BUFFER+strlen(BUFFER)));
                //output plaintext
            }

            output << ip << endl;

        }
        else {
            //encipher the line
            char *msg = formCipheredMessage(CTEXT, ip, encoded_msg);
            //print the cipher in groups of five to the ouput file
            printCipherToFile(output, msg);
        }
    }

    //empty the rest of the buffer
    groupBUFFER(output, strlen(BUFFER));

    //notify user where plaintext and ciphertext files are
    cout << "Plaintext file is: " << inp_file << endl;
    cout << "Encrypted file is: " << outp_file << endl << endl;
}

    //don't forget to close the files
    input.close();
    output.close();

    //return success of the operation
    return success;
}//end encryptText()


//----------------------------------------------------------------
//Function: formatData()
//Parameters: data - the array we want to format
//Return Type: None
//Purpose: Get rid of all spaces in the array.
//----------------------------------------------------------------
```

3

Chapter

```
void formatData(char data[]){

    for (int mx=0, nx=0; (*(data+nx) != '\0'); nx++){
        if (*(data+nx) == ' '){
            //do nothing - skip over the space in the data
        }
        else {
            *(data+mx++) = *(data+nx);
        }
    }

    //don't forget to add the null terminator
    *(data+mx) = '\0';

    return;
}//end formatData()




//------------------------------------------------------------------
//Function: formCipheredMessage()
//Parameters:  CTEXT - the cipher alphabet we will use for substitution
//             MESSAGETOCIPHER - the user's message
//             enc_message - the enciphered message to be determined
//Return Type: char* - a pointer to the encoded information.
//Purpose: Encipher the user's message.
//------------------------------------------------------------------
char* formCipheredMessage(const char CTEXT[], const char MESSAGETOCIPHER[],

                          char enc_message[]){

    int length = strlen(MESSAGETOCIPHER)+1;

    int encode_value;

    for (int ix=0; ix<length; ix++){

        //test to see if we have an alphabetic character; if not,
        //simply copy it to our encrypted message - this preserves
        //characters such as ' , ! etc...
        if (!isalpha(static_cast<int>(MESSAGETOCIPHER[ix]))){
            enc_message[ix] = MESSAGETOCIPHER[ix];
        }
        else {
```

```
                //valid character - the easy way to calculate the ciphered
                //character is based on the plain text's ascii character value;
                //since it has to be a capital letter, it must be in the range
                //from 65 to 90, with A represented by 65, Z by 90.  By simply
                //subtracting 65 from the encode_value (the integer representation
                //of the plaintext character), we now know what cipher character
                //to use.

                encode_value = toupper(static_cast<int>(MESSAGETOCIPHER[ix]));
                enc_message[ix] = CTEXT[encode_value-SIXTYFIVE];
         }
      }

      //return a reference to the encoded message
      return enc_message;
}//end formCipheredMessage()



//----------------------------------------------------------------
//Function: getFileNames()
//Parameters:  infile_name - the input file
//             outfile_name - the output file we will write the
//             enciphered text to
//Return Type: None
//Purpose: Get file information from the user.
//----------------------------------------------------------------
void getFileNames(char * &infile_name, char * &outfile_name)
{
   char data[SIZE];

   cout << "Enter filename to store/retrieve plaintext message: ";

   cin >> data;

   infile_name = new char[strlen(data) + 1];
   strcpy(infile_name, data);

   cout << "Enter filename to store enciphered message: ";

   cin >> data;

   outfile_name = new char[strlen(data) + 1];
   strcpy(outfile_name, data);
```

3

Chapter

```
        cout << endl;

        return;
}//end getFileNames()


//------------------------------------------------------------------
//Function: getInputType()
//Parameters: None
//Return Type: int - 0 indicates keyboard input, 1 indicates file
//               input
//Purpose: Determines if the user will be manually entering text to
//be enciphered or if the user wants a file to be enciphered.
//------------------------------------------------------------------
int getInputType(void)
{
    char type;
    bool error = false;
    int value;

    do {
        //prompt user for input from file or keyboard
        cout << "Is file input from keyboard (K, k) or file (F, f): ";
        cin >> type;

        //make type an uppercase letter
        type = static_cast<char>(toupper(static_cast<int>(type)));

        //check for an invalid character
        if ((type != 'K') && (type != 'F')){
            cerr << "You have entered an invalid character!" << endl << endl;
            error = true;
        }
        else {
            if (type == 'K')
                value = 0;          //value of 0 represents keyboard input
                else value = 1;     //value of 1 represents file input
            error = false;
        }

    } while (error);

    cout << endl;
```

```
   return value;

}//end getInputType()


//------------------------------------------------------------------
//Function: getKeyword()
//Parameters: text - the keyword that the user enters
//Return Type: None
//Purpose: Prompts the user for a keyword and continues until
//a valid keyword has been entered.
//------------------------------------------------------------------
void getKeyword(char * &text)
{
   bool error = false;

   do {
      char buffer[SIZE];
      cout << "Enter keyword or keyword phrase in UPPERCASE" << endl
           << "do not use spaces or non-alphabetic characters): ";

      cin.getline(buffer, SIZE, '\n');
      text = new char[strlen(buffer) + 1];
      strcpy(text, buffer);

      error = checkInput(text);

   } while (error);

   return;
}//end getKeyword()


//------------------------------------------------------------------
//Function: getMessage()
//Parameters:  input - the name of the input plaintext file
//             output the name of the output ciphertext file
//             msg_to_cipher - the message to be encoded
//             PTEXT[] - the plaintext alphabet
//             CTEXT[] - the ciphertext alphabet
//Return Type: bool, indicating success of operation
//Purpose: Allow the user to manually input text from the keyboard.
//Save the text in plaintext to the input file; encrypt the text
//and save it to the specified output file for later retrieval.
```

```
//----------------------------------------------------------------
bool getMessage(char* input, char* output, char msg_to_cipher[],
                const char PTEXT[], const
char CTEXT[]){

    bool go_on = true, success = false;

    ofstream textFile(input, ios::app);
    ofstream cipherFile(output, ios::app);

    if ((!textFile) || (!cipherFile)){
        //do nothing - error will be noted to user later
    }
    else {

        success = true;

        textFile << "PLAINTEXT:  " << PTEXT << endl;
        textFile << "CIPHERTEXT: " << CTEXT << endl << endl;

        //get the newline character off of the input stream
        cin.get();

        cout << "Enter the message in UPPERCASE or lowercase characters. "
                << endl
            << "Non-alphabetic characters may be entered but are ignored."
                << endl
            << "Use a / at the beginning of each line that should remain"
                << endl
            << "in plaintext and a \\ on a separate line to indicate the"
                << endl
            << "end of an enciphered message." << endl << endl;

        while (go_on) {

            //get the entire line, up to 256 characters
            cin.getline(msg_to_cipher, SIZE, '\n');

            //case user doesn't want the text to be encrypted
            if (msg_to_cipher[0] == '/'){

                if (strlen(BUFFER)>0){
                    //empty whatever is in the buffer
                    groupBUFFER(cipherFile, strlen(BUFFER));
```

```
                //adjust the buffer
                strcpy(BUFFER, (BUFFER+strlen(BUFFER)));
            }

            //output plaintext
            textFile << msg_to_cipher << endl;
            cipherFile << msg_to_cipher << endl;
        }

        //case user is done entering text
        else if (static_cast<int>(msg_to_cipher[0]) == NINETYTWO){
            go_on = false;
        }

        //encrypt the text
        else {
            textFile << msg_to_cipher << endl;
            char enciphered_msg[BIGSIZE];
            formCipheredMessage(CTEXT,msg_to_cipher,enciphered_msg);
            printCipherToFile(cipherFile,enciphered_msg);
        }
        }

    //empty the rest of the buffer
    groupBUFFER(cipherFile, strlen(BUFFER));
    }

    //close the files
    textFile.close();
    cipherFile.close();

    //notify user where plaintext and ciphertext files are
    cout << "\nPlaintext file is: " << input << endl;
    cout << "Encrypted file is: " << output << endl << endl;

    return success;
}//end getMessage()


//----------------------------------------------------------------
//Function: getShiftKey()
//Parameters:  key_desired - uppercase key entered by the user
//Return Type: None
//Purpose: Get the key the user enters; error checking performed
```

3

Chapter

```
                     //until user enters a valid value.
                     //-----------------------------------------------------------------
                     void getShiftKey(char &key_desired){

                        bool error = true;

                        do {
                           //prompt user to enter an uppercase shift key
                           cout << "Enter UPPERCASE Alphabetic Shift Key (CTRL-C to quit): ";
                           cin >> key_desired;

                           int key_value = static_cast<int>(key_desired);

                           //do some error checking
                           if ((key_value < SIXTYFIVE) || (key_value > NINETY)){
                              cerr << "\nYou must enter a letter from A to Z!" << endl << endl;
                           }
                           else {
                              error = false;
                           }
                        } while (error);

                        cout << endl;

                        return;
                     }//end getShiftKey()


                     //-----------------------------------------------------------------
                     //Function: groupBUFFER()
                     //Parameters: out - the output stream we are writing to
                     //            num - the number of characters we want to output
                     //Return Type: None
                     //Purpose: Output the buffer in groups of five characters at a
                     //time.
                     //-----------------------------------------------------------------
                     void groupBUFFER(ofstream out, int num)
                     {

                        for (int kx=0;kx<num;kx++){

                           if ((kx!=0) && (kx%TWENTYFIVE==0)){
                              out << endl;
```

```
      }

      if ((kx!=0) && (kx%FIVE == 0) && (kx%TWENTYFIVE!=0)){
         out << " " << *(BUFFER+kx);
      }
      else {
      out << *(BUFFER+kx);
      }
   }

   out << endl;

   return;
}//end groupBUFFER()



//------------------------------------------------------------------
//Function: printCipherToFile()
//Parameters: op - the output file we are writing to
//            msg - the cipher text we are displaying
//Return Type: None
//Purpose: Group the cipher in 5-block characters in the
//specified output file.
//------------------------------------------------------------------
void printCipherToFile(ofstream op, char msg[]){

   formatData(msg);

   //check to see if there are more than 25 characters
   //in the buffer; if so, print out as many groups of
   //25 as possible
   if (strlen(BUFFER) >= TWENTYFIVE){

      int numchars = (strlen(BUFFER)/TWENTYFIVE)*TWENTYFIVE;
      //print the contents of the buffer to the output stream
      groupBUFFER(op, numchars);
      //shift whatever is left in the buffer
      strcpy(BUFFER, (BUFFER+numchars));
      //append data to the buffer
      strcat(BUFFER, msg);
   }

   //if buffer contents are less than 25, simply append the new
   //data to the buffer
```

```
        else if ((strlen(BUFFER) >= 0) && (strlen(BUFFER) < TWENTYFIVE)){
            strcat(BUFFER, msg);
        }


    return;
}//end printCipherToFile()



//----------------------------------------------------------------
//Function: shiftKeyword()
//Parameters: ctext - the cipher alphabet we are going to shift
//            user_key - the key the user entered
//Return Type: None
//Purpose: Shift the keyword or keyword phrase we will use later to
//encode the user's message.
//----------------------------------------------------------------
void shiftKeyword(char ctext[], const char USER_KEY){

    int location;
    char temp[TWENTYSIX] = {'\0'};

    //find the location of the key in the plaintext
    for (int ix=0; ix<TWENTYSIX; ix++){
        if (USER_KEY == ctext[ix]){
            location = ix;
            break;
        }
    }

    if (location == TWENTYFIVE){
        //do nothing
    }
    else {

        //put into temp all the characters up to and including the shift key
        //location now indicated how many characters, so we must increment by
        //one since the array uses a zero-based index
        strncpy(temp, ctext, location+1);
        //shift all remaining characters in the ciphertext
        strcpy(ctext, (ctext+location+1));
        //concatenate temp back to ctext
        strcat(ctext, temp);
    }
```

```
      return;
}//end shiftKeyword();



//------------------------------------------------------------------
//Function: welcome()
//Parameters: None
//Return Type: None
//Purpose: Prints the program's greeting message.
//------------------------------------------------------------------
void welcome(void)
{
    cout << "CIPHER5.EXE PROGRAM enciphers text based upon the use of a"
              << endl
          << "keyword or keyword phrase and an alphabetic shift key using a"
              << endl
          << "monoalphabetic substitution process." << endl << endl;

    return;
}//end welcome()
//end file cipher5.cpp
```

Deciphering Operations

After developing CIPHER5.BAS and CIPHER5.CPP, it's only logical that a mechanism is required to restore a received message to its original plaintext content. In this section, several previously developed subroutines are modified and incorporated into programs appropriately named DCIPHER5.BAS and DCIPHER5.CPP as they perform the inverse function of CIPHER5.BAS and CIPHER5.CPP. Although you could incorporate deciphering operations into CIPHER5.BAS and CIPHER5.CPP, it is easier to explain deciphering coding operations as a separate entity. In addition, some organizations may prefer to limit non-headquarters or certain corporate locations' capability to deciphering messages and preclude those locations from originating enciphered messages. Thus, the separation of enciphering and deciphering operations may be preferred by some users. For other users who prefer a program that combines both operations, I'll develop such programs using more sophisticated enciphering techniques later in this book. However, because the focus is on the development of modular routines, I'll show you the ease in which modules from both programs can be combined.

Prior to developing the coding required to decipher a message created through the use of a keyword or keyword phrase and an alphabetic shift, it may be useful to review the manual process required to decipher a message enciphered in this manner.

The Decipherment Process

To correctly decipher an enciphered message developed using a keyword or keyword phrase and shift key requires knowledge of both elements. Once both elements are known, you can construct a keyword-based mixed alphabet and shift the alphabet to obtain the cipher alphabet. To initiate the deciphering process, place the cipher alphabet above the plaintext alphabet. For each letter in the enciphered message, first locate its position in the cipher alphabet and extract the plaintext character at the position in the alphabet which equals the position of the enciphered character in the cipher alphabet. For example, assume the keyword phrase was GODSAVETHEQUEEN and that the shift key is the character B. In this case the keyword-based alphabet becomes GODSAVETHQUNBCFIJKLMPRWXYZ. Because the shift key is the character B, shift the keyword-based alphabet until it is positioned so that the character B is on the extreme right. Remember that the alphabetic shift key was previously defined as an uppercase character in the plaintext alphabet that defines the location where the right end of the resulting shifted alphabet ends. Thus, using the shift key character B results in the cipher alphabet becoming: CFIJKLMPRWXYZGODSAVETHQUNB.

Now that you have constructed the cipher alphabet based upon the pre-defined keyword phrase and shift key, place that alphabet above the plaintext alphabet as shown below:

    Cipher alphabet: `CFIJKLMPRWXYZGODSAVETHQUNB`

    Plaintext alphabet: `ABCDEFGHIJKLMNOPQRSTUVWXYZ`

Now suppose the first two groups of five enciphered characters in a received message are LRAKW OVKDP. Searching the cipher alphabet, you would first locate the character L and read down the same position into the plaintext alphabet to extract the character F. Similarly, locating R in the cipher alphabet results in extracting I from the plaintext, A results in extracting R from the plaintext alphabet, K in the cipher alphabet produces E in the plaintext alphabet, and so on. Thus, LRAKW OVKDP in the enciphered message is equivalent to FIREJOSEPH in plaintext. Now that you have a feeling for the manual process required to decipher an enciphered message, let's construct a program to automate this process.

The DCIPHER5.BAS Program

To automate deciphering of a previously enciphered message based upon the use of a keyword or keyword phrase and an alphabetic shift key, I'll first construct a program appropriately named DCIPHER5.BAS. In doing so, I'll use all of the previously developed subroutines included in CIPHER5.BAS as is, or in a slightly modified form. To indicate that a change was made to a previously developed subroutine, I'll prefix its name with the character D to indicate its modification for deciphering a received message.

Listing 3.5 contains the statements that make up the main portion of DCIPHER5.BAS. Similar to the statements in CIPHER5.BAS, a comment of five asterisks is used to denote a PRINT statement included for illustrative purposes and whose elimination will not affect the operation of the program.

Listing 3.5 The main portion of the DCIPHER5.BAS program.

```
REM PROGRAM DCIPHER5.BAS
DIM PLAINTEXT$(26), CIPHERTEXT$(26), KEY$(26)
CLS
GOSUB INITIALIZE
        PRINT "DCIPHER5.BAS PROGRAM deciphers text based upon the use
                of a keyword or keyword"
        PRINT "phrase and an alphabetic shift key using a monoalphabetic
                substitution process."
        PRINT
        INPUT "Enter keyword or keyword phrase in UPPERCASE: ", TEXT$
        PRINT "Plaintext based alphabet is      : ";        '*****
        FOR I = 0 TO 25: PRINT PLAINTEXT$(I); : NEXT I       '*****
        GOSUB KEYWORD                  'form keyword-based mixed alphabet
        PRINT "Keyword-based alphabet is        : "; X$      '*****
1       INPUT "Enter UPPERCASE Alphabetic Shift Key: ", K$
        FOR I = 0 TO 25
        IF K$ = PLAINTEXT$(I) GOTO 2
        NEXT I
        PRINT "You must enter a letter from A to Z"
```

```
        GOTO 1
2       REM Position I represents shift key letter

GOSUB FORMCIPHER                'create cipher alphabet
        PRINT "Shifted keyword mixed alphabet is    : ";        '*****
        FOR I = 0 TO 25: PRINT CIPHERTEXT$(I); : NEXT I: PRINT  '*****
GOSUB INITIALIZE                'reinitialize plaintext array
GOSUB DMSGFILE                  'assign I/O files, place message on a file
GOSUB DCONVERTSTORE             'convert and store plaintext on a file
GOSUB PRTOUT                    'print results
STOP
```

It should be noted that the only difference between the main portion of CIPHER5.BAS and DCIPHER5.BAS is the subroutine names DMSGFILE and DCONVERTSTORE. Since you noted that the character D would be used as a prefix to indicate a change to a previously developed subroutine for decipherment operations, let us focus our attention on those two subroutines.

The DMSGFILE Subroutine

The process of assigning I/O files must be reversed for decipherment. That is, the filename used for the input of the plaintext message in the CIPHER5.BAS program becomes the output file. Similarly, the filename used for the storage of the enciphered message in the CIPHER5.BAS program becomes the input file for decipherment operations. To provide those modifications, you must change the use of the string variables OUTFILE$ and INFILE$ previously used in the subroutine MSGFILE. To change I/O file assignments, simply reverse the use of the previously mentioned string variables.

Listing 3.6 lists the statements in the new subroutine named DMSGFILE, which contains the reversal of I/O file assignments. If you compare this subroutine to the previously developed subroutine MSGFILE, you should note that the difference between the two is limited to the previously mentioned reversal of I/O filename assignments.

Listing 3.6 The DMSGFILE subroutine.

```
DMSGFILE:
        REM Routine to assign I/O files and accept keyboard or file input
        REM and remove spaces between words
                INPUT "Enter filename to store plaintext message,
                        default=MESSAGE.DAT", OUTFILE$
```

```
              IF OUTFILE$ = "" THEN OUTFILE$ = "MESSAGE.DAT"
              INPUT "Enter filename for enciphered message,
                  default=CIPHERTX.DAT", INFILE$
              IF INFILE$ = "" THEN INFILE$ = "CIPHERTX.DAT"
              INPUT "Select keyboard (k) or file (f) message input: ",
                  IN$
              IF IN$ = "F" OR IN$ = "f" THEN RETURN
              OPEN INFILE$ FOR OUTPUT AS #1
      REM Routine to place message on a file removing spaces between
                  words
              PRINT "Enter your message - place a / at the beginning of
                  each line"
              PRINT "that should remain in plaintext and a \ on a
                  separate line"
              PRINT "to indicate the end of the enciphered message"
              PRINT
AGN:          LINE INPUT TEXT$
              IF MID$(TEXT$, 1, 1) = "/" THEN GOTO XT
              NTEXT$ = ""
              FOR I = 1 TO LEN(TEXT$)
              NTEXT$ = NTEXT$ + LTRIM$(MID$(TEXT$, I, 1))
              NEXT I
              WRITE #1, NTEXT$
              IF MID$(TEXT$, 1, 1) = "\" GOTO DONE
              GOTO AGN
XT:           WRITE #1, TEXT$
              GOTO AGN
DONE:           CLOSE #1
RETURN
```

The DCONVERTSTORE Subroutine

The second subroutine that required modification for deciphering is
CONVERTSTORE. As previously discussed, the modified subroutine was
renamed DCONVERTSTORE to reflect its modification for decipherment
operations.

Lisitng 3.7 gives the statements contained in the subroutine
DCONVERTSTORE. Other than changing two REM statements to reflect
the fact that the routine now converts ciphertext to plaintext, the only
additional changes relate to search and replacement operations. The IF
statement in the nested FOR-NEXT loop now compares each character in
the string variable TEXT$ to each character in the CIPHERTEXT$ array

instead of the PLAINTEXT$ array. When a match occurs, the character in TEXT$ is replaced by a character in the array PLAINTEXT$ located at the same position in the array where the character in TEXT$ matched the character in the array CIPHERTEXT$. Thus, DCONVERTSTORE simply makes use of the plaintext alphabet stored in the array PLAINTEXT$ and the ciphertext alphabet stored in the array CIPHERTEXT$ in the reverse manner in which they were used in the subroutine CONVERTSTORE.

Listing 3.7 THE DCONVERTSTORE subroutine.

```
DCONVERTSTORE:
        REM Routine to convert and store plaintext on a file
        OPEN INFILE$ FOR INPUT AS #1
        OPEN OUTFILE$ FOR OUTPUT AS #2
        DO UNTIL EOF(1)
                INPUT #1, TEXT$
                MSGLEN = LEN(TEXT$)
                IF MID$(TEXT$, 1, 1) = "/" THEN GOTO CLEARTXT
                IF MID$(TEXT$, 1, 1) = "\" THEN GOTO DONE1
                REM Convert ciphertext to plaintext
                        FOR I = 1 TO MSGLEN
                        FOR J = 0 TO 25
                        IF MID$(TEXT$, I, 1) = CIPHERTEXT$(J) THEN GOTO GOTIT
                        NEXT J
GOTIT:                  MID$(TEXT$, I, 1) = PLAINTEXT$(J)
                        NEXT I
CLEARTXT:               WRITE #2, TEXT$
        LOOP
DONE1:          CLOSE #2
RETURN
```

Program Operation

To illustrate the operation of the DCIPHER5.BAS program, you can execute it using the previously enciphered message to the fictional JOHN P. BIDDER as input. Regardless of whether you use the keyboard or specify a file for input of the ciphered messaged, the program produces the same result. Figure 3.3 illustrates the execution of DCIPHER5.BAS in which the keyboard is used to enter the received enciphered message. Because the previously developed subroutine PRTOUT was used to display the resulting deciphered message, that message is displayed in groups of five characters as indicated in the lower portion of Figure 3.3. Although the program converted the ciphertext message back into its plaintext character representation, it did not restore the message to its original format with spaces between words and words rebuilt from two or more five-character groupings when it crossed such groupings. Those functions cannot be performed when the encipherment method does not substitute a character for the space character and results in the human recipient of the deciphered message being responsible for understanding how to correctly read the deciphered message.

```
Figure 3.3 The execution of DCIPHER5.BAS

DCIPHER5.BAS PROGRAM deciphers text based upon the use of a
%keyword or keyword phrase and an alphabetic shift key using a
%Monoalphabetic substitution process.

Enter keyword or keyword phrase in UPPERCASE: MICROSOFTWINDOWS
Plaintext-based alphabet is: ABCDEFGHIJKLMNOPQRSTUVWXYZ
Keyword-based alphabet is: MICROSFTWNDABEGHJKLPQUVXYZ
Enter UPPERCASE Alphabetic Shift Key: B
Shifted keyword mixed alphabet is: EGHJKLPQUVXYZMICROSFTWNDAB
Enter filename to store plaintext message, default=MESSAGE.DAT
Enter filename to store enciphered message, default=CIPHERTX.DAT
Select keyboard (k) or file (f) message input: K
Enter your message - place a / at the beginning of each line
%that should remain in plaintext and a \ on a separate line
%to indicate the end of the enciphered message.


/TO: JOHN P. BIDDER
GUJMI ZIOKF QEMFN IQTMJ OKJFK
MFQIT SEMJL IOFQK COICK OFAXX
\
Press return key to display resulting deciphered message.

Resulting deciphered message is:
TO: JOHN P. BIDDER
BIDNO MORET HANTW OHUND REDTE
NTHOU SANDF ORTHE PROPE RTYKK
```

The DCIPHER5.CPP Program

Once again a C++ version of a previously constructed BASIC language program is presented for readers who prefer this programming language. Maintaining our naming conventions, the C++ version of DCIPHER5.BAS is appropriately named DCIPHER5.CPP, while the executable version of the program is named DCIPHER5.EXE. To distinguish the executable version of DCIPHER5.BAS from DCIPHER5.CPP, remember that there are two directories on the CD-ROM accompanying this book and that source and executable BASIC programs are stored in the BASIC directory while C++ source and executable programs are stored in the C directory.

Listing 3.8 contains the complete listing of DCIPHER5.CPP. As you read through the code you will note that, similar to the BASIC program, large segments of code were reused. Of particular interest is the function appropriately named decipher, which locates where the encrypted data is in the ciphertext.

Listing 3.8 The DCIPHER5.CPP program listing.

```
/*
dcipher5.cpp
C++ code written by Jonathan Held
using Microsoft Visual C++, version 5.0, on March 12, 1998.
*/

//standard include files
#include<iostream.h>
#include<fstream.h>
#include<stdlib.h>
#include<string.h>
#include<ctype.h>

//function prototypes
bool checkInput(char * &);
void createAlphabet(char *, char[]);
void decipher(ifstream, ofstream, const char[], char[]);
void formatData(char []);
void getFileNames(char *&, char *&);
void getFileToDecipher(const char[], char[]);
bool getMessage(char* input, char* output, char msg_to_decipher[],
                const char PTEXT[], const char CTEXT[]);
int getInputType();
void getKeyword(char *&);
void getShiftKey(char &);
void shiftKeyword(char [], char);


//constants we will use
const int FIVE = 5, TWENTYFIVE = 25, TWENTYSIX = 26,
```

```
         TWENTYSEVEN = 27, SIXTYFIVE = 65, NINETY = 90,
         NINETYTWO = 92, SIZE = 256;



//------------------------------------------------------------
//Function: main()
//Parameters: None
//Return Type: int - 0 execution is normal, 1 abnormal termination
//Purpose: Runs the main part of the program.
//------------------------------------------------------------
int main()
{
char plaintext[TWENTYSEVEN] = {'A','B','C','D','E','F','G','H',
```

Alternative Relationships

Up to this point the focus has been on using the development of a keyword-based mixed alphabet to create a ciphertext alphabet. Once that was accomplished, an alphabetic shift key was used to further mix the relationship between plaintext and ciphertext alphabets. In performing those tasks, the only information a message recipient requires is the keyword or keyword phrase and the alphabetic shift key to decipher a message through the use of a program. With a little knowledge of the method used to create a keyword-based mixed alphabet and the use of a shift key, most people can learn how to manually decipher a message. The major benefit of the previously described encipherment method is the ability of most persons to manually perform encipherment and decipherment with a minimum of information.

You can extend the use of keyword or keyword phrase mixed alphabets and alphabetic shifting to the plaintext alphabet. In fact, you can develop nine common alphabetic relationships that are listed in Table 3.1. You could also reverse the resulting plaintext, ciphertext, or both plaintext and ciphertext alphabets to further increase the number of alphabetic relationships. However, this may add a degree of confusion to both encipherment and decipherment due to the large number of options users could be forced to consider and remember. To keep your techniques practical, I'll simply illustrate the use of two keyword-based mixed sequence alphabets for enciphering a message and leave it to you to modify CIPHER5.BAS to obtain other plaintext-ciphertext relationships.

Table 3.1 Common alphabetic relationships

plaintext alphabet in normal sequence	ciphertext alphabet in normal sequence and shifted
plaintext alphabet in normal sequence	ciphertext alphabet in keyword mixed sequence
plaintext alphabet in normal sequence	ciphertext alphabet in keyword mixed sequence and shifted
plaintext alphabet in keyword mixed sequence	ciphertext alphabet in normal sequence and shifted
plaintext alphabet in keyword mixed sequence	ciphertext alphabet in keyword mixed sequence
plaintext alphabet in keyword mixed sequence	ciphertext alphabet in keyword mixed sequence and shifted
plaintext alphabet in keyword mixed sequence and shifted	ciphertext alphabet in normal sequence and shifted
plaintext alphabet in keyword mixed sequence and shifted	ciphertext alphabet in keyword mixed sequence
plaintext alphabet in keyword mixed sequence and shifted	ciphertext alphabet in keyword mixed sequence and shifted

To illustrate the use of two keyword-based mixed alphabets, assume the keyword SANDIEGO is used to form the plaintext alphabet and the keyword BALTIMORE is used to form the ciphertext alphabet. Figure 3.4 illustrates the resulting mixed plaintext and ciphertext alphabets.

```
Figure 3.4 Dual mixed alphabet relationship.

Plaintext keyword   = SANDIEGO
Ciphertext keyword  = BALTIMORE

Mixed plaintext alphabet:    SANDIEGOBCFHJKLMPQRTUVWXYZ
Mixed ciphertext alphabet:   BALTIMORECDFGHJKNPQSUVWXYZ
```

Suppose you wish to encode BID. To do so, you would perform the same operation as previously discussed. That is, you would first locate B in the mixed plaintext alphabet and note its position in that alphabet. Next, you would extract the character in the ciphertext alphabet that corresponds to the location of B in the plaintext alphabet, resulting in B being replaced by E. Next, the letter I would be located in the mixed plaintext alphabet; the letter I would be extracted from the ciphertext alphabet. Similarly, D would be replaced by T.

Sometimes luck works both ways. During World War I the British War Office developed a cipher device which they planned to distribute to British forces as a field cipher. So highly regarded was the device that one argument against its adoption for field use was its possible capture and use by the Germans—a situation many high-level personnel in the Allied forces thought would preclude the ability of the Allies to decipher enemy messages. To verify the security afforded by their device, the British submitted five short enciphered messages to the only formal cryptologic organization in the United States.

Located on a 500-acre estate named Riverbank at Geneva, IL, the Department of Ciphers at Riverbank was headed by William Frederick Friedman, considered by some as America's greatest cryptologist. Although Friedman was able to determine the keyword of one of the mixed alphabets, apparently he hit the proverbial "blank wall" in attempting to determine the other keyword. Turning to his wife, he asked her to make her mind a blank and tell him the first word that came to mind when he said a word. When he said the first keyword, "CIPHER," she replied, "MACHINE." The intuitive guess of his wife was correct, and Friedman cabled the plaintext solution of the five messages to London, dooming the adoption of the device many persons were afraid would, if captured by the Germans, preclude the Allies from solving enemy messages.

Weaknesses

Note that although two different keywords were used, many characters in the ciphertext alphabet are the same as their plaintext equivalents, especially towards the end of each alphabet. This is one of several weaknesses of mixed alphabets, as the encipherment of a long message may provide numerous hints concerning the contents of a message when ciphertext and plaintext characters coincide. It is more practical to use one keyword-based alphabet and an appropriate alphabetic shift key to eliminate the overlapping of plaintext and ciphertext characters than to simply use two keyword mixed alphabets.

The second major weakness of all keyword-based monoalphabetic substitution techniques is the fact that a continuous one-for-one character replacement forms the basis of this category of enciphering techniques. This means that the techniques are very vulnerable to decipherment by a person performing a frequency analysis of characters in intercepted enciphered messages. For example, as Samuel Morse noted in developing the assignments of dots and dashes to characters in the English language in forming the code that bears his name, the letter E is the most frequently occurring character, followed by T. Thus, Morse assigned a dot to denote E and a dash to denote T prior to assigning sequences of dots and dashes to denote other characters in his code.

Suppose, for example, that you intercepted a message enciphered using the plaintext-ciphertext relationship illustrated in Figure 3.4. Further assume that you performed a frequency analysis of the characters in the enciphered message and discovered that the letter M occurred most frequently, followed by the character S. In this case, your first attempt to reconstruct the plaintext-ciphertext alphabet relationship in order to decipher the message would result in placing the character E in the plaintext alphabet over the character M in the ciphertext alphabet, followed by placing the character T in the plaintext alphabet over the character S in the ciphertext alphabet. Although a frequency analysis of characters may not provide an exact relationship between plaintext and ciphertext characters, the analysis normally provides enough intelligent clues to conduct a successful decipherment if you gain access to one long message or a few short messages enciphered using the same alphabetic relationship.

Transposition-based Monoalphabetic Substitution

This chapter focuses on three commonly used methods to develop a mixed alphabet. The first two methods are related to the use of arrays, or matrices, while the third method can be considered a position and extraction technique. After you obtain an understanding of the manual process required for the formation of a transposition mixed alphabet and the encipherment of a message using that alphabet, I'll turn your attention to automating the process. I'll show you how to develop a series of subroutines you can use to perform different types of transpositions and then incorporate those subroutines into a program. When possible, previously created subroutines will be used to take advantage of your previous efforts.

Matrix-Based Transposition

By placing an alphabet into an NxN matrix, or array, you can obtain the ability to extract characters in many different ways. For example, consider the sequential plaintext alphabet placed into a 7x4 matrix as illustrated in Figure 4.1. Each character in the alphabet is referenced by a row and column position and can be considered an element in the array or matrix. By extracting matrix elements in a predefined sequence, you can develop a transposed alphabet.

Figure 4.1 Placing the plaintext alphabet into a matrix.
Each character in the matrix is identified by its row and
column position.

```
                         COLUMNS
                1    2    3    4    5    6    7

           1    A    B    C    D    E    F    G
  ROWS     2    H    I    J    K    L    M    N
           3    O    P    Q    R    S    T    U
           4    V    W    X    Y    Z
```

Perhaps the earliest use of a matrix with a cryptographic alphabet can be traced to the Greek writer Polybius. He arranged the Greek alphabet into a square and numbered the rows and columns whose values identified the location of each letter. This enabled each letter to be identified by a pair of numbers that represented the intersection of a row and column in the matrix.

In addition to devising the use of a matrix for cryptographic applications, Polybius suggested the use of his matrix as a mechanism to transmit information by torches. Polybius proposed that letters in the alphabet could be transmitted over relatively long distances by persons holding a different number of torches. For example, a person holding one torch at his right and two to his left would signal the letter located at the intersection of the first row and second column in the matrix.

The formation of an alphabet into a matrix was rediscovered by modern cryptographers and forms the basis for developing a large number of encipherment systems. Some systems convert letters into numbers, while other systems use the matrix to form different types of alphabets based upon the extraction of row and column entries using a predefined algorithm.

If you extract the matrix elements in each column commencing with column seven and then work backwards, extracting the elements in column six, column five, and so on, the transposed alphabet

GNUFMTELSZDKRYCJQXBIPWAHOV is created. If we extracted the matrix elements in a progressive column order, we would obtain the transposed alphabet AHOVBIPWCJQXDKRYELSZFMTGNU.

Unfortunately, the placement of a plaintext alphabet into a matrix results in the development of a transposed alphabet in which several sequences of letters are displaced by fixed positions, making the job of a cryptanalyst easier if he or she attempts to reconstruct the transposed alphabet used to encipher messages. To add a degree of difficulty to any reconstruction attempt, these alphabets are normally developed through the use of a keyword or keyword phrase.

Figure 4.2 illustrates the construction of a keyword-based alphabet fitted into a 7x4 matrix, using KEYWORD as the keyword. Similar to the keyword-based alphabets discussed in Chapter 3, Keyword-Based Monoalphabetic Substitution, you can use either a keyword or keyword phrase to develop a mixed alphabet. Then, by placing the resulting alphabet into a matrix you can develop a transposed keyword-based mixed alphabet. The construction of this alphabet is easy to duplicate, providing the message recipient with an easy mechanism for preparing to decipher a received message. In addition, using a keyword or keyword phrase adds an additional degree of difficulty to a cryptanalyst attempting to decipher a message that intentionally or unintentionally falls into his or her hands.

Figure 4.2 A keyword-based mixed alphabet placed into a matrix. In this example, the keyword KEYWORD was used to form the keyword-based mixed alphabet.

```
                        COLUMNS
                1   2   3   4   5   6   7

            1 | K   E   Y   W   O   R   D
ROWS        2 | A   B   C   F   G   H   I
            3 | J   L   M   N   P   Q   S
            4 | T   U   V   X   Z
```

In examining Figure 4.2, note that the keyword used is seven positions in length and defines the number of columns in the matrix. When developing the keyword-based mixed alphabet, remember to first remove any duplicate letters in the keyword or keyword phrase and then add the remaining letters of the alphabet that are not in the keyword or keyword phrase in the sequence in which they appear in the alphabet. For example, the keyword ALPHA would be reduced to ALPH to eliminate the duplicate A. This would result in the creation of a matrix with four columns.

Simple Transposition

There are several methods that can be used to develop a transposed keyword-based mixed alphabet. Perhaps the most obvious method, referred to as simple transposition, extracts column entries in their column order. The simple transposition of the keyword-based alphabet illustrated in Figure 4.2, in which the keyword is KEYWORD, produces the following keyword-based simple transposed alphabet: KAJTEBLUYCMVWFNXOGPZRHQDIS.

After you obtain the transposed alphabet, you can use it for the plaintext or ciphertext alphabet. In addition, you could create two different transposed alphabets and use one for the plaintext alphabet and the second for the ciphertext alphabet. The examples presented in this chapter restrict the use of transposed alphabets to the ciphertext alphabet.

Encipherment

Similar to previously described manual encipherment processes, you should list the plaintext alphabet above the ciphertext alphabet. For each character in the plaintext message, you would first locate that character in the plaintext alphabet and extract the corresponding character by position in the ciphertext alphabet. Figure 4.3 illustrates the encipherment of the first two characters of a plaintext message using the previously developed keyword-based simple transposed alphabet.

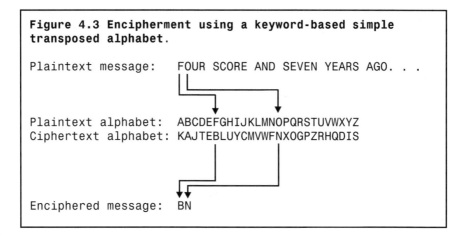

Figure 4.3 Encipherment using a keyword-based simple transposed alphabet.

Decipherment

The decipherment process can be considered the reverse of the previously illustrated encipherment process. That is, you would rearrange your sheet of paper to place the enciphered message at the top of the page. Next, you would list the ciphertext alphabet above the plaintext alphabet. Then, you would take each character in the enciphered message and locate it in the ciphertext alphabet, extracting the plaintext alphabet character in the equivalent position where the ciphertext character was located in the ciphertext alphabet.

Numeric Transposition

Another popular method used to develop a transposed alphabet through the use of a matrix involves the selection of rows based upon the alphabetic position of the character in the keyword. This technique is known as numeric transposition, because a numeric is normally assigned to each column based upon the location of the first character in the column relative to the characters in the adjusted keyword. The characters in each column are then extracted to form the transposed alphabet based upon the numeric value assigned to each column.

Figure 4.4 illustrates the construction of a numeric transposition-based alphabet using the keyword KEYWORD. Note that a numeric is first assigned to each column based upon the position of the first character in each column in the first row of characters. Simply extract the characters in each column based upon the numeric sequence of each column.

```
┌─────────────────────────────────────────────────────────────┐
│ Figure 4.4 Constructing a numeric transposition-based alphabet.│
│                                                               │
│                              COLUMNS                          │
│                     3   2   7   6   4   5   1                 │
│                    ─────────────────────────────             │
│              1  │   K   E   Y   W   O   R   D                 │
│       ROWS   2  │   A   B   C   F   G   H   I                 │
│              3  │   J   L   M   N   P   Q   S                 │
│              4  │   T   U   V   X   Z                         │
│                                                               │
│                                                               │
│       Resulting alphabet:                                     │
│           DISEBLUKAJTOGPZRHQWFNXYCMV                          │
└─────────────────────────────────────────────────────────────┘
```

Encipherment and Decipherment

After you create a numeric-based transposition alphabet, you can use that alphabet as the ciphertext alphabet. You can then encipher and decipher messages in the same manner as previously described for the simple transposition alphabet.

Other Variations

Once a keyword- or keyword phrase-based alphabet is placed into a matrix, you can use several additional extraction techniques to form a transposition alphabet. Other variations you can consider include reversed simple and reversed numeric transpositions as well as different diagonally formed transpositions. Because the simple and conventional numeric transpositions are the primary methods used for the formation of transposed alphabets, I'll leave it as an exercise for readers to develop other types of transposed alphabets.

The use of a matrix for enciphering messages provides a mechanism for supplementing or circumventing the use of more secure systems. During World War II, General Leslie Groves who was in charge of the Manhattan Project, which resulted in the development of the atomic bomb, needed a mechanism to discuss matters of high secrecy over the telephone. General Groves developed a series of 10x10 matrices in which each matrix contained both letters of the alphabet as well as code word characters that represented different laboratory or manufacturing sites.

To reduce the possibility of an overheard telephone conversation being analyzed, General Groves took two actions. First, he developed a different matrix for each person he needed to talk to concerning matters of national security. This reduced the potential effect of the loss of a matrix and made it more difficult for a series of overheard conversations to be analyzed. Secondly, within each matrix, General Groves located multiple copies of frequently occurring letters in the English language, such as the letters A, E, I, O, U, and T. The number of repetitions of a character depended upon the frequency of occurrence of the letter in the alphabet. For example, in one of the general's matrices, he included nine E's and seven T's. This technique considerably reduced the possibility and effectiveness of a frequency analysis being used to decipher an overheard conversation.

4

Chapter

Interval Extraction

The last technique discussed in this chapter that is used to create a program to automate its operation involves the extraction of characters from the plaintext alphabet based upon a predefined interval. As each letter in the alphabet is extracted, it is removed from the plaintext alphabet and entered into the interval extracted alphabet.

Figure 4.5 illustrates two examples of the formation of interval extracted alphabets based upon using an interval of three positions. In the example at the top portion of Figure 4.5, the interval 3 extraction process is applied against a sequential plaintext alphabet. In the example at the bottom of Figure 4.5, the interval 3 extraction process is applied against a keyword-based mixed alphabet using KEYWORD as the keyword. Note the significant differences between the resulting extracted alphabets even though the extraction interval was the same for each example.

```
Figure 4.5 Developing interval extracted alphabet.

Interval 3 extraction of plaintext alphabet
Plaintext alphabet:
    ABCDEFGHIJKLMNOPQRSTUVWXYZ
Resulting interval 3 extracted alphabet:
    CFILORUXAEJNSWBHPVDMYKZTGQ

Interval 3 extraction of keyword-based alphabet
Keyword-based alphabet:
    KEYWORDABCFGHIJLMNPQSTUVXZ
Resulting interval 3 extracted alphabet:
    YRBGJNSVKOCIPUEALTWHXFZQDM
```

Encipherment and Decipherment

Once an interval extracted alphabet is formed, it can be used in the same manner as previously described for the simple and numeric-based transposition alphabets. You could use the interval 3 extracted alphabet produced in Figure 4.5 as the ciphertext alphabet for enciphering a message as previously illustrated in Figure 4.3. Similarly, you can use that alphabet and its relationship to the plaintext alphabet to decipher an enciphered message.

Automating Matrix-Based Systems

Encipherment

To facilitate the automation process required to encipher messages based upon transposition-based mixed alphabets, you can create two new subroutines. One subroutine, which I'll label TRANSPORT, can be used to form either a simple or numeric transposition mixed alphabet sequence based upon the user's preference. The second subroutine, which I'll label INTERVAL, can be used to create an extracted alphabet based upon a pre-defined interval or position. After you create those two subroutines, you can add them to the previously created CIPHER5.BAS program and change the main portion of the program to permit the newly created sub-routines to be invoked. The resulting program, which I'll call CIPHER6.BAS, permits users to dynamically enter the name of the files they wish to use to store an input plaintext message as well as the result-ing enciphered message.

The TRANSPORT Subroutine

Listing 4.1 shows the contents of the subroutine labeled TRANSPORT, which creates either a simple or numeric transposition mixed sequence alphabet. This subroutine includes several unnecessary PRINT statements to illustrate how the program operates. Similar to the previous use of extraneous PRINT statements, I have identified those statements with comments consisting of five asterisks to facilitate their removal.

Listing 4.1 The TRANSPORT subroutine.

```
TRANSPORT:
        REM Routine to form simple or numeric transposition mixed sequence
        REM Initialize 26 by 26 matrix to nulls
                POSITION = 0
                FOR I = 0 TO 26
                FOR J = 0 TO 16
                TRANS$(I, J) = ""
                NEXT J, I
        REM Determine actual matrix size
                COLUMN = LEN(KEYCOL$)
                ROW = 26 / COLUMN - INT(26 / COLUMN)
                IF ROW > 0 THEN ROW = (INT(26 / COLUMN) + 1) ELSE ROW = 26
                        / COLUMN
        REM Place keyword-based alphabet into matrix elements
                PRINT "MATRIX IS:": PRINT
                FOR I = 0 TO ROW - 1
                FOR J = 0 TO COLUMN - 1
                IF POSITION > 25 THEN GOTO ALLDONE
                TRANS$(I, J) = PLAINTEXT$(POSITION)
                PRINT TRANS$(I, J);                    '*****
                POSITION = POSITION + 1
                NEXT J
```

```
                    PRINT                              '*****
ALLDONE:            NEXT I
                    PRINT : PRINT                  '*****
            IF ORDER$ = "NUMERIC" GOTO NUMERIC
            REM Form simple transposition-based mixed alphabet
                    X$ = ""
                    FOR I = 0 TO COLUMN - 1
                    FOR J = 0 TO ROW - 1
                    X$ = X$ + LTRIM$(TRANS$(J, I))
                    NEXT J
                    NEXT I
            REM Place into PLAINTEXT array
                    FOR I = 0 TO 25
                    PLAINTEXT$(I) = MID$(X$, I + 1, 1)
                    NEXT I
            RETURN
            REM Form numeric transposition-based mixed alphabet
NUMERIC:            FOR I = 0 TO COLUMN - 1
                    TEMP$(I) = TRANS$(0, I)'place in temporary storage first row
                    NEXT I
                    FOR I = 0 TO COLUMN - 1'begin sort
                    FOR J = I + 1 TO COLUMN - 1
                    IF TEMP$(I) > TEMP$(J) THEN SWAP TEMP$(I), TEMP$(J)
                    NEXT J
                    NEXT I   'TEMP$ array now contains sorted order of characters
            REM  Compare sorted keyword to first column in matrix, extract
            REM  when they match by getting row contents
                    X$ = ""
                    FOR I = 0 TO COLUMN - 1'
                    FOR J = 0 TO COLUMN - 1
                    IF TEMP$(I) <> TRANS$(0, J) GOTO NMATCH
                    FOR K = 0 TO ROW - 1           'match, get row contents
                    X$ = X$ + LTRIM$(TRANS$(K, J))
                    NEXT K
NMATCH:             NEXT J
                    NEXT I
            REM Place into PLAINTEXT array
                    FOR I = 0 TO 25
                    PLAINTEXT$(I) = MID$(X$, I + 1, 1)
                    NEXT I
RETURN
```

The first group of statements in the subroutine TRANSPORT initializes a
26x26 string matrix labeled TRANS$ to nulls. This matrix permits a keyword

or keyword phrase that can be up to 26 characters in length. The second group of statements determines the actual size of the matrix. Here, the value of COLUMN is the length of the keyword in characters. Thus, a keyword consisting of five characters would require a matrix of five columns and six rows for all 26 letters of the alphabet to fit into the matrix.

The third group of statements places the characters of a keyword-based alphabet into the string array TRANS$. Note that the values for the indices for the nested FOR-NEXT loops are adjusted by subtracting 1 from the values of ROW and COLUMN because the matrix elements commence at position 0,0. Also, note values are assigned to TRANS$ from the string array PLAINTEXT$. The array PLAINTEXT$ contains the keyword developed alphabet which was filled by the prior invoking of the previously described KEYWORD subroutine. You must invoke KEYWORD prior to invoking TRANSPORT. To facilitate passing information to determine the number of columns in the matrix, the statement KEYCOL$=X$ was added to the end of the third group of statements in the KEYWORD subroutine.

4

Chapter

The PRINT statements included in the third group of statements simply display the matrix for your review and will be removed from the subroutine later in this chapter. The IF statement permits the selection of a simple or numeric-based mixed alphabet. If the string variable ORDER$ does not equal "NUMERIC," the simple transposition-based mixed alphabet is formed. This occurs in the fourth statement group which simply adds each character in every row of each column to the string X$ in column sequence. The resulting simple transposition-based mixed alphabet is placed into the string array PLAINTEXT$ and the subroutine ends.

If the user wants a numeric transposition-based mixed alphabet, a branch to the label NUMERIC in the subroutine occurs. At this location, the first character in each column is placed into temporary storage in the string array TEMP$. Next, the contents of TEMP$ are sorted, resulting in that array containing the characters of the keyword in sorted order. This is followed by another group of statements which cycles through the elements of the TEMP$ array. Each element of that array is matched against the first character in each column of the TRANS$ array. When a match occurs, the contents of the column are extracted and added to the string X$, which results in the formation of a numeric transposition mixed sequence alphabet. The last group of statements places the resulting alphabet into the string array PLAINTEXT$.

Listing 4.2 illustrates the modified calling sequence used to invoke the subroutine TRANSPORT. This calling sequence will display the formed matrix, ciphertext alphabet, and plaintext alphabet to enable you to verify the operation of the subroutine. To enable you to use the calling sequence and the TRANSPORT subroutine, the code has been stored on a file labeled CIPHERTR.BAS on the companion CD. The PRINT statements that display the matrix and alphabets will be removed when you develop the program CIPHER6.BAS.

Listing 4.2 The main part of CIPHERTR.BAS and the calling sequence to invoke the TRANSPORT subroutine.

```
REM PROGRAM CIPHERTR.BAS
DIM PLAINTEXT$(26), CIPHERTEXT$(26), KEY$(26), TRANS$(26, 26), TEMP$(26)
        CLS
        PRINT "PROGRAM CIPHERTR.BAS enciphers a message using a
                transposition matrix"
        PRINT "and a monoalphabetic substitution process based upon a
                keyword "
        PRINT "or keyword phrase and an alphabetic shift key."
        PRINT
GOSUB INITIALIZE
        INPUT "Enter keyword or keyword phrase in UPPERCASE: ", TEXT$
        PRINT "Plaintext based alphabet is    : ";          '*****
        FOR I = 0 TO 25: PRINT PLAINTEXT$(I); : NEXT I      '*****
GOSUB KEYWORD                  'form keyword-based mixed alphabet
        PRINT "Keyword-based alphabet is      : "; X$       '*****
        INPUT "Enter transposition matrix method - SIMPLE or NUMERIC :",
ORDER$
GOSUB TRANSPORT
        PRINT ORDER$; " Transposition Alphabet is         :"; X$
1       INPUT "Enter UPPERCASE Alphabetic Shift Key: ", K$
        FOR I = 0 TO 25
        IF K$ = PLAINTEXT$(I) GOTO 2
        NEXT I
        PRINT "You must enter a letter from A to Z"
        GOTO 1
2       REM Position I represents shift key letter

GOSUB FORMCIPHER              'create cipher alphabet
        PRINT "Shifted keyword mixed alphabet is           : ";        '*****
        FOR I = 0 TO 25: PRINT CIPHERTEXT$(I); : NEXT I: PRINT        '*****
```

```
GOSUB INITIALIZE        'reinitialize plaintext array
GOSUB MSGFILE           'assign I/O files, place message on a file
GOSUB CONVERTSTORE      'convert and store ciphertext on a file
GOSUB PRTOUT            'print results
STOP
```

The CIPHERTR.BAS Program

Figure 4.6 illustrates the execution of the program CIPHERTR.BAS to encipher a message based upon the use of a simple transposition mixed
sequence alphabet and an alphabetic shift key. This example uses the keyword KEYWORD and the alphabetic shift character C. Note the display of
the 4-row-by-7-column matrix formed by the TRANSPORT subroutine.
Because a simple transposition method was selected, the letters in the
matrix are extracted in column order, KAJT followed by EBLU, and so on.
This is verified by the line after the end of the matrix display.

4

Chapter

**Figure 4.6 The execution of CIPHERTR.BAS program using a simple
transposition keyword mixed alphabet.**

```
Program CIPHERTR.BAS enciphers a message using a transposition
matrix and a monoalphabetic substitution process based on a
keyword or keyword phrase and an alphabetic shift key.
Enter keyword or keyword phrase in UPPERCASE: KEYWORD
Plaintext-based alphabet is: ABCDEFGHIJKLMNOPQRSTUVWXYZ
Keyword-based alphabet is: KEYWORDABCFGHIJLMNPQSTUVXZ
Enter transposition matrix method - SIMPLE OR NUMERIC: SIMPLE
MATRIX IS:

KEYWORD
ABCFGHI
JLMNPQS
TUVXZ


SIMPLE Transposition Alphabet is: KAJTEBLUYCMVWFNXOGPZRHQDIS
Enter UPPERCASE Alphabetic Shift Key: C
Shifted keyword mixed alphabet is: MVWFNXOGPZRHQDISKAJTEBLUYC
Enter filename to store plaintext message, default=MESSAGE.DAT
Enter filename to store enciphered message, default=CIPHERTX.DAT
Select keyboard (k) or file (f) message input: K
Enter your message - place a / at the beginning of each line that
should remain in plaintext and a \ on a separate line to indicate
the end of the enciphered message
```

```
/TO: BILL
/FROM: AL
MEET ME IN ST LOUIS ON FRIDAY FEBRUARY
THIRTEEN AT NINE PM
\
Press Return key to display resulting enciphered message

Resulting enciphered message is:
TO: BILL
FROM: AL
QNNTQ NPDJT HIEPJ IDXAP FMYXN
VAEMA YTGPA TNNDM TDPDN SQXXX
```

As in previous examples, an alphabetic shift key character results in the shift of a previously developed alphabet so that the position of the shift key letter is rotated to the right of the alphabet. Entering the shift key C rotates the simple transposition alphabet by ten positions.

The plaintext alphabet should be compared to the shifted keyword mixed alphabet for the encipherment of a message, because the latter alphabet is the ciphertext alphabet. In this example the message to be enciphered is MEET ME IN ST LOUIS ON FRIDAY FEBRUARY THIRTEEN AT NINE PM. The M in the plaintext alphabet corresponds to the letter Q in the shifted keyword mixed alphabet. Thus, the first character in the enciphered message is Q. The character E in the message is located in the plaintext alphabet. Because its position corresponds to the position of the character N in the shifted keyword mixed alphabet, replace E with N and continue the process to verify the operation of the portion of the program which enciphers a message based upon a simple transposition mixed alphabet and alphabetic shift key.

Figure 4.7 illustrates the execution of the program CIPHERTR.BAS when a numeric transposition mixed alphabet was selected. Because D is the lowest character in the keyword KEYWORD, the characters in the column headed by D are extracted first. Thus, DIS are the first three letters displayed for the numeric transposition alphabet. Because E is the next lowest letter in the keyword, the contents of the column headed by E are added to the alphabet. Thus, EBLU follows the characters DIS. You can examine the remainder of Figure 4.7 to verify that the message is indeed enciphered correctly by using the relationship between the plaintext and shifted keyword mixed alphabets displayed in that illustration.

```
Figure 4.7 The execution of CIPHERTR.BAS program using a numeric
transposition keyword mixed alphabet.

Program CIPHERTR.BAS enciphers a message using a transposition
matrix and a monoalphabetic substitution process based on a
keyword or keyword phrase and an alphabetic shift key.
Enter keyword or keyword phrase in UPPERCASE: KEYWORD
Plaintext-based alphabet is: ABCDEFGHIJKLMNOPQRSTUVWXYZ
Keyword-based alphabet is: KEYWORDABCFGHIJLMNPQSTUVXZ
Enter transposition matrix method - SIMPLE OR NUMERIC: NUMERIC
MATRIX IS:

KEYWORD
ABCFGHI
JLMNPQS
TUVXZ

NUMERIC Transposition Alphabet is: DISEBLUKAJTOGPZRHQWFNXYCMV
Enter UPPERCASE Alphabetic Shift Key: C
Shifted keyword mixed alphabet is: MVDISEBLUKAJTOGPZRHQWFNXYC
Enter filename to store plaintext message, default=MESSAGE.DAT
Enter filename to store enciphered message, default=CIPHERTX.DAT
Select keyboard (k) or file (f) message input: K
Enter your message - place a / at the beginning of each line that
should remain in plaintext and a \ on a separate line to indicate
the end of the enciphered message

/TO: BILL
/FROM: AL
MEET ME IN ST LOUIS ON FRIDAY FEBRUARY
THIRTEEN AT NINE PM
\
Press Return key to display resulting enciphered message

Resulting enciphered message is:
TO: BILL
FROM: AL
TSSQT SUOHQ JGWUH GOERU IMYES
VRWMR YQLUR QSOM  QOUOS PTXX
```

The INTERVAL Subroutine

Listing 4.3 contains the contents of the subroutine INTERVAL, which
forms an interval extracted alphabet based upon a predefined interval.
That interval is passed to the subroutine in the variable INTERVAL.

Listing 4.3 The INTERVAL subroutine used to form an interval extracted alphabet.

```
INTERVAL:
        REM Subroutine to form interval extracted alphabet
        COUNT = 0
        I = INTERVAL - 1  'adjust since array starts at 0
        X$ = ""
        DO UNTIL COUNT >= 26
                X$ = X$ + PLAINTEXT$(I)
                COUNT = COUNT + 1
                I = I + INTERVAL
                IF I >= 26 THEN I = I - 26
        LOOP
        REM Put back into PLAINTEXT$ array
        FOR I = 0 TO 25
        PLAINTEXT$(I) = MID$(X$, I + 1, 1)
        NEXT I
RETURN
```

Note in Listing 4.3 that the interval value is decreased by 1 since the array starts at element 0. The DO UNTIL COUNT loop extracts each character from the string array PLAINTEXT$ until all of the characters are extracted. Note that whenever I equals or exceeds 26, you should reset I to I-26. This recirculates the sequence. Also note that since you are using the string array PLAINTEXT$, you must invoke the subroutine KEYWORD prior to invoking the subroutine INTERVAL if you wish to use an interval extraction based upon a keyword mixed alphabet. Similar to the TRANSPORT subroutine, conclude the INTERVAL subroutine by placing the interval extracted alphabet back into the array PLAINTEXT$.

The TRANSPORT.CPP Program

Prior to developing the program CIPHER6 that will encipher messages based upon any one of the three alphabetic formation techniques previously presented in this chapter, let's turn our attention to C++ coding of the subroutine TRANSPORT and the program CIPHERTR. The C++ versions of both are included on the CD-ROM in the C directory as both source and executable files.

Listing 4.4 lists the statements in the C++ version of TRANSPORT, which is stored on the CD-ROM under the filename TRANSPORT.CPP. The executable version of TRANSPORT.CPP is stored on the CD-ROM in the C directory under the filename TRANSPORT.EXE.

Listing 4.4 The TRANSPORT.CPP program listing.

```
/*
transport.cpp
C++ code written by Jonathan Held using Microsoft Visual C++, version
5.0, on March 21, 1998.
*/

//standard include files
#include<iostream.h>
#include<assert.h>
#include<string.h>
#include<ctype.h>

//function prototypes
bool checkInput(char * &);
void createCipherStream(char *, char[]);
void createMatrix(char ** &, const char [], const int, const int);
int findLowestValue(int *&, const int);
int getKeyword(char *&);
void printMatrix(char ** &, const int, const int);
void reviseCipherStream(char **&, char [], const int, const int);
void deleteMatrix(char **&, const int, const int);

//constants we will use
const int TWENTYFIVE = 25, TWENTYSIX = 26,
          TWENTYSEVEN = 27, SIXTYFIVE = 65, NINETY = 90,
          NINETYTWO = 92, SIZE = 256;

//-----------------------------------------------------------------
//Function: main()
//Parameters: None
//Return Type: int - 0 execution is normal, 1 abnormal termination
//Purpose: Runs the main part of the program.
//-----------------------------------------------------------------
int main()
{
    char plaintext[TWENTYSEVEN] = {'A','B','C','D','E','F','G','H',
                                   'I','J','K','L','M','N','O','P',
                                   'Q','R','S','T','U','V','W','X',
                                   'Y','Z', '\0'};
```

```
char cipherStream[TWENTYSEVEN] = {'\0'};
char ** cMatrix;
char *keyword;
int rows, columns;

//get the keyword we are going to use, determine number of rows
//and columns of our matrix
columns = getKeyword(keyword);
rows = TWENTYSIX/columns;

//integer division requires that we check and see if there is a
//remainder; if so, we need to add one extra row to our matrix
if (TWENTYSIX%columns){
    rows++;
}

//create the initial ciphertext stream
createCipherStream(keyword, cipherStream);

//insert the stream into our matrix
createMatrix(cMatrix, cipherStream, rows, columns);

reviseCipherStream(cMatrix, cipherStream, rows, columns);


//echo to the user what we have
cout << "\nPlaintext-based alphabet is: " << plaintext << endl
     << "Keyword-based alphabet is:   " << cipherStream << endl << endl;

//delete the dynamically allocated matrix
deleteMatrix(cMatrix, rows, columns);

delete keyword;

return 0;
}//end main()



//----------------------------------------------------------------
//Function: checkInput()
//Parameters: input - the keyword the user entered
//Return Type: bool - true if the input string contains an error,
//                    false otherwise
//Purpose: Checks the user's keyword for invalid characters.
```

```
//-----------------------------------------------------------------
bool checkInput(char * &input)
{
   bool error = false;
   int count = strlen(input);

   for (int ix=0; ix<count; ix++){

      int char_value = static_cast<int>(*(input+ix));
      //determine if the user did not enter an uppercase character
      if ((char_value < SIXTYFIVE) || (char_value > NINETY)){
         error = true;
         cerr << "You entered an invalid keyword!" << endl << endl;
         break;
      }
   }

   return error;
}//end checkInput()


//-----------------------------------------------------------------
//Function: createCipherStream()
//Parameters: input - the keyword the user entered
//            cipher - the keyword alphabet that will be constructed
//Return Type: None
//Purpose: Creates a preliminary cipher stream that will be used to
//form the cipher matrix.
//-----------------------------------------------------------------
void createCipherStream(char *input, char stream[])
{
   bool used[TWENTYSIX];
   int index = 0,
       count = strlen(input);

   //no characters are initially used
   for (int ix=0; ix<TWENTYSIX; ix++){
      used[ix] = false;
   }

   //keep track of each character used, start forming the keyword
   //alphabet
   for (int jx=0; jx<count; jx++){
```

```
         //get each character of the input string (integer value)
         int char_value = static_cast<int>(*(input+jx));

         if (used[char_value-SIXTYFIVE]){
            //do nothing - the character was already used
         }
         else {
            //mark as used and add to the keyword alphabet
            used[char_value-SIXTYFIVE] = true;
            *(stream+index++) = static_cast<char>(char_value);
         }
      }

      //go through the list of characters used - those which weren't
      //used should be added to the keyword alphabet
      for (int kx=0; kx<TWENTYSIX; kx++){

         if (!(used[kx])){
            *(stream+index++) = static_cast<char>(SIXTYFIVE+kx);
         }
      }

      return;
}//end createCipherStream()


//----------------------------------------------------------------
//Function: createMatrix()
//Parameters: matrix - the matrix we are going to create
//            CSTREAM - the initial cipher stream based on the
//                         user's keyword
//            ROWS - the number of rows in the matrix
//            COLS - the number of columns in the matrix
//Return Type: None
//Purpose: Creates a numeric key transposed matrix, identical to
//figure 4.4.
//----------------------------------------------------------------
void createMatrix(char ** &matrix, const char CSTREAM[], const int ROWS,
                  const int COLS)
{
   int count = 0;

   //dynamically allocate memory for the RxC matrix
   //we use assert to ensure that memory was allocated;
```

```
   //if not, then the program will terminate abnormally
   assert(matrix = new char*[ROWS]);
   for (int ix=0; ix<ROWS; ix++){
      *(matrix + ix) = new char[COLS];
   }

   //fill in the matrix
   for (int jx=0; jx<ROWS; jx++){
      for (int kx=0; kx<COLS; kx++){
      //we only want to enter a character into the matrix
      //twenty-six times - most of the time we allocate
      //a matrix larger than what we will need to use; when
      //we have more than 26 characters, we simply insert a
      //null terminator into the matrix
         if (count < TWENTYSIX)
            *(*(matrix+jx)+kx) = CSTREAM[count++];
      else
            *(*(matrix+jx)+kx) = '\0';
      }
   }

   //print the resulting matrix
   printMatrix(matrix, ROWS, COLS);

   return;
}//end createMatrix()


//-----------------------------------------------------------------
//Function: deleteMatrix()
//Parameters: matrix - the matrix we are going to destroy
//            R - the number of rows in the matrix
//            C - the number of columns in the matrix
//Return Type: None
//Purpose: Destroys the dynamically allocated matrix!
//-----------------------------------------------------------------
void deleteMatrix(char **&matrix, const int R, const int C)
{
   for (int ix=0; ix<R; ix++)
      delete [] *(matrix+ix);

   delete [] matrix;

   return;
```

```
}//end deleteMatrix()



//-----------------------------------------------------------------
//Function: findLowestValue()
//Parameters: values - the ASCII values of all characters in the
//                      top row of the matrix
//            COLS - the number of columns in the matrix
//Return Type: int - the column we want.
//Purpose: Determines what column we are going to extract from
//the matrix and put into the cipher stream.
//-----------------------------------------------------------------
int findLowestValue(int *&values, const int COLS)
{
    int loc=0, lowest=999;

    for (int ix = 0; ix < COLS; ix++){
       if (*(values+ix) != 999){
          if (*(values+ix) < lowest){
             lowest = *(values+ix);
             loc = ix;
          }
       }
    }

    *(values+loc) = 999;

    return loc;
}//end findLowestValue()



//-----------------------------------------------------------------
//Function: getKeyword()
//Parameters: text - the keyword that the user enters
//Return Type: int - the length of the keyword
//Purpose: Prompts the user for a keyword and continues until
//a valid keyword has been entered.  Returns the length of the
//keyword.
//-----------------------------------------------------------------
int getKeyword(char * &text)
{
    bool error = false;
    char buffer[SIZE];
```

```
        do {
           cout << "Enter keyword or keyword phrase in UPPERCASE" << endl
                 << "do not use spaces or non-alphabetic characters): ";

           cin.getline(buffer, SIZE, '\n');
           assert(text = new char[strlen(buffer) + 1]);
           strcpy(text, buffer);

           error = checkInput(text);

           //delete text if there was an error
           if (error){
              delete [] text;
           }

        } while (error);

        cout << endl;

        return strlen(buffer);
}//end getKeyword()


//------------------------------------------------------------------
//Function: printMatrix()
//Parameters: the_matrix - the matrix we want to display
//             ROWS - the number of rows in the matrix
//             COLS - the number of columns in the matrix
//Return Type: None
//Purpose: Displays the matrix.
//------------------------------------------------------------------
void printMatrix(char ** &the_matrix, const int ROWS, const int COLUMNS)
{
    cout << "The matrix is:" << endl << endl;

    for (int ix=0; ix<ROWS; ix++){

        for (int kx=0; kx<COLUMNS; kx++){
            cout << *(*(the_matrix+ix)+kx) << " ";
        }

        cout << endl;
    }
```

```
         return;
}//end printMatrix()


//------------------------------------------------------------------
//Function: reviseCipherStream()
//Parameters: MATRIX - the numeric keyed transposed matrix
//            cipher - the cipher stream that was originally created
//                     when the user entered a keyword
//            R - the number of rows in the matrix
//            C - the number of columns in the matrix
//Return Type: None
//Purpose: Overwrites the cipher stream initially created with the
//one we get by taking columns out of the matrix.
//------------------------------------------------------------------
void reviseCipherStream(char ** &MATRIX, char cipher[], const int R,
                        const int C)
{
    bool done = false;
    int counter = 0;

    //place ASCII values of first row's characters into a table;
    //we will use these values to determine the order in which
    //we pull columns out of the matrix
    int *top_row_ASCII_values = new int[C];
    assert(top_row_ASCII_values);

    //no cast to integer type required since this is already taken
    //care of for us
    for (int ix=0; ix<C; ix++){
        *(top_row_ASCII_values + ix) = *((*MATRIX)+ix);
    }

    for (int jx=0; jx<C; jx++){

        //find out what column we want
        int col = findLowestValue(top_row_ASCII_values, C);

        //put contents of the column into the cipher stream, but
        //only do this when we have a character!
        for (int kx=0; kx<R; kx++){
            if ((*(*(MATRIX+kx)+col)) != '\0'){
                cipher[counter++] = (*(*(MATRIX+kx)+col));
            }
```

```
      }
   }

   //destroy dynamically allocated memory
   delete [] top_row_ASCII_values;

   return;
}//end reviseCipherStream()
//end file transport.cpp
```

In examining the TRANSPORT.CPP listing shown in Listing 4.4, note that the function createMatrix is used to create a numeric key transposed matrix which is identical to Figure 4.4. This subroutine dynamically allocates memory based upon the rows and columns. Note that the function deleteMatrix is included in the program to remove any previously allocated matrix. This is good programming practice.

Two additional functions that warrant a bit of attention are findLowestValue and reviseCipherStream. The function findLowestValue is used to determine the column that is going to be used for extraction and placed into the cipher stream, while the function reviseCipherStream is used to overwrite the cipher stream initially created with the one obtained by taking columns out of the matrix.

The CIPHERTR.CPP Program

Listing 4.5 lists the statements in the C++ program CIPHERTR.CPP, which provides a similar capability to CIPHERTR.BAS. That is, this program enciphers a message based upon the use of a simple transposition mixed-sequence alphabet and an alphabet shift key. Although the listing is lengthy and the program is included on the CD-ROM, it is included in its entirety here as doing so provides you with the ability to note the relationship between functions and the order by which they are invoked. Due to the extensive documentation contained within the program listing, it is left for you to examine the listing and the remarks which illustrate how the program operates.

Listing 4.5 The CIPHERTR.CPP program listing.

```
/*
ciphertr.cpp
C++ code written by Jonathan Held
using Microsoft Visual C++, version 5.0, on March 23, 1998.
```

```
*/

//standard include files
#include<iostream.h>
#include<assert.h>
#include<string.h>
#include<ctype.h>
#include<fstream.h>

//function prototypes
bool checkInput(char * &);
void createCipherStream(char *, char[]);
void createMatrix(char ** &, const char [], const int, const int);
void display(char *);
bool encryptText(char *, char *, const char [], const char[], char []);
void deleteMatrix(char **&, const int, const int);
int findLowestValue(int *&, const int);
void formatData(char []);
char* formCipheredMessage(const char[], const char [], char []);
void getFileNames(char *&, char *&);
int getInputType(void);
int getKeyword(char *&);
bool getMessage(char*, char*, char [], const char[], const char[]);
void getShiftKey(char &);
void groupBUFFER(ofstream, int);
void numericExtraction(char **&, char [], const int, const int);
void printCipherToFile(ofstream, char[]);
void printMatrix(char ** &, const int, const int);
void reviseCipherStream(char **&, char [], const int, const int);
void shiftKeyword(char [], const char);
void simpleExtraction(char **&, char [], const int, const int);
int typeOfExtraction(void);

//constants we will use
const int FIVE = 5, TWENTYFIVE = 25, TWENTYSIX = 26,
        TWENTYSEVEN = 27, SIXTYFIVE = 65, NINETY = 90,
        NINETYTWO = 92, SIZE = 256, BIGSIZE = 1000;

char BUFFER[BIGSIZE] = {'\0'};
//-----------------------------------------------------------------
//Function: main()
//Parameters: None
//Return Type: int - 0 execution is normal, 1 abnormal termination
//Purpose: Runs the main part of the program.
```

```
//-----------------------------------------------------------------
int main()
{
   char plaintext[TWENTYSEVEN] = {'A','B','C','D','E','F','G','H',
                                  'I','J','K','L','M','N','O','P',
                                  'Q','R','S','T','U','V','W','X',
                                  'Y','Z', '\0'};

   char cipherStream[TWENTYSEVEN] = {'\0'};
   char message_to_cipher[SIZE], enciphered_message[SIZE];

   char ** cMatrix;
   char *keyword, key, *infile, *outfile;
   int rows, columns, input_type;
   bool success;

   //get the keyword we are going to use, determine number of rows
   //and columns of our matrix
   columns = getKeyword(keyword);
   rows = TWENTYSIX/columns;

   //integer division requires that we check and see if there is a
   //remainder; if so, we need to add one extra row to our matrix
   if (TWENTYSIX%columns){
      rows++;
   }

   //create the initial ciphertext stream
   createCipherStream(keyword, cipherStream);

   //echo to the user what we have
   cout << "Plaintext-based alphabet is: " << plaintext << endl
        << "Keyword-based alphabet is:   " << cipherStream << endl << endl;

   //insert the stream into our matrix
   createMatrix(cMatrix, cipherStream, rows, columns);

   reviseCipherStream(cMatrix, cipherStream, rows, columns);

   getShiftKey(key);
   shiftKeyword(cipherStream, key);

   getFileNames(infile, outfile);
```

4

Chapter

```
   //query the user as to whether we are deciphering keyboard
   //or file input
   input_type = getInputType();

   //process file input
   if (input_type){
      success = encryptText(infile, outfile, plaintext, cipherStream,
               enciphered_message);
   }
   else {
      cout << "Use a \'/\' to leave a line in plaintext." << endl
           << "Use a \'\\' to indicate end of message input. " << endl;
      success = getMessage(infile, outfile, message_to_cipher, plaintext,
cipherStream);
   }

   //report success of operation
   if (!success){
      cerr << "Error: Invalid filename specified. Goodbye." << endl;
   }
   else {
      cout << "Press return to display resulting enciphered message."
               << endl;
      //get the newlines off the current input stream
      cin.get();
      if (input_type == 1){
         cin.get();
      }
      display(outfile);
   }

   //delete the dynamically allocated matrix
   deleteMatrix(cMatrix, rows, columns);

   delete keyword;

   return (!success);
}//end main()


//----------------------------------------------------------------
//Function: checkInput()
//Parameters: input - the keyword the user entered
//Return Type: bool - true if the input string contains an error,
```

```
//              false otherwise
//Purpose: Checks the user's keyword for invalid characters.
//------------------------------------------------------------------
bool checkInput(char * &input)
{
   bool error = false;
   int count = strlen(input);

   for (int ix=0; ix<count; ix++){

      int char_value = static_cast<int>(*(input+ix));
      //determine if the user did not enter an uppercase character
      if ((char_value < SIXTYFIVE) || (char_value > NINETY)){
         error = true;
         cerr << "You entered an invalid keyword!" << endl << endl;
         break;
      }
   }

   return error;
}//end checkInput()


//------------------------------------------------------------------
//Function: createCipherStream()
//Parameters: input - the keyword the user entered
//            cipher - the keyword alphabet that will be constructed
//Return Type: None
//Purpose: Creates a preliminary cipher stream that will be used to
//form the cipher matrix.
//------------------------------------------------------------------
void createCipherStream(char *input, char stream[])
{
   bool used[TWENTYSIX];
   int index = 0,
       count = strlen(input);

   //no characters are initially used
   for (int ix=0; ix<TWENTYSIX; ix++){
      used[ix] = false;
   }

   //keep track of each character used, start forming the keyword
   //alphabet
```

```
    for (int jx=0; jx<count; jx++){

        //get each character of the input string (integer value)
        int char_value = static_cast<int>(*(input+jx));

        if (used[char_value-SIXTYFIVE]){
            //do nothing - the character was already used
        }
        else {
            //mark as used and add to the keyword alphabet
            used[char_value-SIXTYFIVE] = true;
            *(stream+index++) = static_cast<char>(char_value);
        }
    }

    //go through the list of characters used - those which weren't
    //used should be added to the keyword alphabet
    for (int kx=0; kx<TWENTYSIX; kx++){

        if (!(used[kx])){
            *(stream+index++) = static_cast<char>(SIXTYFIVE+kx);
        }
    }

    return;
}//end createCipherStream()


//------------------------------------------------------------------
//Function: createMatrix()
//Parameters: matrix - the matrix we are going to create
//            CSTREAM - the initial cipher stream based on the
//                      user's keyword
//            ROWS - the number of rows in the matrix
//            COLS - the number of columns in the matrix
//Return Type: None
//Purpose: Creates a numeric key transposed matrix, identical to
//figure 4.4.
//------------------------------------------------------------------
void createMatrix(char ** &matrix, const char CSTREAM[], const int ROWS,
                  const int COLS)
{
    int count = 0;
```

```
   //dynamically allocate memory for the RxC matrix
   //we use assert to ensure that memory was allocated;
   //if not, then the program will terminate abnormally
   assert(matrix = new char*[ROWS]);
   for (int ix=0; ix<ROWS; ix++){
      *(matrix + ix) = new char[COLS];
   }

   //fill in the matrix
   for (int jx=0; jx<ROWS; jx++){
      for (int kx=0; kx<COLS; kx++){
      //we only want to enter a character into the matrix
      //twenty-six times - most of the time we allocate
      //a matrix larger than what we will need to use; when
      //we have more than 26 characters, we simply insert a
      //null terminator into the matrix
         if (count < TWENTYSIX)
            *(*(matrix+jx)+kx) = CSTREAM[count++];
      else
            *(*(matrix+jx)+kx) = '\0';
      }
   }

   return;
}//end createMatrix()


//------------------------------------------------------------------
//Function: encryptText()
//Parameters:  inp_file - the name of the input plaintext file
//          outp_file - the name of the output ciphertext file
//          PTEXT[] - the plaintext alphabet
//          CTEXT[] - the ciphertext alphabet
//          encoded_msg[] - the message to be encoded
//Return Type: bool, indicating success of operation
//Purpose: Used to encrypt file input.  Takes each line of the input
//file, encrypts it, and saves the result to the specified output
//file.
//------------------------------------------------------------------
bool encryptText(char * inp_file, char * outp_file, const char PTEXT[],
                const char CTEXT[], char encoded_msg[])
{
   bool success = false;
```

```
        char ip[SIZE];

        //declare file stream objects
        ifstream input(inp_file, ios::in);
        ofstream output(outp_file, ios::app);

        if ((!input) || (!output)){
           //do nothing - I/O error; user will be notified upon
           //procedure's return to main()
        }
        else {

           success = true;

           //print plaintext and ciphertext alphabets to the
           //output file
           output << "PLAINTEXT:  " << PTEXT << endl;
           output << "CIPHERTEXT: " << CTEXT << endl << endl;

           while (input.getline(ip, BIGSIZE, '\n')){

              //check to see if the user wants the line to appear in plain text
              if (ip[0] == '/'){

                 if (strlen(BUFFER)>0){

                 //empty whatever is in the buffer
                 groupBUFFER(output, strlen(BUFFER));
                 //adjust the buffer
                 strcpy(BUFFER, (BUFFER+strlen(BUFFER)));
                 //output plaintext
                 }

              output << ip << endl;

              }
              else {
                 //encipher the line
                 char *msg = formCipheredMessage(CTEXT, ip, encoded_msg);
                 //print the cipher in groups of five to the ouput file
                 printCipherToFile(output, msg);
              }
           }
```

```
        //empty the rest of the buffer
        groupBUFFER(output, strlen(BUFFER));
        //notify user where plaintext and ciphertext files are
        cout << "Plaintext file is: " << inp_file << endl;
        cout << "Encrypted file is: " << outp_file << endl << endl;
    }

    //don't forget to close the files
    input.close();
    output.close();

    //return success of the operation
    return success;
}//end encryptText()


//------------------------------------------------------------------
//Function: deleteMatrix()
//Parameters: matrix - the matrix we are going to destroy
//            R - the number of rows in the matrix
//            C - the number of columns in the matrix
//Return Type: None
//Purpose: Destroys the dynamically allocated matrix!
//------------------------------------------------------------------
void deleteMatrix(char **&matrix, const int R, const int C)
{
    for (int ix=0; ix<R; ix++)
        delete [] *(matrix+ix);

    delete [] matrix;

    return;
}//end deleteMatrix()


//------------------------------------------------------------------
//Function: display()
//Parameters: name - the name of the file the user wants displayed
//Return Type: None
//Purpose: Echoes the resulting output file to the screen.
//------------------------------------------------------------------
void display(char *name)
{
    ifstream infile(name, ios::in);
```

```
        char input[SIZE];

        if (!(infile)){
           cerr << "Unable to open input file for display." << endl;
        }
        else {
           while (infile.getline(input, SIZE, '\n')){
              cout << input << endl;
           }
        }

        return;
}//end display()


//------------------------------------------------------------------
//Function: findLowestValue()
//Parameters: values - the ASCII values of all characters in the
//                     top row of the matrix
//            COLS - the number of columns in the matrix
//Return Type: int - the column we want.
//Purpose: Determines what column we are going to extract from
//the matrix and put into the cipher stream.
//------------------------------------------------------------------
int findLowestValue(int *&values, const int COLS)
{
        int loc=0, lowest=999;

        for (int ix = 0; ix < COLS; ix++){
           if (*(values+ix) != 999){
              if (*(values+ix) < lowest){
                 lowest = *(values+ix);
                 loc = ix;
              }
           }
        }

        *(values+loc) = 999;

        return loc;
}//end findLowestValue()
```

```
//-----------------------------------------------------------------
//Function: formatData()
//Parameters: data - the array we want to format
//Return Type: None
//Purpose: Get rid of all spaces in the array.
//-----------------------------------------------------------------
void formatData(char data[]){

    for (int mx=0, nx=0; (*(data+nx) != '\0'); nx++){
        if (*(data+nx) == ' '){
            //do nothing - skip over the space in the data
        }
        else {
            *(data+mx++) = *(data+nx);
        }
    }

    //don't forget to add the null terminator
    *(data+mx) = '\0';

    return;
}//end formatData()




//-----------------------------------------------------------------
//Function: formCipheredMessage()
//Parameters:  CTEXT - the cipher alphabet we will use for substitution
//             MESSAGETOCIPHER - the user's message
//             enc_message - the enciphered message to be determined
//Return Type: char* - a pointer to the encoded information.
//Purpose: Encipher the user's message.
//-----------------------------------------------------------------
char* formCipheredMessage(const char CTEXT[], const char MESSAGETOCIPHER[],
                          char enc_message[]){

    int length = strlen(MESSAGETOCIPHER)+1;

    int encode_value;

    for (int ix=0; ix<length; ix++){

        //test to see if we have an alphabetic character; if not,
        //simply copy it to our encrypted message - this preserves
        //characters such as ' , ! etc...
```

```
        if (!isalpha(static_cast<int>(MESSAGETOCIPHER[ix]))){
          enc_message[ix] = MESSAGETOCIPHER[ix];
        }
        else {
          //valid character - the easy way to calculate the ciphered
          //character is based on the plain text's ascii character value;
          //since it has to be a capital letter, it must be in the range
          //from 65 to 90, with A represented by 65, Z by 90.  By simply
          //subtracting 65 from the encode_value (the integer representation
          //of the plaintext character), we now know what cipher character
          //to use.

          encode_value = toupper(static_cast<int>(MESSAGETOCIPHER[ix]));
          enc_message[ix] = CTEXT[encode_value-SIXTYFIVE];
        }
    }

  //return a reference to the encoded message
  return enc_message;
}//end formCipheredMessage()


//----------------------------------------------------------------
//Function: getInputType()
//Parameters: None
//Return Type: int - 0 indicates keyboard input, 1 indicates file
//            input
//Purpose: Determines if the user will be manually entering text to
//be enciphered or if the user wants a file to be enciphered.
//----------------------------------------------------------------
int getInputType(void)
{
  char type;
  bool error = false;
  int value;

  do {
    //prompt user for input from file or keyboard
    cout << "Is file input from keyboard (K, k) or file (F, f): ";
    cin >> type;

    //make type an uppercase letter
    type = static_cast<char>(toupper(static_cast<int>(type)));
```

```
      //check for an invalid character
      if ((type != 'K') && (type != 'F')){
         cerr << "You have entered an invalid character!" << endl << endl;
         error = true;
      }
      else {
         if (type == 'K')
            value = 0;       //value of 0 represents keyboard input
            else value = 1;   //value of 1 represents file input
         error = false;
      }

   } while (error);

   cout << endl;

   return value;

}//end getInputType()


//----------------------------------------------------------------
//Function: getFileNames()
//Parameters:  infile_name - the input file
//             outfile_name - the output file we will write the
//             enciphered text to
//Return Type: None
//Purpose: Get file information from the user.
//----------------------------------------------------------------
void getFileNames(char * &infile_name, char * &outfile_name)
{
   char data[SIZE];

   cout << "Enter filename to store/retrieve plaintext message: ";

   cin >> data;

   infile_name = new char[strlen(data) + 1];
   strcpy(infile_name, data);

   cout << "Enter filename to store enciphered message: ";

   cin >> data;
```

```
      outfile_name = new char[strlen(data) + 1];
      strcpy(outfile_name, data);

      cout << endl;

      return;
}//end getFileNames()




//-----------------------------------------------------------------
//Function: getKeyword()
//Parameters: text - the keyword that the user enters
//Return Type: int - the length of the keyword
//Purpose: Prompts the user for a keyword and continues until
//a valid keyword has been entered.  Returns the length of the
//keyword.
//-----------------------------------------------------------------
int getKeyword(char * &text)
{
      bool error = false;
      char buffer[SIZE];

      do {
         cout << "Enter keyword or keyword phrase in UPPERCASE" << endl
              << "do not use spaces or non-alphabetic characters): ";

         cin.getline(buffer, SIZE, '\n');
         assert(text = new char[strlen(buffer) + 1]);
         strcpy(text, buffer);

         error = checkInput(text);

         //delete text if there was an error
         if (error){
            delete [] text;
         }

      } while (error);

      cout << endl;

      return strlen(buffer);
}//end getKeyword()
```

```
//----------------------------------------------------------------
//Function: getMessage()
//Parameters:  input - the name of the input plaintext file
//             output the name of the output ciphertext file
//             msg_to_cipher - the message to be encoded
//             PTEXT[] - the plaintext alphabet
//             CTEXT[] - the ciphertext alphabet
//Return Type: bool, indicating success of operation
//Purpose: Allow the user to manually input text from the keyboard.
//Save the text in plaintext to the input file; encrypt the text
//and save it to the specified output file for later retrieval.
//----------------------------------------------------------------
bool getMessage(char* input, char* output, char msg_to_cipher[],
                const char PTEXT[], const char CTEXT[])
{
   bool go_on = true, success = false;

   ofstream textFile(input, ios::app);
   ofstream cipherFile(output, ios::app);

   if ((!textFile) || (!cipherFile)){
      //do nothing - error will be noted to user later
   }
   else {

      success = true;

      textFile << "PLAINTEXT:  " << PTEXT << endl;
      textFile << "CIPHERTEXT: " << CTEXT << endl << endl;

      //get the newline character off of the input stream
      cin.get();

      cout << "Enter the message in UPPERCASE characters: " << endl;

      while (go_on) {

         //get the entire line, up to 256 characters
         cin.getline(msg_to_cipher, SIZE, '\n');

         //case user doesn't want the text to be encrypted
         if (msg_to_cipher[0] == '/'){

            if (strlen(BUFFER)>0){
```

4

Chapter

```
                        //empty whatever is in the buffer
                        groupBUFFER(cipherFile, strlen(BUFFER));
                        //adjust the buffer
                        strcpy(BUFFER, (BUFFER+strlen(BUFFER)));
                    }

                    //output plaintext
                    textFile << msg_to_cipher << endl;
                    cipherFile << msg_to_cipher << endl;
              }

              //case user is done entering text
              else if (static_cast<int>(msg_to_cipher[0]) == NINETYTWO){
                  go_on = false;
              }

              //encrypt the text
              else {
                  textFile << msg_to_cipher << endl;
                  char enciphered_msg[BIGSIZE];
                  formCipheredMessage(CTEXT,msg_to_cipher,enciphered_msg);
                  printCipherToFile(cipherFile,enciphered_msg);
              }
          }

      //empty the rest of the buffer
      groupBUFFER(cipherFile, strlen(BUFFER));
      }

      //close the files
      textFile.close();
      cipherFile.close();

      //notify user where plaintext and ciphertext files are
      cout << "\nPlaintext file is: " << input << endl;
      cout << "Encrypted file is: " << output << endl << endl;

      return success;
}//end getMessage()


//----------------------------------------------------------------
//Function: getShiftKey()
//Parameters:  key_desired - uppercase key entered by the user
```

```
//Return Type: None
//Purpose: Get the key the user enters; error checking performed
//until user enters a valid value.
//----------------------------------------------------------------
void getShiftKey(char &key_desired)
{
   bool error = true;

   do {
      //prompt user to enter an uppercase shift key
      cout << "Enter UPPERCASE Alphabetic Shift Key (CTRL-C to quit): ";
      cin >> key_desired;

      int key_value = static_cast<int>(key_desired);

      //do some error checking
      if ((key_value < SIXTYFIVE) || (key_value > NINETY)){
         cerr << "\nYou must enter a letter from A to Z!" << endl << endl;
      }
      else {
         cout << endl;
         error = false;
      }
   } while (error);

   return;
}//end getShiftKey()



//----------------------------------------------------------------
//Function: groupBUFFER()
//Parameters: out - the output stream we are writing to
//            num - the number of characters we want to output
//Return Type: None
//Purpose: Output the buffer in groups of five characters at a
//time.
//----------------------------------------------------------------
void groupBUFFER(ofstream out, int num)
{

   for (int kx=0;kx<num;kx++){

      if ((kx!=0) && (kx%TWENTYFIVE==0)){
         out << endl;
```

```
        }

        if ((kx!=0) && (kx%FIVE == 0) && (kx%TWENTYFIVE!=0)){
            out << " " << *(BUFFER+kx);
        }
        else {
        out << *(BUFFER+kx);
        }
    }

    out << endl;

    return;
}//end groupBUFFER()


//-----------------------------------------------------------------
//Function: numericExtraction()
//Parameters: MATRIX - the matrix we want to form the cipher from
//            cipher - the cipher stream we will create
//            R - the number of rows in the matrix
//            C - the number of columns in the matrix
//Return Type: None
//Purpose: Creates the cipher stream we will use to encrypt files
//by pulling off the columns from the matrix in alphabetical order
//based on the character in the top row, and inserting them into
//the cipher array.
//-----------------------------------------------------------------
void numericExtraction(char **& MATRIX, char cipher[], const int R,
                       const int C)
{
    int counter = 0;

    //place ASCII values of first row's characters into a table;
    //we will use these values to determine the order in which
    //we pull columns out of the matrix
    int *top_row_ASCII_values = new int[C];
    assert(top_row_ASCII_values);

    //no cast to integer type required since this is already taken
    //care of for us
    for (int ix=0; ix<C; ix++){
        *(top_row_ASCII_values + ix) = *((*MATRIX)+ix);
```

```
        }

        for (int jx=0; jx<C; jx++){

            //find out what column we want
            int col = findLowestValue(top_row_ASCII_values, C);

            //put contents of the column into the cipher stream, but
            //only do this when we have a character!
            for (int kx=0; kx<R; kx++){
                if ((*(*(MATRIX+kx)+col)) != '\0'){
                    cipher[counter++] = (*(*(MATRIX+kx)+col));
                }
            }
        }

        //destroy dynamically allocated memory
        delete [] top_row_ASCII_values;

        return;
}//end numericExtraction()


//-----------------------------------------------------------------
//Function: printCipherToFile()
//Parameters: op - the output file we are writing to
//            msg - the cipher text we are displaying
//Return Type: None
//Purpose: Group the cipher in 5-block characters in the
//specified output file.
//-----------------------------------------------------------------
void printCipherToFile(ofstream op, char msg[])
{
    formatData(msg);

    //check to see if there are more than 25 characters
    //in the buffer; if so, print out as many groups of
    //25 as possible
    if (strlen(BUFFER) >= TWENTYFIVE){

        int numchars = (strlen(BUFFER)/TWENTYFIVE)*TWENTYFIVE;
        //print the contents of the buffer to the output stream
        groupBUFFER(op, numchars);
```

```
      //shift whatever is left in the buffer
      strcpy(BUFFER, (BUFFER+numchars));
      //append data to the buffer
      strcat(BUFFER, msg);
   }

   //if buffer contents are less than 25, simply append the new
   //data to the buffer
   else if ((strlen(BUFFER) >= 0) && (strlen(BUFFER) < TWENTYFIVE)){
      strcat(BUFFER, msg);
   }

   return;
}//end printCipherToFile()


//-----------------------------------------------------------------
//Function: printMatrix()
//Parameters: the_matrix - the matrix we want to display
//            ROWS - the number of rows in the matrix
//            COLS - the number of columns in the matrix
//Return Type: None
//Purpose: Displays the matrix.
//-----------------------------------------------------------------
void printMatrix(char ** &the_matrix, const int ROWS, const int COLUMNS)
{
   cout << "\nThe matrix is:" << endl << endl;

   for (int ix=0; ix<ROWS; ix++){

      for (int kx=0; kx<COLUMNS; kx++){
         cout << *(*(the_matrix+ix)+kx) << " ";
      }

      cout << endl;
   }

   return;
}//end printMatrix()


//-----------------------------------------------------------------
//Function: reviseCipherStream()
//Parameters: MATRIX - the numeric keyed transposed matrix
```

```
//              cipher - the cipher stream that was originally created
//                       when the user entered a keyword
//              R - the number of rows in the matrix
//              C - the number of columns in the matrix
//Return Type: None
//Purpose: Overwrites the cipher stream initially created with the
//one we get by taking columns out of the matrix.
//-----------------------------------------------------------------
void reviseCipherStream(char ** &MATRIX, char cipher[], const int R,
                        const int C)
{
    int extract_type = typeOfExtraction();

    if (!(extract_type)){
        simpleExtraction(MATRIX, cipher, R, C);
    }
    else {
        numericExtraction(MATRIX, cipher, R, C);
    }

    //print the resulting matrix
    printMatrix(MATRIX, R, C);

    if (!(extract_type))
        cout << "\nSIMPLE Transposition alphabet is: " << cipher << endl
                << endl;
    else
        cout << "\nNUMERIC Transposition alphabet is: " << cipher << endl
                << endl;

    return;
}//end reviseCipherStream()


//-----------------------------------------------------------------
//Function: shiftKeyword()
//Parameters: ctext - the cipher alphabet we are going to shift
//            user_key - the key the user entered
//Return Type: None
//Purpose: Shift the keyword or keyword phrase we will use later to
//encode the user's message.
//-----------------------------------------------------------------
void shiftKeyword(char ctext[], const char USER_KEY)
{
```

```
        int location;
        char temp[TWENTYSIX] = {'\0'};

        //find the location of the key in the plaintext
        for (int ix=0; ix<TWENTYSIX; ix++){
           if (USER_KEY == ctext[ix]){
              location = ix;
              break;
            }
        }

        if (location == TWENTYFIVE){
             //do nothing
        }
        else {

           //put into temp all the characters up to and including the shift key
           //location now indicated how many characters, so we must increment by
           //one since the array uses a zero-based index
           strncpy(temp, ctext, location+1);
           //shift all remaining characters in the ciphertext
           strcpy(ctext, (ctext+location+1));
           //concatenate temp back to ctext
           strcat(ctext, temp);
        }

        cout << "Shifted keyword-mixed alphabet is: " << ctext << endl << endl;

        return;
}//end shiftKeyword();


//------------------------------------------------------------------
//Function: simpleExtraction()
//Parameters: MATRIX - the matrix we want to form the cipher from
//            cipher - the cipher stream we will create
//            R - the number of rows in the matrix
//            C - the number of columns in the matrix
//Return Type: None
//Purpose: Creates the cipher stream we will use to encrypt files
//by pulling off the columns from left to right and inserting them
//into the cipher array.
//------------------------------------------------------------------
```

```
void simpleExtraction(char **& MATRIX, char cipher[], const int R,
                      const int C)
{
    int counter = 0;

    for (int ix=0; ix<C; ix++){
        for (int kx=0; kx<R; kx++){
            if ((*(*(MATRIX+kx)+ix)) != '\0'){
                cipher[counter++] = (*(*(MATRIX+kx)+ix));
            }
        }
    }

    return;
}//end simpleExtraction()


//---------------------------------------------------------------
//Function: typeOfExtraction()
//Parameters:  None
//Return Type: int - 0 denotes SIMPLE extraction, 1 NUMERIC
//Purpose: Determines what type of extraction the user wants to
//perform.
//---------------------------------------------------------------
int typeOfExtraction()
{
    char type[SIZE];
    int ret_value;

    do {
        cout << "Enter transposition matrix method - SIMPLE or NUMERIC: ";
        cin >> type;
    } while (strcmp(type, "SIMPLE") && strcmp(type, "NUMERIC"));

    if (!strcmp(type, "SIMPLE"))
        ret_value = 0;
    else
        ret_value = 1;

    return ret_value;
}//end typeOfExtraction
//end file ciphertr.cpp
```

4

Chapter

The CIPHER6.BAS Program

To illustrate the execution of the interval extraction subroutine, I'll incorporate that routine into a program which enciphers messages based upon any one of the three alphabet formation techniques presented earlier in this chapter—interval extraction, simple transposition, and numeric transposition. This program, which is contained on the file CIPHER6.BAS on the companion CD-ROM, contains extraneous PRINT statements highlighted with five asterisks as comments which were included to facilitate explaining the operation of the program. You may want to remove those statements from the program if you wish to use it or distribute it to associates for use.

Listing 4.6 contains the statements that make up the main portion of the CIPHER6.BAS program. The first group of statements starting with the label "START" simply displays the program's options, accepts the user-specified enciphering method, and assigns a value to the string variable ORDER$ based upon the type of enciphering technique selected.

Listing 4.6 The main portion of the CIPHER6.BAS program.

```
REM PROGRAM CIPHER6.BAS
DIM PLAINTEXT$(26), CIPHERTEXT$(26), KEY$(26), TRANS$(26, 26), TEMP$(26)
START:  CLS
        PRINT "PROGRAM CIPHER6.BAS ENCIPHERS A MESSAGE USING ONE"
        PRINT "OF THE FOLLOWING TECHNIQUES TO FORM A CIPHER ALPHABET"
        PRINT " (1) INTERVAL EXTRACTION SEQUENCE"
        PRINT " (2) SIMPLE TRANSPOSITION SEQUENCE"
        PRINT " (3) NUMERIC TRANSPOSITION SEQUENCE"
        PRINT
        INPUT "Enter method to form enciphered message 1, 2 or 3: ", X
        IF X < 1 OR X > 3 THEN GOTO START
        IF X = 2 THEN ORDER$ = "SIMPLE"
        IF X = 3 THEN ORDER$ = "NUMERIC"
        IF X > 1 THEN GOTO TRAN
        INPUT "Enter the interval as a numeric between 1 and 25: ", INTERVAL
TRAN:   INPUT "Enter keyword or keyword phrase in UPPERCASE: ", TEXT$
        PRINT
GOSUB INITIALIZE
        PRINT "Plaintext based alphabet is    : ";          '*****
        FOR I = 0 TO 25: PRINT PLAINTEXT$(I); : NEXT I      '*****
GOSUB KEYWORD                   'form keyword based mixed alphabet
        PRINT "Keyword based alphabet is      : "; X$       '*****
```

```
ON X GOSUB INTERVAL, TRANSPORT, TRANSPORT
        IF X = 1 THEN PRINT "Interval Alphabet is              : "; X$
        IF X > 1 THEN PRINT ORDER$; " Transposition Alphabet is :"; X$
1       INPUT "Enter UPPERCASE Alphabetic Shift Key: ", K$
        FOR I = 0 TO 25
        IF K$ = PLAINTEXT$(I) GOTO 2
        NEXT I
        PRINT "You must enter a letter from A to Z"
        GOTO 1
2       REM Position I represents shift key letter

GOSUB FORMCIPHER              'create cipher alphabet
        PRINT "Shifted keyword mixed alphabet is    : ";          '*****
        FOR I = 0 TO 25: PRINT CIPHERTEXT$(I); : NEXT I: PRINT    '*****
GOSUB INITIALIZE              'reinitialize plaintext array
GOSUB MSGFILE                 'assign I/O files, place message on a file
GOSUB CONVERTSTORE            'convert and store ciphertext on a file
GOSUB PRTOUT                  'print results
STOP
```

4

Chapter

If an interval extraction technique is selected, the user is prompted to enter the interval to be used. Regardless of the enciphering method selected, the user is then prompted to enter a keyword or keyword phrase that will be used to form a keyword-based mixed alphabet. Both the plaintext alphabet and keyword-based mixed alphabet are displayed through the use of extraneous PRINT statements you can remove. You should note that the subroutines INITIALIZE and KEYWORD, as well as the other subroutines invoked from the main portion of CIPHER6.BAS, contain the statements previously described in this book and will not be reviewed again.

The ON X GOSUB statement causes a branch to the INTERVAL or TRANSPORT subroutine based upon the user-selected encipherment method that was assigned to the variable X. After one of those subroutines is invoked, the appropriate alphabet is displayed by the use of extraneous IF-THEN PRINT statements that can be removed from the program. The program accepts an alphabetic shift key, invokes the FORMCIPHER subroutine, and displays the shifted keyword mixed alphabet which, in effect, is the cipher alphabet. Again, you can remove the extraneous PRINT statements if you so desire. Thereafter, the program invokes four more subroutines that reinitialize the plaintext array, assign I/O files and place a message on a file, convert and store the ciphertext on a file, and print the results of the encipherment operation.

Figure 4.8 illustrates the execution of CIPHER6.BAS when an interval extraction technique is used to form a cipher alphabet. In this example, the keyword MICROSOFT was used to form the keyword-based alphabet. It is that alphabet that is used as the basis for forming the interval alphabet. Because 3 was entered as the extraction interval, every third character in the keyword-based alphabet is removed to form the interval alphabet. Thus, C is extracted, followed by S, and so on from the keyword-based alphabet.

```
Figure 4.8 The execution of CIPHER6.BAS.

Program CIPHER6.BAS enciphers a message using one of the
following techniques to form a cipher alphabet.
    (1) Interval Extraction Sequence
    (2) Simple Transposition Sequence
    (3) Numeric Transposition Sequence
Enter method to form enciphered message 1, 2, or 3: 1
Enter the interval as a numeric between 1 and 25: 3
Enter keyword or keyword phrase in UPPERCASE: MICROSOFT

Plaintext-based alphabet is: ABCDEFGHIJKLMNOPQRSTUVWXYZ
Keyword-based alphabet is: MICROSFTABDEGHJKLNPQUVWXYZ
Interval alphabet is: CSAEJNUXMRFBGKPVYIOTDHLQWZ
Enter UPPERCASE Alphabetic Shift Key: B
Shifted keyword mixed alphabet is: GKPVYIOTDHLQWZCSAEJNUXMRFB
Enter filename to store plaintext message, default=MESSAGE.DAT
Enter filename to store enciphered message, default=CIPHERTX.DAT
Select keyboard (k) or file (f) message input: K
Enter your message - place a / at the beginning of each line
that should remain in plaintext and a \ on a separate line to
indicate the end of the enciphered message

/TO: DAN
/FROM: GEORGE
WE MUST MEET QUICKLY TO DISCUSS THE USE
OF THE ENGLISH LANGUAGE AND SPELLING OF
COMMONLY USED FOODE ·
\
Press Return key to display resulting enciphered message

Resulting enciphered message is:
TO: DAN
FROM: GEORGE
MYWUJ NWYYN AUDPL QFNCV DJPUJ
JNTYU JYCIN TYYZO QDJTQ GZOUG
OYGZV SYQQ  DZOCI PCWWC ZQFUJ
YVICC VYXXX
```

The selection of B as the shift key causes the interval alphabet to be rotated so that the character B in the alphabet is positioned at the extreme right. The resulting shifted keyword mixed alphabet formed using an interval extraction method represents the ciphertext alphabet. Thus, first locate each character in the message in the plaintext alphabet and then extract the character in the equivalent position in the shifted-keyword mixed alphabet.

Note that the message WE MUST MEET... results in the enciphered message MYWUJ NWYYN... You can verify the accuracy of the encipherment process by noting that the position of W in the plaintext message is equivalent to M in the shifted keyword mixed alphabet, E has the same position as Y, and so on, verifying the accuracy of the enciphering process.

The CIPHER6.CPP Program

Continuing our presentation of C++ versions of each BASIC language version, Listing 4.7 contains the program listing of CIPHER6.CPP. As you review the program listing, you will note that an extensive effort was made to make the program as "crash-free" as possible, as well as to incorporate the functionality of the BASIC language version of the program. When you examine the program listing, you may wish to focus your attention upon the functions interval, which creates the cipher stream based on interval extraction, and numericExtraction, which creates the cipher stream used to encrypt files by pulling off the columns from the matrix in alphabetical order based on the character in the top row and inserting them into the cipher array. Although many of the previously developed C++ functions are included once again in this program listing, the listing is presented in its entirety to facilitate reference to the relationship between functions as well as the manner by which they operate.

Listing 4.7 The CIPHER6.CPP program listing.

```
/*
cipher6.cpp
C++ code written by Jonathan Held using Microsoft Visual C++,
version 5.0, on March 24, 1998.
*/
```

```
//standard include files
#include<iostream.h>
#include<assert.h>
#include<string.h>
#include<ctype.h>
#include<fstream.h>

//function prototypes
bool checkInput(char * &);
void createCipherStream(char *, char[]);
void createMatrix(char ** &, const char [], const int, const int);
void display(char *);
bool encryptText(char *, char *, const char [], const char[], char []);
void deleteMatrix(char **&, const int, const int);
int findLowestValue(int *&, const int);
void formatData(char []);
char* formCipheredMessage(const char[], const char [], char []);
void getFileNames(char *&, char *&);
int getInputType(void);
int getKeyword(char *&);
bool getMessage(char*, char*, char [], const char[], const char[]);
void getShiftKey(char &);
void groupBUFFER(ofstream, int);
void interval(char[]);
void numericExtraction(char **&, char [], const int, const int);
void printCipherToFile(ofstream, char[]);
void printMatrix(char ** &, const int, const int);
void reviseCipherStream(char **&, char [], const int, const int,
                        const int);
void shiftKeyword(char [], const char);
void simpleExtraction(char **&, char [], const int, const int);
int welcome(void);

//constants we will use
const int ONE = 1, TWO = 2, THREE = 3, FIVE = 5, TWENTYFIVE = 25,
        TWENTYSIX = 26, TWENTYSEVEN = 27, SIXTYFIVE = 65,
        NINETY = 90, NINETYTWO = 92, SIZE = 256, DUMMY_VAL = 999,
        BIGSIZE = 1000;
char BUFFER[BIGSIZE] = {'\0'};
//------------------------------------------------------------------
//Function: main()
//Parameters: None
//Return Type: int - 0 execution is normal, 1 abnormal termination
//Purpose: Runs the main part of the program.
```

```
//------------------------------------------------------------------
int main()
{
    char plaintext[TWENTYSEVEN] = {'A','B','C','D','E','F','G','H',
                                   'I','J','K','L','M','N','O','P',
                                   'Q','R','S','T','U','V','W','X',
                                   'Y','Z', '\0'};

    char cipherStream[TWENTYSEVEN] = {'\0'};
    char message_to_cipher[SIZE], enciphered_message[SIZE];

    char ** cMatrix;
    char *keyword, key, *infile, *outfile;
    int rows, columns, input_type, encipher_type;
    bool success;


    encipher_type = welcome();

    if (encipher_type == ONE){
        getKeyword(keyword);
        createCipherStream(keyword, cipherStream);
        cout << "Keyword-based alphabet is: "
                << cipherStream << endl << endl;
        interval(cipherStream);
    }
    else {
        //get the keyword we are going to use, determine number of rows
        //and columns of our matrix
        columns = getKeyword(keyword);
        rows = TWENTYSIX/columns;

        //integer division requires that we check and see if there is a
        //remainder; if so, we need to add one extra row to our matrix
        if (TWENTYSIX%columns){
            rows++;
        }

        //create the initial ciphertext stream
        createCipherStream(keyword, cipherStream);

        //echo to the user what we have
        cout << "Plaintext-based alphabet is: " << plaintext << endl
```

```
                          << "Keyword-based alphabet is:    " << cipherStream << endl
                              << endl;

         //insert the stream into our matrix
         createMatrix(cMatrix, cipherStream, rows, columns);

         reviseCipherStream(cMatrix, cipherStream, rows, columns,
                     encipher_type);

     }

     getShiftKey(key);
     shiftKeyword(cipherStream, key);

     getFileNames(infile, outfile);

     input_type = getInputType();

     //process file input
     if (input_type){
        success = encryptText(infile, outfile, plaintext, cipherStream,
                    enciphered_message);
     }
     else {
        cout << "Use a \'/\' to leave a line in plaintext." << endl
             << "Use a \'\\' to indicate end of message input. " << endl;
        success = getMessage(infile, outfile, message_to_cipher, plaintext,
cipherStream);
     }

     //report success of operation
     if (!success){
        cerr << "Error: Invalid filename specified. Goodbye." << endl;
     }
     else {
        cout << "Press return to display resulting enciphered message."
                 << endl;
        //get the newlines off the current input stream
        cin.get();
        if (input_type == ONE){
           cin.get();
        }
        display(outfile);
```

```
      }

      //delete dynamically allocated memory accordingly
      if (encipher_type != ONE)
         deleteMatrix(cMatrix, rows, columns);

      delete [] infile;
      delete [] outfile;
      delete [] keyword;

      return (!success);
}//end main()



//-----------------------------------------------------------------
//Function: checkInput()
//Parameters: input - the keyword the user entered
//Return Type: bool - true if the input string contains an error,
//                    false otherwise
//Purpose: Checks the user's keyword for invalid characters.
//-----------------------------------------------------------------
bool checkInput(char * &input)
{
   bool error = false;
   int count = strlen(input);

   for (int ix=0; ix<count; ix++){

      int char_value = static_cast<int>(*(input+ix));
      //determine if the user did not enter an uppercase character
      if ((char_value < SIXTYFIVE) || (char_value > NINETY)){
         error = true;
         cerr << "You entered an invalid keyword!" << endl << endl;
         break;
      }
   }

   if (count == 0){
      cerr << "You entered an invalid keyword!" << endl << endl;
      error = true;
   }

   return error;
```

4

Chapter

```
}//end checkInput()


//------------------------------------------------------------------
//Function: createCipherStream()
//Parameters: input - the keyword the user entered
//            cipher - the keyword alphabet that will be constructed
//Return Type: None
//Purpose: Creates a preliminary cipher stream that will be used to
//form the cipher matrix.
//------------------------------------------------------------------
void createCipherStream(char *input, char stream[])
{
   bool used[TWENTYSIX];
   int index = 0,
       count = strlen(input);

   //no characters are initially used
   for (int ix=0; ix<TWENTYSIX; ix++){
      used[ix] = false;
   }

   //keep track of each character used, start forming the keyword
   //alphabet
   for (int jx=0; jx<count; jx++){

      //get each character of the input string (integer value)
      int char_value = static_cast<int>(*(input+jx));

      if (used[char_value-SIXTYFIVE]){
         //do nothing - the character was already used
      }
      else {
         //mark as used and add to the keyword alphabet
         used[char_value-SIXTYFIVE] = true;
         *(stream+index++) = static_cast<char>(char_value);
      }
   }

   //go through the list of characters used - those which weren't
   //used should be added to the keyword alphabet
   for (int kx=0; kx<TWENTYSIX; kx++){

      if (!(used[kx])){
```

```
            *(stream+index++) = static_cast<char>(SIXTYFIVE+kx);
      }
   }

   return;
}//end createCipherStream()



//----------------------------------------------------------------
//Function: createMatrix()
//Parameters: matrix - the matrix we are going to create
//            CSTREAM - the initial cipher stream based on the
//                         user's keyword
//            ROWS - the number of rows in the matrix
//            COLS - the number of columns in the matrix
//Return Type: None
//Purpose: Creates a numeric key transposed matrix, identical to
//figure 4.4.
//----------------------------------------------------------------
void createMatrix(char ** &matrix, const char CSTREAM[], const int ROWS,
                  const int COLS)
{
   int count = 0;

   //dynamically allocate memory for the RxC matrix
   //we use assert to ensure that memory was allocated;
   //if not, then the program will terminate abnormally
   assert(matrix = new char*[ROWS]);
   for (int ix=0; ix<ROWS; ix++){
      *(matrix + ix) = new char[COLS];
   }

   //fill in the matrix
   for (int jx=0; jx<ROWS; jx++){
      for (int kx=0; kx<COLS; kx++){
      //we only want to enter a character into the matrix
      //twenty-six times - most of the time we allocate
      //a matrix larger than what we will need to use; when
      //we have more than 26 characters, we simply insert a
      //null terminator into the matrix
         if (count < TWENTYSIX)
            *(*(matrix+jx)+kx) = CSTREAM[count++];
            else
            *(*(matrix+jx)+kx) = '\0';
```

```
      }
   }

   return;
}//end createMatrix()



//-----------------------------------------------------------------
//Function: encryptText()
//Parameters:  inp_file - the name of the input plaintext file
//             outp_file - the name of the output ciphertext file
//             PTEXT[] - the plaintext alphabet
//             CTEXT[] - the ciphertext alphabet
//             encoded_msg[] - the message to be encoded
//Return Type: bool, indicating success of operation
//Purpose: Used to encrypt file input.  Takes each line of the input
//file, encrypts it, and saves the result to the specified output
//file.
//-----------------------------------------------------------------
bool encryptText(char * inp_file, char * outp_file, const char PTEXT[],
                 const char CTEXT[], char encoded_msg[])
{
   bool success = false;
   char ip[SIZE];

   //declare file stream objects
   ifstream input(inp_file, ios::in);
   ofstream output(outp_file, ios::app);

   if ((!input) || (!output)){
      //do nothing - I/O error; user will be notified upon
      //procedure's return to main()
   }
   else {

      success = true;

      //print plaintext and ciphertext alphabets to the
      //output file
      output << "PLAINTEXT:  " << PTEXT << endl;
      output << "CIPHERTEXT: " << CTEXT << endl << endl;

      while (input.getline(ip, BIGSIZE, '\n')){
```

```
        //check to see if the user wants the line to appear in plain text
        if (ip[0] == '/'){

            if (strlen(BUFFER)>0){

            //empty whatever is in the buffer
            groupBUFFER(output, strlen(BUFFER));
            //adjust the buffer
            strcpy(BUFFER, (BUFFER+strlen(BUFFER)));
            //output plaintext
             }

        output << ip << endl;

        }
        else {
            //encipher the line
            char *msg = formCipheredMessage(CTEXT, ip, encoded_msg);
            //print the cipher in groups of five to the ouput file
            printCipherToFile(output, msg);
        }
    }

    //empty the rest of the buffer
    groupBUFFER(output, strlen(BUFFER));

    //notify user where plaintext and ciphertext files are
    cout << "Plaintext file is: " << inp_file << endl;
    cout << "Encrypted file is: " << outp_file << endl << endl;
    }

    //don't forget to close the files
    input.close();
    output.close();

    //return success of the operation
    return success;
}//end encryptText()


//----------------------------------------------------------------
//Function: deleteMatrix()
//Parameters: matrix - the matrix we are going to destroy
//            R - the number of rows in the matrix
```

```
//               C - the number of columns in the matrix
//Return Type: None
//Purpose: Destroys the dynamically allocated matrix!
//-----------------------------------------------------------------
void deleteMatrix(char **&matrix, const int R, const int C)
{
    for (int ix=0; ix<R; ix++)
        delete [] *(matrix+ix);

    delete [] matrix;

    return;
}//end deleteMatrix()



//-----------------------------------------------------------------
//Function: display()
//Parameters: name - the name of the file the user wants displayed
//Return Type: None
//Purpose: Echoes the resulting output file to the screen.
//-----------------------------------------------------------------
void display(char *name)
{
    ifstream infile(name, ios::in);
    char input[SIZE];

    if (!(infile)){
        cerr << "Unable to open input file for display." << endl;
    }
    else {
        while (infile.getline(input, SIZE, '\n')){
            cout << input << endl;
        }
    }

    return;
}//end display()



//-----------------------------------------------------------------
//Function: findLowestValue()
//Parameters: values - the ASCII values of all characters in the
//                     top row of the matrix
//            COLS - the number of columns in the matrix
```

```
//Return Type: int - the column we want.
//Purpose: Determines what column we are going to extract from
//the matrix and put into the cipher stream.
//----------------------------------------------------------------
int findLowestValue(int *&values, const int COLS)
{
   int loc=0, lowest = DUMMY_VAL;

   for (int ix = 0; ix < COLS; ix++){
      if (*(values+ix) != DUMMY_VAL){
         if (*(values+ix) < lowest){
            lowest = *(values+ix);
            loc = ix;
         }
      }
   }

   *(values+loc) = DUMMY_VAL;

   return loc;
}//end findLowestValue()



//----------------------------------------------------------------
//Function: formatData()
//Parameters: data - the array we want to format
//Return Type: None
//Purpose: Get rid of all spaces in the array.
//----------------------------------------------------------------
void formatData(char data[]){

   for (int mx=0, nx=0; (*(data+nx) != '\0'); nx++){
      if (*(data+nx) == ' '){
         //do nothing - skip over the space in the data
      }
      else {
         *(data+mx++) = *(data+nx);
      }
   }

   //don't forget to add the null terminator
   *(data+mx) = '\0';

   return;
```

```
    }//end formatData()


    //-----------------------------------------------------------------
    //Function: formCipheredMessage()
    //Parameters:  CTEXT - the cipher alphabet we will use for substitution
    //             MESSAGETOCIPHER - the user's message
    //             enc_message - the enciphered message to be determined
    //Return Type: char* - a pointer to the encoded information.
    //Purpose: Encipher the user's message.
    //-----------------------------------------------------------------
    char* formCipheredMessage(const char CTEXT[], const char MESSAGETOCIPHER[],
                          char enc_message[])
    {
       int length = strlen(MESSAGETOCIPHER)+1;

       int encode_value;

       for (int ix=0; ix<length; ix++){

          //test to see if we have an alphabetic character; if not,
          //simply copy it to our encrypted message - this preserves
          //characters such as ' , ! etc...
          if (!isalpha(static_cast<int>(MESSAGETOCIPHER[ix]))){
             enc_message[ix] = MESSAGETOCIPHER[ix];
          }
          else {
             //valid character - the easy way to calculate the ciphered
             //character is based on the plain text's ascii character value;
             //since it has to be a capital letter, it must be in the range
             //from 65 to 90, with A represented by 65, Z by 90.  By simply
             //subtracting 65 from the encode_value (the integer representation
             //of the plaintext character), we now know what cipher character
             //to use.

             encode_value = toupper(static_cast<int>(MESSAGETOCIPHER[ix]));
             enc_message[ix] = CTEXT[encode_value-SIXTYFIVE];
          }
       }

       //return a reference to the encoded message
       return enc_message;
    }//end formCipheredMessage()
```

```
//----------------------------------------------------------------
//Function: getInputType()
//Parameters: None
//Return Type: int - 0 indicates keyboard input, 1 indicates file
//                input
//Purpose: Determines if the user will be manually entering text to
//be enciphered or if the user wants a file to be enciphered.
//----------------------------------------------------------------
int getInputType(void)
{
   char type;
   bool error = false;
   int value;

   do {
      //prompt user for input from file or keyboard
      cout << "Is file input from keyboard (K, k) or file (F, f): ";
      cin >> type;

      //make type an uppercase letter
      type = static_cast<char>(toupper(static_cast<int>(type)));

      //check for an invalid character
      if ((type != 'K') && (type != 'F')){
         cerr << "You have entered an invalid character!" << endl << endl;
         error = true;
      }
      else {
         if (type == 'K')
            value = 0;          //value of 0 represents keyboard input
            else value = 1;     //value of 1 represents file input
         error = false;
      }

   } while (error);

   cout << endl;

   return value;
}//end getInputType()


//----------------------------------------------------------------
//Function: getFileNames()
```

```
//Parameters:  infile_name - the input file
//             outfile_name - the output file we will write the
//             enciphered text to
//Return Type: None
//Purpose: Get file information from the user.
//-----------------------------------------------------------------
void getFileNames(char * &infile_name, char * &outfile_name)
{
   char data[SIZE];

   cout << "Enter filename to store/retrieve plaintext message: ";

   cin >> data;

   infile_name = new char[strlen(data) + 1];
   strcpy(infile_name, data);

   cout << "Enter filename to store enciphered message: ";

   cin >> data;

   outfile_name = new char[strlen(data) + 1];
   strcpy(outfile_name, data);

   cout << endl;

   return;
}//end getFileNames()


//-----------------------------------------------------------------
//Function: getKeyword()
//Parameters: text - the keyword that the user enters
//Return Type: int - the length of the keyword
//Purpose: Prompts the user for a keyword and continues until
//a valid keyword has been entered.  Returns the length of the
//keyword.
//-----------------------------------------------------------------
int getKeyword(char * &text)
{
   bool error = false;
   char buffer[SIZE];

   do {
```

```
      cout << "Enter keyword or keyword phrase in UPPERCASE" << endl
                  << "do not use spaces or non-alphabetic characters): ";

      cin.getline(buffer, SIZE, '\n');
      assert(text = new char[strlen(buffer) + 1]);
      strcpy(text, buffer);

      error = checkInput(text);

      //delete text if there was an error
      if (error){
         delete [] text;
      }

   } while (error);

   cout << endl;

   return strlen(buffer);
}//end getKeyword()



//------------------------------------------------------------------
//Function: getMessage()
//Parameters:  input - the name of the input plaintext file
//             output the name of the output ciphertext file
//             msg_to_cipher - the message to be encoded
//             PTEXT[] - the plaintext alphabet
//             CTEXT[] - the ciphertext alphabet
//Return Type: bool, indicating success of operation
//Purpose: Allow the user to manually input text from the keyboard.
//Save the text in plaintext to the input file; encrypt the text
//and save it to the specified output file for later retrieval.
//------------------------------------------------------------------
bool getMessage(char* input, char* output, char msg_to_cipher[],
                const char PTEXT[],
                const char CTEXT[])
{
   bool go_on = true, success = false;

   ofstream textFile(input, ios::app);
   ofstream cipherFile(output, ios::app);
```

```cpp
if ((!textFile) || (!cipherFile)){
   //do nothing - error will be noted to user later
}
else {

   success = true;

   textFile << "PLAINTEXT:  " << PTEXT << endl;
   textFile << "CIPHERTEXT: " << CTEXT << endl << endl;

   //get the newline character off of the input stream
   cin.get();

   cout << "Enter the message in UPPERCASE characters: " << endl;

   while (go_on) {

      //get the entire line, up to 256 characters
      cin.getline(msg_to_cipher, SIZE, '\n');

      //case user doesn't want the text to be encrypted
      if (msg_to_cipher[0] == '/'){

         if (strlen(BUFFER)>0){
            //empty whatever is in the buffer
            groupBUFFER(cipherFile, strlen(BUFFER));
            //adjust the buffer
            strcpy(BUFFER, (BUFFER+strlen(BUFFER)));
         }

         //output plaintext
         textFile << msg_to_cipher << endl;
         cipherFile << msg_to_cipher << endl;
         }

      //case user is done entering text
      else if (static_cast<int>(msg_to_cipher[0]) == NINETYTWO){
         go_on = false;
         }

      //encrypt the text
      else {
         textFile << msg_to_cipher << endl;
         char enciphered_msg[BIGSIZE];
```

```
                formCipheredMessage(CTEXT,msg_to_cipher,enciphered_msg);
                printCipherToFile(cipherFile,enciphered_msg);
                }
        }

    //empty the rest of the buffer
    groupBUFFER(cipherFile, strlen(BUFFER));
    }

    //close the files
    textFile.close();
    cipherFile.close();

    //notify user where plaintext and ciphertext files are
    cout << "\nPlaintext file is: " << input << endl;
    cout << "Encrypted file is: " << output << endl << endl;

    return success;
}//end getMessage()


//----------------------------------------------------------------
//Function: getShiftKey()
//Parameters:  key_desired - uppercase key entered by the user
//Return Type: None
//Purpose: Get the key the user enters; error checking performed
//until user enters a valid value.
//----------------------------------------------------------------
void getShiftKey(char &key_desired)
{
    bool error = true;

    do {
        //prompt user to enter an uppercase shift key
        cout << "Enter UPPERCASE Alphabetic Shift Key (CTRL-C to quit): ";
        cin >> key_desired;

        int key_value = static_cast<int>(key_desired);

        //do some error checking
        if ((key_value < SIXTYFIVE) || (key_value > NINETY)){
            cerr << "\nYou must enter a letter from A to Z!" << endl << endl;
        }
        else {
```

4

Chapter

```
            cout << endl;
            error = false;
        }
    } while (error);

    return;
}//end getShiftKey()


//-----------------------------------------------------------------
//Function: groupBUFFER()
//Parameters: out - the output stream we are writing to
//            num - the number of characters we want to output
//Return Type: None
//Purpose: Output the buffer in groups of five characters at a
//time.
//-----------------------------------------------------------------
void groupBUFFER(ofstream out, int num)
{

    for (int kx=0;kx<num;kx++){

        if ((kx!=0) && (kx%TWENTYFIVE==0)){
            out << endl;
        }

        if ((kx!=0) && (kx%FIVE == 0) && (kx%TWENTYFIVE!=0)){
            out << " " << *(BUFFER+kx);
        }
        else {
                out << *(BUFFER+kx);
        }
    }

    out << endl;

    return;
}//end groupBUFFER()


//-----------------------------------------------------------------
//Function: interval()
//Parameters:  ctext - the cipher stream we are modifying
//Return Type: None
```

```
//Purpose: Create the cipher stream based on interval extraction.
//----------------------------------------------------------------
void interval(char ctext[])
{
   int interval, pos;
   char temp[TWENTYSEVEN];

   cout << "Enter the interval as a numeric between 1 and 25: ";
   cin >> interval;

   while ((interval < ONE) || (interval > TWENTYFIVE)){
      cerr << "\aInterval must be between 1 and 25." << endl;
      cerr << "Enter interval: ";
      cin >> interval;
   }

   for (int ix=0; ix<TWENTYSIX; ix++)
      temp[ix] = ctext[ix];

   for (int jx=0; jx<TWENTYSIX; jx++){
      pos = (((jx+1)*interval)-1)%TWENTYSIX;
      ctext[jx] = temp[pos];
   }

   cout << "\nInterval-based alphabet is " << ctext << endl << endl;

   return;
}//end interval()


//----------------------------------------------------------------
//Function: numericExtraction()
//Parameters: MATRIX - the matrix we want to form the cipher from
//            cipher - the cipher stream we will create
//            R - the number of rows in the matrix
//            C - the number of columns in the matrix
//Return Type: None
//Purpose: Creates the cipher stream we will use to encrypt files
//by pulling off the columns from the matrix in alphabetical order
//based on the character in the top row, and inserting them into
//the cipher array.
//----------------------------------------------------------------
void numericExtraction(char **& MATRIX, char cipher[], const int R,
                       const int C)
```

Chapter **4**

```
{
   int counter = 0;

   //place ASCII values of first row's characters into a table;
   //we will use these values to determine the order in which
   //we pull columns out of the matrix
   int *top_row_ASCII_values = new int[C];
   assert(top_row_ASCII_values);

   //no cast to integer type required since this is already taken
   //care of for us
   for (int ix=0; ix<C; ix++){
      *(top_row_ASCII_values + ix) = *((*MATRIX)+ix);
   }

   for (int jx=0; jx<C; jx++){

      //find out what column we want
      int col = findLowestValue(top_row_ASCII_values, C);

      //put contents of the column into the cipher stream, but
      //only do this when we have a character!
      for (int kx=0; kx<R; kx++){
         if ((*(*(MATRIX+kx)+col)) != '\0'){
            cipher[counter++] = (*(*(MATRIX+kx)+col));
         }
      }
   }

   //destroy dynamically allocated memory
   delete [] top_row_ASCII_values;

   return;
}//end numericExtraction()


//-----------------------------------------------------------------
//Function: printCipherToFile()
//Parameters: op - the output file we are writing to
//            msg - the cipher text we are displaying
//Return Type: None
//Purpose: Group the cipher in 5-block characters in the
//specified output file.
//-----------------------------------------------------------------
```

```
void printCipherToFile(ofstream op, char msg[]){

    formatData(msg);

    //check to see if there are more than 25 characters
    //in the buffer; if so, print out as many groups of
    //25 as possible
    if (strlen(BUFFER) >= TWENTYFIVE){

        int numchars = (strlen(BUFFER)/TWENTYFIVE)*TWENTYFIVE;
        //print the contents of the buffer to the output stream
        groupBUFFER(op, numchars);
        //shift whatever is left in the buffer
        strcpy(BUFFER, (BUFFER+numchars));
        //append data to the buffer
        strcat(BUFFER, msg);
    }

    //if buffer contents are less than 25, simply append the new
    //data to the buffer
    else if ((strlen(BUFFER) >= 0) && (strlen(BUFFER) < TWENTYFIVE)){
        strcat(BUFFER, msg);
    }

    return;
}//end printCipherToFile()


//-----------------------------------------------------------------
//Function: printMatrix()
//Parameters: the_matrix - the matrix we want to display
//            ROWS - the number of rows in the matrix
//            COLS - the number of columns in the matrix
//Return Type: None
//Purpose: Displays the matrix.
//-----------------------------------------------------------------
void printMatrix(char ** &the_matrix, const int ROWS, const int COLUMNS)
{
    cout << "\nThe matrix is:" << endl << endl;

    for (int ix=0; ix<ROWS; ix++){

        for (int kx=0; kx<COLUMNS; kx++){
            cout << *(*(the_matrix+ix)+kx) << " ";
```

```
        }

        cout << endl;
    }

    return;
}//end printMatrix()


//-----------------------------------------------------------------
//Function: reviseCipherStream()
//Parameters: MATRIX - the numeric keyed transposed matrix
//            cipher - the cipher stream that was originally created
//                     when the user entered a keyword
//            R - the number of rows in the matrix
//            C - the number of columns in the matrix
//Return Type: None
//Purpose: Overwrites the cipher stream initially created with the
//one we get by taking columns out of the matrix.
//-----------------------------------------------------------------
void reviseCipherStream(char ** &MATRIX, char cipher[], const int R,
                        const int C, const int enc_type)
{
    if (enc_type == TWO){
        simpleExtraction(MATRIX, cipher, R, C);
    }
    else {
        numericExtraction(MATRIX, cipher, R, C);
    }

    //print the resulting matrix
    printMatrix(MATRIX, R, C);

    if (enc_type == TWO)
        cout << "\nSIMPLE Transposition alphabet is: " << cipher << endl
                << endl;
    else
        cout << "\nNUMERIC Transposition alphabet is: " << cipher << endl
                << endl;

    return;
}//end reviseCipherStream()
```

```
//------------------------------------------------------------------
//Function: shiftKeyword()
//Parameters: ctext - the cipher alphabet we are going to shift
//            user_key - the key the user entered
//Return Type: None
//Purpose: Shift the keyword or keyword phrase we will use later to
//encode the user's message.
//------------------------------------------------------------------
void shiftKeyword(char ctext[], const char USER_KEY)
{
   int location;
   char temp[TWENTYSIX] = {'\0'};

   //find the location of the key in the plaintext
   for (int ix=0; ix<TWENTYSIX; ix++){
     if (USER_KEY == ctext[ix]){
        location = ix;
        break;
      }
   }

   if (location == TWENTYFIVE){
           //do nothing
   }
   else {

      //put into temp all the characters up to and including the shift key
      //location now indicated how many characters, so we must increment by
      //one since the array uses a zero-based index
      strncpy(temp, ctext, location+1);
      //shift all remaining characters in the ciphertext
      strcpy(ctext, (ctext+location+1));
      //concatenate temp back to ctext
      strcat(ctext, temp);
   }

   cout << "Shifted keyword-mixed alphabet is: " << ctext << endl << endl;

   return;
}//end shiftKeyword();


//------------------------------------------------------------------
//Function: simpleExtraction()
```

```
//Parameters: MATRIX - the matrix we want to form the cipher from
//           cipher - the cipher stream we will create
//           R - the number of rows in the matrix
//           C - the number of columns in the matrix
//Return Type: None
//Purpose: Creates the cipher stream we will use to encrypt files
//by pulling off the columns from left to right and inserting them
//into the cipher array.
//-----------------------------------------------------------------
void simpleExtraction(char **& MATRIX, char cipher[], const int R,
                      const int C)
{
   int counter = 0;

   for (int ix=0; ix<C; ix++){
      for (int kx=0; kx<R; kx++){
         if ((*(*(MATRIX+kx)+ix)) != '\0'){
            cipher[counter++] = (*(*(MATRIX+kx)+ix));
            }
         }
      }

   return;
}//end simpleExtraction()


//-----------------------------------------------------------------
//Function: welcome()
//Parameters:  None
//Return Type: int - method the cipher stream will be created;
//1 is interval, 2 is simple, 3 is numeric
//Purpose: Allow the user to select which method he/she wants
//to use to create the cipher stream.
//-----------------------------------------------------------------
int welcome()
{
   int type;

   cout << "Program cipher6.cpp enciphers a message using one" << endl
        << "of the following techniques to form a cipher alphabet:"
                 << endl << endl
             << "(1) Interval Extraction Sequence" << endl
             << "(2) Simple Transposition Sequence" << endl
             << "(3) Numeric Transposition Sequence" << endl << endl
```

```
                 << "Enter method to form enciphered message 1, 2 or 3: ";

    cin >> type;

    while ((type <ONE) || (type > THREE)){
        cerr << "\aYou must enter a number between 1 and 3!" << endl;
        cerr << "Choice: ";
        cin >> type;
    }

    //get the newline off the stream
    cin.get();
    cout << endl;

    return type;
}//end welcome()
//end file cipher6.cpp
```

Decipherment

You can easily construct a program to decipher messages previously enciphered through the use of an interval extraction, simple transposition, or
numeric transposition sequence used to form a cipher alphabet. In doing
so, you can use the subroutines contained in the previously created
DCIPHER5.BAS program, change the main portion of the program to
reflect the selection of one of the three decipherment techniques under
consideration, and add the subroutines INTERVAL and TRANSPORT. The
resulting programs, which are contained on the files DCIPHER6.BAS and
DCIPHER6.CPP on the companion CD-ROM, are named as such since
they are to be used to decipher messages previously enciphered through
the use of the CIPHER6.BAS and CIPHER6.CPP programs.

The DCIPHER6.BAS Program

Listing 4.8 lists the statements in the main program of the
DCIPHER6.BAS program. You should note that the main portion of
DCIPHER6.BAS is almost an exact duplicate of CIPHER6.BAS, with the
differences between programs related to the use of the term "decipher" in
place of "encipher" and the inclusion of the subroutines DMSGFILE and
DCONVERTSTORE in place of MSGFILE and CONVERTSTORE. As
explained previously, the prefix D on a subroutine is used to indicate a
modification to a previously developed subroutine which results in a

deciphering operation in place of an enciphering operation. Similar to other programs in this chapter, a comment consisting of five asterisks is used to indicate an extraneous PRINT statement included for explanation purposes but which can be removed from the program if you so desire.

Listing 4.8 The main portion of the DCIPHER6.BAS program.

```
REM PROGRAM DECIPHER.BAS
DIM PLAINTEXT$(92), CIPHERTEXT$(36, 92), KEY$(92)
        CLS
        PRINT "DECIPHER.BAS PROGRAM deciphers text based upon the use"
        PRINT "of enciphering techniques contained in the book:"
        PRINT "ELECTRONIC MAIL PRIVACY:USING PRACTICAL ENCIPHERING
                TECHNIQUES"
        PRINT
        PRINT "This program supports the use of upper and lower case
                letters,"
        PRINT "digits, punctuation characters and other characters whose
                ASCII"
        PRINT "values range between 32 and 128, but EXCLUDES the use of the"
        PRINT "foward slash (/), backslash (\) and double quote characters."
        PRINT
        PRINT
AGN1:   INPUT "Enter your secret code (6 characters required) : "; CODE$
        IF LEN(CODE$) = 6 THEN GOTO OK
        CLS
        PRINT "Your secret code must be 6 characters - please try again"
        PRINT
        GOTO AGN1
OK:     CLS
GOSUB INITIALIZE                'initialize plaintext values
GOSUB SETUP                     'obtain random seed and position in seed
GOSUB DMSGFILE                  'assign I/O files, place message on a file
GOSUB KEYWORD                   'form keyword based alphabet of 96 characters
GOSUB PFORMCIPHER               'create 36 cipher alphabets
GOSUB RDCONVERTSTORE            'convert and store ciphertext on a file
GOSUB PRTOUT                    'print results
STOP
```

```
Figure 4.9 Enciphering a sample message using the CIPHER6.BAS
program.

/TO FIDEL
/FROM GORBY
PLEASE NOTE THAT A FEW CHANGES IN THE EAST
NOW WARRANT YOUR CONSIDERATION OF CHANGING
CUBAN ECONOMY TO THE CAPITALISTIC SYSTEM STOP
OTHERWISE REMEMBER FAMOUS FATE OF ROMANIAN LEADER
STOP BEST REGARDS STOP
\
Press Return key to display the resulting enciphered message

Resulting enciphered message is
TO FIDEL
FROM GORBY
YOUGI UVZLU LEGLG XUWNE GVAUI
RVLEU UGILV ZWWGF FGVLD ZPFNZ
VIRQU FGLRZ VZXNE GVARV ANPJG
VUNZV ZSDLZ LEUNG YRLGO RILRN
IDILU SILZY ZLEUF WRIUF USUSJ
UFXGS ZPIXG LUZXF ZSGVR BFOUG
QUFIL ZYJUI LFUAG FQIIL ZYXXX
```

To illustrate the use of DCIPHER6.BAS, let's execute CIPHER6.BAS. Figure 4.9 illustrates the plaintext message and its resulting enciphered message when an interval extraction sequence of 3, keyword of MAYDECEMBER, and alphabetic shift key of B are used to form the shifted keyword mixed alphabet.

Figure 4.10 illustrates the use of the DCIPHER6.BAS program to decipher our previously enciphered message. Note that the message recipient must know the type of technique used to encipher the message, the keyword or keyword phrase, and the alphabetic shift key. In addition, when an interval extraction technique is used, the recipient must also know the interval used for extraction.

Figure 4.10 Deciphering the message created using CIPHER6.BAS through the use of the DCIPHER6.BAS program.

```
Program DCIPHER6.BAS deciphers a message using one of the
following techniques to form a cipher alphabet
    (1) Interval Extraction Sequence
    (2) Simple Transposition Sequence
    (3) Numeric Transposition Sequence
Enter method to form enciphered message 1, 2, or 3: 1
Enter the interval as a numeric between 1 and 25: 3
Enter keyword or keyword phrase in UPPERCASE: MAYDECEMBER

Plaintext-based alphabet is: ABCDEFGHIJKLMNOPQRSTUVWXYZ
Keyword-based alphabet is: MAYCEDBRFGHIJKLNOPQSTUVWXZ
Interval alphabet is: YCFILPTWMDBGJNQUXAERHKOSVZ
Enter UPPERCASE alphabet shift key: B
Shifted keyword mixed alphabet is: GJNQUXAERHKOSVZYCFILPTWMDB
Enter filename to store plaintext message, default=MESSAGE.DAT
Enter filename to store enciphered message, defualt=CIPHERTX.DAT
Select keyboard (k) or file (f) message input: F
Press Return key to display resulting deciphered message

Resulting deciphered message is:
TO FIDEL
FROM GORBY
PLEAS ENOTE THATA FEWCH ANGES
INTHE EASTN OWWAR RANTY OURCO
NSIDE RATIO NOFCH ANGIN GCUBA
NECON OMYTO THECA PITAL ISTIC
SYSTE MSTOP OTHER WISER EMEMB
ERFAM OUSFA TEOFR OMANI ANLEA
DERST OPBES TREGA RDSST OPXXX
```

Because the author of this book is not a good typist, file input was selected in place of keyboard input. Because the program was created using the same PRTOUT subroutine used by enciphering programs to display the resulting deciphered message, that message is displayed in groups of five characters.

The inclusion of PRINT statements to display the four alphabets developed by the program can be used to trace the operation of the program. In addition, you can use the positional relationship between the plaintext alphabet characters and the characters in the shifted keyword mixed alphabet to verify the deciphering of the message contained in Figure 4.9 into the plaintext shown at the bottom of Figure 4.10. For example, the first group of five enciphered characters in Figure 4.9 is YOUGI. Locating

Y in the shifted keyword mixed alphabet in Figure 4.10 and reading upward to the plaintext alphabet results in the extraction of the character P. Similarly, O becomes L, U becomes E, G becomes A, and I becomes S. Thus, if you desire you can easily verify the operation of the program. Once you are satisfied with its operation or do not wish to probe its operation, you can remove the extraneous print statements that display the different alphabets.

The DCIPHER6.CPP Program

Similar to the program DCIPHER6.BAS, its C++ version which is stored on the CD-ROM under the filename DCIPHER6.CPP has a large number of functions used in the same manner as its encipher version. Thus, in this section we will focus our attention on examining the function that provides the program with its decipherment capability. That function is the decipher function whose statements are given in Listing 4.9. Listing 4.9 includes a number of built-in comments that define the logic of the program. You can find the complete program and the executable version on the CD-ROM in the C directory.

4

Chapter

Listing 4.9 The C++ decipher function used in the program DCIPHER6.CPP.

```
//------------------------------------------------------------------
//Function: decipher()
//Parameters: in - the input file we are deciphering
//            out - the output file we are writing the deciphered
//                  text to
//            PTEXT - the plaintext alphabet (used to decipher)
//            ctext - the ciphertext
//Return Type: None
//Purpose: Decipher the input file and write the contents to the
//output file specified by the user.
//------------------------------------------------------------------
void decipher(ifstream in, ofstream out, const char PTEXT[], char ctext[])
{
   char enc_file_data[SIZE];

   //continue this process until we get to the end of the file
   while (in.getline(enc_file_data, SIZE, '\n')){
      if (enc_file_data[0] == '/'){
         out << enc_file_data << endl;
      }
```

```
        else {
          //format the data - i.e., get rid of all spaces
                formatData(enc_file_data);

            //dump data to file
            for (int ix=0; ix<strlen(enc_file_data); ix++){

          //used to keep track of what plaintext character
              //we are going to use
              int jx;

              for (jx=0; jx<TWENTYSIX; jx++){
              //find where the encrypted data is in the
              //ciphertext - this location corresponds to
              //the plaintext character location
                  if (enc_file_data[ix] == ctext[jx])
                  break;
              }

          //conditionals for grouping by five and inserting
              //new lines
              if (!(ix%TWENTYFIVE))
                  out << endl;

              if ((ix!=0) && (!(ix%FIVE))){
                out << " " << PTEXT[jx];
              }
              else {
                  out << PTEXT[jx];
              }
          }
        }
    }

    return;
}//end decipher()
```

Monoalphabetic Combinations

Regardless of the technique or techniques used to form a monoalphabetic cipher alphabet, the maximum number of trials necessary to correctly decipher a message remains the same. That number is 26!, which is approximately 4.0329E+26—a very large number. However, that large number can be very deceptive, as it is relatively easy for a trained cryptanalyst to decipher a lengthy message by a frequency analysis of the characters in the enciphered message. For example, E is the most common letter in the English language, followed by the letter T, which has the next highest frequency of occurrence. By performing a frequency analysis of the characters in an enciphered message a trained analyst may be able to note that E was replaced by one character, T by another, and so on. By deciphering a few characters correctly, patterns may become visually identifiable. For example, deciphering three enciphered characters as EET may provide the analyst with a clue that the character prefixing the first deciphered E is the plaintext M. This monoalphabetic substitution weakness means you should keep messages relatively short to hinder the possibility of a frequency analysis being used as a wedge by a cryptanalyst to initiate the deciphering of your message. This weakness also resulted in the development of polyalphabetic substitution encipherment and pseudo-random encipherment techniques—topics I will cover in the next two chapters of this book.

4

Chapter

One of the more interesting matrix-based enciphering techniques operates upon pairs of characters to reduce the potential for a frequency analysis providing an easy mechanism to decipher messages. Although referred to as the Playfair cipher after Lyon Playfair, a scientist of Victorian England and the Deputy Speaker of the House of Commons, in actuality, the cipher was developed by Playfair's friend and close associate Charles Wheatstone.

The Playfair cipher system is based upon the formation of a keyword mixed alphabet that is contained in a 5x5 matrix, where the letters I and J are regarded as identical and combined to reduce the English alphabet to 25 letters. Thus, the use of the keyword QUALE would result in the following alphabetic matrix being used for encipherment.

```
Q    U    A    L    E
B    C    D    F    G
H    I/J  K    M    N
O    P    R    S    T
V    W    X    Y    Z
```

The encipherment of messages occurs using pairs of letters—a technique referred to as digraphic encipherment. The rules governing the encipherment of each pair of characters is based upon the relationship of the letters to one another in the keyword-based matrix. Because there are only three possible relationships between letters in the matrix, there are three rules that govern encipherment.

If a pair of letters falls within the same row, they are replaced by the letters to their right, with each row considered cyclical so that the letter to the right of the last letter in a row becomes the first letter in the row. Thus, the pair of letters ST would be replaced by TO, while QU would be replaced by UA.

The second rule governing the encipherment of pairs of letters is applicable to letters that appear in the same column. Similar to the rule governing the replacement of pairs of letters contained in the same row, letters that appear in the same column are replaced by the letter beneath each letter. Here, the cyclical provision results in the letter below the last letter in the column being the letter at the top of the column. Thus, DR would be enciphered as KX, while ZE would be enciphered as EG.

The third rule governing encipherment is applicable to the situation in which a pair of plaintext letters is not located in a common row or column. When this occurs, each letter is replaced by the letter located in its own row at the column position occupied by the other plaintext letter. Thus, under this rule DE would be replaced by GA, while TH would be replaced by ON.

To further reduce the ability of frequency analysis as a decipherment tool, any double letter occurring in a pair is separated by the use of an X. Thus, HOLLY would become HOLXLY if the pair of L letters was on a pair boundary.

The use of digraphs by the Playfair cipher extends the cipher combinations from 26 letters when a one-for-one monoalphabetic substitution process is used to either 625 or 676 digraphs, depending upon the manner in which the I/J letter combination is used. Not only does this technique provide a substantial expanded base of characters for a frequency analysis, but it results in forcing an analysis to be performed on letter pairs whose frequency of occurrence has substantially less divergence than single letters. For example, the two most common letters in the English language, E and T, have an average frequency of approximately 12 percent and 9 percent, respectively. In comparison, the two most common letter pairs, TH and HE, have a frequency of occurrence of 3.5 percent and 2.5 percent.

During World War II, the Playfair cipher was used by Australian coast watchers hiding on many Japanese occupied islands in the South Pacific. Using the keys ROYAL NEW ZEALAND NAVY and PHYSICAL EXAMINATION, messages were transmitted concerning the loss of PT 109 which led to the rescue of Lieutenant John F. Kennedy and his PT boat crew.

4

Chapter

Chapter 5

Polyalphabetic Substitution

The conclusion of Chapter 4, Transposition-Based Monoalphabetic Substitution, briefly discussed a major weakness of monoalphabetic substitution-based enciphering techniques. That weakness is its susceptibility to frequency analysis: A relatively long message can be used as a guide for a trial-and-error process in which the most commonly occurring letters in a plaintext alphabet are substituted for the most frequently occurring characters in the enciphered message. A trained cryptanalyst can use this technique as a wedge to further deciphering operations because the correct substitution of one plaintext character for an enciphered character is carried through the entire enciphered message when a monoalphabetic substitution process is employed.

One method used to overcome the weakness of a monoalphabetic substitution system is the use of a polyalphabetic substitution system. Unlike a monoalphabetic substitution system in which each plaintext character is mapped to a fixed ciphertext character, a polyalphabetic substitution system permits each plaintext character to be mapped into a different ciphertext character for a specified number of occurrences prior to being mapped back into its original ciphertext character. The number of different ciphertext characters each plaintext character can be mapped into depends upon the number of ciphertext alphabets used. The number of ciphertext alphabets used defines the period or cyclic redundancy of repetition of the mapping process.

Although a manual enciphering process becomes more difficult to perform as the number of ciphertext alphabets increases, the use of computers significantly reduces this difficulty. This chapter first examines the construction and utilization of several polyalphabetic substitution systems. Similar to previous chapters, this chapter shows you how to

Lawyer and architect Leon Battista Alberti is considered by many to be the father of Western cryptology. The author of the most comprehensive manuscript on cryptanalysis for its time, Alberti is also credited with the invention of polyalphabetic substitution and enciphered code in the fifteenth century.

Alberti's efforts in the development of a polyalphabetic substitution system took the form of a disk constructed through the use of two copper plates. The circumference of each plate was divided into 24 equal parts known as cells. The larger copper plate, which was stationary, contained the letters of the alphabet entered into each cell in their alphabetic sequence. The letters H, K, and Y were not included as Alberti did not feel they were necessary. Because the letters J, U, and W were not in his alphabet, he inscribed the numbers 1 to 4 to complete the entries in the cells of the fixed plate.

The second plate, whose diameter was smaller than the stationary plate, had 24 cells into which the letters of the Latin alphabet were inscribed in a random order. This plate was movable and was placed over the larger plate, with both plates attached to one another by a needle affixed through the center of both plates. This resulted in the needle providing a relationship between the movable and fixed plate cell entries.

Alberti's cipher disk enabled the relationship between the plaintext alphabet contained on the circumference on the fixed plate and the ciphertext alphabet contained on the circumference on the movable plate to be altered. To do so simply required the placement of a letter in the movable disk so it was positioned toward a letter on the outer disk. Because each new setting of Alberti's disk created a new cipher alphabet, each setting resulted in the altering of the plaintext-ciphertext encipherment relationship and enabled encipherment to occur using a polyalphabetic substitution process. All that was required to successfully encipher and decipher messages was for each party to have identical disks and agree upon the initial index letter of the movable disk and a method to change the use of the index.

construct enciphering and deciphering programs to automate the use of polyalphabetic substitution systems to encipher and decipher messages. This chapter also discusses several variations you may wish to consider in developing different types of polyalphabetic substitution systems.

Simple Polyalphabetic Substitution Systems

One of the earliest polyalphabetic substitution systems is known as the Vigenére cipher after its inventor, Blaise de Vigénere. First published in 1586, the Vigenére cipher is based upon the development of a tableau in which all possible displaced alphabets are positioned one under another, commencing with the original alphabet in the top row.

The Vigenére Cipher

Figure 5.1 illustrates the basic Vigenére tableau which consists of 26 rows, with each row containing 26 letters. Note that the Vigenére tableau can be represented as a 26x26 matrix consisting of 676 elements. In fact, the tableau contained in Figure 5.1 was created by the execution of the program POLY1.BAS whose contents are shown in Listing 5.1.

5

Chapter

```
Figure 5.1. Basic Vigenére tableau.

  ABCDEFGHIJKLMNOPQRSTUVWXYZ

A ABCDEFGHIJKLMNOPQRSTUVWXYZ
B BCDEFGHIJKLMNOPQRSTUVWXYZA
C CDEFGHIJKLMNOPQRSTUVWXYZAB
D DEFGHIJKLMNOPQRSTUVWXYZABC
E EFGHIJKLMNOPQRSTUVWXYZABCD
F FGHIJKLMNOPQRSTUVWXYZABCDE
G GHIJKLMNOPQRSTUVWXYZABCDEF
H HIJKLMNOPQRSTUVWXYZABCDEFG
I IJKLMNOPQRSTUVWXYZABCDEFGH
J JKLMNOPQRSTUVWXYZABCDEFGHI
K KLMNOPQRSTUVWXYZABCDEFGHIJ
L LMNOPQRSTUVWXYZABCDEFGHIJK
M MNOPQRSTUVWXYZABCDEFGHIJKL
N NOPQRSTUVWXYZABCDEFGHIJKLM
O OPQRSTUVWXYZABCDEFGHIJKLMN
P PQRSTUVWXYZABCDEFGHIJKLMNO
Q QRSTUVWXYZABCDEFGHIJKLMNOP
```

```
R  RSTUVWXYZABCDEFGHIJKLMNOPQ
S  STUVWXYZABCDEFGHIJKLMNOPQR
T  TUVWXYZABCDEFGHIJKLMNOPQRS
U  UVWXYZABCDEFGHIJKLMNOPQRST
V  VWXYZABCDEFGHIJKLMNOPQRSTU
W  WXYZABCDEFGHIJKLMNOPQRSTUV
X  XYZABCDEFGHIJKLMNOPQRSTUVW
Y  YZABCDEFGHIJKLMNOPQRSTUVWX
Z  ZABCDEFGHIJKLMNOPQRSTUVWXY
```

The POLY1.BAS Program

The POLY1.BAS program uses the previously developed INITIALIZE subroutine to initialize the letters of the alphabet into the string array PLAINTEXT$. The subroutine TABLE is used to fill the two-dimensional string array labeled TABLEAU$ with a sequence of 26 alphabets. Through the use of a nested pair of FOR-NEXT loops and a mod 26 operator, each row in the string array labeled TABLEAU$ is assigned an alphabet in which row *n* has a displacement of one character position with respect to row *n*-1. To illustrate the operation of the subroutine TABLE, note that when J is 0, I will vary from 0 to 25. Thus, the use of TABLEAU$(J,I) results in row 0 being assigned the values of PLAINTEXT$((I+0) mod 26), the non-displaced alphabet. Once the inner I loop is completed, J is incremented by 1 to a value of 1 and the I loop is again varied from 0 to 25. This results in TABLEAU$(J,I) having Row 1 assigned the alphabet displaced by one position, since PLAINTEXT$((I+J) mod 26) results in a value of 1 for J shifting the assignment of plaintext letters to TABLEAU$ by one position.

The subroutine PRINTIT was created to print the tableau as well as the row and column labels that represent vertically and horizontally positioned alphabets. This subroutine was developed simply to display the tableau, and its row and column positioning elements were used for the extraction of characters from the tableau during the enciphering process as we will shortly observe.

Listing 5.1 The POLY1.BAS program listing.

```
REM PROGRAM POLY1.BAS
DIM PLAINTEXT$(26), TABLEAU$(26, 26)
     CLS
```

```
GOSUB INITIALIZE
GOSUB TABLE
GOSUB PRINTIT
STOP
INITIALIZE:
        RESTORE
        REM Initialize plaintext values
        FOR I = 0 TO 25
        READ PLAINTEXT$(I)
        NEXT I
        DATA "A","B","C","D","E","F","G","H","I","J","K","L","M","N"
        DATA "O","P","Q","R","S","T","U","V","W","X","Y","Z"
RETURN
TABLE:
        FOR J = 0 TO 25
        FOR I = 0 TO 25
        TABLEAU$(J, I) = PLAINTEXT$((I + J) MOD 26)
        NEXT I
        NEXT J
RETURN
PRINTIT:
        PRINT "  ";
        FOR I = 0 TO 25: PRINT PLAINTEXT$(I); : NEXT I: PRINT : PRINT
        FOR J = 0 TO 25
        PRINT PLAINTEXT$(J); " ";
        FOR I = 0 TO 25
        PRINT TABLEAU$(J, I);
        NEXT I
        PRINT
        NEXT J
RETURN
```

The POLY1.CPP Program

To add a bit of diversity, the C++ program version of POLY1.BAS was written to display one line at a time, requiring you to hit Enter at the end of each line to proceed to the next line. Listing 5.2 contains the listing of the program POLY1.CPP. Both that program and the executable version of the program named POLY1.EXE are stored in the C directory on the companion CD-ROM.

Listing 5.2 The POLY1.CPP program listing.

```
/*poly1.cpp
C++ code written by Jonathan Held, March 26, 1998,
using Microsoft's Visual C++ version 5.0.
*/

//standard include files
#include <iostream.h>

//constant we will use
const int TWENTYSIX = 26, TWENTYSEVEN = 27, SIZE = 256;

//function prototypes
void initialize(char [][TWENTYSEVEN], const char []);
void printHeader(const char[]);
void printTable(const char [][TWENTYSEVEN]);


//------------------------------------------------------------------
//Function: main()
//Parameters:  None
//Return type: None
//Purpose: Demonstrates a simple Vigenere tableau.
//------------------------------------------------------------------
int main()
{
    char plaintext[TWENTYSEVEN] = {'A','B','C','D','E','F','G','H',
                                   'I','J','K','L','M','N','O','P',
                                   'Q','R','S','T','U','V','W','X',
                                   'Y','Z','\0'};

    char table[TWENTYSIX][TWENTYSEVEN];

    initialize(table, plaintext);
    printHeader(plaintext);
    printTable(table);

    return 0;
}//end main()


//------------------------------------------------------------------
//Function: initialize()
//Parameters:  tbl - the two-dimensional Vigenere tableau
```

```
//              PTEXT - the plaintext alphabet
//Return type: None
//Purpose: Creates the Vigenere tableau by performing a shift on
//the plaintext alphabet for each Vigenere row entry.
//-----------------------------------------------------------------
void initialize(char tbl[][TWENTYSEVEN], const char PTEXT[])
{
   for (int ix=0; ix<TWENTYSIX; ix++){
      for (int jx=0; jx<TWENTYSIX; jx++){
         tbl[ix][jx] = PTEXT[(ix+jx)%TWENTYSIX];
      }
      tbl[ix][TWENTYSIX] = '\0';
   }

   return;
}//end initialize()




//-----------------------------------------------------------------
//Function: printHeader()
//Parameters:  PTEXT - the plaintext alphabet (also serves as the
//             Vigenere column header
//Return type: None
//Purpose: Prints the Vigenere column header and informs the user
//to hit enter after each line of the table is printed.
//-----------------------------------------------------------------
void printHeader(const char PTEXT[])
{
   cout << "Hit enter at the end of each line" << endl
        << "to proceed to the next. " << endl << endl;

   cout << "\t";

   for (int ix=0; ix<TWENTYSIX; ix++)
      cout << PTEXT[ix];

   cout << endl << endl;
   return;
}//end printHeader()




//-----------------------------------------------------------------
//Function: printTable()
//Parameters:  TABLE - the two-dimensional Vigenere tableau
```

```
//Return type: None
//Purpose: Creates the Vigenere tableau by performing a shift on
//the plaintext alphabet for each Vigenere row entry.
//----------------------------------------------------------------
void printTable(const char TABLE[][TWENTYSEVEN])
{
   char junk[SIZE];

   for (int ix=0; ix<TWENTYSIX; ix++){
      cout << TABLE[ix][0] << "\t";
      cout << TABLE[ix];

      //get any characters the user may have types off
      //the input stream and discard them
      cin.getline(junk, SIZE, '\n');
   }

   return;
}//end printTable()
//end file poly1.cpp
```

Encipherment

To use the Vigenére cipher system, first select a keyword or keyword phrase. This keyword or keyword phrase, unlike those used in a keyword-based mixed alphabet, can retain repeating characters. For example, SECRET is a valid Vigenére cipher keyword, although it would be modified to SECRT if used to develop a keyword-based mixed alphabet.

Once the Vigenére keyword or keyword phrase is selected, it is repeated in tandem with the characters in the plaintext message as the plaintext message is encoded. On a repeating basis, one character from the plaintext message and one character from the keyword are used as row and column header indices. The location within the tableau where the indices intersect points to the ciphertext character which is extracted from the tableau.

Figure 5.2 illustrates an example of a Vigenére encipherment using the keyword SECRET. Due to the symmetrical structure of the tableau, you can use either the row or column for the plaintext character pointer and the opposite row or column for the keyword character pointer. For example, using the plaintext character for the row position and the keyword character for the column position results in the extraction of the cipher-text character E when the plaintext character is M and the keyword character is S. If you reverse the assignment of rows and columns, the use of the column character M and the row character of S as pointers also results in the extraction of the ciphertext character E.

Although the use of a Vigenére cipher negates the use of a letter frequency count as a decipherment wedge by a cryptanalyst, this cipher system has one serious deficiency. This deficiency is known as the "probable word" attack in which a cryptanalyst first selects a word considered likely to be in the plaintext message. Then, the cryptanalyst performs a modulo 26 subtraction of each character in that word from all possible locations in the ciphertext, examining the sequence of characters produced by the modulo 26 subtraction process for a recognizable word or word fragment.

```
Figure 5.2 A Vigenére encipherment.

Keyword:            SECRETSECRETSECRETSECRE

Plaintext:          MEETMEINSTLOUISTOMORROW

Ciphertext:         EIGKQXARUKPHMMUKSFGVTFA
```

During World War I, the Italians used an encipher system known as cifrario tascabile, or "pocket cipher," that was a modified Vigenére cipher with the digits added to the end of the plaintext alphabet, while the cipher alphabets consisted of the digits 10 to 45 in sequence. Radiograms intercepted by the Austrians that were enciphered using the cifrario tascabile usually required less than half a day for trained cryptanalysts to decipher, and provided them with a wealth of information, including the ability to respond to an Italian offensive before the offensive was launched!

Other Polyalphabetic Substitution Methods

As previously explained, a major weakness of the Vigenére cipher system is its susceptibility to a probable word attack. This susceptibility results from the use of a repeating keyword whose characters are continuously used as pointers with each plaintext character for the extraction of a ciphertext character from the tableau. To counter this susceptibility you can develop a large number of different polyalphabetic substitution methods—a few of which we will investigate in this section. However, prior to doing so let us examine the major elements of a periodic polyalphabetic substitution system.

Periodic Polyalphabetic Substitution

A periodic polyalphabetic substitution system contains one plaintext alphabet and two or more cipher alphabets. The plaintext alphabet is considered to be the primary alphabet because it serves as an extraction pointer to a column location within each cipher alphabet row. The cipher alphabets provide the characters for extraction that yield the ciphertext and are referred to as secondary alphabets.

Figure 5.3 illustrates a simple example of a periodic polyalphabetic substitution system. In this example, the plaintext alphabet is the simple sequential English alphabet A through Z, with position one commencing with the letter A. The secondary cipher alphabets are a sequence of five plaintext alphabets shifted by one, two, three, four, and five character positions. The first cipher alphabet is indicated by the row header C1, while succeeding cipher alphabets are indicated by row headers C2, C3, C4, and C5.

```
Figure 5.3 Periodic polyalphabetic substitution system.

Plaintext alphabet:
        ABCDEFGHIJKLMNOPQRSTUVWXYZ

Cipher alphabets:
C1      BCDEFGHIJKLMNOPQRSTUVWXYZA
C2      CDEFGHIJKLMNOPQRSTUVWXYZAB
C3      DEFGHIJKLMNOPQRSTUVWXYZABC
C4      EFGHIJKLMNOPQRSTUVWXYZABCD
C5      FGHIJKLMNOPQRSTUVWXYZABCDE
```

Operation

The operation of a periodic polyalphabetic substitution system involves locating the plaintext character in the plaintext alphabet. Next, the match position is located and serves as a pointer to the extraction of a cipher character from the first cipher alphabet. The second plaintext character is then matched against the plaintext alphabet, and the match position serves as a mechanism to extract the second cipher character from the second cipher alphabet. This process continues until a character is extracted from the last cipher alphabet. At this point the process begins anew with the result of the next plaintext match causing an extraction to occur from the first cipher alphabet.

To illustrate the use of a periodic polyalphabetic substitution system, encipher the message FIRE FRED using the system illustrated in Figure 5.3. Locating F in the plaintext and using that character location as a pointer to the first cipher alphabet (C1) results in the extraction of the cipher character G. Next, locating I in the plaintext and using its position as a pointer to the second cipher alphabet (C2) results in the extraction of the cipher character K. Similarly, R is enciphered as U, E is enciphered as I, and F is enciphered as K. Because you have now used the last cipher alphabet, encipher R, which is the sixth character in the plaintext message, using the first cipher alphabet, resulting in R being enciphered as S. Similarly, E is enciphered using the second cipher alphabet as G, while D is enciphered using the third cipher alphabet to obtain its replacement by G. Thus, the message FIRE FRED is enciphered as GKUIKSGG.

In the example shown in Figure 5.3, there was a total of five cipher alphabets. This means that the use of each cipher alphabet is repeated for every five characters in the plaintext—this polyalphabetic substitution system is then said to have a period of five. Unfortunately, this also means that if a cryptanalyst can determine the repetition period of the cipher alphabets, he or she can perform a series of character frequency analyses that could eventually result in the decipherment of an intercepted message. To add a degree of difficulty to the life of a cryptanalyst, you can consider a variety of techniques to reduce the potential of analysis and decipherment.

5

Chapter

Reducing Probability of Decipherment

One method that can be used to reduce the potential threat of analysis and decipherment is to extend its repetition period. Although this is time consuming when performed manually and subject to an increased probability of an enciphering error as the number of cipher alphabets increases, you can easily accomplish this through automation via a computer. Because you would also want to eliminate the use of a simple displacement for creating the cipher alphabets, you can use several methods to accomplish this. First, you can base the creation of the plaintext and each ciphertext alphabet upon the use of a keyword or keyword phrase. For example, assume you use the keyword MICROSOFT for the plaintext alphabet and the keyword phrase WINDOWS ARE FUN for the ciphertext alphabets. You can use the first keyword in its normal manner, and the second keyword can be used vertically as a mechanism to establish shifted cipher alphabets.

Figure 5.4 illustrates the use of a keyword-based periodic polyalphabetic substitution system using the keyword MICROSOFT to form the plaintext alphabet, while the keyword phrase WINDOWS ARE FUN is used to form shifted cipher alphabets. You should note that the plaintext keyword-based alphabet at the top of Figure 5.4 serves as a position pointer to each cipher alphabet. Concerning the cipher alphabet, you should note that since I will shortly develop a program using 26 cipher alphabets incorporated into a matrix, I labeled the cipher alphabets 0 to 25 to correspond to the array index that will be used. You should also note that the use of a vertical keyword or keyword phrase to form cipher alphabets positions the keyword or keyword phrase characters to the extreme right of the matrix in the last column. For example, in cipher alphabet 0 W is rotated to the last column; hence, the first column commences with the character X. Similarly, in Row 1 (cipher alphabet 1) the character I in the keyword phrase WINDOWSAREFUN is positioned in the last column, which makes the character J the first character in Row 1.

Figure 5.4 A plaintext keyword-based alphabet and polyalphabetic ciphertext matrix using a shifted keyword-based alphabet.

```
    MICROSFTABDEGHJKLNPQUVWXYZ

0   XYZABCDEFGHIJKLMNOPQRSTUVW
1   JKLMNOPQRSTUVWXYZABCDEFGHI
2   OPQRSTUVWXYZABCDEFGHIJKLMN
3   EFGHIJKLMNOPQRSTUVWXYZABCD
4   PQRSTUVWXYZABCDEFGHIJKLMNO
5   TUVWXYZABCDEFGHIJKLMNOPQRS
6   BCDEFGHIJKLMNOPQRSTUVWXYZA
7   STUVWXYZABCDEFGHIJKLMNOPQR
8   FGHIJKLMNOPQRSTUVWXYZABCDE
9   GHIJKLMNOPQRSTUVWXYZABCDEF
10  VWXYZABCDEFGHIJKLMNOPQRSTU
11  CDEFGHIJKLMNOPQRSTUVWXYZAB
12  DEFGHIJKLMNOPQRSTUVWXYZABC
13  HIJKLMNOPQRSTUVWXYZABCDEFG
14  IJKLMNOPQRSTUVWXYZABCDEFGH
15  KLMNOPQRSTUVWXYZABCDEFGHIJ
16  LMNOPQRSTUVWXYZABCDEFGHIJK
17  MNOPQRSTUVWXYZABCDEFGHIJKL
18  NOPQRSTUVWXYZABCDEFGHIJKLM
19  QRSTUVWXYZABCDEFGHIJKLMNOP
20  RSTUVWXYZABCDEFGHIJKLMNOPQ
21  UVWXYZABCDEFGHIJKLMNOPQRST
22  WXYZABCDEFGHIJKLMNOPQRSTUV
23  YZABCDEFGHIJKLMNOPQRSTUVWX
24  ZABCDEFGHIJKLMNOPQRSTUVWXY
25  ABCDEFGHIJKLMNOPQRSTUVWXYZ
```

5

Chapter

One weakness of polyalphabetic substitution systems was discovered by Auguste Kerckhoffs, a Dutchman born in 1835 who became a naturalized citizen of France. Author of *La Cryptographie militaire*, considered one of the most extensive works on cryptanalysis, Kerckhoffs developed a general solution for polyalphabetic substitution systems that has deciphered many "unbreakable" messages.

Under the Kerckhoffs method, a group of several intercepted messages is aligned so that the position of each enciphered character in each message is aligned by column. If the same key is used for the encipherment of each message, the letters in each column represent an encipherment process in which the same ciphertext alphabet was used. Thus, each column can be attacked as if it represented a monoalphabetic substitution by performing a frequency analysis of the letters in each column. Of course, if you change the key used to govern the enciphering process, the frequency of key changes and the number of messages enciphered by any one key determines the ability of the Kerckhoffs process to be used against your messages. If you transmit only a few messages with each key prior to changing the key, a frequency analysis of your messages on a column-by-column basis will more than likely produce meaningless results. If you transmit a large number of messages but change keys frequently, your message groups enciphered by a common key will probably be sufficient for a cryptanalyst to apply Kerckhoffs' method. Thus, you must balance both the change in keys and the number of messages enciphered using a key.

The POLY2.BAS Program

Now that you have reviewed a few techniques to construct a series of cipher alphabets, I'll show you how to develop a program to encipher a message using a polyalphabetic substitution technique. This program is stored in the file POLY2.BAS on the companion CD-ROM, and, for simplicity of illustration, will use 26 cipher alphabets.

Listing 5.3 contains the main portion of POLY2.BAS. After using four
PRINT statements to display information about the program, the first
INPUT statement assigns the plaintext keyword or keyword phrase to the
string variable TEXT$. The subroutine INITIALIZE is then invoked to
form the plaintext alphabet and the subroutine KEYWORD is invoked to
form a keyword-based mixed alphabet. This is followed by a FOR-NEXT
loop which assigns the keyword-based alphabet to the string array
PLAIN$, since the string array PLAINTEXT$ will be reused. Once the
ciphertext keyword or keyword phrase is entered, it is assigned to the
string variable TEXT$ and the subroutines INITIALIZE and KEYWORD are
invoked again to form the ciphertext keyword-based mixed alphabet. This
alphabet is placed into the array CIPHER$ through the use of a
FOR-NEXT loop. Then, a series of four subroutines is invoked. Subroutines PFORMCIPHER and PCONVERTSTORE are modified versions of the
subroutines FORMCIPHER and CONVERTSTORE previously developed,
with the prefix P used to denote its modification for polyalphabetic use.
Subroutines MSGFILE and PRTOUT remain the same and will not be discussed further.

Listing 5.3 The main portion of the POLY2.BAS program.

```
REM PROGRAM POLY2.BAS
DIM PLAINTEXT$(26), PLAIN$(26), CIPHER$(26), CIPHERTEXT$(26), KEY$(26)
        CLS
        PRINT "POLY2.BAS PROGRAM enciphers text based upon the use of
                two keywords"
        PRINT "or keyword phrases using a polyalphabetic substitution
                process using"
        PRINT "26 cipher alphabets."
        PRINT
        INPUT "Enter plaintext keyword or keyword phrase in UPPERCASE: ",
                TEXT$
GOSUB INITIALIZE                  'initialize plaintext alphabet
GOSUB KEYWORD                     'form keyword based mixed alphabet
        FOR I = 0 TO 25: PLAIN$(I) = PLAINTEXT$(I): NEXT I
        INPUT "Enter ciphertext keyword or keyword phrase in UPPERCASE:",
                TEXT$
GOSUB INITIALIZE                  're-initialize plaintext alphabet
GOSUB KEYWORD
```

```
        FOR I = 0 TO 25: CIPHER$(I) = PLAINTEXT$(I): NEXT I
GOSUB PFORMCIPHER                'create 26 cipher alphabets
GOSUB MSGFILE                    'assign I/O files, place message on a file
GOSUB PCONVERTSTORE              'convert and store ciphertext on a file
GOSUB PRTOUT                     'print results
STOP
```

The PFORMCIPHER Subroutine

Listing 5.4 illustrates the statements contained in the subroutine PFORMCIPHER. As noted from the REM statement at the beginning of this subroutine, its function is to form 26 ciphertext alphabets using the first keyword character as a basis for generating each alphabet.

Listing 5.4 The PFORMCIPHER subroutine.

```
PFORMCIPHER:
        REM routine to form 26 CIPHERTEXT alphabets based upon the first
            keyword character
        FOR ZI = 0 TO 25
        GOSUB INITIALIZE
        FOR J = 0 TO 25
        IF CIPHER$(ZI) = PLAINTEXT$(J) THEN GOTO GOTYA
        NEXT J
GOTYA:  J = J + 1
        FOR K = 0 TO 25
        CIPHERTEXT$(ZI) = CIPHERTEXT$(ZI) + PLAINTEXT$((K + J) MOD 26)
        NEXT K
        NEXT ZI
        LPRINT TAB(5);
RETURN
```

The subroutine PFORMCIPHER contains three FOR-NEXT loops. The outer loop uses the index ZI which varies from 0 to 25 and is used to develop 26 ciphertext alphabets. After the first FOR statement, invoke the subroutine INITIALIZE to set the plaintext alphabet in its sequence into the array PLAINTEXT$. The FOR-NEXT loop using the index J then compares the character in the appropriate location of the string array CIPHER$ to each character in PLAINTEXT$ until a match occurs. When a match occurs, the character in the string array CIPHER$, which represents the first character in the ciphertext alphabet ZI, is matched to position J in the plaintext alphabet and a branch to the label GOTYA occurs.

Because you want to shift the matched character to the last column, increment J by 1 prior to using the FOR-NEXT loop with K as the index to form the ciphertext alphabet. The execution of the subroutine PFORMCIPHER produces the 26x26-character matrix previously illustrated in Figure 5.4, as CIPHERTEXT$(ZI) varies from 0 to 25 when WINDOWSAREFUN is used as the ciphertext keyword phrase.

The PCONVERTSTORE Subroutine

The subroutine PCONVERTSTORE is similar to the subroutine CONVERTSTORE, although it is modified to sequentially pick a ciphertext character from each cipher alphabet in sequence until the last alphabet is reached. The ciphertext character extraction process begins anew with the first cipher alphabet.

Listing 5.5 contains the statements in the subroutine PCONVERTSTORE. The statement that sets the variable C to a value of 0 also sets the pointer to the first cipher alphabet. The next modification to CONVERTSTORE is the replacement of the string array PLAINTEXT$ by the string array PLAIN$ in the first IF statement in the subroutine. This statement mates a character from the plaintext stored in the string variable TEXT$ to a character in the string variable PLAIN$ which contains the keyword-based mixed plaintext alphabet. When a match occurs, J points to the location in the keyword-based mixed alphabet that serves as a pointer to each cipher alphabet for the extraction to a cipher character. However, when you branch to the label GOTIT, you must increment J by 1 because you incremented J by that amount in the subroutine PFORMCIPHER.

Listing 5.5 The PCONVERTSTORE subroutine.

```
PCONVERTSTORE:
      REM Routine to convert and store ciphertext on a file
      OPEN INFILE$ FOR INPUT AS #1
      OPEN OUTFILE$ FOR OUTPUT AS #2
      C = 0                            'first alphabet pointer
      DO UNTIL EOF(1)
              INPUT #1, TEXT$
              MSGLEN = LEN(TEXT$)
              IF MID$(TEXT$, 1, 1) = "/" THEN GOTO CLEARTXT
              IF MID$(TEXT$, 1, 1) = "\" THEN GOTO DONE1
```

```
              REM Convert plaintext to ciphertext
                      FOR I = 1 TO MSGLEN
                      FOR J = 0 TO 25
                      IF MID$(TEXT$, I, 1) = PLAIN$(J) THEN GOTO GOTIT
                      NEXT J
GOTIT:                MID$(TEXT$, I, 1) = MID$(CIPHERTEXT$(C), J + 1, 1)
                      C = C + 1
                      IF C = 26 THEN C = 0      'reset to first alphabet
                      NEXT I
CLEARTXT:             WRITE #2, TEXT$
       LOOP
DONE1:        CLOSE #2
RETURN
```

Once a match occurs and you branch to the label GOTIT, the character in the string TEXT$ is replaced by a character from the cipher alphabet whose index value is C at position J+1 through the use of the MID$ statement. C is then incremented by 1 to point to the next cipher alphabet. However, if C equals 26 it is reset to a value of 0 to point back to the first cipher alphabet.

Program Execution

Figure 5.5 illustrates an example of the execution of POLY2.BAS using MICROSOFT as the plaintext keyword and WINDOWSAREGREAT as the ciphertext keyword phrase. I purposely changed the ciphertext keyword from WINDOWSAREFUN to WINDOWSAREGREAT to illustrate one deficiency of keyword-based polyalphabetic substitution systems—common keywords or keyword phrases. (The POLY2.BAS program enciphers text based on the use of two keywords or keyword phrases using a polyalphabetic substitution process using 26 cipher alphabets.)

Figure 5.5 The execution of POLY2.BAS.

```
Enter plaintext keyword or keyword phrase in UPPERCASE: MICROSOFT
Enter ciphertext keyword or keyword phrase in UPPERCASE: WINDOWSAREGREAT
Enter filename to store plaintext message, default=MESSAGE.DAT
Enter filename to store enciphered message, default=CIPHERTX.DAT
Select keyboard (k) or file (f) message input: K
Enter your message - place a / at the beginning of each line
that should remain in plaintext and a \ on a separate line
to indicate the end of the enciphered message

/TO ROSS THE BOSS
/FROM JUDY
YOU CONFUSED PICK UP THE BALL AND GET
OFF THE COURT WITH THE QUOTE WHEN THE
GOING GETS TOUGH THE TOUGH GET GOING
\
Press Return key to display resulting enciphered message

Resulting enciphered message is:

TO ROSS THE BOSS
FROM JUDY
VNIGT KHMKR FUEJX EDTAB ACMOH
RHVZL TZHZS RXGXK PGMTA XEFPS
DHIFB PGOAD PKWTP TTRQT RKDHD
LKHBD ARBEI EJHMO
```

At this point it may be useful to manually encipher a portion of the clear-text message YOU CONFUSED... to develop the enciphered message VNIGT KHMKR EUEIX... shown in the lower portion of Figure 5.5. Using the keyword-based mixed plaintext alphabet at the top of Figure 5.4, locate Y and extract the character in the Y column from the first cipher alphabet, obtaining the character V. Next, locate the character O in the keyword-based mixed plaintext alphabet and extract the character in the plaintext O column from the second cipher alphabet to obtain the character N. Similarly, U in the plaintext message results in I being extracted from the third cipher alphabet, and so on.

In Figure 5.4, the ciphertext keyword phrase WINDOWSAREFUN was used, while the ciphertext keyword phrase WINDOWSAREGREAT was used when the program POLY2.BAS was executed. Because both keyword phrases have the first 10 characters in common, of which 9 are used to form cipher alphabets due to a duplicate W, the first 9 cipher alphabets are the same for both keyword phrases. This means that the use of a polyalphabetic substitution system will be more secure if you avoid industry-specific keyword or keyword phrases as well as other terms someone may be able to correctly guess based upon your or other employees' work habits.

The COUNT.CPP Program

As a "bonus" for readers who have followed the alphabets in this chapter, I will provide a bonus program in this section in addition to the customary C++ version of a previously explained BASIC program. The bonus C++ program is appropriately named COUNT.CPP as it counts the characters in a file, performing a frequency analysis.

Listing 5.6 contains a listing of the statements in the C++ bonus program. Although the program COUNT.CPP was written to analyze encrypted files that contain uppercase alphabetic characters, you can easily modify it to operate on all characters in the character set by changing its computeFrequencyCount function. This modification is left as an exercise for you to perform.

Listing 5.6 The COUNT.CPP program listing.

```
/*
count.cpp
C++ code written by Jonathan Held, March 27, 1998,
using Microsoft's Visual C++ version 5.0.
*/

//standard include files
#include <assert.h>
#include <ctype.h>
#include <iostream.h>
#include <iomanip.h>
#include <fstream.h>
#include <string.h>
```

```
//function prototypes
bool computeFrequencyCount(const char *&, const char*&);
void displayOutput(ofstream, const char *&);
void getFileNames(char *&, char *&);
void initialize(void);
void welcome(void);

//constants
const int TWENTYSIX = 26, SIXTYFIVE = 65, NINETY = 90,
          ONE_HUNDRED = 100, SIZE = 256;

//globals
int count[TWENTYSIX];
int total_characters = 0;


//-----------------------------------------------------------------
//Function: main()
//Parameters:  None
//Return type: int
//Purpose: Performs a frequency analysis on encrypted text that
//was enciphered using monoalphabetic substitution techniques.
//-----------------------------------------------------------------
int main()
{
   bool success = false;
   char *inp_file, *op_file;

   welcome();
   initialize();
   getFileNames(inp_file, op_file);
   success = computeFrequencyCount(inp_file, op_file);

   if (!success){
      cerr << "\a\nProblem opening input file and/or "
           << "writing to output file!" << endl
         << "Program terminating abnormally." << endl;
   }

   delete [] inp_file;
   delete [] op_file;

   return (success);
}//end main
```

5

Chapter

```
//------------------------------------------------------------------
//Function: computeFrequencyCount()
//Parameters:  INP - the name of the input file
//             OP - the name of the output file
//Return type: bool, true if we are successful, false otherwise
//Purpose: Computes the frequency count of an encrypted file by
//reading a line of text, analyzing the line one character at a
//time, indexing into the global count array and incrementing the
//count of that character, and continuing until it reaches the
//end of the line.  This process is continued until the eof is
//reached.  Since all characters are uppercase, we index into the
//count array on the ASCII value of the character minus 65.  Hence,
//an A is at index 0 (65-65=0), and Z is at index 25 (90-65=25).
//------------------------------------------------------------------
bool computeFrequencyCount(const char *&INP, const char *&OP)
{
   bool success = false;
   char temp[SIZE];

   ifstream input(INP, ios:: in);
   ofstream output(OP, ios:: out);

   //if we can't open the input file, we need to report the
   //error to the user
   if ((!input) || (!output)){
      //do nothing
   }
   else {
      success = true;

      //read each character
      char one_character;

      //character's ASCII value
      int value;

      //perform frequency count on each line
      while (input.getline(temp, SIZE, '\n')){

         for (int ix=0; ix<strlen(temp); ix++){

            one_character = *(temp+ix);
            value = static_cast<int>(one_character);
```

```
                //check for a valid character
                if ((value >= SIXTYFIVE) || (value <= NINETY)){

                      //increment the number of characters
                   total_characters++;

                         //add the count of the character to the array
                         count[value - SIXTYFIVE] += 1;
                         }
                   }
            }

      //check for no characters in the input file
      if (total_characters == 0){
         success = false;
      }
      else {
         //echo the output to the screen and save it to a file
         displayOutput(output, OP);
      }
   }

   return success;
}//end computeFrequencyCount()


//-----------------------------------------------------------------
//Function: displayOutput()
//Parameters:  OUTFILE - the file we are writing the results to
//             FILE_NAME - the name of the output file
//Return type: None
//Purpose: Displays the results to the screen and saves them to a
//file named FILE_NAME.
//-----------------------------------------------------------------
void displayOutput(ofstream OUTFILE, const char*& FILE_NAME)
{
   cout << "Frequency count is: " << endl << endl;
   OUTFILE << "Frequency count is: " << endl << endl;

   cout << "Character" << "\t" << "Count" << "\t" << "Frequency" << endl;
   OUTFILE << "Character" << "\t" << "Count" << "\t" << "Frequency" <<
endl;

   for (int ix=0; ix<TWENTYSIX; ix++){
```

```
        cout << setw(4) << static_cast<char>(ix + SIXTYFIVE) << "\t\t"
                << setw(3) << count[ix] << "\t"
                << static_cast<float>(count[ix])/total_characters*ONE_HUNDRED
                << "%" << endl;
    OUTFILE << setw(4) << static_cast<char>(ix + SIXTYFIVE) << "\t\t"
                 << setw(3) << count[ix] << "\t"
                << static_cast<float>(count[ix])/total_characters*ONE_HUNDRED
                << "%" << endl;

    }

    cout << "\nTotal number of characters is: " << total_characters << endl;
    cout << "Data saved to file " << FILE_NAME << endl;
    OUTFILE << "\nTotal number of characters is: " << total_characters <<
endl;

    return;
}//end displayOutput()



//---------------------------------------------------------------
//Function: getFileNames()
//Parameters:  input - the input file
//             output - the output file where the frequency data
//                      will be saved
//Return type: None
//Purpose: Queries the user for the input and output file names.
//---------------------------------------------------------------
void getFileNames(char *&input, char *&output)
{
    char temp[SIZE];
    int char_count = 0;

    cout << "Input file (the file you want to perform" << endl
         << "the frequency count on): ";

    cin.getline(temp, SIZE, '\n');
    char_count = strlen(temp);

    assert(input = new char[char_count+1]);
    strcpy(input, temp);

    cout << "\nOutput file: ";
```

```
      cin.getline(temp, SIZE, '\n');
      char_count = strlen(temp);

      assert(output = new char[char_count+1]);
      strcpy(output, temp);
      return;
}//end getFileNames()




//------------------------------------------------------------------
//Function: initialize()
//Parameters:  None
//Return type: None
//Purpose: Initializes the character count to 0 for each character
//in the global count array.
//------------------------------------------------------------------
void initialize()
{
   for (int ix=0; ix<TWENTYSIX; ix++){
      count[ix] = 0;
   }

   return;
}//end initialize




//------------------------------------------------------------------
//Function: welcome()
//Parameters:  None
//Return type: None
//Purpose: Describes the count.cpp program.
//------------------------------------------------------------------
void welcome(void)
{
   cout << "Program count.cpp performs a frequency count "
        << "on an encrypted file." << endl
        << "Results can be used to help decipher messages "
        << "that used a mono-" << endl
        << "alphabetic substitution scheme." << endl << endl;

   return;
}//end welcome()
//end file count.cpp
```

5

Chapter

The POLY2.CPP Program

The program POLY2.CPP, which represents the C++ language version of the POLY2.BAS program, was developed as a continuation of our strategy of providing encryption examples in both languages. Listing 5.7 includes the POLY2.CPP program listing. The actual program, as well as the executable version of the program, are located in the C directory on the CD-ROM. Concerning the executable version of the program, its filename follows the naming convention used in this book, resulting in the filename POLY2.EXE. To distinguish the executable versions of the BASIC and C++ programs from one another, it is important to remember that although they have the same filename, they are located in different directories. That is, the file POLY2.EXE located in the directory BASIC represents the executable version of the program POLY2.BAS while the file POLY2.EXE located in the C directory represents the executable version of the program POLY2.CPP.

Listing 5.7 The POLY2.CPP program listing.

```
/*poly2.cpp
C++ code written by Jonathan Held, April 1, 1998,
using Microsoft's Visual C++ version 5.0.
*/

//standard includes
#include<iostream.h>
#include<assert.h>
#include<string.h>
#include<ctype.h>
#include<fstream.h>

//constants we will use
const int FIVE = 5, TWENTYFIVE = 25, TWENTYSIX = 26,
          TWENTYSEVEN = 27, SIXTYFIVE = 65, NINETY = 90,
          NINETYTWO = 92, SIZE = 256, BIGSIZE = 1000;

//function prototypes
bool checkInput(char * &);
void createStream(char *, char []);
void createTable(char [][TWENTYSEVEN], const char [], const char []);
void display(char *);
void formatData(char []);
```

```
bool encryptText(char *, char *, const char PTEXT[],
                        const char [][TWENTYSEVEN], char []);

char* formCipheredMessage(const char [], const char [][TWENTYSEVEN],
                        const char[], char []);

void getFileNames(char *&, char *&);
int getInputType(void);
int getKeyword(char *&);

bool getMessage(char *, char *, const char [],
                        const char [][TWENTYSEVEN], char []);

void groupBUFFER(ofstream, int);
void printCipherToFile(ofstream, char[]);
bool writeMatrixToFile(const char [], const char [][TWENTYSEVEN]);

char BUFFER[BIGSIZE] = {'\0'};

//------------------------------------------------------------------
//Function: main()
//Parameters: None
//Return Type: int - 0 means program terminated normally
//Purpose: Runs the main part of the program.
//------------------------------------------------------------------
int main()
{

    char plaintext[TWENTYSEVEN] = {'A','B','C','D','E','F','G','H',
                                   'I','J','K','L','M','N','O','P',
                                   'Q','R','S','T','U','V','W','X',
                                   'Y','Z','\0'};

    char *ptext_keyword, *ctext_keyword, *infile, *outfile;

    //p_stream is used to help form the alphabetic-shifted cipher
    //alphabets
    char p_stream[TWENTYSIX] = {'\0'};

    //c_stream represented the top row of the polyalphabetic ciphertext
    //matrix
    char c_stream[TWENTYSIX] = {'\0'};
```

```
//table is the actual polyalphabetic ciphertext matrix
char table[TWENTYSIX][TWENTYSEVEN], message_to_cipher[SIZE];

int type_of_input;
bool success = false;

cout << "Enter plaintext keyword or keyword phrase in UPPERCASE: ";
getKeyword(ptext_keyword);
cout << "Enter ciphertext keyword or keyword phrase in UPPERCASE: ";
getKeyword(ctext_keyword);
createStream(ptext_keyword, p_stream);
createStream(ctext_keyword, c_stream);
createTable(table, plaintext, c_stream);
getFileNames(infile, outfile);
type_of_input = getInputType();

//handle file input
if (type_of_input){
    success = encryptText(infile, outfile, p_stream, table,
                          message_to_cipher);
}
//keyboard input
else {
  success = getMessage(infile, outfile, p_stream, table,
                       message_to_cipher);
}

//report success of operation
if (!success){
   cerr << "Error: Invalid filename specified. Goodbye." << endl;
}
else {
   cout << "Press return to display resulting enciphered message."
           << endl;
   //get the newlines off the current input stream
   cin.get();

   if (type_of_input){
      cin.get();
   }

   display(outfile);
}
```

```
    writeMatrixToFile(p_stream, table);

    delete [] ptext_keyword;
    delete [] ctext_keyword;

    return (0);
}//end main()



//------------------------------------------------------------------
//Function: checkInput()
//Parameters: input - the keyword the user entered
//Return Type: bool - true if the input string contains an error,
//                    false otherwise
//Purpose: Checks the user's keyword for invalid characters.
//------------------------------------------------------------------
bool checkInput(char * &input)
{
    bool error = false;
    int count = strlen(input);

    for (int ix=0; ix<count; ix++){

        int char_value = static_cast<int>(*(input+ix));
        //determine if the user did not enter an uppercase character
        if ((char_value < SIXTYFIVE) || (char_value > NINETY)){
            error = true;
            cerr << "\aYou entered an invalid keyword!" << endl << endl
              << "Re-enter keyword: ";
            break;
        }
    }

    //check for just the newline and no other characters entered
    if (count == 0){
        cerr << "\aYou entered an invalid keyword!" << endl << endl
                << "Re-enter keyword: ";
        error = true;
    }

    return error;
}//end checkInput()
```

```
//------------------------------------------------------------------
//Function: createStream()
//Parameters: input - the keyword the user entered
//            stream - streams used in the polyalphabetic cipher
//                      matrix.
//Return Type: None
//Purpose: Creates a preliminary stream that will be used in
//conjunction with the polyalphabetic cipher matrix.
//------------------------------------------------------------------
void createStream(char *input, char stream[])
{
   bool used[TWENTYSIX];
   int index = 0,
      count = strlen(input);

   //no characters are initially used
   for (int ix=0; ix<TWENTYSIX; ix++){
      used[ix] = false;
   }

   //keep track of each character used, start forming the keyword
   //alphabet
   for (int jx=0; jx<count; jx++){

      //get each character of the input string (integer value)
      int char_value = static_cast<int>(*(input+jx));

      if (used[char_value-SIXTYFIVE]){
         //do nothing - the character was already used
      }
      else {
         //mark as used and add to the keyword alphabet
         used[char_value-SIXTYFIVE] = true;
         *(stream+index++) = static_cast<char>(char_value);
      }
   }

   //go through the list of characters used - those which weren't
   //used should be added to the keyword alphabet
   for (int kx=0; kx<TWENTYSIX; kx++){

      if (!(used[kx])){
         *(stream+index++) = static_cast<char>(SIXTYFIVE+kx);
      }
```

```
   }

   stream[TWENTYSIX] = '\0';

   return;
}//end createStream()



//----------------------------------------------------------------
//Function: createTable()
//Parameters: tbl - the polyalphabetic ciphertext matrix we are
//                  creating
//            PTEXT - the plaintext alphabet we use to form
//                    shifted keyword alphabets; starting position
//                    within the plaintext alphabet is determined by
//                    the cipher stream
//            CSTREAM - the cipher stream that represents the top
//                      row of the polyalphabetic ciphertext matrix
//Return Type: None
//Purpose: Creates a polyalphabetic ciphertext matrix.  Each character
//in the cipherstream represents a row in the polyalphabetic ciphertext
//matrix; this row is a shifted alphabet that starts at the character
//subsequent to the cstream character.
//----------------------------------------------------------------
void createTable(char tbl[][TWENTYSEVEN], const char PTEXT[],
                         const char CSTREAM[])
{
   for (int ix=0; ix<TWENTYSIX; ix++){
      int start_pos = (static_cast<int>(CSTREAM[ix]) - SIXTYFIVE + 1) %
                      TWENTYSIX;
         for (int jx=0; jx<TWENTYSIX; jx++){
               tbl[ix][jx] = PTEXT[(start_pos + jx) % TWENTYSIX];
         }
      tbl[ix][TWENTYSIX] = '\0';
   }

   return;
}//end createTable()



//----------------------------------------------------------------
//Function: display()
//Parameters: name - the name of the file the user wants displayed
//Return Type: None
```

```cpp
//Purpose: Echoes the resulting output file to the screen.
//----------------------------------------------------------------
void display(char *name)
{
    ifstream infile(name, ios::in);
    char input[SIZE];

    if (!(infile)){
       cerr << "Unable to open input file for display." << endl;
    }
    else {
       while (infile.getline(input, SIZE, '\n')){
          cout << input << endl;
       }
    }

    cout << endl;

    return;
}//end display()


//----------------------------------------------------------------
//Function: encryptText()
//Parameters: inp_file - the name of the input plaintext file
//            outp_file - the name of the output file to save the
//                        encrypted text
//            PSTREAM[] - the top row of the polyalphabetic ciphertext
//                        matrix
//            TBL[][] - the polyalphabetic ciphertext matrix
//         encoded_msg[] - the message to be encoded
//Return Type: bool, indicating success of operation
//Purpose: Used to encrypt file input.  Takes each line of the input
//file, encrypts it, and saves the result to the specified output
//file.
//----------------------------------------------------------------
bool encryptText(char * inp_file, char * outp_file, const char PSTREAM[],
                 const char TBL[][TWENTYSEVEN], char encoded_msg[])
{
    bool success = false;
    char ip[SIZE];

    //declare file stream objects
    ifstream input(inp_file, ios::in);
```

```
ofstream output(outp_file, ios::app);

if ((!input) || (!output)){
   //do nothing - I/O error; user will be notified upon
   //procedure's return to main()
}
else {

   success = true;

   while (input.getline(ip, BIGSIZE, '\n')){

      //check to see if the user wants the line to appear in plaintext
      if (ip[0] == '/'){

         if (strlen(BUFFER)>0){

               //empty whatever is in the buffer
               groupBUFFER(output, strlen(BUFFER));
               //adjust the buffer
               strcpy(BUFFER, (BUFFER+strlen(BUFFER)));
               //output plaintext
            }

      output << ip << endl;

      }
      else {
         //encipher the line
         char *msg = formCipheredMessage(PSTREAM, TBL, ip, encoded_msg);
         //print the cipher in groups of five to the ouput file
         printCipherToFile(output, msg);
      }
   }

   //empty the rest of the buffer
   groupBUFFER(output, strlen(BUFFER));

   //notify user where plaintext and ciphertext files are
   cout << "Plaintext file is: " << inp_file << endl;
   cout << "Encrypted file is: " << outp_file << endl << endl;
}

//don't forget to close the files
```

```
      input.close();
      output.close();

      //return success of the operation
      return success;
}//end encryptText()



//------------------------------------------------------------------
//Function: formatData()
//Parameters: data - the array we want to format
//Return Type: None
//Purpose: Get rid of all spaces in the array.
//------------------------------------------------------------------
void formatData(char data[])
{
    for (int mx=0, nx=0; (*(data+nx) != '\0'); nx++){
        if (*(data+nx) == ' '){
            //do nothing - skip over the space in the data
        }
        else {
            *(data+mx++) = *(data+nx);
        }
    }

    //don't forget to add the null terminator
    *(data+mx) = '\0';

    return;
}//end formatData()



//------------------------------------------------------------------
//Function: formCipheredMessage()
//Parameters: PSTREAM - the top row of the polyalphabetic cipher matrix
//            TBL - the actual polyalphabetic cipher matrix
//            MESSAGETOCIPHER - the message we want to encipher
//            enc_message - the enciphered message
//Return Type: char* - a pointer to the encoded information.
//Purpose: Encipher the user's message.
//------------------------------------------------------------------
char* formCipheredMessage(const char PSTREAM[], const char
TBL[][TWENTYSEVEN],
                          const char MESSAGETOCIPHER[], char enc_message[])
```

```
{
   int length = strlen(MESSAGETOCIPHER)+1;

   //location identifies where in the CSTREAM character the plaintext
   //character is
   int location = 0;

   //use this variable to keep track of which cipher alphabet
   //we are using - making it a static ensures that its value
   //is preserved when we make subsequent function calls
   static int which_cipher_alphabet = 0;

   for (int ix=0; ix<length; ix++){

      //test to see if we have an alphabetic character; if not,
      //simply copy it to our encrypted message - this preserves
      //characters such as ' , ! etc...
      if (!isalpha(static_cast<int>(MESSAGETOCIPHER[ix]))){
         enc_message[ix] = MESSAGETOCIPHER[ix];
      }
      else {

         //find the location of the character we want to
            //encipher in the CSTREAM
            for (int jx=0; jx<TWENTYSIX; jx++){
               if (MESSAGETOCIPHER[ix] == PSTREAM[jx]){
                  location = jx;
                  break;
               }
            }

         enc_message[ix] =
TBL[which_cipher_alphabet%TWENTYSIX][location];

         //go to the next cipher alphabet
           which_cipher_alphabet++;
      }
   }

   //return a reference to the encoded message
   return enc_message;
}//end formCipheredMessage()
```

5

Chapter

```
//------------------------------------------------------------------
//Function: getFileNames()
//Parameters:  infile_name - the input file
//             outfile_name - the output file we will write the
//             enciphered text to
//Return Type: None
//Purpose: Get file information from the user.
//------------------------------------------------------------------
void getFileNames(char * &infile_name, char * &outfile_name)
{
    char data[SIZE];

    cout << "Enter filename to store/retrieve plaintext message: ";

    cin >> data;

    infile_name = new char[strlen(data) + 1];
    strcpy(infile_name, data);

    cout << "Enter filename to store enciphered message: ";

    cin >> data;

    outfile_name = new char[strlen(data) + 1];
    strcpy(outfile_name, data);

    cout << endl;

    return;
}//end getFileNames()


//------------------------------------------------------------------
//Function: getInputType()
//Parameters: None
//Return Type: int - 0 indicates keyboard input, 1 indicates file
//                   input
//Purpose: Determines if the user will be manually entering text to
//be enciphered or if the user wants a file to be enciphered.
//------------------------------------------------------------------
int getInputType(void)
{
    char type;
    bool error = false;
```

```
    int value;

    do {
        //prompt user for input from file or keyboard
        cout << "Is file input from keyboard (K, k) or file (F, f): ";
        cin >> type;

        //make type an uppercase letter
        type = static_cast<char>(toupper(static_cast<int>(type)));

        //check for an invalid character
        if ((type != 'K') && (type != 'F')){
            cerr << "You have entered an invalid character!" << endl << endl;
            error = true;
        }
        else {
            if (type == 'K')
                value = 0;        //value of 0 represents keyboard input
                else value = 1;   //value of 1 represents file input
            error = false;
        }

    } while (error);

    cout << endl;

    return value;
}//end getInputType()


//------------------------------------------------------------------
//Function: getKeyword()
//Parameters: text - the keyword that the user enters
//Return Type: int - the length of the keyword
//Purpose: Prompts the user for a keyword and continues until
//a valid keyword has been entered.  Returns the length of the
//keyword.
//------------------------------------------------------------------
int getKeyword(char * &text)
{
    bool error = false;
    char buffer[SIZE];
```

```
    do {

        cin.getline(buffer, SIZE, '\n');
        assert(text = new char[strlen(buffer) + 1]);
        strcpy(text, buffer);

        error = checkInput(text);

        //delete text if there was an error
        if (error){
            delete [] text;
        }

    } while (error);

    cout << endl;

    return strlen(buffer);
}//end getKeyword()



//-------------------------------------------------------------
//Function: getMessage()
//Parameters:  input - the name of the input plaintext file
//             output the name of the output ciphertext file
//             msg_to_cipher - the message to be encoded
//             PSTREAM - the top row of the polyalphabetic ciphertext
//                       matrix; used to index into the actual table
//             TBL - the polyalphabetic ciphertext matrix
//Return Type: bool, indicating success of operation
//Purpose: Allow the user to manually input text from the keyboard.
//Save the text in plaintext to the input file; encrpyt the text
//and save it to the specified output file for later retrieval.
//-------------------------------------------------------------
bool getMessage(char* input, char* output, const char PSTREAM[],
                          const char TBL[][TWENTYSEVEN], char
msg_to_cipher[])
{
    bool go_on = true, success = false;

    ofstream textFile(input, ios::app);
    ofstream cipherFile(output, ios::app);

    if ((!textFile) || (!cipherFile)){
```

```
        //do nothing - error will be noted to user later
}
else {

    success = true;

    //get the newline character off of the input stream
    cin.get();

    cout << "Enter the message in UPPERCASE or lowercase characters. "
            << endl
        << "Non-alphabetic characters may be entered but are ignored."
            << endl
        << "Use a / at the beginning of each line that should remain"
            << endl
        << "in plaintext and a \\ on a separate line to indicate the"
            << endl
        << "end of an enciphered message." << endl << endl;

    while (go_on) {

        //get the entire line, up to 256 characters
        cin.getline(msg_to_cipher, SIZE, '\n');

        //case user doesn't want the text to be encrypted
        if (msg_to_cipher[0] == '/'){

            if (strlen(BUFFER)>0){
                //empty whatever is in the buffer
                groupBUFFER(cipherFile, strlen(BUFFER));
                //adjust the buffer
                strcpy(BUFFER, (BUFFER+strlen(BUFFER)));
            }

            //output plaintext
            textFile << msg_to_cipher << endl;
            cipherFile << msg_to_cipher << endl;
             }

        //case user is done entering text
        else if (static_cast<int>(msg_to_cipher[0]) == NINETYTWO){
            go_on = false;
             }
```

```
                          //encrypt the text
                          else {
                              textFile << msg_to_cipher << endl;
                              char enciphered_msg[BIGSIZE];
                              formCipheredMessage(PSTREAM, TBL, msg_to_cipher,enciphered_msg);
                              printCipherToFile(cipherFile,enciphered_msg);
                              }
                      }

              //empty the rest of the buffer
              groupBUFFER(cipherFile, strlen(BUFFER));
              }

       //close the files
       textFile.close();
       cipherFile.close();

       //notify user where plaintext and ciphertext files are
       cout << "\nPlaintext file is: " << input << endl;
       cout << "Encrypted file is: " << output << endl << endl;

       return success;
}//end getMessage()


//----------------------------------------------------------------
//Function: groupBUFFER()
//Parameters: out - the output stream we are writing to
//            num - the number of characters we want to output
//Return Type: None
//Purpose: Output the buffer in groups of five characters at a
//time.
//----------------------------------------------------------------
void groupBUFFER(ofstream out, int num)
{
   for (int kx=0;kx<num;kx++){

       if ((kx!=0) && (kx%TWENTYFIVE==0)){
          out << endl;
       }

       if ((kx!=0) && (kx%FIVE == 0) && (kx%TWENTYFIVE!=0)){
          out << " " << *(BUFFER+kx);
       }
```

```
        else {
                out << *(BUFFER+kx);
        }
    }

    out << endl;

    return;
}//end groupBUFFER()


//----------------------------------------------------------------
//Function: printCipherToFile()
//Parameters: op - the output file we are writing to
//            msg - the cipher text we are displaying
//Return Type: None
//Purpose: Group the cipher in 5-block characters in the
//specified output file.
//----------------------------------------------------------------
void printCipherToFile(ofstream op, char msg[])
{
    formatData(msg);

    //check to see if there are more than 25 characters
    //in the buffer; if so, print out as many groups of
    //25 as possible
    if (strlen(BUFFER) >= TWENTYFIVE){

        int numchars = (strlen(BUFFER)/TWENTYFIVE)*TWENTYFIVE;
        //print the contents of the buffer to the output stream
        groupBUFFER(op, numchars);
        //shift whatever is left in the buffer
        strcpy(BUFFER, (BUFFER+numchars));
        //append data to the buffer
        strcat(BUFFER, msg);
    }

    //if buffer contents are less than 25, simply append the new
    //data to the buffer
    else if ((strlen(BUFFER) >= 0) && (strlen(BUFFER) < TWENTYFIVE)){
        strcat(BUFFER, msg);
    }

    return;
```

```
    }//end printCipherToFile()


    //------------------------------------------------------------------
    //Function: writeMatrixToFile()
    //Parameters: CSTREAM - the top row of the polyalphabetic cipher matrix
    //            TBL - the actual matrix
    //Return Type: bool - indicates success of the operation
    //Purpose: Prints the matrix to a file "table.dat" for future
    //reference.
    //------------------------------------------------------------------
    bool writeMatrixToFile(const char PSTREAM[], const char TBL[][TWENTYSEVEN])
    {
        ofstream output("table.dat", ios::out);
        bool success = false;

        if (output){
            success = true;
            output << PSTREAM << endl << endl;
            for (int ix=0; ix<TWENTYSIX; ix++)
                output << TBL[ix] << endl;
        }

        cout << "Polyalphabetic matrix was written to file table.dat"
            << endl << endl;

        output.close();

        return success;
    }//end writeMatrixToFile()
    //end file poly2.cpp
```

The DPOLY2.BAS Program

Earlier in this chapter you developed the programs POLY2.BAS and
POLY2.CPP to encipher messages using a polyalphabetic substitution
technique. Because you need a mechanism to automate the decipherment
of such messages, I will now focus your attention upon the development
of a program to reverse the encipherment process. I will label these two
programs DPOLY2.BAS and DPOLY2.CPP to denote that they decipher
messages enciphered using the POLY2.BAS and POLY2.CPP programs.

In this section you will first examine the operation of the BASIC program DPOLY2.BAS. Once this is accomplished I will turn your attention to the statements in the C++ version of the program.

Listing 5.8 shows the statements in the main portion of the program DPOLY2.BAS developed to decipher messages previously enciphered using the program POLY2.BAS. When you examine Listing 5.8, you will note that the only differences between the main portion of the programs are changes to PRINT statements that essentially replace "cipher" with "decipher" and the prefix of two subroutines by the character D to denote major changes to previously developed subroutines without that prefix. Because the only subroutines that were significantly changed were MSGFILE and PCONVERTSTORE, I will focus on these two subroutines.

Listing 5.8. The main portion of the DPOLY2.BAS program.

```
REM PROGRAM DPOLY2.BAS
DIM PLAINTEXT$(26), PLAIN$(26), CIPHER$(26), CIPHERTEXT$(26), KEY$(26)
        CLS
        PRINT "DPOLY2.BAS PROGRAM deciphers text previously enciphered
               using two keywords"
        PRINT "or keyword phrases and a polyalphabetic substitution
               process using"
        PRINT "26 cipher alphabets."
        PRINT
        INPUT "Enter plaintext keyword or keyword phrase in UPPERCASE: ",
               TEXT$
GOSUB INITIALIZE                 'initialize plaintext alphabet
GOSUB KEYWORD                    'form keyword based mixed alphabet
        FOR I = 0 TO 25: PLAIN$(I) = PLAINTEXT$(I): NEXT I
        INPUT "Enter ciphertext keyword or keyword phrase in UPPERCASE:",
               TEXT$
GOSUB INITIALIZE                 're-initialize plaintext alphabet
GOSUB KEYWORD
        FOR I = 0 TO 25: CIPHER$(I) = PLAINTEXT$(I): NEXT I
GOSUB PFORMCIPHER                'create 26 cipher alphabets
GOSUB DMSGFILE                   'assign I/O files, place message on a file
GOSUB DPCONVERTSTORE             'convert and store ciphertext on a file
GOSUB PRTOUT                     'print results
STOP
```

The DMSGFILE Subroutine

The major differences between the previously developed subroutine
MSGFILE and the subroutine DMSGFILE are related to the assignment of
the string variables OUTFILE$ and INFILE$. In the subroutine DMSGFILE,
these assignments are reversed from their assignment in MSGFILE.
Because the contents of the subroutine DMSGFILE were described as part
of our description of the program DCIPHER6.BAS and other programs in
Chapter 4, you should refer to that chapter for information concerning
this subroutine and the program listing.

The DPCONVERTSTORE Subroutine

The statements used to form the subroutine DPCONVERTSTORE are contained in Listing 5.9. Unlike the subroutine PCONVERTSTORE, which
converts a plaintext message to ciphertext and stores the message in
ciphertext on a disk file, DPCONVERTSTORE performs a reverse process.
That is, the subroutine DPCONVERTSTORE converts an enciphered message to plaintext and stores the plaintext message on a disk file.

Listing 5.9. The DPCONVERTSTORE subroutine listing.

```
DPCONVERTSTORE:
        REM Routine to convert and store ciphertext on a file
        OPEN INFILE$ FOR INPUT AS #1
        OPEN OUTFILE$ FOR OUTPUT AS #2
        C = 0                               'first alphabet pointer
        DO UNTIL EOF(1)
                INPUT #1, TEXT$
                MSGLEN = LEN(TEXT$)
                IF MID$(TEXT$, 1, 1) = "/" THEN GOTO CLEARTXT
                IF MID$(TEXT$, 1, 1) = "\" THEN GOTO DONE1
                REM Convert plaintext to ciphertext
                        FOR I = 1 TO MSGLEN
                        FOR J = 0 TO 25
                        IF MID$(TEXT$, I, 1) = MID$(CIPHERTEXT$(C), J + 1,
                                1) THEN GOTO GOTIT
                        NEXT J
GOTIT:                  MID$(TEXT$, I, 1) = PLAIN$(J)
                        C = C + 1
                        IF C = 26 THEN C = 0      'reset to first alphabet
                        NEXT I
```

```
CLEARTXT:                    WRITE #2, TEXT$
        LOOP
DONE1:          CLOSE #2
RETURN
```

When you compare the subroutine DPCONVERTSTORE to the subroutine PCONVERTSTORE, you should note that the difference between the two subroutines is limited to the structure of an IF statement in each subroutine and the statement at label GOTIT. In PCONVERTSTORE, the first IF statement is used to match each character in the string variable TEXT$ to a character in the keyword-based alphabet stored in the array PLAIN$ and use the location of the match as a pointer into a cipher alphabet. In the subroutine DPCONVERTSTORE, each character is matched to the cipher alphabet whose value is C at position J+1.

In the subroutine PCONVERTSTORE, a branch to the label GOTIT results in the replacement of a plaintext character (MID$(TEXT$,I,1)) by a ciphertext character (MID$(CIPHERTEXT$(C),J+1,1)) in the cipher alphabet C at position J+1. In the subroutine DPCONVERTSTORE, you should replace each enciphered character with its equivalent plaintext character. Because a match using the previously described IF statement results in the location of the correct alphabet and location within the alphabet, we then set each character in TEXT$ to the array element PLAIN$(J) to extract the appropriate plaintext character. This allows you to convert the ciphertext back into its equivalent plaintext character.

Program Execution

To verify the operation of the program DPOLY2.BAS, execute it using the same plaintext and ciphertext keywords used to encipher your message using the POLY2.BAS program. Figure 5.6 illustrates the execution of the DPOLY2.BAS program using the plaintext keyword MICROSOFT and the ciphertext keyword phrase WINDOWSAREGREAT. The lower portion of this example shows the resulting deciphered message. You will note that this message is the same message that was entered as plaintext when the program POLY2.BAS was executed in Figure 5.5.

5

Chapter

```
Figure 5.6 The execution of the program DPOLY2.BAS.

DPOLY2.BAS PROGRAM deciphers text previously enciphered using two
keywords
or keyword phrases and a polyalphabetic substitution process using
26 cipher alphabets.

Enter plaintext keyword or keyword phrase in UPPERCASE: MICROSOFT
Enter ciphertext keyword or keywork phrase in UPPERCASE: WINDOWSAREGREAT
Enter filename to store plaintext message, default=MESSAGE.DAT
Enter filename for enciphered message, default=CIPHERTX.DAT
Select keyboard (k) or file (f) message input: F
Press Return key to display resulting deciphered message

Resulting deciphered message is:
TO ROSS THE BOSS
FROM JUDY
YOUCO NFUSE DPICK UPTHE BALLA
NDGET OFFTH ECOUR TWITH THEQU
OTEWH ENTHE GOING GETST OUGHT
HETOU GHGET GOING
```

Other differences between DPOLY2.BAS and POLY2.BAS relate to PRINT statements that were changed to display "deciphered" instead of "enciphered" in the subroutine PRTOUT. Because this was an insignificant change, I did not change the name of the subroutine; however, the PRINT statements in the subroutine were changed when the program was stored on the file DPOLY2.BAS on the companion CD-ROM.

The DPOLY2.CPP Program

In concluding this chapter, dual coverage of BASIC and C++ programs will be continued by turning your attention to the C++ version of DPOLY2. That program, which has the filename DPOLY2.CPP, is contained on the CD-ROM in the C directory.

Listing 5.10 contains a listing of the statements in the header and the main function of DPOLY2.CPP. In examining the listing shown in Listing 5.10 you will note that many functions used in the program POLY2.CPP are reused, such as checkInput, createStream, and createTable. Thus, in this section I will focus your attention on the key difference between the two programs. That difference is primarily in the inclusion of the functions decipher and getFileToDecipher. Listing 5.11 lists the statements in those two functions. Since each function is explicitly documented through the use of comments, I will leave it to you to review the statements for each function.

Listing 5.10 Header and function main statements in DPOLY2.CPP.

```
/*DPOLY2.CPP
C++ code written by Jonathan Held
Using Microsoft's Visual C++ Version 5.0
*/

//standard includes
#include<iostream.h>
#include<assert.h>
#include<string.h>
#include<ctype.h>
#include<fstream.h>
#include<stdlib.h>

//constants we will use
const int FIVE = 5, TWENTYFIVE = 25, TWENTYSIX = 26,
          TWENTYSEVEN = 27, SIXTYFIVE = 65, NINETY = 90,
          NINETYTWO = 92, SIZE = 256, BIGSIZE = 1000;

//function prototypes
bool checkInput(char * &);
void createStream(char *, char []);
void createTable(char [][TWENTYSEVEN], const char [], const char []);
void decipher(ifstream, ofstream, const char[], char[]);
void display(char *);
void formatData(char []);
void getFileNames(char *&, char *&);
void getFileToDecipher(const char[], char[][TWENTYSEVEN]);
int getInputType(void);
int getKeyword(char *&);
bool getMessage(char*, char*, char [], const char[], const
                char[][TWENTYSEVEN]);


//----------------------------------------------------------------
//Function: main()
//Parameters: None
//Return Type: int - 0 means program terminated normally
//Purpose: Runs the main part of the program.
```

```
//-----------------------------------------------------------------
int main()
{

    char plaintext[TWENTYSEVEN] = {'A','B','C','D','E','F','G','H',
                                   'I','J','K','L','M','N','O','P',
                                   'Q','R','S','T','U','V','W','X',
                                   'Y','Z','\0'};

    char *ptext_keyword, *ctext_keyword, *infile, *outfile;

    //p_stream is used to help form the alphabetic-shifted cipher
    //alphabets
    char p_stream[TWENTYSIX] = {'\0'};

    //c_stream represented the top row of the polyalphabetic ciphertext
    //matrix
    char c_stream[TWENTYSIX] = {'\0'};

    //table is the actual polyalphabetic ciphertext matrix
    char table[TWENTYSIX][TWENTYSEVEN];

    char enc_msg[SIZE];

    int type_of_input;
    bool success = false;

    cout << "Enter plaintext keyword or keyword phrase in UPPERCASE: ";
    getKeyword(ptext_keyword);
    cout << "Enter ciphertext keyword or keyword phrase in UPPERCASE: ";
    getKeyword(ctext_keyword);
    createStream(ptext_keyword, p_stream);
    createStream(ctext_keyword, c_stream);
    createTable(table, plaintext, c_stream);
    type_of_input = getInputType();

    if (type_of_input){
       //decipher accordingly
       getFileToDecipher(p_stream, table);
    }
    else {
       getFileNames(infile, outfile);
       getMessage(infile, outfile, enc_msg, p_stream, table);
       cout << "Press return to display the deciphered text." << endl;
```

```
        display(outfile);
    }

    return 0;
}
```

Listing 5.11 Statements in the decipher and *getFileToDecipher* functions from the program DPOLY2.CPP.

```
//-----------------------------------------------------------------
//Function: decipher()
//Parameters: in - the input file we are deciphering
//            out - the output file we are writing the deciphered
//                  text to
//            PSTREAM - the plaintext alphabet (used to decipher)
//            TBL - the polyalphabetic substitution table
//Return Type: None
//Purpose: Decipher the input file and write the contents to the
//output file specified by the user.
//-----------------------------------------------------------------
void decipher(ifstream in, ofstream out, const char PSTREAM[], const
            char TBL[][TWENTYSEVEN])
{
    char enc_file_data[SIZE];
    static int which_cipher_alphabet = 0;

    //continue this process until we get to the end of the file
    while (in.getline(enc_file_data, SIZE, '\n')){

        if (enc_file_data[0] == '/'){
            out << enc_file_data << endl;
        }
        else {
            //format the data - i.e., get rid of all spaces
                formatData(enc_file_data);

            //dump data to file
            for (int ix=0; ix<strlen(enc_file_data); ix++){

            //used to keep track of what plaintext character
              //we are going to use
              int jx;
```

```
                    for (jx=0; jx<TWENTYSIX; jx++){
                //find where the encrypted data is in the
                //ciphertext - this location corresponds to
                //the plaintext character location
                if (enc_file_data[ix] == TBL[which_cipher_alphabet%TWENTYSIX][jx])
                   break;
        }

        //conditionals for grouping by five and inserting
           //new lines
           if (!(ix%TWENTYFIVE))
              out << endl;

           if ((ix!=0) && (!(ix%FIVE))){
              out << " " << PSTREAM[jx];
           }
           else {
              out << PSTREAM[jx];
           }

              which_cipher_alphabet++;
        }
     }
   }

   return;
}//end decipher()


   //------------------------------------------------------------------
   ///-----------------------------------------------------------------
   //Function: getFileToDecipher()
   //Parameters: PSTREAM - the plaintext stream at the top of the
   //            polyalphabetic substitution table
   //            TBL - the polyalphabetic table
   //Return Type: None
   //Purpose: Prompt the user for the name of the encrypted file
   //and the file the user wants to store the decrypted text to.
   //------------------------------------------------------------------
   void getFileToDecipher(const char PSTREAM[], char TBL[][TWENTYSEVEN])
   {
      char fileinput[SIZE], fileoutput[SIZE];

      cout << "Enter name of file to decipher: ";
```

```
    cin >> fileinput;

    ifstream input(fileinput, ios::in);

    if (!(input)){
       cerr << "Input file not available. Exiting program." << endl;
       exit(EXIT_FAILURE);
    }

    cout << "Enter name of file for output: ";
    cin >> fileoutput;
    ofstream output(fileoutput, ios::out);   .

    if (!(output)){
       cerr << "Output file not created.  Exiting program." << endl;
       exit(EXIT_FAILURE);
    }

    decipher(input, output, PSTREAM, TBL);

    //don't forget to close the files
    input.close();
    output.close();

    cout << "\nDeciphered text is in " << fileoutput << endl;
    cout << "\nPress return to display deciphered text." << endl;
    cin.get();
    cin.get();

    display(fileoutput);

    return;
}//end getFileToDecipher()


//----------------------------------------------------------------
```

Chapter 6

Using Random Numbers

Through the use of random numbers you can decrease the decipherment capability of people who illicitly gain access to an enciphered message. In fact, the use of a true random number sequence as an enciphering key theoretically makes it impossible for a person to decipher that message. Unfortunately, the use of a true random number sequence is beyond the capability of most organizations due to the time, cost, and the effort required to provide the sequence to others who must use it to decipher messages. Thus, most random number sequences are actually pseudo-random number sequences that, with varying degrees of difficulty, can be duplicated.

This chapter first discusses the ways in which true random number sequences are developed and why they are impractical for most persons and organizations. Next, you will examine the built-in random number generator included in most programming languages and learn how to use that facility to create a pseudo-random number sequence that can serve as an enciphering and deciphering key. This discussion is followed by the construction of a series of programs that illustrate the use of computer-generated random number sequences to encipher and decipher messages.

6

Chapter

Random Numbers and Random Number Sequences

Random numbers are unordered numbers that are independent of preceding and succeeding numbers. Thus, a random number sequence is an unordered series of random numbers.

The use of random number sequences in cryptology provides a mechanism to create an unbreakable enciphered message. To illustrate this, assume the random number sequence you obtain (through a process described later in this chapter) is converted into a binary sequence. Also assume that each plaintext character in your message is converted into a binary sequence. You could use modulo 2 addition to add the plaintext and random number binary values to produce an enciphered binary sequence. If the recipient has the same random number sequence, he or she would use modulo 2 subtraction to subtract the binary values of the random numbers from the enciphered binary sequence to reproduce the plaintext message. Because the binary random number sequence functions as a unique key known only to the message encipherer and message decipherer, any person who illicitly obtains a copy of the enciphered message cannot decipher the message.

The father of the application of modulo 2 arithmetic to encipherment systems was Gilbert Vernam. Working in downtown Manhattan for American Telephone & Telegraph Company during 1917, Vernam was assigned to a project to investigate the security of the telegraph.

In 1917, the Baudot code was used for the transmission of information via telegraph. In this code, characters were represented by a predefined sequence of a combination of five marks and spaces which represented different levels of current that would be placed on the telegraph line to identify a character. Automated telegraph operations used punched paper tape for both offline message preparation as well as message transmission and reception. Marks were represented by holes, and spaces were represented by leaving the tape intact.

After studying telegraph operations, Vernam proposed punching a "key" tape consisting of randomly selected characters literally pulled from a hat. He proposed electromechanically adding the pulses on the keytape to the pulses of plaintext characters as follows:

plaintext		key		ciphertext
mark	+	mark	=	space
mark	+	space	=	mark
space	+	mark	=	mark
space	+	space	=	space

With Vernam's method, if you assign a binary 1 to a mark and a binary 0 to a space, you have modulo 2 addition forming the ciphertext. Thus, it should not be surprising that Vernam's method for reconstructing the plaintext characters was based upon modulo 2 subtraction.

Vernam's encipherment ideas were converted from paper to hardware by the construction of two devices during 1918. These devices were connected to two teletypewriters and their successful use represents the beginning of automated cryptographic operations.

Generating Random Number Sequences

A true random number sequence is not only an unordered sequence of numbers but also a non-reproducible sequence. According to rumors, certain spy agencies monitor natural processes, such as the height of solar flares on the sun or the number of gamma rays emitted by decaying radioactive material per unit period of time, to develop a sequence of non-reproducible random numbers. These numbers are converted to a binary sequence for use as a key by equipment manufactured to encipher and decipher messages. Diskettes or tapes containing random binary sequences that serve as an enciphering and deciphering key are then prepared for use during different time periods and those disks are sent by courier to government locations where communications security (COMSEC) equipment that uses such disks is located. COMSEC personnel then load the appropriate disks at predefined times to change the keys, since the duplicate use of a binary key sequence would eliminate the reproducibility of the key and make the messages enciphered using a repeating key susceptible to decipherment by foreign governments monitoring communications.

The time, effort, and cost associated with developing true random number sequences and distributing those sequences for use normally restricts its use to government institutions. Commercial products that encipher messages and data files normally do so through the use of pseudo-random number sequences.

6

Chapter

Pseudo-random Number Sequences

A pseudo-random number sequence is based on the use of an algorithm to generate a sequence of numbers. Any person who has access to the algorithm can exercise the algorithm and will eventually be able to reproduce the pseudo-random number sequence used by another person. Although this means that the use of pseudo-random number sequences makes an enciphered message decipherable by an unauthorized party, the time and effort required to do so may preclude this from actually happening. Some algorithms may generate millions to tens or hundreds of billions of unique key sequences, forcing those who illicitly obtain access to an enciphered message to use powerful mainframe computers for months or years in an attempt to decipher a message. The selection of an algorithm to generate pseudo-random numbers can provide a very high level of security even though the resulting enciphered message based on the use of that algorithm is breakable. One algorithm which provides a reasonable number of random number sequences is built into the BASIC programming language in the form of the RND function.

The RND Function

The BASIC RND function invokes a routine which generates pseudo-random decimal numbers in the range 0 to 1. In most versions of BASIC, including QuickBASIC, the format of the RND function is RND[(x)], where the value of x determines how the function generates the next random number. Table 6.1 indicates the number returned by the function based upon different argument values.

Table 6.1. Returned RND function number.

Argument Value	Number Returned
x<0	Always returns the same number for any given x.
x>0 or x omitted	Returns the next random number in the sequence.
x=0	Returns the last number generated.

When using the RND function in a program with a value of $x>0$, the same sequence of random numbers is generated each time you execute the program. This generation is illustrated in Listing 6.1 in which the top portion lists a simple program which prints five random numbers through the use of the RND function, while the lower portion shows the results obtained by executing the program three times. Note that each sequence of random numbers generated by the program is exactly the same.

Listing 6.1. Using the RND function.

```
FOR I = 1 TO 5
PRINT RND(I);
NEXT I
PRINT
```

.7055475	.533424	.5795186	.2895625	.301948
.7055475	.533424	.5795186	.2895625	.301948
.7055475	.533424	.5795186	.2895625	.301948

Using random numbers for enciphering and deciphering messages dates to the modern spy. During World War II, Nazi agents, as well as Allied spies working in occupied Europe and in neutral countries, enciphered and deciphered messages based upon the use of what is known as a one-time pad.

Each one-time pad consists of a series of pages with each page containing a sequence of random numbers, usually blocked into groups of five digits for convenience. Each page of random numbers was to be used one time, providing the basis for the name of the pad.

To use this method, a spy first prepares his or her message in plaintext, positioning the characters in the message into groups of five letters. Then, the value of each letter in the group is added (using modulo 26 arithmetic) to the value of each random digit to produce the enciphered message. The following example illustrates the enciphering operation attributed to agent Maxwell Smart.

plaintext message	SENDM	OREMO	NEYNO	WXXXX
random digits	15829	31276	50341	92371
modulo 26 addition				
enciphered message	TJVFV	RSGTU	SEBRP	FZAEY

At the spy's home base, the received message is decoded through the use of a second one-time pad whose contents match the contents of the pad used by the spy. For example,

6

Chapter

the received enciphered message would be deciphered as follows:

received message	TJVFV	RSGTU	SEBRP	FZAEY
random digits	15829	31276	50341	92371
modulo 26 subtraction	SENDM	OREMO	NEYNO	WXXXX

Unless the one-time pad falls into the hands of enemy agents, the resulting enciphered message is unbreakable. This technique is so secure that its use has been documented in many spy trials occurring during the Cold War, although the capture of the spies was attributed to factors other than the ability of counterspies to read enciphered messages.

RANDOMIZE Statement

The use of an easily duplicated random number sequence clearly limits its usefulness as an encryption and decryption key. Fortunately, BASIC contains a statement that can be used to reseed the random number generator and produce a different sequence of random numbers. The statement that reseeds the random number generator is the RANDOMIZE statement whose format is RANDOMIZE[*expression*]. Note that the random number sequence uses the seed to generate a new sequence of random numbers, with the first number becoming a new seed. That new seed is then used to generate a newer seed, and so on, based upon the algorithm used by BASIC to generate random numbers. Thus, the seed generated by the use of the RANDOMIZE statement governs the location where the random number generation process begins.

If the optional expression in the RANDOMIZE statement is omitted, BASIC will pause and display the message "Random Number Seed (-32768 to 32767)?" To change the sequence of random numbers generated by the use of a RND function, you can place a RANDOMIZE statement at the beginning of a program. Listing 6.2 illustrates this concept, with the top portion containing a small program listing that includes the RANDOMIZE statement, while the lower portion shows the results of executing the program three times. Note that the use of a different seed results in the generation of a new random number sequence.

Listing 6.2 Using the RANDOMIZE statement.

```
RANDOMIZE
FOR I = 1 TO 5
PRINT RND(I);
NEXT I
PRINT
```

```
Random-number seed (-32768 to 32767)? -5
.4362451       .3257061       .2495473       .1388514       .1759562
Random-number seed (-32768 to 32767)? -5
.4362451       .3257061       .2495473       .1388514       .1759562
Random-number seed (-32768 to 32767)? 0
.7641413       .3576428       .1068624       .7075312       4.804176E-02
```

Because the value of the random number seed can range from -32678 to 32767, you can obtain the ability to generate 65,536 different random number sequences through the use of the RANDOMIZE statement. You can consider using a variable with a RANDOMIZE statement. Reading the value for the variable from the keyboard serves as a mechanism to provide a program user with the ability to specify the random number sequence to be used to encipher and decipher messages. The seed value then becomes the "code" or "key" for the enciphering and deciphering process.

Working with Random Numbers

Because a majority of the applications for random numbers are for numbers in some range other than 0 to 1, you need a mechanism to change those numbers to integers. That mechanism is obtained by multiplying the value of RND by 10^n, where n defines the number of integers you need from 1 to 6. You can then use the BASIC INT function to obtain the integer value of the resulting computation. For example, INT(RND*100) would produce integers whose values are between 0 and 99, while INT(RND*1000) would produce integers whose values are between 0 and 999.

The RANDOM1.BAS Program

The top portion of Listing 6.3 contains the program listing of RANDOM1.BAS. The lower portion shows the results obtained when the program is executed three times. This program generates random numbers between 0 and 25 based upon the use of the RND function and reseeds the random number generator by specifying a reseeding position. You should note that the program simply discards any number exceeding 25 to smooth the resulting random numbers to the range 0 to 25.

Listing 6.3 The RANDOM1.BAS program listing and sample execution with different values assigned to the RANDOMIZE statement.

```
REM Program RANDOM1.BAS
REM routine to generate random numbers between 0 and 25
       CLS
start: INPUT "Enter a number, 0 to terminate: ", y
       IF y = 0 THEN STOP
       RANDOMIZE (y)
       FOR I = 1 TO 75
       x = INT(RND(I) * 100)
       IF x > 25 THEN GOTO skip
       PRINT x;
skip:  NEXT I
       PRINT
       GOTO start


Enter a number, 0 to terminate: 5
23 7 19 18 22 6 17 15 1 3 17 23 20 13 14
Enter a number, 0 to terminate: 7
11 5 16 20 16 3 15 4 4 23 4 4 24 23 21 19 8 3 11 6 3
Enter a number, 0 to terminate: 9
1 14 14 22 7 22 7 19 23 4 20 9 2 23 5 15 11
Enter a number, 0 to terminate: 0
```

The RANDOM2.BAS Program

Listing 6.4 contains the program listing and sample execution of the program RANDOM2.BAS. This simple program was developed to illustrate how you can use random numbers to encipher messages. In this example, our plaintext alphabet is restricted to the 26 uppercase letters. This alphabet is initialized by the INITIALIZE subroutine. Next, the program uses a user-entered number to seed the random number generator and accepts a one-line message read into the string variable TEXT$. The characters in that message are then placed into the string array KEY$.

Listing 6.4 The RANDOM2.BAS program listing and its repeated execution using different random seed numbers and the same plaintext message.

```
REM Program RANDOM2.BAS
REM Sample program to demonstrate use of random numbers for enciphering
DIM KEY$(80), PLAINTEXT$(26)
CLS
        PRINT "Program RANDOM2.BAS to demonstrate use of random numbers and"
        PRINT "random number seed in enciphering operations"
GOSUB INITIALIZE
START: PRINT
        INPUT "Enter a random seed number, 0 to terminate ", Y
        IF Y = 0 THEN STOP
        RANDOMIZE (Y)
        INPUT "Enter a one line message in UPPERCASE: ", TEXT$
        FOR I = 1 TO LEN(TEXT$)
        KEY$(I) = MID$(TEXT$, I, 1)
        NEXT I
REM Encipher
        PRINT "Enciphered message is               : ";
        FOR I = 1 TO LEN(TEXT$)
        FOR J = 0 TO 25
        IF PLAINTEXT$(J) = KEY$(I) GOTO GOTIT    'locate character position
        NEXT J                                   ' in plaintext array
GOTIT: X = INT(RND * 100)                        'get random number
        IF X > 25 THEN GOTO GOTIT                ' less than 25
        Z = (J + X) MOD 26                       'use MOD 26 addition to add
        PRINT PLAINTEXT$(Z);                     'display enciphered
character
        NEXT I
        GOTO START
INITIALIZE:
        RESTORE
        REM Initialize plaintext values
        FOR I = 0 TO 25
        READ PLAINTEXT$(I)
        NEXT I
        DATA "A","B","C","D","E","F","G","H","I","J","K","L","M","N"
        DATA "O","P","Q","R","S","T","U","V","W","X","Y","Z"
RETURN
```

```
Program RANDOM2.BAS to demonstrate use of random numbers and
random number seed in enciphering operations

Enter a random seed number, 0 to terminate 5
Enter a one-line message in UPPERCASE: FIREFREDNOW
Enciphered message is : CPKWBXVSORN
Enter a random seed number, 0 to terminate 8
Enter a one-line message in UPPERCASE: FIREFREDNOW
Enciphered message is: RDMXNQVCJXE
Enter a random seed number, 0 to terminate 51
Enter a one-line message in UPPERCASE: FIREFREDNOW
Enciphered message is: ZXDDMCBNHGZ
Enter a random seed number, 0 to terminate 0
```

The routine labeled ENCIPHER matches each character in the message that was placed in the string array KEY$ to a plaintext character. When a match is found, a branch to the label GOTIT occurs, and a two-digit random number is obtained. Next, the program discards the random number if it exceeded 25 and obtains a new random number, forcing x to be between 0 and 25.

Once an acceptable value of x is obtained, the index value of J, which represents the plaintext character location in the alphabet, is added via modulo 26 addition to the random number. By restricting the largest random number to 25 and the plaintext character position to 26, the largest number produced by adding the two becomes 51. Performing modulo 26 addition prevents a resulting number occurring from different additions, such as would be the case if a random number added to the index resulted in a value of 52 or more. For example, 1 mod 26 is 1, but so is 53 mod 26 and 79 mod 26. By limiting the maximum value of the sum of the index and random number to 51, you ensure you can correctly decipher a message that was enciphered using the technique previously described.

The RANDOM1.CPP Program

Since the purpose of this book is to acquaint you with both BASIC and C++ encryption and decryption coding methods, let's turn our attention to two C++ random number programs. The first program, RANDOM1.CPP, prompts you for a seed and uses that seed to generate a sequence of random numbers between 1 and 100, only displaying those numbers that are less than 25.

The top portion of Listing 6.5 contains the statement in the program RANDOM1.CPP, while the lower portion shows three examples of its execution. Although this program was written to attempt to duplicate the program RANDOM1.BAS, the lack of a C++ RANDOMIZE statement resulted in the development of the function getSeed which is used to return a user-entered seed value. That value is used with the C++ function SRAND to generate 75 random numbers, with only those numbers whose values do not exceed 25 being displayed.

If you compare the random numbers shown at the bottom of Listing 6.5 to those produced by the execution of the BASIC version of the program, you will note different results even though the same seed values were used. These differences result from the fact that most programming languages use a different algorithm to generate random numbers.

Listing 6.5 The RANDOM1.CPP program listing and its repeated execution using different random seed numbers.

```
/*
random1.cpp
C++ code written by Jonathan Held on April 26, 1998,
using Microsoft Visual C++ version 5.0

Author's note: In C++, if you wish to randomize without
having to enter a seed each time, you can use the
statement:

   srand(time(NULL));

This causes the computer to read its clock to obtain the
value for the seed automatically.  The time function (found
in the library time.h) returns the current "calendar time"
in seconds.
*/

#include <iostream.h>
#include <stdlib.h>

//function prototypes
unsigned getSeed(void);
void generateNumbers(const unsigned);


//----------------------------------------------------------------
```

```
//Function: main()
//Parameters: None
//Return Type: int - 0 if program terminated normally
//Purpose: driver that makes calls to various procedures defined
//in random1.cpp
//-------------------------------------------------------------------
int main(){

    unsigned seed;

    while (seed = getSeed())
        generateNumbers(seed);

    return 0;
}//end main()




//-------------------------------------------------------------------
//Function: getSeed()
//Parameters: none
//Return Type: unsigned int - the seed the client entered
//Purpose: gets the seed for the random number generator.  If the
//user enters a negative number, it causes the seed to underflow to
//a very high non-negative number.
//-------------------------------------------------------------------
unsigned getSeed(){

    unsigned seed_Number;

    cout << "Enter seed, 0 to terminate: ";
    cin >> seed_Number;

    return seed_Number;
}//end getSeed()




//-------------------------------------------------------------------
//Function: generateNumbers()
//Parameters: unsigned int - the seed the client entered
//Return Type: None
//Purpose: Generates random numbers between 1 and 100 and prints
//only those numbers that are less than 25.  Note that if you
//enter the same seed number at different times, you get the same
//"random" number sequence.  Using the srand(time(NULL)) will
```

```
//lessen the chance that the same seed is used twice to generate
//random numbers.
//----------------------------------------------------------------
void generateNumbers(const unsigned SEED){

    int ran_num;

    srand(SEED);

    for (int ix=0; ix < 75; ix++){
       ran_num = 1 + rand() % 100;
       if (ran_num < 25)
          cout << ran_num << " ";
    }

    cout << endl << endl;

    return;
}//end generateNumbers()
//end file random1.cpp

A:\c>random1
Enter seed, 0 to terminate: 5
15 22 8 8 18 12 23 11 16 23 7 16 20 16 13 6 5 18 2 11 7

Enter seed, 0 to terminate: 7
23 16 22 17 19 10 2 16 13 13 2 14 4 12 20 18 20 4 20 20

Enter seed, 0 to terminate: 9
10 23 12 18 3 13 17 18 2 5 11 20 9 5 15 22

Enter seed, 0 to terminate:
```

The RANDOM2.CPP Program

Continuing our exploration of C++ and random numbers, the
RANDOM2.CPP program listing is shown in the top portion of Listing 6.6.
This program is equivalent to RANDOM2.BAS to encode your message
using random numbers. The lower portion of Listing 6.6 illustrates several examples of the execution of the program. When comparing the
results to the results obtained by the execution of RANDOM2.BAS, you
will note that the use of the same seed values produces different results
based upon differences between the two programs in their built-in random number generators. As you will note, RANDOM2.CPP uses random

numbers greater than 25 and adds that number to the location of each character in the plaintext array. The sum is then divided by 26 in the same manner as RANDOM2.BAS.

Both RANDOM1.CPP and RANDOM2.CPP and their executable files are contained on the CD-ROM accompanying this book. The executable versions are named RANDOM1.EXE and RANDOM2.EXE. All four programs are located in the C directory on the CD-ROM.

Listing 6.6 The RANDOM2.CPP program listing and its repeated execution using different random seed numbers.

```
/*
random2.cpp
C++ code written by Jonathan Held on April 28, 1998,
using Microsoft Visual C++ version 5.0
*/

#include <iostream.h>
#include <stdlib.h>
#include <string.h>
#include <assert.h>

//function prototypes
bool checkInput(char *&);
char* encipher(char *&);
void formatData(char []);
void getMessage(char *&);
unsigned int getSeed(void);
void gotit(const char [], char *&, const int, int);

const int BUFFER_SIZE = 256;


//------------------------------------------------------------------
//Function: main()
//Parameters: None
//Return Type: int - 0 if program terminated normally
//Purpose: driver that makes calls to various procedures defined
//in random1.cpp
//------------------------------------------------------------------
int main(){
```

```
   unsigned int seed;
   char *message, *result;

   while (seed = getSeed()) {
      srand(seed);
      getMessage(message);
      cout << "\nYou entered: " << message << endl;
      result = encipher(message);
      cout << "Enciphered message is " << result << endl << endl;
      delete message;
   }

   return 0;
}//end main()

//-----------------------------------------------------------------
//Function: checkInput()
//Parameters: input - the message the user entered
//Return Type: bool - true if the input string contains an error,
//                    false otherwise
//Purpose: Checks the user's keyword for invalid characters.
//-----------------------------------------------------------------
bool checkInput(char * &input)
{
   bool error = false;
   int count = strlen(input);

   for (int ix=0; ix<count; ix++){

      int char_value = static_cast<int>(*(input+ix));
      //determine if the user did not enter an uppercase character
      if ((char_value < 65) || (char_value > 90)){
         error = true;
         cerr << "\aYou entered an invalid message!" << endl << endl;
         break;
      }
   }

   if (count == 0){
      cerr << "\aYou entered an invalid message!" << endl << endl;
      error = true;
   }
```

```
        return error;
    }//end checkInput()



    //------------------------------------------------------------------
    //Function: encipher()
    //Parameters: inp - the user's input that will be enciphered
    //Return Type: char * - a pointer to the encrypted string
    //Purpose: returns a pointer to the encrypted text
    //------------------------------------------------------------------
    char* encipher(char *&inp){

        //yet another, and easier way to represent the plaintext
        //array
        const char plaintext[] = "ABCDEFGHIJKLMNOPQRSTUVWXYZ";
        int index = 0;

        char *encrypted = new char[strlen(inp)+1];
        assert(encrypted);

        for (int ix=0; ix < strlen(inp); ix++){
            for (int jx=0; jx <26; jx++){
                if (plaintext[jx] == inp[ix]){
                    gotit(plaintext, encrypted, jx, index++);
                    break;
                }
            }
        }

        //don't forget to insert the null terminator
        encrypted[strlen(inp)] = '\0';

        return encrypted;
    }//end encipher();



    //------------------------------------------------------------------
    //Function: formatData()
    //Parameters: data - the array we want to format
    //Return Type: None
    //Purpose: Get rid of all spaces in the array.
    //------------------------------------------------------------------
    void formatData(char data[]){
```

```
    for (int mx=0, nx=0; (*(data+nx) != '\0'); nx++){
        if (*(data+nx) == ' '){
            //do nothing - skip over the space in the data
        }
        else {
            *(data+mx++) = *(data+nx);
        }
    }

    //don't forget to add the null terminator
    *(data+mx) = '\0';

    return;
}//end formatData()




//-----------------------------------------------------------------
//Function: getMessage()
//Parameters: input - user's one-line message
//Return Type: None
//Purpose: Gets a one-line message from the user.
//-----------------------------------------------------------------
void getMessage(char *&input){

    char buffer[BUFFER_SIZE] = {'\0'};
    bool error = false;

    do{
        cout << "Enter a one-line message (no spaces) in UPPERCASE: ";
        cin.getline(buffer, BUFFER_SIZE, '\n');
        assert(input = new char[strlen(buffer) + 1]);
        strcpy(input, buffer);
        formatData(input);
        error = checkInput(input);

        if (error)
            delete input;

    } while (error);

    return;
}//getMessage()
```

6

Chapter

```
//-------------------------------------------------------------------
//Function: getSeed()
//Parameters: none
//Return Type: unsigned int - the seed the client entered
//Purpose: gets the seed for the random number generator.  If the
//user enters a negative number, it causes the seed to underflow to
//a very high non-negative number.  If the user enters an
//alphanumeric sequence, e.g., "A123", then seed_Number is set to
//zero.
//-------------------------------------------------------------------
unsigned getSeed(){

    unsigned int seed_Number;

    cout << "Enter seed, 0 (or non-digit) to terminate: ";
    cin >> seed_Number;
    cin.ignore();

    return seed_Number;
}//end getSeed()



//-------------------------------------------------------------------
//Function: gotit()
//Parameters: p_text - the plaintext array, i.e., characters "A-Z"
//            enc_msg - a pointer to the message that will be encoded
//            loc - the location of each encoded character in the
//            plaintext array
//Return Type: None
//Purpose: encodes the user's input using random numbers
//-------------------------------------------------------------------
void gotit(const char p_text[], char *&enc_msg, int loc, int index){

    int random_num, z;

    do {
       random_num = rand() % 100;
    } while (random_num > 25);

    z = (loc + random_num) % 26;
    enc_msg[index] = p_text[z];

    return;
}//end gotit()
```

```
//end file random2.cpp
A:\c>RANDOM2
Enter seed, 0 (or non-digit) to terminate: 5
Enter a one-line message (no spaces) in UPPERCASE: FIREFREDNOW

You entered: FIREFREDNOW
Enciphered message is TDYLWCANCKC

Enter seed, 0 (or non-digit) to terminate: 8
Enter a one-line message (no spaces) in UPPERCASE: FIREFREDNOW

You entered: FIREFREDNOW
Enciphered message is QLEGOKYPGRV

Enter seed, 0 (or non-digit) to terminate: 51
Enter a one-line message (no spaces) in UPPERCASE: FIREFREDNOW

You entered: FIREFREDNOW
Enciphered message is KIYOSXAWQTW

Enter seed, 0 (or non-digit) to terminate:
```

Modulo 26 Arithmetic

To better understand the routine necessary to decipher the previously enciphered series of messages that used a random number-based enciphering program requires a review of modulo 26 addition and modulo 26 subtraction. Suppose the position values of the first four characters in a plaintext message with respect to their location in the sequential plaintext alphabet are 6, 2, 4, and 18, while a randomly generated number sequence based upon a defined seed was 12, 14, 22, and 17.

The top of Figure 6.1 illustrates the enciphering process performed through the use of modulo 26 addition. Once the enciphered characters reach their destination, the same sequence of random numbers is used to reconstruct the original characters. However, this time modulo 26 subtraction is performed as illustrated in the bottom portion of Figure 6.1. When performing modulo 26 subtraction, if the numerator is smaller than the subtrahend you "borrow" 1, which in effect has a decimal value of 26, prior to performing the required subtraction. Thus, 9-17 becomes (26+9)-17, or 18, when modulo 26 subtraction is performed.

```
Figure 6.1. Enciphering and deciphering using modulo 26 addition
and subtraction.


Enciphering using modulo 26 addition
character value                                    6     2     4    18
random number                                     12    14    22    17

modulo 26 addition result
represents enciphered character value             18    16     0     9


Deciphering using modulo 26 subtraction

enciphered character value                        18    16     0     9
random number                                     12    14    22    17

modulo 26 subtraction result
represents plaintext character value               6     2     4    18
```

Now that you have an appreciation of the modulo subtraction process, let's focus our attention upon a small program developed to decipher a previously enciphered one-line message based upon a specified seed for the BASIC random number generator.

The DRANDOM2.BAS Program

Listing 6.7 contains the statements in the program DRANDOM2.BAS and three examples of its execution. In keeping with the file naming conventions previously established, I labeled the program DRANDOM2.BAS to indicate that it deciphers a message previously enciphered using the program RANDOM2.BAS.

Listing 6.7 The DRANDOM2.BAS program listing and its repeated execution using different random seed numbers and different ciphertext messages to re-create a common plaintext message.

```
REM Program DRANDOM2.BAS
DIM KEY$(80), PLAINTEXT$(26)
CLS
        PRINT "Program DRANDOM2.BAS to demonstrate use of random numbers
                and"
        PRINT "random number seed in deciphering operations"
GOSUB INITIALIZE
```

```
START: PRINT
       INPUT "Enter a random seed number, 0 to terminate ", Y
       IF Y = 0 THEN STOP
       RANDOMIZE (Y)
       INPUT "Enter a one line message in UPPERCASE: ", TEXT$
       FOR I = 1 TO LEN(TEXT$)
       KEY$(I) = MID$(TEXT$, I, 1)
       NEXT I
REM Decipher
       PRINT "Deciphered message is                : ";
       FOR I = 1 TO LEN(TEXT$)
       FOR J = 0 TO 25
       IF PLAINTEXT$(J) = KEY$(I) GOTO GOTIT
       NEXT J
GOTIT: X = INT(RND * 100)
       IF X > 25 THEN GOTO GOTIT
       IF J < X THEN J = J + 26
       Z = J - X
       PRINT PLAINTEXT$(Z);
       NEXT I
       GOTO START
INITIALIZE:
        RESTORE
        REM Initialize plaintext values
        FOR I = 0 TO 25
        READ PLAINTEXT$(I)
        NEXT I
        DATA "A","B","C","D","E","F","G","H","I","J","K","L","M","N"
        DATA "O","P","Q","R","S","T","U","V","W","X","Y","Z"
RETURN
```

Program DRANDOM2.BAS to demonstrate use of random numbers and random number seed in deciphering operations

```
Enter a random seed number, 0 to terminate 5
Enter a one line message in UPPERCASE: CPKWBXVSORN
Deciphered message is                : FIREFREDNOW
Enter a random seed number, 0 to terminate 8
Enter a one line message in UPPERCASE: RDMXNQVCJXE
Deciphered message is                : FIREFREDNOW
Enter a random seed number, 0 to terminate 51
Enter a one line message in UPPERCASE: ZXDDMCBNHGZ
Deciphered message is                : FIREFREDNOW
Enter a random seed number, 0 to terminate 0
```

After entering the random number generator's seed number and the one-line enciphered message, the decipher routine matches each character in the message against the plaintext alphabet stored in the array PLAINTEXT$. Once a match occurs, you have located the correct position value or location of the ciphertext character in the plaintext character in the plaintext alphabet—a value assigned to the variable J. After the value of J is obtained, a branch to the label GOTIT occurs and a random number between 0 and 25 is extracted. Because you must perform modulo 26 subtraction to reconstruct the plaintext character, compare the value of J to the value of x and increase J by 26 if the value of J is less than x. Then we subtract the value of x from the value of J, in effect performing modulo 26 subtraction. As indicated in the lower portion of Listing 6.7, this process enables you to reconstruct the plaintext message.

A comparison of the execution of RANDOM2.BAS and DRANDOM2.BAS contained in the lower portions of Listings 6.4 and 6.7 verifies the correctness of the deciphering process. That is, plaintext messages enciphered using a defined random number seed value in Listing 6.4 are entered as ciphertext messages in Listing 6.7 with the same seed number. This results in the correct decipherment of each message into its original plaintext contents.

The DRANDOM2.CPP Program

Listing 6.8 lists the statements in the C++ program DRANDOM2.CPP. This program represents the C++ version of DRANDOM2.BAS and can be considered to represent the decipher version of RANDOM2.CPP. That is, a message enciphered using RANDOM2.CPP can be deciphered using DRANDOM2.CPP as long as you enter the same seed for each program. Figure 6.2 illustrates the execution of RANDOM2.EXE and DRANDOM2.EXE using the same seed number. As indicated in Figure 6.2, the message HELP was enciphered as QAJA by RANDOM2.EXE based upon the use of 9 for the seed. Then DRANDOM2.EXE was executed using the same seed value; however, the one-line message input to the program is QAJA, which results in the deciphered message HELP.

Listing 6.8 The DRANDOM2.CPP program listing.

```cpp
/*
drandom2.cpp
C++ code written by Jonathan Held on May 1, 1998,
using Microsoft Visual C++ version 5.0
*/

#include <iostream.h>
#include <stdlib.h>
#include <string.h>
#include <assert.h>

//function prototypes
bool checkInput(char *&);
char* decipher(char *&);
void formatData(char []);
void getMessage(char *&);
unsigned int getSeed(void);
void gotit(const char [], char *&, const int, int);

const int BUFFER_SIZE = 256;

//-----------------------------------------------------------------
//Function: main()
//Parameters: None
//Return Type: int - 0 if program terminated normally
//Purpose: driver that makes calls to various procedures defined
//in random1.cpp
//-----------------------------------------------------------------
int main(){

   unsigned int seed;
   char *message, *result;

   while (seed = getSeed()) {
      srand(seed);
      getMessage(message);
      cout << "\nYou entered: " << message << endl;
      result = decipher(message);
      cout << "Deciphered message is " << result << endl << endl;
      delete message;
   }
```

```
      return 0;
}//end main()



//------------------------------------------------------------------
//Function: checkInput()
//Parameters: input - the message the user entered
//Return Type: bool - true if the input string contains an error,
//                    false otherwise
//Purpose: Checks the user's keyword for invalid characters.
//------------------------------------------------------------------
bool checkInput(char * &input)
{
   bool error = false;
   int count = strlen(input);

   for (int ix=0; ix<count; ix++){

      int char_value = static_cast<int>(*(input+ix));
      //determine if the user did not enter an uppercase character
      if ((char_value < 65) || (char_value > 90)){
         error = true;
         cerr << "\aYou entered an invalid message!" << endl << endl;
         break;
      }
   }

   if (count == 0){
      cerr << "\aYou entered an invalid message!" << endl << endl;
      error = true;
   }

   return error;
}//end checkInput()



//------------------------------------------------------------------
//Function: decipher()
//Parameters: inp - the user's input that will be deciphered
//Return Type: char * - a pointer to the decrypted string
//Purpose: returns a pointer to the decrypted text
//------------------------------------------------------------------
char* decipher(char *&inp){
```

```cpp
//yet another, and easier way to represent the plaintext
//array
const char plaintext[] = "ABCDEFGHIJKLMNOPQRSTUVWXYZ";
int index = 0;

char *decrypted = new char[strlen(inp)+1];
assert(decrypted);

for (int ix=0; ix < strlen(inp); ix++){
   for (int jx=0; jx <26; jx++){
      if (plaintext[jx] == inp[ix]){
            gotit(plaintext, decrypted, jx, index++);
            break;
         }
      }
   }

//don't forget to insert the null terminator
decrypted[strlen(inp)] = '\0';

return decrypted;
}//end encipher();


//------------------------------------------------------------------
//Function: formatData()
//Parameters: data - the array we want to format
//Return Type: None
//Purpose: Get rid of all spaces in the array.
//------------------------------------------------------------------
void formatData(char data[]){

   for (int mx=0, nx=0; (*(data+nx) != '\0'); nx++){
      if (*(data+nx) == ' '){
         //do nothing - skip over the space in the data
      }
      else {
         *(data+mx++) = *(data+nx);
      }
   }

   //don't forget to add the null terminator
   *(data+mx) = '\0';
```

```
    return;
}//end formatData()


//------------------------------------------------------------------
//Function: getMessage()
//Parameters: input - user's one-line message
//Return Type: None
//Purpose: Gets a one-line message from the user.
//------------------------------------------------------------------
void getMessage(char *&input){

    char buffer[BUFFER_SIZE] = {'\0'};
    bool error = false;

    do{
        cout << "Enter a one-line message (no spaces) in UPPERCASE: ";
        cin.getline(buffer, BUFFER_SIZE, '\n');
        assert(input = new char[strlen(buffer) + 1]);
        strcpy(input, buffer);
        formatData(input);
        error = checkInput(input);

        if (error)
            delete input;

    } while (error);

    return;
}//getMessage()



//------------------------------------------------------------------
//Function: getSeed()
//Parameters: none
//Return Type: unsigned int - the seed the client entered
//Purpose: gets the seed for the random number generator.  If the
//user enters a negative number, it causes the seed to underflow to
//a very high non-negative number.  If the user enters an
//alphanumeric sequence, e.g., "A123", then seed_Number is set to
//zero.
//------------------------------------------------------------------
unsigned getSeed(){
```

```
    unsigned int seed_Number;

    cout << "Enter seed, 0 (or non-digit) to terminate: ";
    cin >> seed_Number;
    cin.ignore();

    return seed_Number;
}//end getSeed()


//-------------------------------------------------------------------
//Function: gotit()
//Parameters: p_text - the plaintext array, i.e., characters "A-Z"
//            enc_msg - a pointer to the message that will be encoded
//            loc - the location of each encoded character in the
//            plaintext array
//Return Type: None
//Purpose: encodes the user's input using random numbers
//-------------------------------------------------------------------
void gotit(const char p_text[], char *&dec_msg, int loc, int index){

    int random_num, z;

    do {
        random_num = rand() % 100;
    } while (random_num > 25);

    if (loc < random_num)
            loc+= 26;

    z = loc - random_num;
    dec_msg[index] = p_text[z];

    return;
}//end gotit()
//end file drandom2.cpp
```

```
Figure 6.2 Using the C++ executable file DRANDOM2.EXE to decipher a
one-line message enciphered using RANDOM2.EXE.

C:\>random2
Enter seed, 0 (or non-digit) to terminate: 9
Enter a one-line message (no spaces) in UPPERCASE: HELP

You entered: HELP
Enciphered message is QAJA

Enter seed, 0 (or non-digit) to terminate: 0

C:\>DRANDOM2
Enter seed, 0 (or non-digit) to terminate: 9
Enter a one-line message (no spaces) in UPPERCASE: QAJA

You entered: QAJA
Deciphered message is HELP

Enter seed, 0 (or non-digit) to terminate:
```

Constructing an Enciphering Program

Now that you have reviewed the operation and utilization of the BASIC RANDOMIZE statement, the RND function, and the equivalent C++ statement, you have the foundation that enables you to construct enciphering programs which will use the built-in BASIC random number generator and the equivalent C++ statements. However, since that random number generator is available to anyone who has a computer and appropriate software, an intercepted enciphered message could be easily deciphered if you simply use a numeric value for selecting an available random number seed. This is because there are a limited number of random number seeds from which you can select in comparison to the number of combinations obtained by mixing up an alphabet. Prior to creating your random number-based enciphering program, first focus your attention upon extending the random process to obtain a much larger series of possible enciphering combinations.

Extending the Random Process

As previously mentioned in this chapter, the BASIC random number seed varies from -32768 to 32767, providing a total of 65,536 random number sequences (remember that a seed value of 0 also produces a sequence). Therefore, a person who intercepts or otherwise obtains a copy of your enciphered message can decipher that message by trying each random number seed. This obviously takes some time; however, it subjects the contents of your enciphered message to decipherment through the use of a well-known maximum number of decipherment attempts.

There are numerous methods you can consider to extend the level of security in using BASIC's and C++'s random number generators. For example, to obtain an additional level of security you can consider using two key numbers in your encipherment and decipherment process. The first key number, as previously explained, selects the random number seed. The second number would either directly or indirectly set the beginning location in the random number sequence selected. This process could theoretically result in an infinite number of combinations an unauthorized person might be faced with during an illegal decipherment process.

The top of Listing 6.9 contains a routine designed to generate random numbers between 0 and 25 based upon a defined seed and location within the selected seed. The bottom portion of Listing 6.9 shows the results obtained by executing the program three times. In examining Listing 6.9, note that each time the program was executed, the same seed was executed, but the position in the seed was changed by the use of a FOR-NEXT loop in which the statement dummy=RND is executed x times, where x represents the value of the location in the seed. The first random number considered for use by the program is located at position $x+1$ in the selected seed.

Listing 6.9 The routine to generate a random number sequence based upon a defined seed and a location in the seed.

```
REM routine to generate random numbers between 0 and 25
REM based on a defined seed and location in the seed

start:  INPUT "Enter your key numbers separated by commas: ", y, x
            RANDOMIZE (y)
```

```
            FOR i = 1 to x: dummy = RND: NEXT I
            FOR i = 1 to 75
            x = INT(RND(i) * 100)
            IF x > 25 THEN GOTO skip
            PRINT x;
skip:   NEXT I
            PRINT
```

```
Enter your key numbers separated by commas: 1,1
 10 10 10 5 21 22 11 4 5 18 21 15 17 8 15 13 15 9
Enter your key numbers separated by commas: 1,50
 17 8 15 13 15 9 10 16 12 18 6 0 15 9 23 5 11
Enter your key numbers separated by commas: 1,100
 15 9 23 5 11 3 14 2 10 13 6 4 10 10 23 22 5 11 13 8 2 21
```

The use of a FOR-NEXT statement to select a location in a random number sequence places a limit on the location within the sequence you can begin your encipherment process. This is because each version of BASIC and C++ has a limit on the maximum value that can be assigned to a variable. For example, the maximum value of an integer is 32,767 in QuickBASIC, while a long integer can have a value up to 2,147,483,647 in that language. You can also use single- or double-precision numeric variables to extend the maximum value allowed by the language and the number of combinations allowed in selecting a position within a random number sequence. However, the use of high numbers, whether they are integers or numerics, can result in significant user waiting periods while the computer cycles through a large number of random numbers within a particular random number seed to locate the desired position within a random number sequence. For example, the execution of the FOR-NEXT loop FOR I = 1 TO x shown at the top of Listing 6.9 could result in the user of the program waiting for several minutes if an extremely large value was entered for x and the program was executed on an old 8088-based computer.

In addition to a long waiting period, the use of a large number is difficult to remember and might restrict the use of the preceding example to a simple low value or easy-to-remember number, such as 500, 1,000, and so on. The use of a number limited to 1,000 or so still significantly extends the number of combinations resulting from the selection of a random number sequence and position within the sequence. For 1,000 positions within a sequence, the total number of combinations an unauthorized person would need to try to decipher a message would be extended to 65,536,000 since there are 65,536 different random number seeds. Even if the right combination was discovered halfway through the search sequence, this could result in over 32 million combinations being used for the attempted decipherment. For a message such as BID THIRTY TWO MILLION ON TUESDAY AT THE AUCTION, any decipherment that occurs after Tuesday may be worthless. The use of two keys that select a random number sequence and position within the sequence may provide a significant level of message protection for many users. However, recognizing the need of most users for an extra level of protection, I'll demonstrate a few easy-to-implement techniques that can be used to obtain that desired additional level of protection.

Extending the Combinations

You can substantially increase both the number of combinations available for starting the random number sequence to be used in a program as well as the speed in which the user of the program obtains access to the sequence. To accomplish this, use a third key to increment the FOR-NEXT loop to both speed up the positioning process as well as increase the number of combinations an unauthorized party must try in an attempt to decipher an enciphered message.

The top portion of Listing 6.10 contains the program listing for entering a three-number sequence to select a position within a random number sequence defined by a random number seed from which to commence the encipherment process at the next random number position. In this example, the first number is assigned to the variable x, and is used to select the random number seed sequence. The second number entered is assigned to the variable y and defines the limit of the FOR-NEXT loop. The value of the third number entered is assigned to the variable z and defines the increment used in the FOR-NEXT loop. Each of the numbers can be considered to represent a key. You can consider this elementary program a random number generator based upon the use of a three-numeric key sequence.

6

Chapter

Listing 6.10 Sample program that uses three numbers to rapidly position the starting point within a random number sequence of a defined random number seed.

```
INPUT "Enter your three key numbers, each separated by a comma: ", x, y, z
RANDOMIZE (x)
FOR i = 1 to y STEP z
dummy = RND
NEXT I
FOR I = 1 TO 10
PRINT INT(RND * 100)
NEXT I
PRINT
```

```
Enter your three key numbers, each separated by a   comma: 12,24,4
 1 87 10 94 95 82 26 71 21 57
Enter your three key numbers, each separated by a   comma: 12,24,9
 50 27 89 1 87 10 94 95 82 26
Enter your three key numbers, each separated by a   comma: 12,240,9
 31 88 52 70 32 72 70 37 95 12
Enter your three key numbers, each separated by a   comma: 12,110543,43
 3 3 17 51 70 18 51 35 79 27
Enter your three key numbers, each separated by a   comma: 110543,1993,12
 65 34 48 63 89 66 63 2 41 29
```

The lower portion of Listing 6.10 illustrates the results obtained from executing the program five times in sequence using different key combinations.

The first two examples illustrated at the bottom of Listing 6.10 could have used the month and day of the month for the first two keys and an hour for the third key. The third example could have used the Julian day for the day instead of the day of the month. In the fourth example, the second key could be a person's date of birth. In the fifth example, perhaps the first key is the person's date of birth, while the second and third keys are the current year and month.

Regardless of the manner in which values are assigned to each key, the use of three keys can provide an extremely large number of combinations. However, the key (no pun intended) to obtaining a large number of combinations is the mechanism used to generate key values. By selecting easy-to-remember but relatively large values for each of the three keys, you can force an unauthorized person with access to a deciphering program to obtain the power of a mainframe or modern Pentium II computer to decipher your message. For example, using a date in the form of *mmddyy* for the first key, a year in the form of *yyyy* for the second key, and a number in the form of *dd* for the third key could result in up to 10 billion possible combinations an unauthorized person obtaining access to an enciphered message might have to try in an attempt to decipher your message! Now that's a significant order of magnitude beyond the 65,536 random number seed sequences and adds a degree of decipherment difficulty that corresponds to a level of protection afforded by many commercially available systems whose purchase price significantly exceeds the cost of this book.

Creating Your Own Random Number Generator

Although the preceding three key examples indicated a series of approximately 10 billion combinations would be required, when you use a built-in random number generator you simplify the life of code-breakers. This is because if they have a bit of knowledge concerning the random number generation scheme you are using, it is a relatively simple process to program a computer to cycle through every possible combination. Because of this, the use of a built-in random number generator entails a bit of a risk. Although it could take a long time to lock onto your random number sequence, who would have expected desktop computers to operate at 400 MHZ a few years ago? This means that the months, days, or hours of attack required today may be reduced to days, hours, or minutes tomorrow. Recognizing this fact, let's examine how you can easily create your own pseudo-random number generator. Because there are an infinite number of equations you could use to create your own generator, doing so can make the life of a code-breaker significantly more difficult.

Because a pseudo-random number generator requires an equation, let's define one. Let's assume the following equation is your magic formula for generating a random number:

$$INTEGER \left(\frac{MYRANDOM * 37 + 462}{42} \right)$$

Although it may appear the preceding formula represents a randomly developed equation, let me explain its operation to shed light on how you can develop your own random number generator. If you assume that the variable MYRANDOM ranges between 0 and 100, then the maximum value of the preceding formula becomes:

$$INTEGER \left(\frac{100 * 37 + 462}{42} \right) \text{ or } 99$$

Thus, your magic formula would return values from 11 to 99, as when MYRANDOM has a value of zero the formula returns a value of 11.

To use a magic formula, you could accept a number from the keyboard and assign its value to the variable MYRANDOM. After computing a pseudo-random number, you could both use that number and assign its value to MYRANDOM to generate a second pseudo-random number. For example, assume you entered 10 from the keyboard. The first time the magic formula is computed you would obtain:

$$INTEGER \left(\frac{10 * 37 + 462}{42} \right) \text{ or } 19$$

Using 19 as input to the formula, you would obtain:

$$INTEGER \left(\frac{19 * 37 + 462}{42} \right) \text{ or } 27$$

Although the preceding magic formula was rather simplistic, it illustrates how you can create your own pseudo-random number generator. In concluding this chapter, I'll illustrate the creation of a program to generate pseudo-random numbers without using a language's built-in random number generator function.

Program Development

In this section, you will construct a program for enciphering and deciphering based upon the use of Microsoft's QuickBASIC random number generator, as well as a C++ equivalent. To do so, you will develop a mechanism to obtain a position in the random number generator which is difficult to duplicate.

To develop a subroutine to obtain a difficult-to-duplicate position within the random number generator, you must consider both the number of character positions you will use in a code your program will operate upon to obtain a location in the random number generator as well as the characters that can be used for each position. For example, a two-position code restricted to numerics is limited to containing values from 00 to 99, or 100 (10^2) combinations. If those two positions can contain alphanumeric characters, each position can contain 36 combinations, while the two positions represent a total of 36^2, or 1,296, combinations.

Table 6.2 lists the number of combinations resulting from the use of code lengths varying from 1 to 10 positions, with each position containing up to 10 (numeric only), 26 (alphabetic only), 36 (alphanumeric), and 128 (any seven-bit ASCII) permissible characters. As indicated in Table 6.2, an expansion of the number of code positions and/or the number of characters permitted to be entered in each position significantly increases the possible number of code combinations. Because most people can easily remember a six-position code, use this type of code to develop a mechanism to obtain a difficult-to-duplicate position within the built-in BASIC random number generator. Using six positions and allowing alphanumeric characters to be placed in each position results in 2,176,782,336 possible combinations! If you extend the characters that can be placed into each code position to the normal ASCII code, you would obtain $439*10^{10}$ possible combinations. Because characters should be converted to their ASCII numeric representation to use for positioning purposes, you need a mechanism to perform this operation.

Table 6.2 Code combinations based upon code length and characters allowed.

X	$10\wedge X$	$26\wedge X$	$36\wedge X$	$128\wedge X$
1	100.00E-01	260.00E-01	360.00E-01	128.00E+00
2	100.00E+00	676.00E+00	129.60E+01	163.84E+02
3	100.00E+01	175.76E+02	466.56E+02	209.72E+04
4	100.00E+02	456.98E+03	167.96E+04	268.44E+06
5	100.00E+03	118.81E+05	604.66E+05	343.60E+08
6	100.00E+04	308.92E+06	217.68E+07	439.80E+10
7	100.00E+05	803.18E+07	783.64E+08	562.95E+12
8	100.00E+06	208.83E+09	282.11E+10	720.58E+14
9	100.00E+07	542.95E+10	101.56E+12	922.34E+16
10	100.00E+08	141.17E+12	365.62E+13	118.06E+19

Listing 6.11 illustrates a short segment of code to read characters and display their ASCII values. In this example, the program executes continuously until a break occurs. After reading a string that is assigned to the string variable A$, the program obtains the length of the string. Next, a FOR-NEXT loop extracts each character from the string through the use

6

Chapter

of the MID$ function and prints the ASCII value of each character through the use of the ASC function. The lower portion of Listing 6.11 illustrates the resulting ASCII values of each character from six strings entered as codes. Note that the code can be all alphabetic (GODAWGS), numeric (362436), alphanumeric (NINE9), or include special characters such as the exclamation mark that are included in the normal ASCII character set (POWER!).

Listing 6.11 Using ASCII character values.

```
CLS
START:
            INPUT A$
            X = LEN(A$)
            FOR I = 1 TO X
            PRINT ASC(MID$(A$, I, 1)); " ";
            NEXT I
            PRINT
GOTO START

? GODAWGS
 71    79    68    65    87    71    83
? YEATIGERS
 89    69    65    84    73    71    69    82    83
? 362436
 51    54    50    52    51    54
? POWER!
 80    78    87    69    82    33
? NINE9
 78    73    78    69    57
? $39.99
 36    51    57    46    57    57
?
```

At the top of Listing 6.12 you will find a C++ version of the BASIC program in Listing 6.11. The C++ version looks at each character entered. This can result in an interesting display that may require a bit of interpretation. Thus, let's examine the output of the program shown in the lower portion of Listing 6.12.

In examining the execution of the program ASCII.CPP, note that if you enter characters separated by a space, such as "1 2 4 6," the ASCII value of 32 which represents a space will be displayed. Thus, the ASCII values for the sequence "1 2 4 6" is displayed as "49 32 50 32 52 32 54." The preceding is true for both alphabetic and numeric characters as indicated by the entry of the character sequence "A B C D" in the lower portion of Listing 6.12.

Listing 6.12 The ASCII.CPP program listing and sample execution.

```
/*
ASCII.cpp
C++ code written by Jonathan Held, May 8, 1998, using Microsoft's
Visual C++ version 5.0.
*/


#include <iostream.h>
#include <string.h>
#include <iomanip.h>



//-----------------------------------------------------------------
//Function: main()
//Parameters: None
//Return Type: int - 0 means program terminated normally, any other
//value indicated abnormal termination
//Purpose: Runs the main part of the program.
//-----------------------------------------------------------------
int main(){
   char buffer[1000];
   const char *spacing = "               ";
   cout << "Use CTRL-C to terminate program." << endl << endl;
   while(true){

      cout << "Enter a sequence of characters: ";
      cin.getline(buffer, 1000, '\n');
      cout << endl << "ASCII values: ";
      int ix = strlen(buffer);
```

```
        for (int jx=0; jx<ix; jx++){
           if ((jx!=0) && (!(jx%10)))
               cout << endl << spacing;
           cout << setw(3) << (int) buffer[jx] << " ";
        }
        cout << endl << endl;
    }
    return 0;
}//end main()
//end file listing
```

```
C:\>ASCII
Use CTRL-C to terminate program.

Enter a sequence of characters: 12

ASCII values:  49  50

Enter a sequence of characters: 1 2 4 6

ASCII values:  49  32  50  32  52  32  54

Enter a sequence of characters: A B C D

ASCII values:  65  32  66  32  67  32  68
```

At this point it may be useful to examine a six-position code used to perform a series of manipulations to obtain a position within a random number seed. Although I will review one series of manipulations, a six-character code provides 6!, or 720, possible methods by which the characters can be used if they are used one character at a time. If you desire, you can change the method of code character manipulations to fit your specific requirements.

To manipulate the six-position code, first multiply the ASCII value of each of the first two characters in the code to use as the RANDOMIZE seed setting. Next, multiply the ASCII values of the third and fourth characters in the code to serve as a first limit for entry into a position within the selected seed. Use the ASCII value of the fifth code character to increment towards the limit. As a further offset into the random number sequence, multiply the ASCII values of the fifth and sixth code characters and use the result as a second limit. Then, sequence towards that limit using the ASCII value of the fourth code character as a mechanism for incrementing towards that limit.

The use of the six-character grouping we previously discussed is illustrated graphically in Figure 6.3. An analysis of the combinations obtained from the use of that code is warranted, as it indicates how good intentions can go astray and why many persons throughout the history of mankind have become so involved in developing "unbreakable" techniques that they literally couldn't see the trees in the forest and did not understand the weakness they created in their quest for increasing the complexity of their code design.

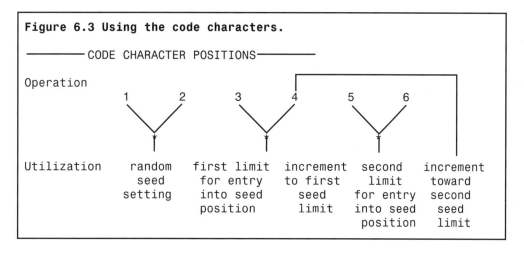

Figure 6.3 Using the code characters.

In Figure 6.3 the use of a two-character position to generate a seed setting when each position is restricted to alphanumeric characters reduces the number of seed combinations to 36^2, or 1,296, which is significantly less than the maximum number of seed settings supported in BASIC. The entry into the selected seed is based upon the multiplication of the value of code positions three and four, which are added to the product of the values of code positions five and six. This means that the maximum value of the displacement into the selected seed is 2,592 positions when code positions are limited to alphanumeric characters. Thus, the maximum number of combinations one has to try in an attempt to locate the position within a selected seed for enciphering a message becomes 1,296 seeds * 2,592 positions, or 3,359,232 combinations! Although this is still a formidable number, it is certainly less formidable than the maximum number of combinations that can be obtained from a six-character position code. You may wish to consider alternative methods to use the characters in a code to initiate a random number sequence within a seed at a defined position. Later in this chapter I will discuss an alternative method you can consider for the use of the characters in a code to initiate a sequence of random numbers. However, for the moment I will focus on the way you can code the previously described code character manipulations for use in programs that encipher and decipher messages based upon the use of the built-in BASIC random number generator. I will also develop programs that will accept any ASCII character in each code position. This will significantly extend the number of possible combinations others must try in an attempt to decipher a message enciphered through the use of the program RANDOM3.BAS developed later in this chapter. For example, with each character code position capable of containing any conventional ASCII character, the use of code positions one and two for selecting the seed increases the number of seeds capable of being used to 127 * 127, or 16,129. Once you have an appreciation for the coding and operation of "secret" code-based programs, you will learn how you can make those "secret" codes even less vulnerable. Following our customary method, once I describe a BASIC program, I will then indicate the appropriate C++ program.

The POSITION.BAS Program

The top of Listing 6.13 gives the statements in the demonstration program POSITION.BAS which accepts a "secret" code up to six characters in length and uses the ASCII values of those characters in the manner previously discussed as a mechanism for positioning into a place in the random number generator. In this program, the subroutine SETUP actually performs the previously described manipulation of the ASCII value of each code character. The lower portion of Listing 6.13 illustrates the execution of the program using five different "secret" codes. The program displays the numeric (ASCII) value of each code character and the first five random numbers following the execution of the positioning subroutine. Any ASCII character can be used for each code character; however, control characters that are non-printable are obviously not printed when used as code characters.

Listing 6.13 The POSITION.BAS program listing and examples of its repeated execution.

```
REM Program POSITION.BAS demonstrates the positioning to a place in the
REM random number generator based upon a secret code up to 6 characters
AGN:
        INPUT "Enter your secret code (6 characters maximum) : "; CODE$
        IF LEN(CODE$) > 6 THEN GOTO AGN
GOSUB SETUP
        PRINT "Numeric value of code characters : ";
        FOR I = 1 TO 6
        PRINT CODE(I); " ";
        NEXT I
        PRINT : PRINT "1st five random numbers : ";
        FOR I = 1 TO 5: PRINT RND; : NEXT I: PRINT : PRINT
        STOP
SETUP:
        REM routine to position random number generator
        FOR I = 1 TO LEN(CODE$)
        CODE(I) = ASC(MID$(CODE$, I, 1))
        NEXT I
        SEED = CODE(1) * CODE2
        MAX = CODE(3) * CODE(4)
        RANDOMIZE SEED
        FOR I = 1 TO MAX STEP CODE(5)                'position into sequence
        DUMMY = RND
        NEXT I
        FOR I = 1 TO CODE(5) * CODE(6) STEP CODE(4) 'further offset into
sequence
        DUMMY = RND
        NEXT I
RETURN
```

```
Enter your secret code (6 characters maximum) : ? HELPME
Numeric value of code characters :  72   69   76   80   77   69
1st five random numbers :  .8671363  .3378422  .4237103  .6096486  .9087062

Enter your secret code (6 characters maximum) : ? 9NINES
Numeric value of code characters :  57   78   73   78   69   83
1st five random numbers :  .4766153  .8707944  .8031864  .3487226  .6214768

Enter your secret code (6 characters maximum) : ? 382438
Numeric value of code characters :  51   56   50   52   51   56
```

6

Chapter

```
1st five random numbers :   .944414  .949271  .5596389  .7912182
9.593111E-02

Enter your secret code (6 characters maximum) : ? 3CARDS
Numeric value of code characters :  51   67   65   82   68   83
1st five random numbers :   .4237103  .6096486  .9087062  .8784156  .0561406

Enter your secret code (6 characters maximum) : ? helpme
Numeric value of code characters :  104  101  108  112  109  101
1st five random numbers :   .5051253  .7871563  .9859242  .1925381  .3514438
```

The POSITION.CPP Program

Continuing our dual language approach to illustrate major encryption coding techniques, the top portion of Listing 6.14 contains the program listing for the C++ version of POSITION.BAS. This program, which has the filename POSITION.CPP, is contained on the CD-ROM in the C directory. Similarly, the executable version of this program is stored under the name POSITION.EXE in the same directory. The lower portion of Listing 6.14 illustrates two examples of the execution of POSITION.CPP. If you compare the execution of POSITION.CPP to the execution of POSITION.BAS, you will note that the use of the same secret code produces different results. As previously explained, the random number generators used in BASIC and C++ differ and result in the difference between the results display when executing POSITION.BAS and POSITION.CPP.

Listing 6.14 The POSITION.CPP program listing and examples of the execution of the program.

```
/*
position.cpp
C++ code written by Jonathan Held, May 8, 1998, using Microsoft's
Visual C++ version 5.0.
*/

//standard includes
#include <iostream.h>
#include <string.h>
#include <stdlib.h>
#include <iomanip.h>

//function prototypes
void firstFiveRndNumbers(char *);
```

```
void getCode(char *&);
void numericValues(char *);
//-------------------------------------------------------------------
//Function: main()
//Parameters: None
//Return Type: int - 0 means program terminated normally, any other
//value means abnormal termination
//Purpose: Runs the main part of the program.
//-------------------------------------------------------------------
int main(){

    cout << "\aHit CTRL-C to terminate this progam." << endl << endl;
    while (true){
        char * the_Code;
        getCode(the_Code);
        numericValues(the_Code);
        firstFiveRndNumbers(the_Code);
        cout << endl;
    }
    return 0;
}//end main()


//-------------------------------------------------------------------
//Function: firstFiveRndNumbers()
//Parameters: the_Code - a pointer to the keyword entered by the
//client
//Return Type: None
//Purpose: Generates the first five random numbers in the sequence.
//Random number generation is done based on a six-character code,
//entered by the client.
//-------------------------------------------------------------------
void firstFiveRndNumbers(char *the_Code){

    int seed = (int)*the_Code * (int)(*(the_Code+1));
    int max = (int)(*(the_Code+2)) * (int)(*(the_Code+3));
    float dummy;
    int increment;
    srand(seed);
    cout << "1st five random numbers: ";
    increment = (int) (*(the_Code + 4));

 for (int ix=1; ix<max; ix+=increment)
     dummy = ((float) rand() )/RAND_MAX;
```

```
        max = (int)(*(the_Code + 4)) * (int) (*(the_Code+5));

    for (int jx=1; jx<max; jx+=increment)
        dummy = ((float) rand() )/RAND_MAX;

    for (int kx=1; kx<=5; kx++)
        cout << ((float) rand() )/RAND_MAX << " ";

    cout << endl;
    return;
}//end firstFiveRndNumbers()
//------------------------------------------------------------------
//Function: getCode()
//Parameters: the_Code - the code that will be entered by the client
//Return Type: None
//Purpose: Prompts the client for a keyword of at least six characters.
//Checks the length of the keyword entered to make sure it has the
//required number of characters.  If it doesn't, it prints an error
//message and prompts for a keyword again.
//------------------------------------------------------------------
void getCode(char *&the_Code){

    int length;
    bool go_on = true;
    char buffer[1000];
    while(go_on){
        cout << "Enter your secret code (6 characters minimum): ";
        cin >> buffer;
        length = strlen(buffer);
        if (length < 6) {
            cerr << "\aCode must be 6 characters or more!"
                    << endl << endl;
        }
        else {
                the_Code = new char[length];
                strcpy(the_Code, buffer);
                go_on = false;
        }
    }
    return;
}//end getCode()
//------------------------------------------------------------------
//Function: numericValues()
//Parameters: the_Code - the code entered by the client
```

```
//Return Type: None
//Purpose: Displays the ASCII values of the characters in the
//keyword.
//----------------------------------------------------------------
void numericValues(char *the_Code){

   char *alias = the_Code;
   int count = 0;
   char *spacing = "                                    ";
   cout <<         "Numeric value of code characters: ";
   while (*alias){
      if ((count !=0) && (!(count%10)))
         cout << endl << spacing;
         cout << setw(4) << (int) (*alias++);
            count++;
      }

   cout << endl;
   return;
}//end numericValues()
//end file position.cpp

A:\c>position
Hit CTRL-C to terminate this progam.

Enter your secret code (6 characters minimum): HELPME
Numeric value of code characters:   72  69  76  80  77  69
1st five random numbers: 0.856807 0.441908 0.621845 0.638844 0.32

Enter your secret code (6 characters minimum): 9NINES
Numeric value of code characters:   57  78  73  78  69  83
1st five random numbers: 0.516404 0.737236 0.561724 0.396344 0.16
```

The RTEST.BAS Program

One of the concerns you may have at this point is the possibility that each random seed results in a sequence of random numbers that repeat. To determine if this is a potential problem, a program was developed to generate the first five random numbers in a seed as two-digit integers and cycle through the seed looking for a match.

Listing 6.15 gives the statements in this program that was labeled RTEST.BAS. Figure 6.4 illustrates the results of the execution of RTEST.BAS when 1 was entered as the seed number. After a period of waiting, I terminated the execution of the program by entering a CTRL-BREAK key sequence because more than 5.7 million numbers had been tested without encountering a duplicate sequence of five numbers. With over 64,000 possible seeds and over 5.7 million non-repeating random number sequences per seed, it is obvious that it will be very difficult to duplicate a position selected by a well-thought-out code word that is manipulated in a well-thought-out manner.

Listing 6.15 The RTEST.BAS program listing, which tests for a repeated sequence within a random number seed.

```
REM Random sequence test program RTEST.BAS
        CLS
        PRINT "TEST FOR 5 REPEATED DIGITS AT BEGINNING OF SEQUENCE"
        POSITION = 3
        INPUT "Enter random generator seed number "; x
        RANDOMIZE x
        FOR I = 1 TO 5  'get first five random numbers as 2-digit integers
        A(I) = INT(RND * 100)
        NEXT I
        k = 1
again:  FOR I = 1 TO 5   'get next group of five random numbers as
                  2-digit integers
        b(I) = INT(RND * 100)
        NEXT I
        FOR I = 1 TO 5     'do they match?
        IF A(I) <> b(I) THEN GOTO skip
        NEXT I
        LOCATE POSITION, 1
        PRINT "match occured at number =", k
        POSITION = POSITION + 1
        GOTO again
skip:   k = k + (6 - I)
        LOCATE 1, 60
        PRINT "search at #"; k
        GOTO again
```

Figure 6.4 Sample execution of the RTEST.BAS program.

```
TEST FOR 5 REPEATED DIGITS AT BEGINNING OF SEQUENCE      search at # 5738617
Enter random generator seed number ? 1
```

Now that you have a subroutine that can be used for positioning with the BASIC and C++ random number generation routines, you can develop enciphering programs.

The RANDOM3.BAS Program

Listing 6.16 contains the statements in the main portion of the enciphering program stored in the file RANDOM3.BAS on the BASIC directory on the companion CD-ROM. This program was constructed to encipher messages using the built-in BASIC random number generator using the previously described subroutine SETUP to obtain a difficult-to-duplicate position within the random number generator.

Listing 6.16 Statements in the main portion of the RANDOM3.BAS program.

```
REM Program RANDOM3.BAS
        CLS
        DIM PLAINTEXT$(25)
        PRINT "RANDOM3.BAS - A program which enciphers messages"
        PRINT "using the built-in BASIC random number generator"
        PRINT
RTN:
        INPUT "Enter your secret code (6 characters maximum) : "; CODE$
        IF LEN(CODE$) > 6 THEN GOTO RTN
GOSUB INITIALIZE               'initialize plaintext values
GOSUB SETUP                    'obtain random seed and position in seed
GOSUB MSGFILE                  'assign I/O files, place message on a file
GOSUB RCONVERTSTORE            'convert and store ciphertext on a file
GOSUB PRTOUT                   'print results
STOP
```

When you examine the statements contained in Listing 6.16, note that the only new subroutine is RCONVERTSTORE, with the prefix R in the name of the subroutine used to identify its modification for use in our random program operation. Thus, in discussing the operation of this program, I will focus attention upon the new subroutine developed for use in the program.

The RCONVERTSTORE Subroutine

Listing 6.17 lists the statements in the subroutine RCONVERTSTORE. The difference between this subroutine and the previously described

CONVERTSTORE subroutine are the statements bounded by the FOR-NEXT loop.

Listing 6.17 Statements in the RCONVERTSTORE subroutine.

```
RCONVERTSTORE:
        REM Routine to convert and store ciphertext on a file
        OPEN INFILE$ FOR INPUT AS #1
        OPEN OUTFILE$ FOR OUTPUT AS #2
        DO UNTIL EOF(1)
                INPUT #1, TEXT$
                MSGLEN = LEN(TEXT$)
                IF MID$(TEXT$, 1, 1) = "/" THEN GOTO CLEARTXT
                IF MID$(TEXT$, 1, 1) = "\" THEN GOTO DONE1
                REM Convert plaintext to ciphertext
                        FOR I = 1 TO MSGLEN
                        X = INT(RND * 100)        'get 2-digit integer
                        X = INT(X / 3.85)         'smooth to 0 to 25
                        FOR J = 0 TO 25
                        IF MID$(TEXT$, I, 1) = PLAINTEXT$(J) THEN GOTO
                                                        GOTIT
                        NEXT J
GOTIT:                  MID$(TEXT$, I, 1) = PLAINTEXT$((X + J) MOD 26)
                        NEXT I
CLEARTXT:               WRITE #2, TEXT$
        LOOP
DONE1:          CLOSE #2
RETURN
```

When converting the subroutine for operation with random numbers, the statement X=INT(RND*100) obtains a one- or two-digit number between 0 and 99. The next statement lowers the maximum resulting value of the modified random number by dividing the number by 3.85 and taking the integer of the result. This smooths the random number to a value between 0 and 25, which is equivalent to the index values in the array PLAINTEXT in which the plaintext alphabet is stored.

The inner FOR-NEXT loop which increments J from 0 to 25 compares each character from a line of input from file #1 to a letter in the string array PLAINTEXT$. When a match occurs, J represents the position in the array PLAINTEXT$ where the match occurred. The branch to the label GOTIT results in the mod 26 addition of the value of J to the smoothed value of the extracted random number. The mod 26 addition of X and J is then used as an index to extract a new character from the string array PLAINTEXT$, which is used to replace the plaintext character in TEXT$. The subroutine RCONVERTSTORE uses the plaintext character set as a mechanism to generate ciphertext based upon the previously described algorithm.

Figure 6.5 illustrates the execution of the program RANDOM3.BAS. In this example, the code 9LIVES was used to obtain a position in the BASIC random number generator. Because the program uses the previously developed PRTOUT subroutine, the resulting enciphered message is printed in groups of five characters as illustrated at the bottom of Figure 6.5.

```
Figure 6.5 Execution of RANDOM3.BAS.

RANDOM3.BAS - A program which enciphers messages
using the built-in BASIC random number generator

Enter your secret code (6 characters maximum) : ? 9LIVES
Enter filename to store plaintext message, default=MESSAGE.DAT
Enter filename to store enciphered message, default=CIPHERTX.DAT
Select keyboard (k) or file (f) message input: K
Enter your message - place a / at the beginning of each line
that should remain in plaintext and a \ on a separate line
to indicate the end of the enciphered message

/TO:   ALL REGIONAL OFFICE MANAGERS
/FROM: PRESIDENT LES MISERABLES
TO PREVENT A CHAPTER ELEVEN ALL EMPLOYEES MUST WORK A DOUBLE SHIFT
CHRISTMAS DAY WITHOUT PAY STOP MANAGERS ARE RESPONSIBLE FOR
IMPLEMENTING THIS POLICY STOP HAVE A NICE DAY
\

Resulting enciphered message is:
TO:   ALL REGIONAL OFFICE MANAGERS
FROM: PRESIDENT LES MISERABLES
PIXHK FQCZV FIZDH PUMJQ NYKQT
RIQSC YDABH RDYDI GVHCS AIFIL
XJUJB LAHEM GOUCF HWVLY KVCTD
BDPYC NJXGB NEGEF OJSDR NMJJH
IVXCB PQORW NXFUF GPISJ QDYGJ
KHFCZ RMREC IMJNN TCIXX
```

6
Chapter

The RANDOM3.CPP Program

Continuing a presentation of C++ coding examples, Listing 6.18 lists the statements in the file RANDOM3.CPP. This file, along with its executable version named RANDOM3.EXE, is stored in the C directory on the companion CD-ROM.

In examining the program listing contained in Listing 6.18, note the functions encryptKeyboardText and encryptFile. The first function writes text entered via the keyboard to an input file and encrypts it to an output file. The second function, encryptFile, encrypts the contents of an input file. Two additional functions that warrant your attention include getCode and setupSeed as a pointer into the C++ random number generator. Since the executable version of RANDOM3.CPP produces similar results to the execution of RANDOM3.BAS, I will leave it to you to use the program.

Listing 6.18 The RANDOM3.CPP program listing.

```
/*
random3.cpp
C++ code written by Jonathan Held, May 14, 1998, using Microsoft's
Visual C++ version 5.0.
*/

//standard includes
#include <iostream.h>
#include <string.h>
#include <stdlib.h>
#include <iomanip.h>
#include <fstream.h>

//function prototypes
void setupSeed(char *);
void display(char *);
void encrypt(ofstream, char []);
void encryptKeyboardText(char *, char *);
bool encryptFile(char *, char *);
void formatData(char []);
void getCode(char *&);
void getFileNames(char * &, char * &);
int getInputType(void);
void groupBUFFER(ofstream, char [], int);


//-------------------------------------------------------------------
//Function: main()
//Parameters: None
//Return Type: int - 0 means program terminated normally, any other
//value means abnormal termination
//Purpose: Runs the main part of the program.
```

```
//------------------------------------------------------------------
int main(){

    char * the_Code, *infile, *outfile;
    int input_type;

    getCode(the_Code);
    setupSeed(the_Code);
    getFileNames(infile, outfile);
    input_type = getInputType();

    //do something with file input first
    if (input_type){
        encryptFile(infile, outfile);
        cin.get();
        display(outfile);
    }
    else {
        encryptKeyboardText(infile, outfile);
        display(outfile);
    }

    return 0;
}//end main()


//------------------------------------------------------------------
//Function: display()
//Parameters: name - the name of the file the user wants displayed
//Return Type: None
//Purpose: Echoes the resulting output file to the screen.
//------------------------------------------------------------------
void display(char *name)
{
    const int SIZE = 256;
    ifstream infile(name, ios::in);
    char input[SIZE];

    cout << "Press return to display the encrypted file.";
    cin.getline(input, SIZE, '\n');
    strcpy(input, input+strlen(input));

    if (!(infile)){
        cerr << "Unable to open input file for display." << endl;
```

6

Chapter

```
      }
    else {
        while (infile.getline(input, SIZE, '\n')){
           cout << input << endl;
        }
    }

    cout << endl;

    infile.close();

    return;
}//end display()



//-----------------------------------------------------------------
//Function: encrypt()
//Parameters: wt - the output stream
//            text - the text that needs to be encrypted
//Return Type: None
//Purpose: Performs the encryption of the client's text based on
//random numbers.
//-----------------------------------------------------------------
void encrypt(ofstream wt, char text[]){

    const int SIZE = 256;

    char plaintext[] = "ABCDEFGHIJKLMNOPQRSTUVWXYZ";
    int x, ix, jx, location;

    for (ix=0; ix < strlen(text); ix++){
       x = (rand() % 26);

       for (jx=0; jx < strlen(plaintext); jx++){
          if (text[ix] == plaintext[jx])
          location = jx;
       }

       text[ix] = plaintext[(x + location)%26];
    }

    groupBUFFER(wt, text, strlen(text));
    return;
}//end encrypt()
```

```
//------------------------------------------------------------------
//Function: encryptKeyboardText
//Parameters: in - the input file name
//            op  - the output file name
//Return Type: None
//Purpose: Writes the client's text to an input file and encrypts
//it to an output file.
//------------------------------------------------------------------
void encryptKeyboardText(char *in, char *op){

   const int SIZE = 256;
   const int NEW_LINE = 92;
   char buffer[SIZE];
   bool go_on = true;

   ofstream input(in, ios:: out);
   ofstream output(op, ios::out);

   if ((!input) || (!output)){
      cerr << "Unable to open file " << in << " or " << op
              << "." << endl;
   }
   else {
      cout << "Enter the message in UPPERCASE or lowercase characters. "
              << endl
              << "Non-alphabetic characters may be entered but are
                  ignored." << endl
              << "Use a / at the beginning of each line that should
                  remain" << endl
              << "in plaintext and a \\ on a separate line to indicate
                  the" << endl
              << "end of an enciphered message." << endl << endl;

      while (go_on){

         cin.getline(buffer, SIZE, '\n');

         input << buffer << endl;

         if (buffer[0] == '/'){
         output << buffer << endl;
      }
      else if (((int) buffer[0]) == NEW_LINE){
        go_on = false;
```

```
                }
        else {
                formatData(buffer);
                  encrypt(output, buffer);
                }
        }
    }

    input.close();
    output.close();

    cout << "Plaintext saved in " << in << endl
         << "Encrypted text in  " << op << endl << endl;

  return;
}//end encryptKeyboardText()



//------------------------------------------------------------------
//Function: encryptFile()
//Parameters: inp - the input file name
//            op  - the output file name
//Return Type: bool indicating success of the operation
//Purpose: Encrypts the contents of a file.
//------------------------------------------------------------------
bool encryptFile(char *inp, char *op){

    const int SIZE = 256;
    char buffer[256];
    bool success = false;

    //declare file stream objects
    ifstream input(inp, ios::in);
    ofstream output(op, ios::out);

    if ((!input) || (!output)){
            cerr << "Unable to open/write to files " << inp << " or "
                    << op << "." << endl;
    }
    else {
       success = true;
       while (input.getline(buffer, SIZE, '\n')){

          if (buffer[0] == '/'){
```

```
                  output << buffer << endl;
                  strcpy(buffer, buffer+strlen(buffer));
        }
          else {
            formatData(buffer);
            encrypt(output, buffer);
          }
      }
    }

    input.close();
    output.close();

    return success;
}//end encryptFile()



//-----------------------------------------------------------------
//Function: formatData()
//Parameters: data - the array we want to format
//Return Type: None
//Purpose: Get rid of all spaces in the array.
//-----------------------------------------------------------------
void formatData(char data[])
{
    for (int mx=0, nx=0; (*(data+nx) != '\0'); nx++){
      if (*(data+nx) == ' '){
          //do nothing - skip over the space in the data
      }
      else {
          *(data+mx++) = *(data+nx);
      }
    }

    //don't forget to add the null terminator
    *(data+mx) = '\0';

    return;
}//end formatData()



//-----------------------------------------------------------------
//Function: getCode()
//Parameters: the_Code - the code that will be entered by the client
```

6

Chapter

```
//Return Type: None
//Purpose: Prompts the client for a keyword of at least six characters.
//Checks the length of the keyword entered to make sure it has the
//required number of characters.  If it doesn't, it prints an error
//message and prompts for a keyword again.
//------------------------------------------------------------------
void getCode(char *&the_Code){

    int length;
    bool go_on = true;
    char buffer[1000];

    while(go_on){

        cout << "Enter your secret code (6 characters minimum): ";
        cin >> buffer;
        length = strlen(buffer);

        if (length < 6) {
        cerr << "\aCode must be 6 characters or more!"
             << endl << endl;
        }
        else {
            the_Code = new char[length];
            strcpy(the_Code, buffer);
            go_on = false;
        }
    }

    return;
}//end getCode()



//------------------------------------------------------------------
//Function: getFileNames()
//Parameters:  infile_name - the input file
//             outfile_name - the output file we will write the
//             enciphered text to
//Return Type: None
//Purpose: Get file information from the user.
//------------------------------------------------------------------
void getFileNames(char * &infile_name, char * &outfile_name)
{
    const int SIZE = 256;
```

```
   char data[SIZE];

   cout << "Enter filename to store/retrieve plaintext message: ";

   cin >> data;

   infile_name = new char[strlen(data) + 1];
   strcpy(infile_name, data);

   cout << "Enter filename to store enciphered message: ";

   cin >> data;

   outfile_name = new char[strlen(data) + 1];
   strcpy(outfile_name, data);

   return;
}//end getFileNames()


//------------------------------------------------------------------
//Function: getInputType()
//Parameters: None
//Return Type: int - 0 indicates keyboard input, 1 indicates file
//                input
//Purpose: Determines if the user will be manually entering text to
//be enciphered or if the user wants a file to be enciphered.
//------------------------------------------------------------------
int getInputType(void)
{
   char type;
   bool error = false;
   int value;

   do {
      //prompt user for input from file or keyboard
      cout << "Is file input from keyboard (K, k) or file (F, f): ";
      cin >> type;

      //make type an uppercase letter
      type = static_cast<char>(toupper(static_cast<int>(type)));

      //check for an invalid character
      if ((type != 'K') && (type != 'F')){
```

```
               cerr << "You have entered an invalid character!" << endl << endl;
               error = true;
            }
            else {
               if (type == 'K')
                  value = 0;          //value of 0 represents keyboard input
                  else value = 1;     //value of 1 represents file input
               error = false;
            }

      } while (error);

      cout << endl;

      return value;
}//end getInputType()


//----------------------------------------------------------------
//Function: groupBUFFER()
//Parameters: out - the output stream we are writing to
//            num - the number of characters we want to output
//            buffer - the buffer to be written to the stream
//Return Type: None
//Purpose: Output the buffer in groups of five characters at a
//time.
//----------------------------------------------------------------
void groupBUFFER(ofstream out, char buffer[], int num)
{
   for (int kx=0;kx<num;kx++){

      if ((kx!=0) && (kx%25==0)){
         out << endl;
      }

      if ((kx!=0) && (kx%5 == 0) && (kx%25!=0)){
         out << " " << *(buffer+kx);
      }
      else {
           out << *(buffer+kx);
      }
   }
```

```
    out << endl;

    return;
}//end groupBUFFER()


//-------------------------------------------------------------------
//Function: setupSeed()
//Parameters: the_Code - a pointer to the keyword entered by the
//client
//Return Type: None
//Purpose: Sets up the random number seed based on the keyword
//code entered by the client.
//-------------------------------------------------------------------
void setupSeed(char *the_Code){

    int seed = (int)*the_Code * (int)(*(the_Code+1));
    int max = (int)(*(the_Code+2)) * (int)(*(the_Code+3));
    float dummy;
    int increment;

    srand(seed);

    increment = (int) (*(the_Code + 4));

    for (int ix=1; ix<max; ix+=increment)
        dummy = ((float) rand() )/RAND_MAX;

    max = (int)(*(the_Code + 4)) * (int) (*(the_Code+5));

    for (int jx=1; jx<max; jx+=increment)
        dummy = ((float) rand() )/RAND_MAX;

    return;
}//end setupSeed()
//end file random3.cpp
```

The DRANDOM3.BAS Program

To use consistent naming conventions, I labeled the programs that decipher messages enciphered using RANDOM3.BAS and RANDOM3.CPP as
DRANDOM3.BAS and DRANDOM3.CPP. Listing 6.19 contains the statements in the main part of that program that are very similar to
RANDOM3.BAS. In fact, the only change in addition to changes in the

words in strings located in PRINT statements is the substitution of the subroutines DMSGFILE for MSGFILE and RDCONVERTSTORE for RCONVERTSTORE.

Listing 6.19 Statements in the main portion of the DRANDOM3.BAS program.

```
REM Program DRANDOM3.BAS
        CLS
        DIM PLAINTEXT$(25)
        PRINT "DRANDOM3.BAS - A program which deciphers messages"
        PRINT "using the built-in BASIC random number generator"
        PRINT "that were enciphered using the RANDOM3.BAS program"
        PRINT
RTN:
        INPUT "Enter your secret code (6 characters maximum) : "; CODE$
        IF LEN(CODE$) > 6 THEN GOTO RTN
GOSUB INITIALIZE             'initialize plaintext values
GOSUB SETUP                  'obtain random seed and position in seed
GOSUB DMSGFILE               'assign I/O files, place message on a file
GOSUB RDCONVERTSTORE         'convert and store plaintext on a file
GOSUB PRTOUT                 'print results
STOP
```

The subroutine DMSGFILE essentially adjusts I/O file references to the opposite of the subroutine MSGFILE. The subroutine RDCONVERTSTORE is very similar to the subroutine RCONVERTSTORE, but converts cipher-text to plaintext instead of plaintext to ciphertext.

The RDCONVERTSTORE Subroutine

Listing 6.20 lists the statements in the subroutine RDCONVERTSTORE. In this subroutine a random number is extracted and smoothed to a value between 0 and 25 in the same manner as performed by the subroutine RCONVERTSTORE. Next, each character in the string variable TEXT$ is matched to a character in the string array PLAINTEXT$, with the position of the match assigned to the variable J.

Listing 6.20 Statements in the RDCONVERTSTORE subroutine.

```
RDCONVERTSTORE:
        REM Routine to convert and store plaintext on a file
        OPEN INFILE$ FOR INPUT AS #1
        OPEN OUTFILE$ FOR OUTPUT AS #2
        DO UNTIL EOF(1)
                INPUT #1, TEXT$
                MSGLEN = LEN(TEXT$)
                IF MID$(TEXT$, 1, 1) = "/" THEN GOTO CLEARTXT
                IF MID$(TEXT$, 1, 1) = "\" THEN GOTO DONE1
                REM Convert ciphertext to plaintext
                        FOR I = 1 TO MSGLEN
                        X = INT(RND * 100)          'get 2 digit integer
                        X = INT(X / 3.85)           'smooth to 0 to 25
                        FOR J = 0 TO 25
                        IF MID$(TEXT$, I, 1) = PLAINTEXT$(J) THEN GOTO
                                                GOTIT
                        NEXT J
GOTIT:                  IF J < X THEN J = J + 26
                        MID$(TEXT$, I, 1) = PLAINTEXT$((J - X) MOD 26)
                        NEXT I
CLEARTXT:               WRITE #2, TEXT$
        LOOP
DONE1:          CLOSE #2
RETURN
```

To perform modulo 26 subtraction, the value of J is compared to the value of X. If J is less than X, J is incremented by 26. The value of X is then subtracted from J via modulo 26 arithmetic and the resulting value is used as an index into the string array PLAINTEXT$. The character at the index position represents the plaintext character and it is used to replace the ciphertext character in the variable TEXT$.

Figure 6.6 illustrates the operation of the program DRANDOM3.BAS. In this example the user simply enters a "secret" code and selects the default filenames and file input as the mechanism for reading the previously created enciphered message. The resulting deciphered message in the lower portion of Figure 6.6 is displayed in groups of five characters since the subroutine PRTOUT was used in the program.

6

Chapter

```
Figure 6.6 Execution of the DRANDOM3.BAS program.

DRANDOM3.BAS - A program which deciphers messages
using the built-in BASIC random number generator
that were enciphered using the RANDOM3.BAS program

Enter your secret code (6 characters maximum) : ? 9LIVES
Enter filename to store plaintext message, default=MESSAGE.DAT
Enter filename for enciphered message, default=CIPHERTX.DAT
Select keyboard (k) or file (f) message input: F
Press the Return key to display resulting deciphered message

Resulting deciphered message is:
TO:   ALL REGIONAL OFFICE MANAGERS
FROM: PRESIDENT LES MISERABLES
TOPRE VENTA CHAPT ERELE VENAL
LEMPL OYEES MUSTW ORKAD OUBLE
SHIFT CHRIS TMASD AYWIT HOUTP
AYSTO PMANA GERSA RERES PONSI
BLEFO RIMPL EMENT INGTH ISPOL
ICYST OPHAV EANIC EDAYS TOPXX
```

Readers may be curious as to the effect of entering a different "secret" code during the execution of the program DRANDOM3.BAS. To illustrate the effect, I used the code 9lives instead of 9LIVES. What may appear to be a small code change is a significant change to the mechanism developed for positioning to a place into the BASIC random number generator.

Figure 6.7 illustrates the effect of using the program DRANDOM3.BAS with an invalid secret code. If you compare the decipherment illustrated in Figure 6.6 to the decipherment illustrated in Figure 6.7, you will note that the use of an incorrect code results in a meaningless deciphered message. Thus, it is as important to keep your secret code secure as it is not to lose your code.

```
Figure 6.7 Using DRANDOM3.BAS with an incorrect code.

DRANDOM3.BAS - A program which deciphers messages
using the built-in BASIC random number generator
that were enciphered using the RANDOM3.BAS program

Enter your secret code (6 characters maximum) : ? 9lives
Enter filename to store plaintext message, default=MESSAGE.DAT
Enter filename for enciphered message, default=CIPHERTX.DAT
Select keyboard (k) or file (f) message input: F
Press the Return key to display resulting deciphered message

Resulting deciphered message is:
TO:   ALL REGIONAL OFFICE MANAGERS
FROM: PRESIDENT LES MISERABLES
KZXUS OUBQR CFOHX CTDZK SPXCP
DYYER WEBKG LGHLU WODDM IHMQK
AQLKH FSCKQ MSTEZ YWEJB FHEWH
UTMTX OWIJC DAIBB HZHKA RBBFJ
ILNET XEKQC XDOZG DFVCX HIYRP
LGCMW VUNRU VSVMO CQQKG GKVXX
```

The DRANDOM3.CPP Program

Listing 6.22 lists the statements in the program DRANDOM3.CPP, which represents the C++ version of DRANDOM3.BAS. Similar to previously described programs, both the source code and executable version of the program are stored in the C directory on the companion CD-ROM. The source file is named DRANDOM3.CPP and the executable file is named DRANDOM3.EXE.

In examining the program listing, note that although it is very similar to RANDOM3.CPP, it contains three new functions used to perform decryption operations. Those functions are decrypt, decryptKeyboardText, and decryptFile. The decrypt function performs the decryption of text based on the code used to generate a random number sequence. The decryptKeyboardText function writes text entered from the keyboard to an input file and decrypts the text to an output file. The third new function, decryptFile, performs the actual decryption of the contents of a file. The use of the executable version of DRANDOM.CPP should only be used with encrypted data generated by the executable version of RANDOM.CPP. This is because the BASIC language versions of those programs use a different random number generator, in effect precluding

interoperability between the C++ and BASIC language versions of those
programs.

Listing 6.22 The DRANDOM3.CPP program listing.

```
/*
drandom3.cpp
C++ code written by Jonathan Held, May 15, 1998, using Microsoft's
Visual C++ version 5.0.
*/

//standard includes
#include <iostream.h>
#include <string.h>
#include <stdlib.h>
#include <iomanip.h>
#include <fstream.h>

//function prototypes
void setupSeed(char *);
void display(char *);
void decrypt(ofstream, char []);
void decryptKeyboardText(char *, char *);
bool decryptFile(char *, char *);
void formatData(char []);
void getCode(char *&);
void getFileNames(char * &, char * &);
int getInputType(void);
void groupBUFFER(ofstream, char [], int);


//----------------------------------------------------------------
//Function: main()
//Parameters: None
//Return Type: int - 0 means program terminated normally, any other
//value means abnormal termination
//Purpose: Runs the main part of the program.
//----------------------------------------------------------------
int main(){

    char * the_Code, *infile, *outfile;
    int input_type;

    getCode(the_Code);
    setupSeed(the_Code);
```

```
   getFileNames(infile, outfile);
   input_type = getInputType();

   //do something with file input first
   if (input_type){
      decryptFile(infile, outfile);
      cin.get();
      display(outfile);
   }
   else {
      decryptKeyboardText(infile, outfile);
      display(outfile);
   }

   return 0;
}//end main()


//----------------------------------------------------------------
//Function: display()
//Parameters: name - the name of the file the user wants displayed
//Return Type: None
//Purpose: Echoes the resulting output file to the screen.
//----------------------------------------------------------------
void display(char *name)
{
   const int SIZE = 256;
   ifstream infile(name, ios::in);
   char input[SIZE];

   cout << "Press return to display the encrypted file.";
   cin.getline(input, SIZE, '\n');
   strcpy(input, input+strlen(input));

   if (!(infile)){
      cerr << "Unable to open input file for display." << endl;
   }
   else {
      while (infile.getline(input, SIZE, '\n')){
         cout << input << endl;
      }
   }
```

```
        cout << endl;

        infile.close();

        return;
}//end display()



//-----------------------------------------------------------------
//Function: decrypt()
//Parameters: wt - the output stream
//            text - the text that needs to be decrypted
//Return Type: None
//Purpose: Performs the decryption of the client's text based on
//random numbers.
//-----------------------------------------------------------------
void decrypt(ofstream wt, char text[]){

    const int SIZE = 256;

    char plaintext[] = "ABCDEFGHIJKLMNOPQRSTUVWXYZ";
    int x, location, ix, jx;

    for (ix=0; ix < strlen(text); ix++){
      x = (rand() % 26);

      for (jx=0; jx < strlen(plaintext); jx++){
         if (text[ix] == plaintext[jx])
            location = jx;
      }

      if (location < x)
         location += 26;

      text[ix] = plaintext[(location-x)%26];

    }

    groupBUFFER(wt, text, strlen(text));
    return;
}//end encrypt()



//-----------------------------------------------------------------
```

```
//Function: decryptKeyboardText
//Parameters: in - the input file name
//           op  - the output file name
//Return Type: None
//Purpose: Writes the client's text to an input file and decrypts
//it to an output file.
//----------------------------------------------------------------
void decryptKeyboardText(char *in, char *op){

   const int SIZE = 256;
   const int NEW_LINE = 92;
   char buffer[SIZE];
   bool go_on = true;

   ofstream input(in, ios:: out);
   ofstream output(op, ios::out);

   if ((!input) || (!output)){
      cerr << "Unable to open file " << in << " or " << op
                << "." << endl;
   }
   else {
      cout << "Enter the message in UPPERCASE or lowercase characters.
               " << endl
             << "Non-alphabetic characters may be entered but are
                ignored." << endl
             << "Use a / at the beginning of each line that should
                remain" << endl
             << "in plaintext and a \\ on a separate line to indicate
                the" << endl
             << "end of an enciphered message." << endl << endl;

      while (go_on){

         cin.getline(buffer, SIZE, '\n');

         input << buffer << endl;

         if (buffer[0] == '/'){
             output << buffer << endl;
           }
           else if (((int) buffer[0]) == NEW_LINE){
               go_on = false;
           }
```

6

Chapter

```
            else {
            formatData(buffer);
                decrypt(output, buffer);
            }
        }
    }

    input.close();
    output.close();

    cout << "Plaintext saved in " << in << endl
         << "Encrypted text in  " << op << endl << endl;

  return;
}//end decryptKeyboardText()


//------------------------------------------------------------------
//Function: decryptFile()
//Parameters: inp - the input file name
//            op  - the output file name
//Return Type: bool indicating success of the operation
//Purpose: decrypts the contents of a file.
//------------------------------------------------------------------
bool decryptFile(char *inp, char *op){

    const int SIZE = 256;
    char buffer[256];
    bool success = false;

    //declare file stream objects
    ifstream input(inp, ios::in);
    ofstream output(op, ios::out);

    if ((!input) || (!output)){
                cerr << "Unable to open/write to files " << inp << " or "
                        << op << "." << endl;
    }
    else {
        success = true;
        while (input.getline(buffer, SIZE, '\n')){

            if (buffer[0] == '/'){
                output << buffer << endl;
```

```
                        strcpy(buffer, buffer+strlen(buffer));
          }
              else {
                formatData(buffer);
                decrypt(output, buffer);
              }
        }
    }

    input.close();
    output.close();

    return success;
}//end decryptFile()



//------------------------------------------------------------------
//Function: formatData()
//Parameters: data - the array we want to format
//Return Type: None
//Purpose: Get rid of all spaces in the array.
//------------------------------------------------------------------
void formatData(char data[])
{
    for (int mx=0, nx=0; (*(data+nx) != '\0'); nx++){
       if (*(data+nx) == ' '){
          //do nothing - skip over the space in the data
       }
       else {
          *(data+mx++) = *(data+nx);
       }
    }

    //don't forget to add the null terminator
    *(data+mx) = '\0';

    return;
}//end formatData()



//------------------------------------------------------------------
//Function: getCode()
//Parameters: the_Code - the code that will be entered by the client
//Return Type: None
```

```
//Purpose: Prompts the client for a keyword of at least six characters.
//Checks the length of the keyword entered to make sure it has the
//required number of characters.  If it doesn't, it prints an error
//message and prompts for a keyword again.
//------------------------------------------------------------------
void getCode(char *&the_Code){

    int length;
    bool go_on = true;
    char buffer[1000];

    while(go_on){

        cout << "Enter your secret code (6 characters minimum): ";
        cin >> buffer;
        length = strlen(buffer);

        if (length < 6) {
        cerr << "\aCode must be 6 characters or more!"
                << endl << endl;
        }
        else {
            the_Code = new char[length];
            strcpy(the_Code, buffer);
            go_on = false;
        }
    }

    return;
}//end getCode()



//------------------------------------------------------------------
//Function: getFileNames()
//Parameters:  infile_name - the input file
//             outfile_name - the output file we will write the
//             enciphered text to
//Return Type: None
//Purpose: Get file information from the user.
//------------------------------------------------------------------
void getFileNames(char * &infile_name, char * &outfile_name)
{
```

```
   const int SIZE = 256;
   char data[SIZE];

   cout << "Enter filename to store/retrieve plaintext message: ";

   cin >> data;

   infile_name = new char[strlen(data) + 1];
   strcpy(infile_name, data);

   cout << "Enter filename to store enciphered message: ";

   cin >> data;

   outfile_name = new char[strlen(data) + 1];
   strcpy(outfile_name, data);
   return;
}//end getFileNames()


//------------------------------------------------------------------
//Function: getInputType()
//Parameters: None
//Return Type: int - 0 indicates keyboard input, 1 indicates file
//                   input
//Purpose: Determines if the user will be manually entering text to
//be enciphered or if the user wants a file to be enciphered.
//------------------------------------------------------------------
int getInputType(void)
{
   char type;
   bool error = false;
   int value;

   do {
      //prompt user for input from file or keyboard
      cout << "Is file input from keyboard (K, k) or file (F, f): ";
      cin >> type;

      //make type an uppercase letter
      type = static_cast<char>(toupper(static_cast<int>(type)));
```

```
            //check for an invalid character
            if ((type != 'K') && (type != 'F')){
                cerr << "You have entered an invalid character!" << endl << endl;
                error = true;
            }
            else {
                if (type == 'K')
                    value = 0;         //value of 0 represents keyboard input
                    else value = 1;    //value of 1 represents file input
                error = false;
            }

        } while (error);

        cout << endl;

        return value;
}//end getInputType()

//------------------------------------------------------------------
//Function: groupBUFFER()
//Parameters: out - the output stream we are writing to
//            num - the number of characters we want to output
//            buffer - the buffer to be written to the stream
//Return Type: None
//Purpose: Output the buffer in groups of five characters at a
//time.
//------------------------------------------------------------------
void groupBUFFER(ofstream out, char buffer[], int num)
{
    for (int kx=0;kx<num;kx++){

        if ((kx!=0) && (kx%25==0)){
            out << endl;
        }

        if ((kx!=0) && (kx%5 == 0) && (kx%25!=0)){
            out << " " << *(buffer+kx);
        }
        else {
            out << *(buffer+kx);
        }
    }
```

```
        out << endl;

        return;
}//end groupBUFFER()


//------------------------------------------------------------------
//Function: setupSeed()
//Parameters: the_Code - a pointer to the keyword entered by the
//client
//Return Type: None
//Purpose: Sets up the random number seed based on the keyword
//code entered by the client.
//------------------------------------------------------------------
void setupSeed(char *the_Code){

        int seed = (int)*the_Code * (int)(*(the_Code+1));
        int max = (int)(*(the_Code+2)) * (int)(*(the_Code+3));
        float dummy;
        int increment;
        srand(seed);

        increment = (int) (*(the_Code + 4));

        for (int ix=1; ix<max; ix+=increment)
           dummy = ((float) rand() )/RAND_MAX;

        max = (int)(*(the_Code + 4)) * (int) (*(the_Code+5));

        for (int jx=1; jx<max; jx+=increment)
           dummy = ((float) rand() )/RAND_MAX;

        return;
}//end setupSeed()
//end file drandom3.cpp
```

An Alternative Random Process

A second process readers can consider for generating random numbers for use in enciphering operations is based upon the work of Gilbert Vernam (see the shaded box near the beginning of this chapter). Using Vernam's method, which he employed to develop a long random key from two relatively short random keys, as a foundation, you can perform a similar operation through the use of two random seed numbers.

To develop this alternative process, assume that you retain the use of a six-character "secret" code word. You can use the ASCII values of the code word as a mechanism to select two random number seeds. For each seed selected, you can position yourselves into the random number sequence and extract 1,000 random numbers from the first sequence and 999 from the second. You can then develop a routine I will call ROTOR that operates upon the two random number sequences similar to Mr. Vernam's dual paper tape reader.

When Gilbert Vernam developed the first automatic enciphering system, random characters were literally pulled from a hat. This system was time-consuming, and it limited the number of random characters on the tape to 1,000. Vernam realized that looping the tape repeated the random character sequence used for encipherment operations every 1,000 characters. To overcome this weakness, Vernam designed a special tape reader that read two tapes consisting of randomly selected characters. The contents of each tape were added to one another using modulo addition. When a cycle of the shorter tape was completed, the longer tape was repositioned by one character position and the sequence of modulo addition by character position was repeated. The longer tape contained 1,000 randomly selected characters, and the shorter tape contained 999 randomly selected characters, which resulted in the use of two tapes extending the random character key sequence to 999,000 before the sequence repeated.

By extending the random cipher key from 1,000 to 999,000 characters, the security of Vernam's automated enciphering system was significantly enhanced. This extension permitted hundreds to thousands of messages to be enciphered before a new pair of tapes was necessary to prevent the key from repeating.

The ROTOR.BAS Program

Listing 6.21 contains the statements in the program ROTOR.BAS which is used to illustrate how you can create your own random number sequence generating routing that can be considerably different from that contained in BASIC but is based upon the use of the BASIC random number generator.

Listing 6.21 The ROTOR.BAS program listing.

```
REM PROGRAM ROTOR.BAS
REM This program constructs a new random number sequence of numbers that
REM range in value from 0 to 99 based upon the extraction of random numbers
REM from two seeds whose location are based on the composition of a
REM six-position code word. This sequence repeats after 999,000 characters
REM with the same secret code.
CLS
DIM R1(1000), R2(999)
RTN:
            INPUT "Enter your secret code (6 characters maximum) : "; CODE$
            IF LEN(CODE$) > 6 THEN GOTO RTN
GOSUB SETUP
            P1 = 0
            P2 = 1
            FOR K=1 TO 500
GOSUB ROTOR
            NEXT K
STOP
SETUP:
            REM Routine to extract two random numbers sequences based on
            REM The composition of the secret code
            FOR I = 1 TO LEN(CODE$)
            CODE(I) = ASC(MID$(CODE$, I, 1)
            NEXT I
            SEED1 = CODE(1)*CODE(3)
            X1 = CODE(5)
            DO UNTIL X1<= 4
                                    X1 = X1 / 2
            LOOP
            SEED1 = SEED * X1
            SEED2 = CODE(2) * CODE(4)
            X2 = CODE(6)
            DO UNTIL X2 <= 4
                                    X2 = X2 / 2
```

```
                    LOOP
                    SEED2 = SEED2 * X2
                    RANDOMIZE SEED1
                    MAX = CODE(1) * CODE(3) * CODE(5)
                    FOR I = 1 TO MAX STEP CODE(2)          'position into sequence
                            DUMMY = RND
                    NEXT I
                    FOR I = 1 TO CODE(1) * 500 STEP CODE(3) 'go further into sequence
                            DUMMY = RND
                    NEXT I
                    FOR I = 1 TO 1000                      'obtain first sequence
                            R1(i) = RND                    'of random numbers
                    NEXT I
                    RANDOMIZE SEED2
                    MAX = CODE(2) * CODE(4) * CODE(6)
                    FOR I = 1 TO MAX STEP CODE(4)          'position into next sequence
                            DUMMY = RND
                    NEXT I
                    FOR I = 1 TO CODE(4) * 8307 STEP CODE(2) 'go further into
                                                                    sequence
                            DUMMY = RND
                    NEXT I
                    FOR I = 1 TO 999                       'get second sequence
                            R2(I) = RND
                    NEXT I
RETURN
ROTOR:
                    R = INT(((R1(P1) + R2(P2)) * 100) MOD 99)
                    PRINT USING "## "; R;
                    P1 = P1+ 1
                    IF P1 = 1000 THEN P2 = P2 + 1
                    IF P1 = 1000 THEN P1 = 0
RETURN
```

The two arrays in the program, R1 and R2, function similar to Mr. Vernam's two punched paper tapes. That is, they contain sequences of 1,000 and 999 random numbers, respectively. You can perform a modulo addition operation on the numbers in the two sequences as well as rotate the relationship between the numbers in each sequence to generate a new random number sequence.

After you enter your "secret" code, it is assigned to the string variable CODE$, similar to the previously developed RANDOM3.BAS program. The subroutine SETUP is then invoked. This subroutine obtains a position in a random number sequence similar to the previously developed routine of the same name. However, this routine uses the ASCII value of the "secret" code to obtain two different seed numbers as well as the location for the extraction of random numbers from each seed.

The first seed, specified by the variable SEED1, has its value determined by first multiplying the ASCII value of the first and third characters in the "secret" code. This produces a maximum value of 127*127, or 16,129. Because the number of seeds supported by BASIC is considerably higher, you then extract the ASCII value of the fifth character in the "secret" code and continuously divide it by 2 until it is less than or equal to 4. This results in the extension of the seed to a maximum value of 64,516. Next, the value of a second seed is computed. First, the ASCII values of the second and fourth characters in the "secret" code are multiplied by one another. Then divide the ASCII value of the sixth character in the code by 2 until it is less than or equal to 4, and use that value as a multiplier of the product of the ASCII value of the second and fourth characters. Once the two seeds are computed, you are ready to select each seed and position yourself into the random number sequence in each seed prior to extracting the random numbers and placing them into the R1 and R2 arrays.

After the first seed is selected using the RANDOMIZE SEED1 statement, use a two-step approach to position yourself into the random number sequence within the selected seed. First multiply the ASCII values of the first, third, and fifth characters in the "secret" code to serve as the limit for the first FOR-NEXT loop, assigning the value of the three products to MAX. The ASCII value of the second character in the "secret" code is used as the stepping increment through the FOR-NEXT loop.

To go further into the random number sequence, we use a second FOR-NEXT loop in which the ASCII value of the first character multiplied by 500 serves as the limit of the loop, and the ASCII value of the third character in the "secret" code functions as the stepping mechanism through the loop. Once your positioning is completed, extract 1,000 random numbers which are placed into the array R1.

Using the value computed for the second seed, use the statement RANDOMIZE SEED2 to select that seed. Next, use the ASCII value of the characters in the "secret" code to position yourself into a random number sequence in that seed. Multiply the values of the second, fourth, and sixth characters in the "secret" code to serve as a limit for the FOR-NEXT loop and use the value of the fourth character to step through the loop. To go further into the sequence, another FOR-NEXT loop multiplies the ASCII value of the fourth character by 8,307 and uses the ASCII value of the second character as a mechanism to step through the loop. This is followed by extracting 999 random numbers and placing them into the array R2.

When you examine the contents of the routine SETUP, note that both the ASCII value of the characters in the "secret" code word and the numerics entered in the program to govern the extraction process were used. You can use this subroutine as a guide to develop a random number extraction process that differs from the techniques presented in this book if you wish to obtain an additional degree of message security.

Once the subroutine SETUP is invoked, set the "paper tape" rotation scheme into operation by assigning the value 0 to the variable P1 and 1 to the variable P2. Then, for illustrative purposes, execute the subroutine ROTOR 500 times. If you were to use this subroutine to encipher a message, each time you invoke the subroutine, up to 999,000 times, you would receive a newly created random number whose value would be between 0 and 99. You must consider transmitting messages with less than 999,000 characters as well as the effect of adding a number with that possible variance to the set of values of plaintext characters you wish to encipher. For example, if 32 of the possible resulting character values are between 0 and 31, those enciphered characters become control characters that cannot be transmitted over 7-bit electronic mail systems. Another concern you should think about is the necessity to print copies of enciphered messages, because you cannot print control characters. You may wish to modify the ROTOR subroutine to produce random numbers within a range of values which, when added to the ASCII value of the supported set of plaintext characters, permits transmission over 7-bit electronic mail systems and printing of enciphered messages.

The first statement in the subroutine ROTOR adds the random numbers in the arrays R1 (0) and R2 (1), multiplies the result by 100, performs a modulo 99 operation, and extracts the integer result. After the value of R is printed, the value of P1 which represents the position in the first random number sequence is incremented by 1. Only after all 1,000 random numbers in the array R1 have been added using the first random number in R2 do you re-sequence or rotor the "paper tape." Here, when P1 equals 1,000 we increment P2 by 1 and reset P1 to 0. Each time the sub-routine ROTOR is invoked you would continue this process.

To illustrate the result of the previously described set of routines, Figure 6.8 contains the random numbers generated from the execution of ROTOR.BAS. In this example, the secret code ROUTE9 was used to generate the sequence of 500 random numbers generated by the program.

Figure 6.8 Execution of ROTOR.BAS using the secret code ROUTE9.

```
Enter your secret code (6 characters maximum) : ? ROUTE9
25 60 92 83 71 68 61 21 49 88 65 40 17 31 30   0   9 71 83 43 96 77 77 42 70 61 36
62 47 52 24 44   3 6    34 27 29 21 24 81 23 98 46 75 83 16 26 64 52 26 57   3 72    9
1    18 84 64 25 18 10 38 74 70 68 30 22 88 58 51 10   1 25 77 91   0 18 53 12 11 92
30    4 89 14 19 19 41 97 70 73 65 78 92 34 26 95 75 12 46   7 50 87 32 26 77 71 16
95 44 74 22 62   9   7 70   4 50 12 91 58 55 12 72 96 24 87 28   4   3 78 97 96 44   1
0    60 66 88 42 85 35 70 55   2 52 52 38 89   2 84 25   7 46 84 41 28 91 48 85 21 69
78 26 33 59 47 26 25 33 77   8   1 67 47   9 90 39 26   2 39 35 36 11 29 39 25 66 25
91 81 82 41 73 68 55 44 22 76 94 65 72   9 68 50 19 90 87 28   4 98   0 10 33 21   2
3    0 17 39   89 51 26 38 30   32 91 37 72 21 13 45 63 24 94 48 29 26 18 17 43 57 22
31 35 89 24 53 13 56 53 95 14 98 22 36 83 33   4 51 78 53 58 71 88 40 66 62 92 19
91 39 31 17 72 93 14 72 33 50 35 42 30 58 42 58   7 90 94 86 86 76 77 32 89 69   2
3    56 67 17 62 18 70 76   5 48 32 48 34 46 92 28 44 98 26 94 78 20 11 15 17 31 20
78 72 49 33 54 19 12 75 75 41 15 80 43 15 91 82 62   4   4 27   2 90 63 16 68 26 74
59 26   4   9 80 23 66 95 18 43 29 46 67   6 31   0 50 54 16 87 98   2 24 34 67 84   2
8    78 79 45 86 13 82 40   8 58 46 73 62 59 69 51   9   3 23 72 38 63 10 26 60 76 59
31 96 29 40 95 12 85 94 92 63 26   9 73 81 23 97 97 63 32 20 94   9 20 19 40 63 97
84 72   2   0 43 18 26 79 73 48 92 24 40 74 61   3 64 39 78 40 10 60 72   7 93 86   8
2    39 33 77 10 91   4 12 93 97 28 25 16 74 95 60 24 33 94 56 82 35 79 54 53 53 61
29 93 70 22 45 84   1 45 46 80 35 95 57 88 12 93 20 68   6 35
```

Chapter 7

Developing Practical Programs

This chapter will first discuss the utilization of previously developed subroutines and concepts into programs for enciphering and deciphering operations. Because you may prefer to use a ready-to-run set of enciphering and deciphering programs, this chapter also presents an overview of the use of a special pair of programs which are contained on the CD-ROM that accompanies this book.

Module Utilization

In previous chapters in this book I developed a number of subroutines that perform predefined operations. As I developed specific programs, those programs were constructed based upon the use of a number of subroutines that provided us with the ability to perform modular operations and link those operations together. You should consider using the previously developed series of subroutines, as well as coding some of the concepts discussed in this book to modify those subroutines, as a basis for developing programs to encipher and decipher messages to satisfy specific user requirements. For example, you may require the use of an enciphering program that restricts the permissible range of enciphered characters. This restriction may result from the ability of an electronic mail system to only accept a limited character set or another limitation that affects the range of resulting enciphered characters. By tailoring previously developed routines you can create enciphering and deciphering programs to satisfy those requirements. To assist you in reviewing the functions performed by the BASIC language subroutines developed and contained in this book, Table 7.1 summarizes their primary function.

Table 7.I BASIC language subroutine functionality

Subroutine	Function Performed
INITIALIZE	This subroutine sets the elements in a string array to the uppercase letters of the alphabet.
FORMCIPHER	This subroutine forms a cipher alphabet by using an uppercase shift key character to rotate the plaintext alphabet until the shift key character is on the extreme right.
MSGENCIPHER	This subroutine converts plaintext to ciphertext using a simple monoalphabetic substitution.
GROUPBY5	This subroutine prints a space after the display of each group of five enciphered characters.
MSGFILE	This subroutine assigns I/O files and accepts either keyboard or file input of messages.
CONVERTSTORE	This subroutine reads the contents of a plaintext message from a file, enciphers the message using a monoalphabetic substitution process, and outputs the resulting enciphered message to a file.
PRTOUT	This subroutine prints an enciphered message in groups of five characters, placing a space between each group and padding the last group with X's until it contains five characters.
KEYWORD	This subroutine creates a keyword-based mixed alphabet based upon a keyword or keyword phrase.
TRANSPORT	This subroutine creates a simple or numeric transposition mixed sequence alphabet.
INTERVAL	This subroutine creates an interval extracted mixed alphabet.
MSGDCIPHER	This subroutine uses a monoalphabetic substitution process to convert ciphertext to plaintext.
DMSGFILE	This subroutine is the reverse of the subroutine MSGFILE with respect to I/O file assignment names as the routine accepts files containing a ciphertext and assigns an output file to store plaintext.
DECIPHER	This routine can be considered as the reverse of the subroutine CONVERTSTORE as it converts ciphertext to plaintext.
DPRTOUT	This subroutine prints the resulting deciphered message on a line-by-line basis without character groupings.
DCONVERTSTORE	This subroutine can be considered as the reverse of the subroutine CONVERTSTORE as it converts ciphertext to plaintext.
RCONVERTSTORE	This is the modified version of the subroutine CONVERTSTORE used for random number-based encipherment. The subroutine smooths random numbers to between 0 and 25 for modulo 26 addition to alphabetic plaintext characters to produce enciphered text.
SETUP	This subroutine selects a random number seed and location in the seed based upon the ASCII value of the characters in a "secret" code.

Subroutine	Function Performed
RDCONVERTSTORE	This is the modified version of the subroutine CONVERTSTORE used for deciphering of messages enciphered through the use of the subroutine RCONVERTSTORE.

The ENCIPHER.EXE Program

Up to this point, the programs developed in this book had significant restrictions concerning the character set available for encipherment. For example, most programs restricted the composition of a message to the uppercase alphabet, forcing users to spell out punctuation characters, such as COMMA for a "," and PERIOD or STOP to signify the end of a sentence.

Because you may prefer to type a message following a minimum of constraints, a new set of programs was developed to perform message enciphering and deciphering operations. The enciphering program is contained in the file ENCIPHER.EXE on the CD-ROM in the form of a directly executable file. The source version of the program is stored on the file ENCIPHER.BAS, with both files located in the BASIC directory.

In a previous version of this book, only the executable version of the ENCIPHER program was provided. If you are curious as to why no source version of this program was provided, if you will let your curiosity wait a few minutes, the rationale for only providing executable versions of the pair of programs whose use is described in this chapter will become apparent.

The program ENCIPHER.EXE was created using seven previously developed subroutines as a foundation for enciphering. Listing 7.1 contains the main module of ENCIPHER.BAS, illustrating the sequence in which different subroutines are called. Our examination of the coding used in several subroutines will provide you with the ability to modify one or more subroutines or use different groups of subroutines to tailor an enciphering program to your specific requirements. This will ensure your program differs from this program and will make it much more difficult for someone to decipher a message they may gain access to. In fact, the author recommends that you develop your own program rather than rely upon any program available for use by the general public, since such a program is equivalent to one government providing a cipher machine to another government, especially if the latter is unfriendly. When this occurs, the

7

Chapter

unfriendly government will use the machine to attempt to decipher messages illicitly obtained by putting the machine through its paces, attempting one combination after another. The unfriendly government will more than likely also take the machine apart to determine what weaknesses exist and attempt to exploit those weaknesses. Due to the preceding, not all of the subroutines in the program ENCIPHER.BAS were discussed in the earlier version of this book.

Listing 7.1 The main portion of the ENCIPHER.BAS program.

```
REM PROGRAM ENCIPHER.BAS
DIM PLAINTEXT$(128), CIPHERTEXT$(36, 92), KEY$(128)
     CLS
     PRINT "ENCIPHER.EXE PROGRAM enciphers text based upon the use"
     PRINT "of enciphering techniques contained in the book TOP SECRET:"
     PRINT "TRANSMITTING ELECTRONIC MAIL USING PRACTICAL ENCIPHERING
TECHNIQUES"
     PRINT
     PRINT "This program supports the use of upper and lower case letters,"
     PRINT "digits, punctuation characters and other characters whose ASCII"
     PRINT "values range between 32 and 128, but EXCLUDES the use of the"
     PRINT "foward slash (/), backslash (\) and double quote characters."
     PRINT
     PRINT
AGN1:  INPUT "Enter your secret code (6 characters required) : "; CODE$
     IF LEN(CODE$) = 6 THEN GOTO OK
     CLS
     PRINT "Your secret code must be 6 characters - please try again"
     PRINT
     GOTO AGN1
OK:    CLS
GOSUB INITIALIZE              'initialize plaintext values
GOSUB SETUP                  'obtain random seed and position in seed
GOSUB MSGFILE                'assign I/O files, place message on a file
GOSUB KEYWORD               'form keyword based alphabet of 96 characters
GOSUB PFORMCIPHER          'create 36 cipher alphabets
GOSUB RCONVERTSTORE        'convert and store ciphertext on a file
GOSUB PRTOUT                 'print results
STOP
```

The subroutine INITIALIZE was modified to expand the ability of ENCIPHER.BAS to accept a wider mixture of characters. The subroutine, whose coding is listed in Listing 7.2, was modified to initialize a string array labeled PLAINTEXT$ to all characters whose ASCII values are between 32 and 127, except those characters whose ASCII values equal 34, 47, and 92. The latter restriction eliminates the forward and back-slash characters as well as the quote (") character from use in a message, except the first two characters can be used to denote a message header or the end of a message. In addition, those characters whose ASCII values equal or exceed 128 or are below 32 should not be used in your plaintext message. ASCII characters whose values are below 32 are control charac-ters that are either non-printable or whose printing results in some strange effects, such as horizontal and vertical tabs, form feeds, and so on. This can significantly alter the display of an enciphered message, and the exclusion of those characters enables an enciphered message to more easily be input via the keyboard if this should become necessary. ASCII characters whose values exceed 127 are known as extended ASCII. Sev-eral popular electronic mail systems will not accept those characters, hence, I have excluded their use in both the plaintext message and the resulting ciphertext. The latter is accomplished by structuring the crea-tion of a modulo addition process that results in ciphertext characters whose ASCII values are between 32 and 127. In spite of these restric-tions, the program opens up the vast majority of your keyboard for use in creating messages. You can use all uppercase and lowercase alphabetic characters, the space character, all digits, and most punctuation charac-ters to prepare your message.

Listing 7.2 The modified INITIALIZE subroutine.

```
INITIALIZE:
        RESTORE
        REM Initialize plaintext values
        I = 0
        K = 32
GOOD:   IF K = 47 OR K = 92 OR K = 34 THEN GOTO NOGD'skip \, /  and "
        PLAINTEXT$(I) = CHR$(K)
        I = I + 1
NOGD:   K = K + 1
        IF I < 128 GOTO GOOD
RETURN
```

When you examine the statements in the modified subroutine INITIALIZE, you may note that the variable I serves as the array index, while the variable K serves as the ASCII character value. Thus, when PLAINTEXT$(0)=CHR$(32), the 0 element of the string array

7

Chapter

PLAINTEXT$ is set to a space character. Thus, the coding in Listing 7.2 replaces the use of READ and DATA statements used in previous INITIALIZE subroutines.

Because the subroutine SETUP provides a mechanism to select a random seed and positions you into a seed, in an earlier version of this book I purposely skipped a discussion of the code used in that subroutine (discussing the mechanism used to obtain the seed and position within the seed is similar to giving a burglar the keys to the store). The earlier version offered a reward of $1,000 to the first person who could decode an encrypted file. Although the prize was won, it required approximately a year of effort on the part of many persons until a satisfactory solution was found. Because no prize is now offered, the entire source file is included on the CD-ROM to permit you to experiment in creating different length keys.

The code used in the subroutine KEYWORD is contained in Listing 7.3. This subroutine is most interesting as it uses the "secret" code to develop a 30-character keyword. Note that the expansion of the 6-character "secret" code to a 30-character keyword substitutes the string "9" for the characters "\", "/", and the double quote whose ASCII value is 34. To preclude any extended ASCII characters occurring in the keyword, any character in the expansion process that has an ASCII value above 127 is set to the string "Q." The remaining modules in the subroutine are similar to modules I developed in the original KEYWORD subroutine. The main difference between the remainder of the subroutines concerns the length of the array PLAINTEXT$, which now contains 93 characters and whose element value now ranges from 0 to 92.

Listing 7.3 The KEYWORD subroutine.

```
KEYWORD:
        REM Place entered keyword into KEY$ array 1 character per position
        REM but mix word thru expansion to 30 characters
            MSGLEN = 30
            J = 1
            FOR I = 1 TO 6
AGN2:       IF J >= 31 THEN GOTO NULLIT
            KEY$(J) = MID$(CODE$, I, 1)
            FOR J = J + 1 TO J + 4
            KEY$(J) = CHR$(ASC(MID$(CODE$, I, 1)) + (J - 1))
```

```
                   IF KEY$(J) = "\" OR KEY$(J) = "/" OR KEY$(J) = CHR$(34) THEN
KEY$(J) = "9"
                   IF ASC(KEY$(J)) > 127 THEN KEY$(J) = "Q"
                   NEXT J
INCIT:     NEXT I
           REM ELIMINATE DUPLICATE LETTERS, REPLACE WITH CARRIAGE RETURNS
NULLIT:    K = 2
           FOR I = 1 TO MSGLEN
           FOR J = K TO MSGLEN
           IF KEY$(I) <> KEY$(J) GOTO NOTDUP
           KEY$(J) = CHR$(13)
NOTDUP:    NEXT J
           K = K + 1
           NEXT I
           REM REMOVE CARRIAGE RETURNS IN STRING
           X$ = ""
           FOR I = 1 TO MSGLEN
           IF KEY$(I) = CHR$(13) THEN GOTO ASKP
           X$ = X$ + KEY$(I)
ASKP:      NEXT I
           REM PLACE REVISED KEYWORD WITH NO DUPLICATE LETTERS BACK IN KEY$
           FOR I = 1 TO LEN(X$)
           KEY$(I) = MID$(X$, I, 1)
           NEXT I
           REM COMPARE KEY$ & PLAINTEXT$ ARRAYS, SET PLAINTEXT$ ELEMENT TO CR
WHEN MATCHED
           FOR J = 1 TO LEN(X$)
           FOR K = 0 TO 92
           IF KEY$(J) = PLAINTEXT$(K) THEN PLAINTEXT$(K) = CHR$(13)
           NEXT K
           NEXT J
           REM CREATE ONE STRING
           FOR I = 0 TO 92
           IF PLAINTEXT$(I) = CHR$(13) THEN GOTO SKIP
           X$ = X$ + PLAINTEXT$(I)
SKIP:      NEXT I
           REM PLACE SEQUENCE BACK INTO PLAINTEXT$ ARRAY
           FOR I = 0 TO 92
           PLAINTEXT$(I) = MID$(X$, I + 1, 1)
           NEXT I
RETURN
```

Listing 7.4 contains the code from the modified subroutine PFORMCIPHER. In examining this subroutine, note that it forms a two-dimensional

7

Chapter

ciphertext alphabet. The index JJ varies from 0 to 35 and forms 36 cipher alphabets that are based upon the keyword exploded from the "secret" code. By now you probably recognize that ENCIPHER.BAS uses a combination of random numbers and a rotating ciphertext alphabet to perform encipherment. Exactly how this occurs is illustrated by the code in the modified subroutine RCONVERTSTORE.

Listing 7.4 The modified PFORMCIPHER subroutine.

```
PFORMCIPHER:
        REM routine to form 35 CIPHERTEXT alphabets based upon the
            characters in the code
        FOR JJ = 0 TO 35
        FOR KK = 0 TO 92
        CIPHERTEXT$(JJ, KK) = PLAINTEXT$((KK + JJ) MOD 92)
        NEXT KK
        NEXT JJ
RETURN
```

Listing 7.5 contains the code in the modified subroutine RCONVERTSTORE. In examining the code in the subroutine RCONVERTSTORE, note that after extracting a two-digit random number using X=INT(RND*100), I divide the result by 1.087 and take the integer portion of the result. This smooths the random number to a value between 0 and 92 which corresponds to the 93 elements in the array PLAINTEXT$. Then I compare each character in each line of the plaintext to a character in the array PLAINTEXT$. When a match occurs, I add the index value of the match position in PLAINTEXT$ to the smoothed value of X using mod 92 addition. The result, stored in the variable Z, is used to extract a character from one of the ciphertext alphabets contained in the string array CIPHERTEXT$. Thus, ENCIPHER.BAS uses random numbers to extract characters from a two-dimensional alphabet to obtain enciphered text. The routines used for enciphering illustrate how you can combine two or more techniques to develop your own enciphering program if you wish to do so.

Listing 7.5 The modified RCONVERTSTORE subroutine.

```
RCONVERTSTORE:
    REM Routine to convert and store ciphertext on a file
    OPEN INFILE$ FOR INPUT AS #1
    OPEN OUTFILE$ FOR OUTPUT AS #2
    ALPHA = 0      'first alphabetic pointer
    PRINT "Enciphering operation in progress ";
```

```
          DO UNTIL EOF(1)
                INPUT #1, TEXT$
                PRINT ".";
                MSGLEN = LEN(TEXT$)
                IF MID$(TEXT$, 1, 1) = "/" THEN GOTO CLEARTXT1
                IF MID$(TEXT$, 1, 1) = "\" THEN GOTO DONE2
                REM Convert plaintext to ciphertext
                     FOR I = 1 TO MSGLEN
                     X = INT(RND * 100)        'get 2-digit integer
                     X = INT(X / 1.087)        'smooth to 0 to 92
                     FOR J = 0 TO 92
                     IF MID$(TEXT$, I, 1) = PLAINTEXT$(J) THEN GOTO MATCH
                     NEXT J
MATCH:               Z = (J + X) MOD 92
                     MID$(TEXT$, I, 1) = CIPHERTEXT$(ALPHA, Z)
                     NEXT I
                     ALPHA = ALPHA + 1
                     IF ALPHA = 35 THEN ALPHA = 0'reset alphapet pointer
CLEARTXT1:           WRITE #2, TEXT$
          LOOP
DONE2:    CLOSE #2
                CLOSE #1
RETURN
PRTOUT: REM Subroutine to print results
     PRINT
     INPUT "Press Return key to display resulting enciphered message", p$
     CLS : TEMP$ = ""
     PRINT "Resulting enciphered message is:"
     OPEN OUTFILE$ FOR INPUT AS #2
     DO UNTIL EOF(2)
          INPUT #2, TEXT$
          IF MID$(TEXT$, 1, 1) = "/" THEN PRINT RIGHT$(TEXT$, LEN(TEXT$) - 1)
          IF MID$(TEXT$, 1, 1) = "/" THEN GOTO NOGROUP
          PRINT TEXT$
NOGROUP: LOOP
     CLOSE #1: CLOSE #2
RETURN
```

To provide you with an indication of how to position the random number generator based upon the composition of a secret code, Listing 7.6 gives the contents of the subroutine SETUP. In examining the statements in the subroutine, note that the seed is set to the value of the product of the first and sixth characters in the secret code. Next, the integer value of the product of the ASCII values of the even characters in the six-position code is used as an initial offset, and the product of the ASCII values of the first and third characters in the code are used as a delimiter in a FOR-NEXT loop, with the value of the second character used to step through the loop.

Listing 7.6 The SETUP subroutine positions the random number generator based upon the composition of the secret code.

```
SETUP:
        REM routine to position the random number generator based upon
        REM the composition of the secret code
        FOR I = 1 TO LEN(CODE$)
        CODE(I) = ASC(MID$(CODE$, I, 1))
        NEXT I
        SEED = CODE(1) * CODE(6)
        MAX = INT(CODE(2) * CODE(4) * CODE(6))
        RANDOMIZE SEED
        FOR I = 1 TO MAX STEP (CODE(5) * CODE(1))    'position into sequence
        DUMMY = RND
        NEXT I
        FOR I = 1 TO CODE(1) * CODE(3) STEP CODE(2) 'further offset into
                                                            sequence
        DUMMY = RND
        NEXT I
RETURN
```

The execution of the program ENCIPHER.EXE is illustrated in Figures 7.1 through 7.3. Figure 7.1 illustrates the display of the first screen of the program which first displays information about the program and then prompts you to enter a six-digit "secret" code. Unlike the restrictions on the plaintext characters in a message, the code can consist of most characters in the ASCII character set; however, as discussed in this book, you should select a code that is not difficult to repeat. Thus, I recommend the use of printable characters.

Figure 7.1 The first screen display of the ENCIPHER.EXE program.

ENCIPHER.EXE PROGRAM enciphers text based upon the use
of enciphering techniques contained in the book TOP SECRET:
TRANSMITTING ELECTRONIC MAIL USING PRACTICAL ENCIPHERING TECHNIQUES

This program supports the use of upper and lower case letters,
digits, punctuation characters and other characters whose ASCII
values range between 32 and 128, but EXCLUDES the use of the
foward slash (/), backslash (\) and double quote characters.

Enter your secret code (6 characters required) : ? TESTME

Figure 7.2 illustrates the second screen displayed when the program
ENCIPHER.EXE is executed. This screen first displays information concerning the filenames to be used to store the plaintext and ciphertext messages.
Because the keyboard was selected for entering the plaintext message, the
program then displays information concerning the use of the forward and
backslash characters. As in our previously developed programs, the forward
slash is used to prefix headers that should remain as plaintext, while the
backslash is used to indicate the termination of the message.

Figure 7.2 The second screen displayed upon execution of ENCIPHER.EXE.

Enter filename to store plaintext message, default=MESSAGE.DAT :
Enter filename to store enciphered message, default=CIPHERTX.DAT :
Select keyboard (k) or file (f) message input: k
Enter your message - place a / at the beginning of each line
that should remain in plaintext and a \ on a separate line
to indicate the end of the enciphered message

/TO JIMMY K. ESTES III
/OFFICE MANAGER
/THE WHITE HOUSE
It has come to my attention that we must develop a plan for
moving all personal furnishing out of this building as soon
as possible. The latest poll suggests our days are numbered.
Please prepare the plan and transmit it to me using the cipher
code we previously agreed to use for information of this type.
Your budget for moving is restricted to $123,456.12.
\
Enciphering operation in progress ....
Press Return key to display resulting enciphered message

After the previously discussed information is displayed, you can enter your message. After the backslash character is entered, the program displays the message "Enciphering operation in progress..." Because the program can require from a few seconds to half a minute or more depending upon the computer you use to encipher your message, dots are displayed while the program executes so you will know it is working. Once the encipherment operation is completed, the message "Press Return key to display resulting enciphered message" is displayed. Once you press the Return key, the resulting enciphered message is displayed as illustrated in Figure 7.3. In addition, the enciphered message is also written onto the file CIPHERTX.DAT, so you can transfer that file via a communications program if you so desire.

```
Figure 7.3 The enciphered message created by ENCIPHER.BAS.

Resulting enciphered message is:
TO JIMMY K. ESTES III
OFFICE MANAGER
THE WHITE HOUSE
5V3~3:C-ORCs_(XX&UATiSZ||]kNSosyCM>X^x,:zk[8fOVz7=pO[ofl|F )
CxbfK_;49YU<_m#t.'q[&_jAoek3Pxr4zcQ$Me$'suF+ZOOU[2xlpx|O{y;
[.}]P_{SY:}GLYGcv=HOUz^#r$7!^<]~Co%1c^AINt@&#tLRmpIeXfYv+?_Q
YwN(JBr@`Q@FgTsguZD;3qgYa#zr<OW7xv;.G:dWP7HXF6)zgOW3gC2,R=+#%i
;;+&z?Xway RTZNh9JIDriv)LmO[%U5i,w,>9NQ:5ITQ8ySH>*,S`(#8<U~b~I
12dx:AIC$m{9Cgi_axS8[s#]a<d +CS<)kn_h>6q,KU_`$}$2^RT
```

The DECIPHER.EXE Program

The program DECIPHER.BAS is provided in both source and executable versions on the CD-ROM accompanying this book. Similar to the ENCIPHER.EXE program, the program DECIPHER.EXE operates through the use of three screens. The execution of the program DECIPHER.EXE is illustrated in Figures 7.4 through 7.6.

To illustrate the use of the deciphering program I will use the program to operate upon the previously enciphered message contained on the file CIPHERTX.DAT. Figure 7.4 illustrates the entry of the same "secret" code that was used to encipher our previously created plaintext message.

Figure 7.4 The first screen displayed upon execution of DECIPHER.EXE.

```
DECIPHER.BAS PROGRAM deciphers text based upon the use
of enciphering techniques contained in the book:
ELECTRONIC MAIL PRIVACY:USING PRACTICAL ENCIPHERING TECHNIQUES

This program supports the use of upper and lower case letters,
digits, punctuation characters and other characters whose ASCII
values range between 32 and 128, but EXCLUDES the use of the
foward slash (/), backslash (\) and double quote characters.


Enter your secret code (6 characters required) : ? TESTME
```

Once your "secret" code is entered, the program displays a second screen which, similar to ENCIPHER.EXE, enables you to assign filenames for storing the plaintext and enciphered messages and select keyboard or file input (Figure 7.5). In this example, the default filenames were accepted and once the deciphering operation commenced, an appropriate message was displayed. After the deciphering operation is completed and you press the Return key, the resulting deciphered message is displayed. This is illustrated in Figure 7.6. In comparing the plaintext message in Figure 7.2 to the deciphered message contained in Figure 7.6, you will note they are exactly the same.

Figure 7.5 The second screen displayed upon execution of DECIPHER.EXE.

```
Enter filename to store plaintext message, default=MESSAGE.DAT
Enter filename for enciphered message, default=CIPHERTX.DAT
Select keyboard (k) or file (f) message input: f
Deciphering operation in progress ........
Press Return key to display resulting deciphered message
```

7

Chapter

Figure 7.6 The resulting deciphered message.

Resulting deciphered message is:
TO JIMMY K. ESTES III
OFFICE MANAGER
THE WHITE HOUSE
It has come to my attention that we must develop a plan for
moving all personal furnishing out of this building as soon
as possible. The latest poll suggests our days are numbered.
Please prepare the plan and transmit it to me using the cipher
code we previously agreed to use for information of this type.
Your budget for moving is restricted to $123,456.12.

The Challenge

In concluding this chapter, an enciphered message is presented in Figure 7.7. Unlike the task faced by most cryptanalysts who do not have access to an enciphering system used to create a message, I have considerably simplified the task of those who may wish to decipher this message. This message was enciphered using the directly executable program ENCIPHER.EXE which is contained on the CD-ROM in the BASIC directory. The enciphered message, which is stored on the file CIPHERTX.DAT on the CD-ROM, can be deciphered using the directly executable program DECIPHER.EXE, which is also contained on the CD-ROM. To facilitate your effort, unlike the original version of this book, this new edition contains both source and executable versions of the programs ENCIPHER and DECIPHER.

Figure 7.7 The "challenge" message.

```
"/TO: ZONE MANAGERS"
"/FROM: CORPORATE QUALITY CONTROL"
"RT m,q>>EA5;uSLxo6WOCy|&fHkf,1.8{Nhx)v~3K)O`;PHK`Q21)`D#bnFvweB6l"
"aZ@pk;N<x^1=qg^Hx8=q%pX4}e~X<N*2*@T2I=$fQqR?pAK*kb*6@2wM7Xhls36b"
"iYfAz]8sk~c]8+J8v:RGUlg19;S{ZMA&gxoymv;d#+1#Oeo+@%,w;-2vH^dE.TDwMg{"
":Z}Z7&J{R$usy(I1lBG[EHGCV$mywR6`MnI5:v'?Enl1<QVJ<kDLP-SFvZ]}Iz`bB{=9"
"QDU)|dFqUTpesb k[C[d?eIr _Ansu(yqNJQE*XFb'fIazV>H]|g#rgeve@8.3'IO?6"
"w8D}{mAPP|y3KYsf6QzMUG`YIh1*)9&?FD4l*u5ckeF^7<n9d;%ROp%NDKKmS9Y7+l^`"
"*XLB7^?UMCuW`&*x.q{66jg# >xl2U2%>)[7BH~iP8|j%[>ln(o,3o4cBxy)6[gr"
"Dy''dm#}3a2F^["
```

Providing the deciphering program may simplify the task of deciphering the message. You can consider using a trial-and-error approach by using different "secret" codes in an attempt to decipher the message. As you cycle through various combinations of "secret" codes, one of the points raised a number of times in this book will become apparent—the program provides a level of privacy for electronic transmission that will deter the casual observer of a message from understanding the contents of the message.

The reason for originally providing only directly executable copies of the two programs whose use was described in this chapter was to hide the technique employed to use the "secret" code used by the enciphering program to generate a random number sequence. Although I originally left the door unlocked, I purposely decided not to turn on the lights!

In a future edition of this book, I anticipate extending the coverage of topics to codebreaking. Thus, if you feel you are successful in deciphering the message illustrated in Figure 7.7 and contained on the file SECRET.MSG, please send a description of the approach you used to decipher the message as well as the deciphered message to me via e-mail at 235-8068@mcimail.com.

I would like to consider describing techniques used by you to decipher the message illustrated in Figure 7.7 or even approaches you took that were not successful. Thus, I welcome all reader comments concerning not only the specific message you are challenged to decipher but all aspects of this book.

7

Chapter

Chapter 8

Public Key Encryption

In this concluding chapter, I turn your attention to a relatively new field of encryption when examined against the evolution of encryption techniques dating to before Caesar's time. That field of encryption is referred to as public key encryption, the focus of this chapter.

Unlike the previous coverage of encryption techniques which included a minimal amount of mathematics, any discussion of public key encryption requires an understanding of a considerable number of mathematical operations. Those operations are crucial to understand how public key encryption works. A second difference between this chapter and previous chapters presented in this book concerns the development of programs which will be conspicuous by their omission in this chapter. The reason for this omission is based upon current United States government restrictions on the export of certain types of encryption software. Because neither I nor my publisher can police the sale of this book nor its distribution, it is safer to simply present concepts in this chapter and leave it to you to develop public key software programs if you so desire.

General Operation

Figure 8.1 illustrates the general operation of a public key-based encryption system. In this example, an encryption algorithm (E) is used with a public encryption key (ke) to encipher input (x), producing ciphertext ($Eke(x)$). Decryption employs a decryption algorithm (D) which operates upon a secret decryption key (kd) such that $D(Eke(x))$ restores the encrypted input to its original form. Note that the algorithms E and D are public; however, the decryption key (kd) must be kept secret. When public key-based secure communications occur in the opposite direction,

another key pair must be created, with the recipient becoming the originator and using an encryption key, while the originator becomes the
recipient and uses a secret decryption key. Thus, communication in each
direction requires the use of a public-private key pair.

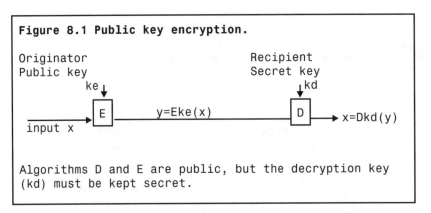

Figure 8.1 Public key encryption.

Algorithms D and E are public, but the decryption key
(kd) must be kept secret.

Authentication Issues

Because the public encryption key is published, anyone can use it to
encrypt a message. This means that it becomes possible for a person to
use a public key to send a false message which, when deciphered, could
appear as a legitimate message. This problem is not normally applicable
to conventional private key systems since the distribution of private keys
are on a controlled basis. This also means that a public key system normally requires a method of authentication, typically accomplished by the
use of a digital signature. However, it is also possible for two persons
using a public key system to authenticate one another by placing a random string into their message and requesting the party they are commu-
nicating with to return the string in their initial reply. Because the
recipient is the only person who can decipher the message, when they
encrypt the message in another public key associated with the originator's private key, the originator can check the message to ensure it was
correctly received. Then, this receipt indicates that the recipient is the
party they claim to be. Figure 8.2 illustrates how two parties can authenticate one another via the use of a public key system.

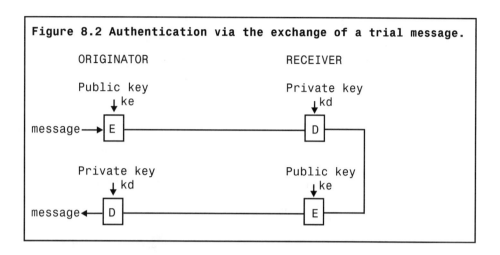

Figure 8.2 Authentication via the exchange of a trial message.

Public vs. Private Key Encryption

In a classic private key cryptosystem, both the sender and receiver of a message must know and use the same secret key. This means both parties must have access to the same key, and if either party should lose or divulge the key, both parties are compromised. Although the use of secret key cryptography dates to before the time of Caesar and is still frequently used in electronic commerce and other business applications, it has several weaknesses in addition to the disclosure of the key compromising messages sent between parties. First, the management of keys can become a daunting task, especially when you have many persons or locations that must communicate with one another and wish to minimize the potential compromise of a key on messages by assigning different keys to each pair of persons or locations that requires secure communications. A second problem associated with secret keys is their distribution. Some organizations initially distribute keys via registered mail, which considerably reduces your ability to promptly respond to changing user requirements. Similarly, if a key should become compromised, the ability to distribute a new key will be dependent upon a telephone call, a courier, or an Express Mail letter, all subject to a security breach.

The Work of Diffie and Hellman

In 1976 the concept of public cryptography was introduced by Whitfield Diffie and Martin Hellman as a mechanism to solve the key management and key distribution problems associated with private key cryptography. In their now-classic paper, they discussed the features of a public key system and noted that such a system should have the following four properties for a given message (M) based upon encryption (E) and decryption (D) procedures:

1. $D(E(M)) = M$
2. Both E and D are easy to compute.
3. It is computationally unfeasible to derive D from E.
4. $E(D(M)) = M$

The first property simply states that once a message is encrypted the application of a decryption procedure will restore it, in effect the same as the property for a private key system. The second property means that for the cryptosystem to be practical, both encryption and decryption should be computationally fast, which also holds for private key cryptology. It is the third property which signifies the key difference between public and private key cryptology, as this property means that encryption is a one-way function and it is not feasible to invert E unless you already know D. This also means that the encryption procedure E can be made public, and only the person who knows D can decrypt the message.

The fourth property indicates that the mapping is one-to-one, meaning that the application of the decryption procedure to a message (M) can be used to verify the person who sent the message, in effect permitting a digital signature.

Under the Diffie-Hellman concept, each person who requires secure communications obtains a pair of keys. One key is referred to as the public key and can be distributed to any person who requires the ability to communicate securely with the person who holds the secret key. The key, no pun intended, to public key encryption is the fact that no third party can determine the composition of the private key from the public key.

It is important to note that the paper presented by Diffie and Hellman provided a concept or framework for the development of public key encryption techniques. However, Diffie-Hellman does not actually represent a public key encryption technique. Although not an actual technique, the work of Diffie and Hellman considerably influenced the development of public key encryption techniques and represents a significant milestone in the field of encryption.

Advantages and Disadvantages

The primary advantage associated with the use of public key cryptology is the increased level of security and convenience it provides, which reduces the effort involved in key management and key distribution associated with a private key system. Since the private key associated with the public key system does not have to be distributed, this both simplifies key management and reduces the possibility of key interception.

The ability to distribute a public key that can encrypt messages that can only be decrypted by the corresponding private key depends upon the selection of an appropriate algorithm. The algorithm must be a one-way function, which from a computational perspective is significantly easier to perform in one direction than from the reverse. For example, the one-way function might be able to be performed in seconds or minutes in the forward direction, but require months or years of trial and error to perform in the opposite direction.

As an example of a one-way function, consider the following equation:

$$y = 5x^4 + 27x^3 + 14x^2 + 12$$

While it is relatively easy and fast to compute y given x, it is much more difficult to compute x given y. Although the time required to execute the one-way function in the forward direction is relatively fast in comparison to the process to perform the reverse, it requires significantly more than the amount of time required to perform private key encryption. This means that public key encryption may not be suitable for certain types of applications, such as high-speed encrypted communications. In such situations, public key cryptology can be used as a supplement to private key cryptology. For example, you could use a public key system to distribute private keys. In fact, a popular application for the use of a public key system by government, industry, and financial organizations is the distribution of private keys via a public key system.

> There was a young fellow named Ben
> Who could only count to modulo ten.
> He said, 'When I go
> past my last little toe
> I shall have to start over again.'
>   -Anonymous

Understanding the Mathematics

The ability to obtain an appreciation for the manner by which public key cryptology operates requires an understanding of a few areas of mathematics that are used to create one-way functions. Thus, prior to turning your attention to the manner by which a popular public key system operates, let me turn your attention to a review of some mathematical concepts.

Most public key systems are based upon finite arithmetic in which numbers are manipulated according to rules that are different from ordinary arithmetic. Because one-way functions used in public key systems are based upon finite arithmetic, and modular arithmetic results in finite sets of numbers, let's commence our review of mathematics with this topic. Since I previously discussed modular arithmetic when developing private key algorithms in this book, I will not turn to this topic in detail.

Modular Arithmetic

Modular arithmetic is a branch of mathematics in which you operate upon a finite set of numbers. For example, the finite set of numbers {0, 1, 2, . . . n-1} are referred to as modulo n arithmetic. Here, n can take any positive integer value except 1 and the result of any arithmetic operation belongs to the same set of n numbers.

Counting in modulo arithmetic goes from 0 to n-1, with the next numbers in the series being 0, 1, . . ., so that the sequence continues and repeats. In fact, when you perform modulo arithmetic, such operations as addition and multiplication are performed as with ordinary arithmetic, with the answer obtained by dividing by n and using the remainder as the result. The result is said to be modulo n, abbreviated as mod n. Thus writing x mod n references the remainder of x when divided by n. To obtain an appreciation for the operation of modulo arithmetic, let me turn your attention to modular addition and modular multiplication.

Modular Addition

When you perform modular addition, the value you obtain for $a+b$ is the same as in normal arithmetic when $a+b<n$. Otherwise, when $a+b>n$, you would subtract n from the sum. If the result is less than n, you would obtain the modulo sum. Otherwise, you would continue to subtract n from the previous result until a value less than n is obtained. This action is equivalent to dividing by n and using the remainder as the result.

For example:

$$8 + 6 + 3 + 9 + 2 + 6 \text{ (modulo 9)} = 7$$

because the sum in normal arithmetic is 34. When divided by 9, you obtain a remainder of 7.

Now it can be told!

Many years ago during the era of communism, I was selected to represent the United States at an engineering conference in Moscow. At that time most home telephones of dissidents and refuseniks were monitored by the KGB; however, most public telephones were not, as there were too many even for the resources of the Soviet spy agency. After meeting with dissidents and refuseniks, I agreed to carry a list of public telephone numbers and calling times out of Moscow so those assisting these harassed persons could communicate with them. Because it wouldn't be smart to simply carry out a list of telephone numbers, those numbers were encoded using modulo 9 arithmetic, and an extra digit was added so that the numbers appeared to represent the combination to a safe or lock. For example:

original telephone number:	4770293
modulo 9 number:	5229706
"safe combination"	522-97-063

Upon return to the free world it was a relatively simple process to convert the "safe combination" back into its telephone number. To do so, all that was required was to add the appropriate digit to each number to obtain nine and discard the last digit. For example, $5 + 4 = 9$, so the first digit is restored to its original value of 4. Similarly, $2 + 7 = 9$, resulting in the second digit of the restored telephone number reconstructed to its original value of 7.

For several years after I visited Moscow, my "modulo 9" number scheme was transported via tourists and in postcards to inform persons in the United States, the United Kingdom, France, and Israel of public telephone numbers they could call, and the date and time to call.

If you perform mod 10 addition, you can simply use the last digit of the answer. Similarly, if you perform mod 100 addition, you can use the last two digits. For example:

$6 + 13 \bmod 10 = 9,$

$114 + 8 \bmod 100 = 2,$ and

$9 + 8 \bmod 10 = 7$

Note that 9, 19, and 29 all represent the same mod 10 number, while 33, 133, and 233 all represent the same mod 100 number. In such situations it is common to use the symbol "@" for equivalence for each series of numbers. Under modular arithmetic two equivalent numbers can be considered as different names for the same mod n number.

Figure 8.3 illustrates results obtained by the construction of a mod 10 addition table. Note that, similar to the sidebar story about my use of modulo 9 addition to encrypt telephone numbers, you can also use a constant modulo 10 as a scheme for encrypting digits. This is because the use of a constant modulo 10 maps each decimal digit into a different decimal digit, such that the process is reversible. In doing so, the use of a constant modulo 10 becomes your "secret" key and decryption is performed by modulo 10 subtraction. Thus, let me turn your attention briefly to modular subtraction.

Figure 8.3 Modulo 10 addition.

	a									
+	0	1	2	3	4	5	6	7	8	9
0	0	1	2	3	4	5	6	7	8	9
1	1	2	3	4	5	6	7	8	9	0
2	2	3	4	5	6	7	8	9	0	1
3	3	4	5	6	7	8	9	0	1	2
4	4	5	6	7	8	9	0	1	2	3
5	5	6	7	8	9	0	1	2	3	4
6	6	7	8	9	0	1	2	3	4	5
7	7	8	9	0	1	2	3	4	5	6
8	8	9	0	1	2	3	4	5	6	7
9	9	0	1	2	3	4	5	6	7	8

(b indicates the left column labels)

Chapter 8

Modular Subtraction

There are several methods you can use to perform modular subtraction. To illustrate these methods, assume you wish to perform the operation (*a-b*) modulo *n*. If *a>b*, you would simply subtract *b* from *a*. If *a<b*, you would add *n* to *a* prior to subtracting *b*. For example, (7–8) modulo 10 is equal to 7+10–8, or 9.

A second method you can use to perform modular subtraction is by adding –*b*, which is referred to as *b*'s additive inverse. Returning to our previous example and noting that the additive inverse of a number is the number you have to add to it to obtain zero, you have:

(7–8) modulo 10 becomes equivalent to 7–(–2) = 9

In the preceding example note that 8's inverse is 2, because in mod 10 arithmetic 8 + 2 = 0. Thus, if the secret key was 8 for encryption, you would add 8 mod 10, while decryption would be performed by adding 2 mod 10.

Modular Multiplication

To continue your examination of modular arithmetic, let me turn your attention to modular multiplication. Figure 8.4 contains a modular 10 multiplication table, indicating the mod 10 values obtained by multiplying each row value by each column value, mod 10. For example, 8*8 mod 10 is 64 mod 10, which is 6 with a remainder of 4 when divided by 10, producing a result of 4.

```
Figure 8.4 Modulo 10 multiplication.
```

	0	1	2	3	4	5	6	7	8	9
0	0	0	0	0	0	0	0	0	0	0
1	0	1	2	3	4	5	6	7	8	9
2	0	2	4	6	8	0	2	4	6	8
3	0	3	6	9	2	5	8	1	4	7
4	0	4	8	2	6	0	4	8	2	6
5	0	5	0	5	0	5	0	5	0	5
6	0	6	2	8	4	0	6	2	8	4
7	0	7	4	1	8	5	2	9	6	3
8	0	8	6	4	2	0	8	6	4	2
9	0	9	8	7	6	5	4	3	2	1

If you examine the multiplication table illustrated in Figure 8.4, you will note that multiplication by 1, 3, 7, and 9 will work as an encryption key since each multiplication results in a one-to-one substitution of the digits. You will also note that multiplication by 0, 2, 4, 5, 6, and 8 will not work as an encryption key. For example, if you attempted to encrypt by multiplying by 2, half the numbers would be duplicates and result in the loss of information. Thus, you would not be able to correctly decrypt using a multiplier of 2.

If you select an appropriate multiplier using modular 10 multiplication, it becomes possible to both encrypt and correctly decrypt data. Concerning the decryption process, similar to modular arithmetic addition, you can undo the effect of modular multiplication by multiplying by an inverse. Here the inverse is known as the multiplicative inverse.

In ordinary arithmetic the multiplicative inverse of x is $1/x$, which results in a fraction when x is an integer. In modular arithmetic, the set of numbers you work with are all integers. Thus, the multiplicative inverse of x, which is written as x^{-1}, is the number by which you multiply x to obtain 1.

For example, consider 5^{-1} mod 4. This means what number multiplied by 5 mod 4 results in a value of 1. Because 5 mod 4 has a value of 1, this is a relatively simple problem whose answer is 1. However, as you will note later in this chapter, finding the multiplicative inverse can become a daunting task.

Returning to Figure 8.4 which contained the modulo 10 multiplication table, only the numbers 1, 3, 7, and 9 have multiplicative inverses modulo 10. For example, 7 is the multiplicative inverse of 3, while 9 is the multiplicative inverse of 1. Thus, encryption could be performed by multiplying by 3 while decryption could be performed by multiplying by 7. Note that both 1 and 9 are their own inverses. Thus, similar to modular addition, modular multiplication could be used to encrypt and decrypt, although you do have to be careful of the manner by which you select digits.

Finding the Multiplicative Inverse

The ability to find a multiplicative inverse in modular arithmetic can be difficult, especially when n is large. For example, if n was a 50-digit number you could spend a considerable period of trial and error time searching for an inverse. Fortunately, the Euclidean algorithm can be used to find the inverse as, given x and n, the algorithm finds the number y such that $x*y$ mod $n = 1$.

The reason multiplicative inverses are important is the fact that they are the only numbers that do not share any common factor other than 1. This means they are in mathematical terms relatively prime numbers. For example, from Figure 8.4 the numbers 1, 3, 7, 9 are the only ones with multiplicative inverses. That is, the largest integer that divides both 3 and 7 is 1. Similarly, the largest integer that divides both 7 and 9 is also 1. In comparison, 2, 4, 6, and 8 do not have a multiplicative inverse modulo 10, and are not relatively prime to 10. For example, 2 divides 4, 6, and 8. This means that you can use mod n multiplication by any number x relatively prime to n as an encryption key since you can multiply x to encrypt and x^{-1} to decrypt. Although whether or not the scheme is secure remains to be determined, this means encryption can occur via multiplication by x mod n, while decryption can occur by multiplying the enciphered data by x^{-1} mod n.

The key, again no pun intended, to the use of numbers that have multiplicative inverses is to use relatively large prime numbers. Thus, prior to moving forward, let's review prime numbers.

Prime Numbers

A prime number is a number greater than 1 that can be divided evenly only by itself and 1. The first 20 prime numbers are 2, 3, 5, 7, 11, 13, 17, 19, 23, 29, 31, 37, 41, 43, 47, 53, 59, 61, 67, and 71. The fundamental Theorem of Arithmetic indicates that primes are the building blocks of the positive integers. In fact, every positive integer is a product of prime numbers. Such products are referred to as composites. Thus, there are three types of natural numbers: primes, composites, and unity.

The ancient Greeks proved mathematically that there are an infinite number of primes and that they are irregularly spaced. During the late 1990s the use of primes in public key cryptology resulted in thousands of persons searching for larger primes. Through the use of specialized software, a prime consisting of 895,932 digits was discovered in 1997.

Three of the more interesting types of primes are Mersenne primes, twin primes, and Sophie Germain primes. Mersenne primes are primes of the form 2^{P} and are the easiest type of number to check for on a binary computer. Although 36 Mersenne primes have been discovered, several regions of numbers between previously identified primes have not been completely searched, and it is not known if the largest is the 36th.

Twin primes are primes of the form p and $p=2$, and differ by two. A Sophie Germain prime is an odd prime p for which $2p+1$ is also a prime. This category of primes was named after Sophie Germain who provided the first case of Fermat's Last Theorem, i.e., $x^n+y^n = z^n$ has no solutions in non-zero integers for $n>2$ for exponents divisible by such primes.

The Euclidean Algorithm

It was briefly mentioned previously that the Euclidean algorithm provides a mechanism to find the multiplicative inverse mod n. Both the Euclidean algorithm and a function developed by Euler known as the totient function play an important role in public key encryption. Thus, prior to directing your attention to a public key algorithm, an additional review of an algorithm and function is warranted.

As you might expect, the Euclidean algorithm was invented by Euclid. While it is conjectured that Euclid was attempting to determine a method to find the greatest common divisor (gcd) of two integers, resulting in the algorithm holding his name, his algorithm can also be used to determine the multiplicative inverse mod n. Thus, it holds an important role in several public key encryption methods.

As a review, the greatest common divisor of two integers is the largest integer that evenly divides both. If the greatest common divisor of two numbers is 1, then those numbers are relatively prime. This means that an algorithm that enables you to efficiently find the gcd of two integers can also determine if the gcd of the two integers is relatively prime. As you will shortly note, if the gcd of two integers is relatively prime, you can find their multiplicative inverse. For example, if you want to find the multiplicative inverse of m mod n, this means you need to find a number μ such that $\mu m = 1$ mod n. This means that μm differs from 1 by a multiple of n. This also means that there is an integer v, such that $\mu n + vm = 1$. As you will soon note, you can use Euclid's algorithm to find μ and v provided $\gcd(m,n) = 1$. If m and n are not relatively prime, you will not be able to determine μ and v, which means that m does not have a multiplicative inverse mod n.

To illustrate the Euclidean algorithm, let's assume you want to compute the gcd of 432 and 252. If you assume the pair x,y with $y<x$, then the smaller number y will have a divisor D such that $x-y$, $x-2y$, etc., also have that divisor unless one of them is zero, a situation which indicates that y divides x and y is the gcd. Thus, you can take $x-ny$ where n is the integer result of dividing x by y, and $x-ny$ is the remainder, which is less than x.

The top portion of Figure 8.5 illustrates generic coding for finding the gcd using the Euclidean algorithm. The lower portion of Figure 8.5 illustrates the use of the Euclidian algorithm for finding the gcd of 432 and 252. Starting with 432 (*a*) and 252 (*b*), you divide *a* by *b* and store the remainder of 180 (*c*). Next you divide *b* by *c* and take the remainder of 72 as *d*. You repeat this sequence of operations until you obtain a zero remainder. The last number before zero, which is 2, is the gcd. If the two numbers have no other common divisor, the number 1 will be the result, indicating that they are relatively prime. An example of the use of the Euclidean algorithm to determine that two numbers have no other common divisor than 1 is shown in Figure 8.6.

Figure 8.5 Finding the greatest common divisor using the Euclidean algorithm.

a. Generic code

```
gcd (a,b)
if(b>a)
        switch (a,b)
while (b>0)
temp=a mod b;
        a=b;
        b=temp;
end
return(a)
```

b. Finding the gcd of 432

```
(a)    432
(b)    252
(c)    180
(d)     72
(e)     36
(f)      2  gcd
(g)      0
```

Figure 8.6 Using the Euclidean algorithm to determine that 19 and 3 are relatively prime to one another.

(a)	19	
(b)	3	
(c)	1	gcd
(d)	0	

The Totient Function

The symbol 0 is known as the totient function, supposedly a contraction of the terms total and quotient. Through the use of the totient function, you can determine how many numbers less than n are relatively prime to n. For example, if n is prime, then the set of integers $\{1, 2, ... n\text{-}1\}$ are relatively prime to n, resulting in $0(n) = n\text{-}1$. If you assume n is a product of two distinct primes, p and q, then there are $(p\text{-}1)*(q\text{-}1)$ numbers relatively prime to n, resulting in $0(n) = (p\text{-}1)(q\text{-}1)$.

As previously indicated, when you construct a table of modulo exponentiation you will note that the results in certain columns are the same. Based upon the research of mathematicians, it turns out that x^y mod n is the same as $x^{(y \bmod 0\,(n))}$ mod n. For example, assume $x = 2$ and $y = 2$. The numbers relatively prime to 10 are $\{1, 3, 7, 9\}$, therefore $0(10) = 4$. Then:

$$x^y \bmod n = 2^2 \bmod 10 = 4$$

and

$$x^{(y \bmod 0(n))} \bmod n = 2^{(2 \bmod 4)} \bmod 10 = 4$$

and

$$y = 3.$$

Then:

$$x^y \bmod 10 = 5^3 \bmod 10 = 5$$

and

$$x^{(y \bmod 0(n))} \bmod n = 5^{(3 \bmod 4)} \bmod 10 = 5$$

The use of the preceding formulas as equivalency is true for all values of n that are primes or any product of distinct primes. One important special case of the preceding is where $y = 1 \bmod 0(n)$. In this situation, for any number x, $x^y = x \bmod n$, which forms the basis for the RSA public key encryption system.

Once you determine a number is a prime through the use of the Euclidean algorithm, you can use the totient function to determine the multiplicative inverse. For example, if n is a prime, then $0(n) = n\text{-}1$. If x is not a multiple of n, then:

   $x^{0(n)} \bmod n = 1$

Then, the multiplicative inverse $x^{-1} \bmod n$ becomes:

   $\text{Inverse} = x^{0(n)-1} \bmod n$

To illustrate this, let's assume you want to determine $5^{-1} \bmod 3$. Since 3 is prime, you would then compute:

   $\text{multiplicative inverse} = 5^{0(3)-1} \bmod 3$

Because:

   $0(3) = 3\text{-}1 = 2$

Then:

   $\text{multiplicative inverse} = 5^{2-1} \bmod 3 = 5 \bmod 3 = 2$

Check the preceding as follows:

   $2 * 5 \bmod 3 = 10 \bmod 3 = 1$

Sure enough, 2 is the multiplicative inverse of 5 mod 3.

Now that you have an appreciation for the general mathematics behind public key cryptology, let me turn your attention to the operation of a popular public key encryption system.

RSA

RSA is a public key encryption system invented by Rivest, Shamir, and Adleman in 1978. Under this technique, both encryption and decryption are performed using exponentiation. RSA obtains security from the difficulty associated with factoring large prime numbers. As you will shortly note, public and private keys are functions of a pair of large prime numbers. Thus, the ability to decipher plaintext from the use of a public key and ciphertext is the equivalent of factoring two large primes.

Using the RSA system, each party generates a public key and a corresponding private key. To do so, two large primes of equal length are selected, *p* and *q*. To facilitate security, each prime should be a minimum of 32 bytes, or 256 bits, in length. Once the two primes are selected, you multiply them together and find their product *n*, which is referred to as the modulus of *pq*.

Public Key Generation

To generate a public key, each person using the RSA algorithm generates their encryption (*e*) and decryption (*d*) keys. The encryption key, *e*, is selected such that it is less than *n* and relatively prime to (*p*-1)(*q*-1), which represents the totient function $0(n)$. This means that *e* and (*p*-1)(*q*-1) have no common factors other than 1. Your public key then becomes the pair <*e,n*>.

Private Key Generation

To compute your private key, you will find another number *d*, such that (*ed*-1) is divisible by (*p*-1)(*q*-1). That is, *d* represents the multiplicative inverse of *e* mod $0(n)$. Then, the private key becomes the pair <*d,n*>. Once your public and private keys are selected, the primes *p* and *q* are no longer needed. Although it is safe to discard them, they should not be revealed.

Message Encipherment

To encipher a message *m* you would first subdivide it into blocks smaller than *n* (*m*<*n*). When working with binary data this would be equivalent to selecting the largest power of 2 less than *n*. You would then use your public key (*e*) to compute ciphertext (*c*) as follows:

$$c = m_i^e \bmod n$$

where m_i represents block *I* of message *m*.

To decrypt a message you would use your private key (*d*) on each ciphertext block c_i as follows:

$$m_i = c_i^d \bmod n$$

To illustrate the use of RSA, let's use a few small primes to facilitate observing the relevant computations. First, let's assume you selected $p = 53$ and $q = 61$. Then:

$n = p*q = 53*61 = 3233$

Next you would randomly select an encryption key, e, such that it has no common factors with 3233. For our example, let's select e to be 41. Then, the private key d would be:

$d = 41^{-1} \bmod 3233$

To compute d, you must obtain the multiplicative inverse of 41 mod 3233. That is, you must determine the number which when multiplied by 41 mod 3233 yields a result of unity. Based upon Euler's application of the totient function, if n is a prime, the $0(n) = n-1$. If p and q are primes and $n = pq$, then $0(n) = (p-1)(q-1)$. Thus, if the gcd $(a,n) = 1$, where x is not a multiple of n, then:

$x^{0(n)} \bmod n = 1$

This means you can compute the multiplicative inverse $x^{-1} \bmod n$ as follows:

$X = x^{0(n)-1} \bmod n$

Returning to your computation, you need to determine the private key d, such that:

$d = 41^{-1} \bmod 3233$

Since 3233 is prime, then $0(3233) = 3233-1 = 3232$. Thus, the inverse of 41 mod 3233 becomes:

$41^{3232-1} \bmod 3233 = 41^{3231} \bmod 3233$

Exponentiation Operations

While it is possible to attempt to raise a number to a large power, doing so will more than likely exhaust the capacity of your computer as there is a finite limit to the size of integers on each computer. Instead of directly raising a number to a power, you can do the modular reduction after each multiply operation. For example, assume you want to compute 123^7 mod 456. Instead of computing 123 multiplied by itself 7 times and then dividing by 456 to obtain the remainder, let's do modular reduction after each multiply. That is:

$123^2 = 123*123 = 15129 \bmod 456 = 81 \bmod 456$

$123^3 = 123*81 \bmod 456 = 9963 \bmod 456 = 387 \bmod 456$

$123^4 = 123*387 \bmod 456 = 47601 \bmod 456 = 177 \bmod 456$

$123^5 = 123*177 \bmod 456 = 21771 \bmod 456 = 339 \bmod 456$

$123^6 = 123*339 \bmod 456 = 41697 \bmod 456 = 201 \bmod 456$

$123^7 = 123*201 \bmod 456 = 24723 \bmod 456 = 99 \bmod 456$

While the preceding method reduces the computation to a series of seven small multiplies and seven small divides, most exponents used with RSA are considerably larger. This means that you would more than likely want to obtain a more efficient method to compute exponents.

To raise a number x to an exponent, you can perform a series of squaring operations. For example:

$123^2 = 123*123 = 15129 \bmod 456 = 81 \bmod 456$

$123^4 = 81*81 = 6561 \bmod 456 = 177 \bmod 456$

While you could continue and square 123 again, obtaining the value of 123^8, unfortunately the 123^7 that you require is not a power of 2. However, if you know what 123^x is, then it is relatively easy to compute 123^{2x}, since you obtain that by squaring 123^x. Similarly, you can compute 123^{2x+1}, as all you need to do is multiply the result obtained by squaring 123^x (123^{2x}) by 123. This means you can perform a sequence of squaring operations to obtain the nearest power of two to the exponent you require, and then multiply the result n times, where n is the difference between the exponent you seek and the nearest computed power of 2. For example:

$123^7 \bmod 456 = 123^2 * 123^2 * 123 * 123 * 123 \bmod 456$

$123^4 \bmod 456 = 177 \bmod 456$

Then:

$123^7 \bmod 456 = 123*123*123*177 \bmod 456$

$= 123*123*339 \bmod 456$

$= 123*201 \bmod 456$

$= 99 \bmod 456$

Note that the preceding method required two squaring and three multiplication operations. You can reduce the number of operations further if you note that $123^a * 123^b = 123^{a+b}$. This means given:

123^2 mod 456 = 81 mod 456

123^7 mod 456 = 387 mod 456

you would compute the following:

$123^6 = 123^2 * 123^4 = 81.387$ mod 456 = 339 mod 456

$123^7 = 123 * 123^6 = 123.339$ mod 456 = 99 mod 456

Note that in this example you would compute 123^2 mod 456, 123^4 mod 456, 123^6 mod 456, and then multiply the last result by 123. This reduces the number of computations to two squares and two multiplies.

If you convert the exponent to binary, you can compute 123 raised to a sequence of powers. For example, 7 is 111_2 which represents the sequence 1_2, 11_2, 111_2. Note that each successive power concatenates one additional bit of the desired exponent. Also note that each successive power (from the most significant bit position) is either twice the preceding power or once or more than twice the preceding power. Thus, you can raise 123 to the first, third, and seventh power by repeated squaring together with multiplication by 123 for the bits that are 1. For example, commencing with the first power you start with:

123 mod 456

To obtain the third power, you would multiply 123 by its square, i.e., 123 (123^2). To then obtain the seventh power, you would obtain the sixth power $(123^3)^2$ and multiply by 123. Thus, raising 123 to the seventh power can be accomplished by repeated squaring and, as required, multiplying by 123 for the bits that are 1. Focusing on exponents:

$7 = (((1)^2 + 1)^2 + 1)$

Then you obtain:

$123^7 = (((123)^2 * 123)^2 * 123)$

Using the preceding method you can perform exponentiation of a base to an exponent as follows:

1. Commence by setting an initial value to 1.

2. Convert the exponent to binary.

3. Read the binary value of the exponent bit by bit from high order to low order and square your value for each position. If the value of the bit position is 1, then multiply by the base. After each operation, perform modular reduction to maintain a relatively small intermediate result.

Now that you have an appreciation for techniques to facilitate exponentiation, let's return to the key computation process. It was noted previously that the inverse of 41 mod 3233 is:

$$41^{3231} \bmod 3233$$

Note that 3231 is 11001001111_2. This means you can compute 41 raised to the 3231 power by squaring 12 times and multiplying 8 times. Although I will leave it as an exercise for you to compute, let's assume the answer was x. You would then publish e and n and keep the value x which represents your secret decryption key. Suppose you want to encrypt the famous message ABADABA... Then, the ASCII value of your message m is:

$$m = 64656467646564...$$

To facilitate computations you would break the message into small blocks. For example:

$$m_1 = 6465$$
$$m_2 = 6467$$
$$m_3 = 6465$$

and so on.

Using the encryption key of 41, the first block would be encrypted as:

$$c_1 = 6465^{41} \bmod 3233$$

Similarly, the second block would be encrypted as follows:

$$c_2 = 6467^{41} \bmod 3233$$

You would continue the same operation on the remaining blocks until you generated the entire encrypted message. As previously discussed, decryption would be performed on a block by block (c_1, c_2...) basis, performing the same exponentiation but using the decryption key whose value is x. Thus:

$$m_1 = c_1{}^x \bmod 3233$$
$$m_2 = c_2{}^x \bmod 3233$$

and so on.

Facilitating the Key Generation Process

Based upon the preceding, the use of RSA depends upon selecting appropriate values for *n, d,* and *e.* As previously noted, selecting those values to obtain an RSA key can be significantly computational intensive. In fact, the selection of values for *n, d,* and *e* can be substantially more computational intensive than using its public and private keys. Fortunately there are a few methods you can apply to reduce your computations.

Locating Large Primes

Although there are an infinite number of primes, you will more than likely select them randomly. This means you will require a mechanism to determine if your random selection is a prime.

One method that can be used to determine if a number *n* is a prime is to divide it by all integers >2 and <= $\sqrt{n}$ and note whether or not the division comes out even. For example, consider the prime 11. The integer of its square root is 3. Then 11/2 and 11/3 do not provide an even number. Thus, 11 is a prime. Now consider 16. Its square root is 4. Then, 16/2, 16/3, and 16/4 provide at least one even number, which means 16 is a non-prime.

While the preceding method provides a mechanism for testing whether or not a number is a prime, as primes get rather lengthy, the time required for such testing becomes impractical. A more practical method to test for a prime is obtained by the use of Euler's totient function. As previously noted, if *n* is prime, then $0(n) = n-1$. When this situation occurs, the function takes on a simpler form and is known as Fermat's theorem.

Fermat's theorem says that if *p* is prime and $0<x<p$, where *x* is relative prime to *n,* then:

$$x^{p-1} = 1 \bmod p$$

Based on Fermat's theorem you would pick a number *x* such that $x<n$ and compute $x^{n-1} \bmod n$. If the answer is not 1, then *n* is not a prime. If the answer is 1, there is a very minute possibility that *n* is not a prime; however, the probability is so small that you can safely consider the number to be a prime.

The steps necessary to locate an appropriate prime can be summarized as follows:

1. Select random number n in an appropriate length. Note that, according to RSA Laboratories, the recommended module sizes are 768 bits for personal use, 1,024 bits for corporate use, and 2,048 bits for extremely important keys, such as the key pair of a certifying authority. Because the two primes (p and q) should be roughly equal in length, the recommendation of a 768-bit modulus for personal use results in each prime having a length of approximately 384 bits.

2. Select a random value for x, such that $x<n$, and compute $x^c \bmod n$, where c represents an odd number for which $n-1=2^b c$ and b is the number of times 2 divides $n-1$, i.e., 2^b is the largest power of 2 that divides $n-1$. If the computation of $x^c \bmod n$ is +1 or -1, n has passed the primary test for the selected value of x. If the computation does not result in +1 or -1, replace the result by its square and determine if the computation produces +1 or -1. If the result is +1, n is not prime as the previous result is a square root of 1 different from +1, -1. If the result is -1, n passes the primary test for x. You would repeat the preceding b-1 times.

3. If n is not a prime, return to step 1.

Summary

The intention of this chapter was to acquaint you with the concept behind public key cryptology to include its mathematics. Although the examples should provide a foundation sufficient for developing programs, a word of caution is in order. Currently, government regulations concerning the export of encryption software with lengthy keys is prohibited. In fact, an office in the government called Munitions Control passes judgment on the ability to export certain types of encryption software and hardware. Because the government has made life difficult for those who have simply posted software on their Web site, you are cautioned to carefully consider how any software you plan to develop that uses keys in excess of 40 bits will be distributed. Otherwise, there is a chance you could experience the necessity to incur a significant amount of legal fees in attempting to explain your actions.

Companion CD-ROM Files

This appendix lists the names of each of the files contained on the companion CD-ROM, as well as a description of the function of each file. To facilitate readers obtaining additional information concerning the operation and utilization of each program, files are listed in this appendix in the order in which they are described in each chapter, by chapter. The .EXE files, which are executable versions of the BASIC and C++ programs, are not listed in the book; however, they are listed below in the same chapter in which the BASIC or C++ program is described.

There are two directories on the CD: BASIC and C. The BASIC directory contains BASIC language source and executable programs, while the C directory contains C++ language source and executable programs. In the chart below, the .EXE file is listed only once with the name of the corresponding program followed by .xxx. The .CPP executable is in the C directory, and the .BAS executable is in the BASIC directory.

Chapter	Filename	Description
2	SHIFT.BAS	This program creates a sequence of shifted alphabets.
	SHIFT.CPP	This program is the C++ version of SHIFT.BAS.
	SHIFT.EXE	This is the executable version of SHIFT.CPP.
	CIPHER1.BAS	This program creates a shifted alphabet based upon the entry of an alphabetic shift key character.
	CIPHER1.CPP	This program is the C++ version of CIPHER1.BAS.
	CIPHER1.EXE	This is the executable version of CIPHER1.xxx.
	CIPHER2.BAS	This program enciphers a one-line message using a cipher alphabet formed by shifting the plaintext alphabet through the use of an alphabetic shift key.
	CIPHER2.CPP	This program is the C++ version of CIPHER2.BAS.
	CIPHER2.EXE	This is the executable version of CIPHER2.xxx.

Chapter	Filename	Description
	CIPHER3.BAS	This program expands upon the functionality of CIPHER2.BAS by adding a routine which displays the resulting enciphered text in groups of five characters.
	CIPHER3.CPP	This program is the C++ version of CIPHER3.BAS.
	CIPHER3.EXE	This is the executable version of CIPHER3.xxx.
	CIPHER4.BAS	This program expands upon the functionality of CIPHER3.BAS by permitting spaces between words in a plaintext message and selectively enciphering the message using a simple monoalphabetic substitution process.
	CIPHER4.CPP	This program is the C++ version of CIPHER4.BAS.
	CIPHER4.EXE	This is the executable version of CIPHER4.xxx.
	DCIPHER4.BAS	This program deciphers a message previously enciphered through the use of CIPHER4.BAS.
	DCIPHER4.CPP	This program is the C++ version of DCIPHER4.BAS.
	DCIPHER4.EXE	This is the executable version of DCIPHER4.xxx.
3	WORD.BAS	This program develops an alphabet based upon the entry of a keyword or keyword phrase.
	WORD.CPP	This program is the C++ version of WORD.BAS.
	WORD.EXE	This is the executable version of WORD.xxx.
	CIPHER5.BAS	This program enciphers a message based upon the use of a keyword or keyword phrase and an alphabetic shift key using a monoalphabetic substitution process.
	CIPHER5.CPP	This program is the C++ version of CIPHER5.BAS.
	CIPHER5.EXE	This is the executable version of CIPHER5.xxx.
	DCIPHER5.BAS	This program deciphers a message enciphered using the program DCIPHER5.BAS.
	DCIPHER5.CPP	This program is the C++ version of DCIPHER5.BAS.
	DCIPHER5.EXE	This is the executable version of DCIPHER5.xxx.
4	CIPHERTR.BAS	This program enciphers a message using a transposition matrix and a monoalphabetic substitution process based upon a keyword or keyword phrase and an alphabetic shift key. This program displays the composition of different alphabets to illustrate the operation of the enciphering process.
	CIPHERTR.CPP	This program is the C++ version of CIPHERTR.BAS.
	CIPHERTR.EXE	This is the executable version of CIPHERTR.xxx.
	TRANSPORT.CPP	This program is a C++ expansion of BASIC's TRANSPORT subroutine.
	TRANSPORT.EXE	This is the executable version of TRANSPORT.CPP.
	CIPHER6.BAS	This program adds an interval extraction capability to CIPHERTR.BAS.
	CIPHER6.CPP	This program is the C++ version of CIPHER6.BAS.
	CIPHER6.EXE	This is the executable version of CIPHER6.xxx.

Chapter	Filename	Description
	DCIPHER6.BAS	This program deciphers messages enciphered using the program CIPHER6.BAS.
	DCIPHER6.CPP	This program is the C++ version of DCIPHER6.BAS.
	DCIPHER6.EXE	This is the executable version of DCIPHER6.xxx.
5	POLY1.BAS	This program creates a Vigenére tableau.
	POLY1.CPP	This program is the C++ version of POLY1.BAS.
	POLY1.EXE	This is the executable version of POLY1.xxx.
	COUNT.CPP	This program performs a frequency count of the contents of an encrypted file.
	COUNT.EXE	This is the executable version of COUNT.CPP.
	POLY2.BAS	This program enciphers a message based upon the use of two keywords or keyword phrases using a polyalphabetic substitution process and 26 cipher alphabets.
	POLY2.CPP	This program is the C++ version of POLY2.BAS.
	POLY2.EXE	This is the executable version of POLY2.xxx.
	DPOLY2.BAS	This program deciphers messages previously enciphered using the program POLY2.BAS.
	DPOLY2.CPP	This program is the C++ version of DPOLY2.BAS.
	DPOLY2.EXE	This is the executable version of DPOLY2.xxx.
6	RANDOM1.BAS	This program generates random numbers between 0 and 25.
	RANDOM1.CPP	This program is the C++ version of RANDOM1.BAS.
	RANDOM1.EXE	This is the executable version of RANDOM1.xxx.
	RANDOM2.BAS	This program demonstrates the use of random numbers to encipher a one-line message.
	RANDOM2.CPP	This program is the C++ version of RANDOM2.BAS.
	RANDOM2.EXE	This is the executable version of RANDOM2.xxx.
	DRANDOM2.BAS	This programs deciphers a one-line message previously enciphered using the program RANDOM2.BAS.
	DRANDOM2.CPP	This program is the C++ version of DRANDOM2.BAS.
	DRANDOM2.EXE	This is the executable version of DRANDOM2.xxx.
	ASCII.CPP	This program displays the ASCII value of characters.
	ASCII.EXE	This is the executable version of ASCII.CPP.
	POSITION.BAS	This program demonstrates the positioning to a place in the BASIC random number generator based upon a "secret" code up to six characters in length.
	POSITION.CPP	This program is the C++ version of POSITION.BAS.
	POSITION.EXE	This is the executable version of POSITION.xxx.
	RTEST.BAS	This program scans a random number seed to locate any sequence of five repeated numbers.
	RTEST.EXE	This is the executable version of RTEST.BAS.
	RANDOM3.BAS	This program enciphers messages using the BASIC random number generator and a six-position "secret" code to locate a starting point in the random number generator.

Chapter	Filename	Description
	RANDOM3.CPP	This program is the C++ version of RANDOM3.BAS.
	RANDOM3.EXE	This is the executable version of RANDOM3.xxx.
	DRANDOM3.BAS	This program deciphers messages previously enciphered using the program RANDOM3.BAS.
	DRANDOM3.CPP	This program is the C++ version of DRANDOM3.BAS.
	DRANDOM3.EXE	This is the executable version of DRANDOM3.xxx.
7	ENCIPHER.BAS	This program performs encipherment using seven previously developed routines.
	ENCIPHER.EXE	This is the executable version of ENCIPHER.BAS.
	DECIPHER.BAS	This program deciphers data previously enciphered using the ENCIPHER.BAS program.
	DECIPHER.EXE	This is the executable version of DECIPHER.BAS.
	SECRET.MSG	This file contains the challenge message that readers can attempt to decipher.

Index

About the CD

The CD-ROM included with this book contains the example programs discussed in the book. Most of the programs are included as BASIC text files (.BAS), C++ text files (.CPP), and executable programs (.EXE).

To copy the software to your hard drive, simply drag and drop the two directories to your drive. As these files require 4.2 megabytes of free space on your hard drive, you may wish to access the files you need directly from the CD, rather than copying them to your hard drive.

See Appendix A for more information about the files on the CD.

 Notice: Opening the CD package makes this book NONRETURNABLE.